Praxis and method

International Library of Sociology

Founded by Karl Mannheim

Editor: John Rex, University of Warwick

Arbor Scientiae
Arbor Vitae

A catalogue of books available in the **International Library of Sociology** and other series of Social Science books published by Routledge & Kegan Paul will be found at the end of this volume.

Praxis and method

A sociological dialogue with Lukács, Gramsci and the early Frankfurt School

Richard Kilminster

Department of Sociology,
University of Leeds

Routledge & Kegan Paul

London, Boston and Henley

First published in 1979
by Routledge & Kegan Paul Ltd
39 Store Street, London WC1E 7DD,
Broadway House, Newtown Road,
Henley-on-Thames, Oxon RG9 1EN and
9 Park Street, Boston, Mass. 02108, USA
Set in 10 on 11 pt Times by
Gloucester Typesetting Co. Ltd, Gloucester
and printed in Great Britain by
Redwood Burn Ltd
Trowbridge and Esher

British Library Cataloguing in Publication Data

Kilminster, Richard

Praxis and method. - (International library of sociology).
1. Communism and society 2. Practice (Philosophy)
I. Title II. Series
301'. 01 HX542 79-40376

ISBN 0 7100 0094 4

To the memory of my parents,
Albert and Christina Kilminster

The variegated canvas of the
world is before me; I stand
over against it; by my
theoretical attitude to it I
overcome its opposition to me
and make its contents my own.
I am at home in the world
when I know it, still more so
when I have understood it.

Hegel

Contents

Acknowledgments

I wish to express my gratitude to Clive Ashworth, Ian Clegg, Doug McEachern, Patrick Hayes, Peter Green, Alan Warde and Scott Beadle, with whom I have had many stimulating discussions about the themes of this book. Zygmunt Bauman, in particular, provided perceptive criticism and guidance when I was preparing an earlier version as a doctoral thesis and Tom Bottomore and Gianfranco Poggi gave helpful critical comments. I have also been sustained by the continuing intellectual encouragement of Norbert Elias. My debt to him is incalculable. As is my gratitude to Bebe Speed for her practical help, forbearance and sympathy.

The author and publisher are grateful for permission to reprint certain materials from the publications listed below:

From W. B. Yeats: 'A Dialogue of Self and Soul' from *The Collected Poems of W. B. Yeats*. Reprinted by permission of M. B. Yeats and the Macmillan Company of London and Basingstoke.

From Max Horkheimer, *Critical Theory*, © S. Fischer Verlag GmbH, Frankfurt am Main. English translation Copyright © 1972 by Herder & Herder, Inc. Reprinted by permission of The Seabury Press, New York and S. Fischer Verlag.

From Georg Lukács, *History and Class Consciousness: Studies in Marxist Dialectics*, translated by Rodney Livingstone. Reprinted by permission of the Merlin Press Ltd.

From *Selections from the Prison Notebooks of Antonio Gramsci* (edited and translated by Quintin Hoare and Geoffrey Nowell-Smith). Reprinted by permission of Lawrence & Wishart, Publishers, London.

Part one

Marx's theory of praxis

Practical philosophy, or more exactly stated, the Philosophy of Praxis, which would realistically influence life and social relationships, the development of truth in concrete activity – this is the overriding destiny of philosophy.

August von Cieszkowski

Part one

Marx's theory of praxis

1 A starting point

It is a mistake to believe that there is one authentic, pure or correct interpretation of Marx's thought (or that of any other theoretician for that matter) which can be held up as what he 'really' meant. All interpretations of this kind are selective and historical since they relate to the different contexts and interests of the expositors and the stage of social development at which they are thus elaborated. There is a tendency among Marxist commentators, for obvious reasons, to portray Marx's writings as more consistent than they are and to suppress omissions, errors, blind spots and unresolved tensions; in short, to transform Marx into a myth. The deification of Marx also carries the temptation to assume that his criticisms of his various theoretical combatants (Hegel, Feuerbach, Bauer, Stirner, Ricardo, Mill, etc.) are definitive, final and unambiguously devastating. It is a theme of this study on the contrary that, seen from a later stage, Marx's assessments of other theorists emerge as frequently selective, partial or simplified in the interest of mounting a critique of societies from the prestigious standpoint of a 'science' of socialism. This contention is followed through in particular in relation to what I argue is Marx's invalid critique of Hegel to demonstrate the selective emphasis present in Marx's interpretation which can be seen to have been uncritically perpetuated later on in the tradition by some of the neo-Marxists treated in this study.

From outside the Marxist camp, however, the older style of 'refutations' of Marx with varying degrees of hostility on the grounds of say failure of his predictions, ambiguities in conceptualizing base and superstructure, erroneous labour theory of value, totalitarian implications, etc. (Leff, Joan Robinson, Popper), has it seems given way in recent years to a tendency in Marxian scholarship positively to seek out unresolved dilemmas, ambivalences or tensions in Marx's work. (This tendency is paralleled in Hegelian studies in the controversy over the supposed conflict in Hegel's work between system and dialectic.) Inconsistencies in Marx's theorizations are often related to such a tension, sometimes held to be Marx's profound perception of an inherent contradiction in the 'human condition' or perhaps the twin horns of a philosophical dilemma which has dogged men from the dawn of history. Tensions or dilemmas championed in Marx's work include those between rationalism and empiricism (Easton);[1] the common one between voluntarism and determinism (in at least Lobkowicz, C. Wright Mills, Robert Vincent Daniels);[2] the Hegelian notion of development versus the Darwinian philosophy of life (Hyppolite);[3] ideas as distorted emanations of the class struggle whilst retaining faith in Reason (Bendix);[4] ethical relativism unreconciled with objective moral superiority of socialism (Kamenka);[5] scientific method based on observed data versus speculatively assumed contradictions in the world (H. B. Acton);[6] future-oriented Marxian man-as-praxis versus the attitude towards the past essential for human historicity being underivable from such practicity (Rotenstreich);[7] between eschatology and dialectics (Avineri);[8] and between regarding human history as essentially open-ended but at the same time trying to foist an empirical closure upon it (Poggi, Bauman).[9] Both the mythologizers and the wilful debunkers generally only incidentally contribute to our understanding of Marx's thought, whereas I think that the revelation of tensions takes scholarship in a far more illuminating direction. However, not only must we be alert to the temptation to hypostatize ambivalences in Marx into timeless co-ordinates of human existence (i.e. the creation of another myth); but also be aware of the danger of remaining in the minutiae of exegesis in Marx's specific theoretical terrain when his transcendence has already been bespoken by the historical process itself. Sociologically speaking, close analysis is required to supplement this work by locating the perceptions of the tensions in Marx to their elaboration from various standpoints at a subsequent stage of development as aspects of later social configurations, through which mediations alone the tensions have their total historical existence.

Schematically, in that latter vein, we can note that the ramifications of the concept of praxis became theoretical issues for social and political theory from the First World War onwards in the works of the writers of the 'Western' Marxist tradition, some of whom are dealt with in this study, whose orientation was primarily philosophical and permeated by *fin de siècle* anti-positivism. The preoccupation with the epistemological aspects of the notion went hand in hand with the preoccupation within Marxism to seek the urgent further praxis of the proletariat (following their mass action in various places during the war and immediately after) to save capitalist society from the 'abyss' through socialist revolution, for which 1917 provided a practical precedent. At the same time the ideologues of the nascent Soviet State came under fire from these theoreticians who saw Marxism as jelling into an implacable, closed orthodoxy informing Bolshevik consolidation, against which they thus formed a heterodox reaction. The theoretical vocabulary of the Western Marxists called up the activistic elements of the Marxian doctrine, notably the early Marxian stress on the 'realization of philosophy' in practice, and the implied sublation of the historically transitory Marxian science of historical materialism itself in the praxis of the proletariat.[10] As is very well known, this tradition became polarized theoretically against the increasingly axiomatized, ideologically frozen Soviet orthodoxy, the debates between which have been relived and reworked more recently by elements of the New Left who have resurrected the earlier concern with praxis and have tended to regard those in the Lukács-Gramsci–Korsch–Frankfurt tradition as the carriers of the 'authentic' Marxism shamelessly distorted by the Soviet theoreticians. Here we have in mind for example the tendency associated with the American journal *Telos*.

Marxists generally have always engaged in debate with other doctrines and theoretical positions prevalent at various stages of the development of Marxism. Hegelianism, Proudhon, various political economists, Vogt, Dühring, the Machists, and so on were combated in theory by Marx and his successors at various points as part of informing current practice within the labour movement. The preoccupation in the post-Lukácsian tradition with the epistemological, philosophical and theoretical questions of the relation between theory and practice was similarly elaborated in a dialogue with contemporary theories, notably a sociology which was largely seen as positivistically inspired, as were the 'orthodox' Marxists who were also being combated. In the work of the 'renegade' tradition the concern with praxis also led to further theoretical reconstructions of the genesis of Marx's thought (in particular his relation to Hegel, which was especially restressed) and created an importance for additional figures such as Cieszkowski, Ruge and Moses Hess. Marx's relation to thinkers such as these was to supplement his already established genesis in the arguments of those anxious to prove above all that Marx's 'definitive' articulation of the level of social development of his time and its tendencies was a praxis orientation. This research provided these later Marxists with a theoretical pedigree to justify the political action they contemplated or advocated at the time.

Again, much of that work has been handed down to later theorists to form routine theoretical positions. For example, the methodological critiques of 'bourgeois social science' and the unquestioning hostility towards 'positivism', which have become part of the reality of contemporary sociology, originated partly in this historically specific tradition of Marxist theory. But they have become perpetuated as theoretical issues in the contemporary context long after their original hortatory purpose has been forgotten. This study reconstructs the genesis of this legacy. Its focus is on the post-Lukácsian activistic strand of Marxist social theory between the wars and up to about the mid-1940s, treated mainly immanently in terms of theoretical issues for sociology associated with the concept of praxis. This focus has meant that two of the most prominent and influential contemporary heirs of that tradition and of orthodox Soviet historical materialism – respectively Jürgen Habermas and Louis Althusser[11] – are not directly dealt with, even though their work handles the same kinds of issues in a new historical situation and also significantly undertakes yet further reconstructions of the theoretical antecedents. However, from time to time various followers of Althusser are discussed in the text and, since the Critical Theorists of the 1930s laid down philosophically some of the basic categories from which the second Frankfurt generation has moved off in their efforts to ground a critical sociology, the first four chapters of Part four can be regarded as a prolegomenon to a study of Habermas.

For all these reasons, we have eschewed commencing with a full-scale exposition of the concept of praxis in Marx and of its significance for his work as a whole and then applying the misleading method of placing this exposition up against what the later writers made of it. This subject not only represents a very well-worn area of scholarship from many perspectives in recent years, but also the nature and significance of Marx's social thought cannot be naïvely assumed as self-evidently available for such an approach since an interpretation would certainly be mediated by the work and influence of the later neo-Marxists who appropriated this their own 'pre-history' in the theoretico-political fashion mentioned earlier. The permeation of sociological culture and expository texts with various traces of these past debates and researches about Marx and the relation between Marxism and sociology is indeed exemplified in the focus and emphases of this study itself. It would be easy uncritically to perpetuate aspects of a historically specific post-Lukácsian Marxist socio-historical self-understanding through the act of reinterpreting that socio-genesis again through the same spectacles, when a potentially more adequate, critical appropriation is possible from a later stage of development. It is through following this line of reasoning that I, for example, take the post-Korschian Western Marxist point that Marx was indeed the only overt 'philosophical social scientist' or 'scientist of human emancipation'. But I argue that that neither exhausts the significance of the Marxian theoretico-social configuration nor demands that we inflate that historically local character (as have some of the writers discussed here) into the inauguration of an absolute dualism of a social science of emancipation versus a social science of justification into which all sociology must be placed.

For all these reasons, my interpretation of Marx, the place of the concept of praxis in his thought and his historical significance is scattered throughout the study, in a dialogue with this particular historical cluster of Western Marxists whose legacy in our present sociological culture first forced us to raise the issues discussed in this study, which has taken us back into the historical genesis of Marx's thought yet again. The brief notes on Marx in the first two chapters thus supplement and help towards uniting the disparate interpretative threads in the text. The standpoint underpinning the study, which guides its particular stresses and emphases, is also elaborated at various points in a debate not only with Marx and with Marxists but with sociology as well, and is more explicitly drawn together in Chapter 18. The work is intended, therefore, to constitute an interlocking theoretical whole of the diverse movements of thought discussed by virtue of its dialogic character, through which the argument passes backwards and forwards across stages of history. The consequent overlapping and interweaving of motifs in the work means that some writers or issues are dealt with under a number of headings and the subjects covered in the individual Parts and Chapters do not always coincide precisely with what their headings announce.

2 Praxis and practice in Hegel and Marx

In the German the word '*Praxis*' carries more or less the same meanings as the English word 'practice', but the dynamic nature of the language can also cope with the two unified connotations given to the term by Marx and by Marxists since Lukács which we will subsequently discuss. In order adequately to encompass these meanings in English, however, entails, I feel, expounding and using a distinction between *practice* and *praxis* which will be followed throughout and exemplified in the discussion of the later Marxists. The significance of the concept of praxis for Marx and the meaning of this suggested dualism are best approached through a very brief discussion of the differences as Marx saw them, between his self-mediating historical dialectic, and that of Hegel, since it was through a stand on the status and possibilities of human action within such a dialectic of history that Marx defines his position and which informs so many of the later post-Lukácsian concerns. This analysis will take us also into the related domains of philosophy and critique in Marx.

The Hegelian conception of dialectical development in the social and natural worlds stressed negativity, that is the dissolution, by the negation inherent in it, of what is taken as immediate reality in any process. Specific states of affairs were regarded as overcome by their negation and carried forward into higher stages of development. The processes overall represented a greater and greater realization of something universal or absolute in reality. Hence it was for Hegel an "uncritical" procedure to presuppose as "valid in their own account" the features of the world which the Kantian analytical method of the Understanding delineates and tabulates.[1] Hegel affirms that the processes of such a historical dialectic always have a positive result, since the course of the moving principle of transition embodied in the world (and so also in the logic of its presentation as analysis) "contains what it results from, absorbed into itself and made part of itself".[2]

Marx, too, always takes the givenness of the thing-like immediacy of the totality at a given stage of development, affirms its immediate force, but then 'recovers' its historical presuppositions. This procedure exemplifies critique, i.e. he demonstrates critically how such a state of affairs came about, how it produced itself as part of a more or less blind self-mediating historical process and then how it will tend to resolve its contradictions into a higher stage.[3] The relatively blind everyday activity which carries this process along we can term *practice*: activity in its "dirty Jewish manifestation", in Marx's words.[4] For Marx this overall process carries with it the concomitant rise to class-consciousness of the proletariat whose 'world-historical' truth, i.e. the potentiality of what they inherently *are* as the bearers of the historical negation of capital, will be realized in the making of a truly 'universal' society serving the interests of all men under communism.

Methodologically, the dialectic in both Hegel and Marx thus possessed two moments, positivity and the moving principle of negativity, welded together in a historical totalizing process. For the post-Hegelians to embrace the positive moment would be to take what is given as read, irrespective of how it produced itself; i.e. merely to affirm what history has handed down. This emphasis tended politically towards conservatism and quietism. Whereas the negative moment (which attracted the Left Hegelians) carried with it for those who were led to stress its simultaneous power as destruction and creation (e.g. Marx, Bakunin, Hess, Lassalle) a radical and revolutionary meaning.[5] Such a dialectic was, in Marx's words, "the scandal and abomination of bourgeoisdom and its doctrinaire professors"[6] who took the existing state of affairs as a positive, fixed datum, in terms of ignoring both its contradictory genesis and its negating tendency.

Marx additionally claimed, as part of his depiction of this world-historical dialectic, to have overcome the Hegelian philosophy as the science of wisdom, as the ethical consummation of all past philosophies surpassed and contained within it. This aspect is developed at greater length later, but some remarks are necessary here. Within Hegel's philosophy were mapped as a development all types of experience as well as the embodiment of the most advanced incorporative stage of that contradictory development of self-consciousness beyond its stage of Spirit to Absolute Knowledge, enshrined in the particularity of the Hegelian savant. Like many of the Left Hegelians, early on Marx wanted to seek to make actuality strive towards its self-realized ideality (to realize philosophy) but quickly came to believe that he needed to move outside Hegelianism in order to be able not only to criticize but also to advocate criticism - as - practice within specific societies; hence the famous "realizing philosophy by abolishing it and abolishing it by realizing it" formula. Marx sought, to use a phrase which came into Marxist currency much later, the "unity of theory and practice",[7] i.e. the carrying through into social reality of what in Hegel had been carried to its ultimate universality only in theory. The pseudo universal interests of the State, actually masquerading particular class interests, were projected by Marx into the world-historical potential of the proletariat in whose revolutionary victory particular and universal interests really coincided. The ideal of a just, rational, self-determining society of human fulfilment embodied in philosophy would then no longer stand over against the real, but philosophy would be sublated as it and the reality progressively met and merged in real human self-conscious praxis.[8] Since Marx himself embodied the most advanced consciousness made possible by the stage of the dialectical development of societal contradictions he himself, like the Hegelians although in a different framework, effectively embodied Absolute Knowledge prior to its further concretization.

In claiming to embody and to be articulating the real tendency of the historical process towards a unified human emancipation, a process he said had been "metaphysically travestied" by Hegel,[9] Marx occupied a powerful practical-theoretical position because, as in Hegel, facts, values and ideals were united in his theory into one organic historical movement. Without conceptualizing the outcome of socialism as being written into the movement of history and scientifically delineable, Marx's dialectical mind realized that nothing would distinguish his socialism from abstract Utopian or gradualist varieties which had also seen class inequality and taken up the proletariat's cause. Marx's historical dialectic of necessity[10] provided him with a unique non-arbitrary potential-oriented scientific certitude for socialism. These two statements by Marx are therefore of great importance in understanding this aspect of his thought:

> Long before me bourgeois historians had described the historical development of this class struggle and bourgeois economists the economic anatomy of the classes. What I did that was new was to demonstrate: (1) that the existence of classes is merely linked to particular historical phases in the development of production, (2) that class struggle necessarily leads to the dictatorship of the proletariat, (3) that this dictatorship itself only constitutes the transition to the abolition of all classes and to a classless society.[11]

> Communism is for us not a state of affairs which is to be established, an ideal to which reality will have to adjust itself. We call communism the real movement which abolishes the present state of things.[12]

The later post-Korschian Critical Theorists were, I think, correct to point out (as we will see in Part four) that *qua* theory, Marx's deliberations were, in their potential-orientation, simultaneously scientific as well as philosophical and 'evaluative'. Commentators have often either misunderstood what they see as the 'unscientific' high moral tone of Marx's writings or alternatively have seen *Capital solely* as a work of social science.[13] Marx's work was, however, gallantly trying to be both, since, although overcome and negated, philosophy was intended to be incorporated into his theory as a layer of critique which guides its focus. Marx's social science did not separate itself from classical philosophy, demolish it in the name of science, and then reject it, but historically reconstituted it as enlightened science to inform the retrieval of social alienation in praxis.

It is mainly in Marx's earlier writings – up to 1845–6 – that he is mostly concerned, like many of the Hegelians at that time, with the post-Hegelian preoccupation with praxis as the way forward from the completion of philosophy in the works of the master. The notion of a 'philosophy of action' was widespread among the Hegelians of the Left and Right. It is to these writings that the later innovators and pedigree seekers in recent praxis-oriented Marxism have turned for their reinterpretations. In the decade 1837–47 Michelet, his pupil August von Cieszkowski (who first systematically advocated praxis after Hegel),[14] Bakunin, Hess, Ruge, Marx and others were all looking to praxis in the world as the conscious road to freedom, however defined. For the Hegelians, theory and practice at the most general level formed a unity and the stage of development of the activity of Spirit as Absolute Knowledge had been historically consummated in them. They had achieved the highest point of the level of wisdom, i.e. as the Absolute conscious of itself, embodied in them after the historical completion of theory in the human practice of history. Cieszkowski's future-oriented "post-theoretical practice"[15] in the sphere of society was advocated in order to pervade reality more fully with Absolute Knowledge in self-conscious praxis (the Left Hegelian position) as against 'inactively' awaiting its fulfilment in the course of time (the Right position).

As will be elaborated in detail at various points later on, because he was anxious, like his post-Lukacsian successors, above all to inform political practice and a critique of a specific social order, and because his critique was mediated by the then fashionable but highly dubious Feuerbachian 'inversion'[16] of Hegel with its return to an anthropological naturalism of sensuous 'immediacy',[17] Marx's general critique of Hegel did not actually adequately engage his thought. As Franz Wiedmann has rightly said of the Marxian 'reversal' of the Hegelian premises,

> Hegel was not turned upside down; instead a non-existent theory was turned into its opposite. Any serious criticism of Hegel would have to begin with his monistic principle.[18]

In the heat of the Young Hegelian debates Marx and Engels sidestepped this monistic principle. The consequent dualistic character of their theories is exemplified in the base and superstructure model of society, which conception also has its ancestry in the related Marxian appeal to a material 'substratum' supposedly denied by Hegel.

But even the most high-flown of the anti-liberal Young Hegelians – Bruno Bauer – never denied the real 'material' conditions of social life and the attendant social evils of poverty and suffering which arose out of them. Marx and Engels unfairly lampooned the ineffectiveness of 'critical criticism' directly to change these real conditions because this was never its intention: its aim was to change people's consciousness. (The Frankfurt School are sometimes similarly wrongly criticized today.) Bauer's point was that to revolutionize these circumstances in themselves through mass action was not enough since this would not change the set of human evaluating attitudes of ignorance, ill-will, habit, superstition and confusion associated with and embodied in them. A revolutionizing of people's ideas away from these uncritical 'dogmatisms' towards a rational, universal, critical, ethical attitude was *logically prior* in order to avoid change merely reinstating a new set of evils.[19] After the publication of *The Holy Family* Bauer quite consistently referred to Marx and Engels as "Feuerbachian dogmatists".[20] But they had inverted a simplified version of Bauer's philosophy of self-consciousness and not Hegel, who was never on his head.

Nor was the appeal to a 'substratum' of material life or to 'sensuousness' uniquely Marxian, for it was also very much a feature of other post-Hegelian theory of the period. Although theirs was a far more crude materialism than Marx's practical, non-ontological social version in which epistemological idealism and materialism were ongoingly sublated in human practice,[21] most of the 'vulgar materialists' of the time (Moleschott, Büchner, Vogt, Lange, Haeckel, Dühring) had also reacted against Hegelianism, which they also saw as panlogism. Interestingly, a contemporary observer of the philosophical scene of the time, the Russian theologian Alexis Khomyakov, rightly remarked of the wave of "neo-German materialism" which followed Hegel that

> Criticism recognized one thing: the complete inadequacy of the Hegelian attempt to create a world without a substratum. Hegel's disciples did not understand that their teacher's whole

problem consisted in exactly this, and they very naively imagined that it would be sufficient to introduce this missing substratum into the system to settle the matter.[22]

In Marx's theory, the 'philosophy of action' and 'materialistic' tendencies of post-Hegelian theory are given a precise sociological and epistemological basis through making what I believe to be both a fateful and a fatal methodological switch in the Hegelian dialectic *vis à vis* the status of finite human activity in the world. Marx rejects Feuerbach's contemplative materialism of immediacy, retaining Hegel's rich mediations and stress on the activity of reality but roots these more in human practice. Marx regards Hegel's dialectic as a coded, mystified way of talking about the real material activity of men in history. Thus Hegelian alienation for Marx is a speculative product of the *real* alienation of men from their externalized creations and from realization of their human potentialities permitted by the level of development of the productive forces of the epoch in which they live. Marx shifts the primary emphasis in the active relation between consciousness and objects in Hegel on to human activity in the world against the resistance of its largely self-made social objectivity. The characteristic of man as an objectifying, externalizing species creates an alienated social world for subsequent generations which appears implacable and opaque. Marx, then, instates the primary importance of mundane, profane human practice as the motor of human life and as the creator of an objectivated social world as against Hegel's apparent stress on the activity of consciousness and consequent demotion of human practice to a secondary status. (Although this stress was more associated with Hegelians like Bauer than with Hegel.)

For Hegel, however, aspects of finite reality are continually cancelled or reflected back into the universal substance of which they are variously conscious, particular, foreign and alien negations, *in and through and embodied in*, the particular historical consciousness and activity of men. There was never an external Spirit-force in Hegel's philosophy. Indeed, if Hegel had been an out-and-out Platonist it would make a sociological critique of his thought rather easier – as Mannheim found later in relation to Max Scheler.[23] In Hegel's system new forms and grades of consciousness (types of experience) are continually posited via the active Notion (*Begriff*) in a process of transition and passing away and this process is represented in particular categorial "determinations" of universals. In Marx, the embodied activity of the Notion seems to have become explicable as an overblown projection of human consciousness of objects in the world – which men only in reality know by their ongoing activity – as being the activity which seems to produce those objects. Marx insists on the relation between consciousness and the objective world as resulting from and being explicable solely in terms of the earthly secular practice of men when, however, this was a straw man in relation to Hegel, for whom such a sensuous, practical approach to Nature was already an aspect of the truth as a developing whole and was incorporated into his system as the "finite teleological standpoint".[24] In Hegel, stated at its most abstract, what is finite, immediate, practical and particular is both particular and universal at the same time, a circumstance which is self-revealed in the course of historico-natural development; whereas in Marx that universality is wrongly held to be a disembodied determinant of particularity and separated from it, to which particularity Marx resorts for an explanation of how that non-existent Hegelian separation is said to occur (e.g. in terms of level of social development, division of labour and commodity fetishism). Marx's basic quarrel is, however, with the Young Hegelians (or with a Hegel filtered through their theoretical vulgarizations) and is based on the desire to develop a scientific theory which he felt could infallibly criticize and inform the changing of existing societies. On this issue, he declared:

> The Germans judge everything from the standpoint of eternity (in terms of the essence of Man), foreigners view everything practically, in terms of actually existing men and circumstances. The thoughts and actions of the foreigner are concerned with *temporariness*, the thoughts and actions of the German with *eternity*.[25]

The question which an over-politicized concern with immediate circumstances suppresses, however, is what is the relation between the temporary and the eternal, the transitory and the permanent, the relative and the absolute? What are the mechanisms of continuity and discontinuity? What are the political implications of these questions? We will return to these issues in later chapters.

Marx's secularizing perspective provided the epistemological position that the 'external' world of Nature is inevitably accessible to men only in a socially humanized form. In Hegel, earlier stages of the self-development of the world are co-present in the totality as various active grades of consciousness (or experience) from in-itselfhood to in-and-for-itselfhood. The ultimate alienation of consciousness is present as historyless Nature which is experienced through finite men mainly as being in-itself. In Marx, men are a conscious part of Nature although Nature is still also experienced as in-itself, as alien. It is the conscious social activity of men to master and appropriate the 'in-itself' of Nature in order to satisfy their needs which determines the extent to which they know it. (Hegel would have accepted this conception of human activity but affirmed its *simultaneous* 'universal' character revealed thereby.) So in Marx Nature has a socially imprinted character and an autonomous role in human affairs at one and the same time. Kolakowski has succinctly encapsulated the epistemological implications of Marx's view as being that "Active contact with the resistance of nature creates knowing man and nature as his object at one and the same time".[26] In the literature, too numerous to cite, this world-constituting practical sense contact usually takes one meaning of the term *praxis*.

Furthermore, the closure of epistemological materialism and idealism in human praxis meant that Marx's social scientific position had effectively abandoned debate in such philosophical categories in favour of the study of the level of social development through which that praxis was mediated and which determined the levels of the 'human' and the 'natural'. (But as we will see, philosophical categories lingered on in Marx.) For Marx 'natural' objects were not, as they were for Feuerbach, eternally existing objects of simple sense certainty but given to men through social development and commerce. This sociological argument was a consequence of regarding the sensuous world, unlike Feuerbach, as constituted by socialized human praxis, as "human sense activity".[27] Marx expresses the unity of the natural and the social thus: "the history of nature and the history of men are dependent on each other so long as men exist".[28]

Neither of the two standard interpretations of Marx's often-quoted remarks about knowledge and practice in the 'Theses on Feuerbach' by the philosophers Ernst Bloch[29] and Nathan Rotenstreich[30] has drawn attention to the Hegelian logic of the Theses or to the full significance of the term "*Diesseitigkeit*" in the most interesting and problematic Thesis, the second. This Thesis reads as follows:

> The question whether human thinking can pretend to objective truth is not a theoretical but a *practical* question. Man must prove the truth, i.e. the reality and power, the 'this-sidedness' [*Diesseitigkeit*] of his thinking in practice. The dispute over the reality or non-reality of thinking that is isolated from practice is a purely *scholastic* question.[31]

Philosophers have tended to concentrate on the significance, largely out of context, of the cryptic statements here and in the other Theses for Marx's status as a philosopher who apparently rewrote the classical notion of truth. But I feel that one should always bear in mind that their Hegelian terminology and general intention only make sense in the specific historical context in which they were written. Failure to realize, for example, the specific meaning of the phrases "prove the truth" and "reality and power" in the post-Hegellan context of the 1840s can lead to serious misunderstandings of Marx's meaning. When these considerations are borne in mind (as will be developed later in this study) Marx can be seen from our later historical stage as having been grappling with the whole problem of the *transcendence* of philosophy as such: both in theory (into social science) and in practice (as human self-determination).

The theoretical "standpoints" discussed in the 'Theses' (e.g. materialism, idealism, abstract individualism) are one-sided moments united in an active concrete totality, a conception which was standard wisdom in Hegelian thought. But for Marx, because of his realist[32] stress on that embodying activity as being solely the constituting accomplishment of secular human sensuous praxis in real life, those positions for him simultaneously coincide with political positions defined along different lines from those of the Hegelians. And Marx's position, the "new materialism", is the authentication, the 'truth' of the other standpoints, having been reached through the Hegelian procedure of traversing them, appropriating them and transcending them: whilst none of the overcome positions are 'false'.[33] Thus, in his commitment to communism Marx was driven to an immanent critique of Hegel, since he saw Hegelianism as rationalizing either conservatism or liberalism or as ineffective verbal radicalism. At the same time, in undertaking an immanent critique of Hegel, Marx reached a higher theoretical standpoint which he believed was able to inform the real political practice he sought. The standpoint of the new theory was a projected, potential, socialized "human society" – communism – already present, implicitly, potentially, in the epoch in which Marx was writing. This could be creatively *made* explicit and real since he believed he had shown that reality was solely the product of human practical sense activity and not of the Hegelian Idea or Bauerian self-consciousness. The historical world was thus potentially rationally changeable by its creators and carriers who could consciously harness the real historical dialectic mystified by Hegel. The stress on the mundane practice of men as the world-constituting real location for understanding history as human history (although for us today hardly debatable, a truism) was of course in Marx's time an important position to maintain against those who seemed to deny it as lower or vulgar activity, both in the interests of secular social science as well as politically. Marx's effort to yoke epistemology and politics is brought out by Ernst Bloch. According to him, Marx maintains that men recognize 'reality' because they produce it. This means that the older theory of truth (correspondence of reality and concept) is for Marx "scholastic" because it assumes a "closed immanence of thought" whereas that correspondence has been created by human activity which maintains it and can thus potentially *change* it.[34]

The 'critical criticism' of Hegelians like Bauer was based on the assumption, according to Marx, that bad aspects of real circumstances were the product of lower categories, i.e. that 'unproved', unillumined, uncritical attitudes were embodied in them. It therefore could only critically compare these bad circumstances with the extent to which they fell short of the pure absolute universal form of higher category. For Marx this left social conditions intact, even though it could be rabidly anti-liberal. At the same time, contemplative materialism for Marx was inherently individualistic and thus politically elitist, advocating changing people's bad circumstances from above in order to change the people themselves. Marx says, however, that since reality is praxically constituted, "practical-critical"[35] activity is possible, i.e. activity which changes the practical, real social circumstances to *make* them better accord with what they 'ideally' could be. (This is another way of talking about the realization and abolition of philosophy in praxis.) The 'ideal' of a better society is no abstraction, but is a potentiality written into the results of the developed and developing historical dialectic of society at any point – "the ensemble of social relations".[36] What man can potentially become depends on the level of social development. (This notion is another way of expressing the conception of man 'proving the truth' in practice, which we will mention in a moment.) If like Feuerbach, however, one fails to see the world completely as a product of sensuous, practical activity then it is not possible, within that theory, to grasp or advocate a change of real circumstances which can be social and revolutionary.

When the ongoing changing of circumstances (the material surroundings of man) through human activity is conceived in that practical conception its potential coincidence with human self-conscious "self-changing" can then be rationally conceived: it is "*revolutionary praxis*".[37] This would be a situation in which, to use Hegelian terms, a process of qualitative change has taken place at the level of the totality from *practice* (more unconscious world-constituting determined activity) to *praxis*, i.e. less determined, more self-conscious practical activity. These considerations also underpin Marx's comment about the "in-itself" to "for-itself"[38] process of the proletariat's acquisition of class-consciousness. The blindly developed, social-structural 'presuppositions' of the historical dialectic whereby men have in their practical activity created both the congruence and incongruence of their thinking with their world are then in self-conscious 'critical' praxis harnessed and society rendered less determining, more directive, planful. And if the theory expressing this process has been adequate and true it will be transcended, i.e. abolished in praxis.[39]

Thesis II operates with a Hegelian theory of truth into which, via the methodological switch mentioned earlier, Marx has injected a practical element. The expression "prove the truth" occurs a great deal in the work of Hegel, for whom truth is the progressive cognitive correspondence through stages of development of an object with its active universal substance: i.e. it connotes progress towards its potentiality via various developing determinations. Each of those stages, in reality and in its concomitant categorial reconstruction as a dialectical proof in a necessary developmental sequence, is said to be the 'truth' of the previous ones and to include them. The next stage is implicit in the present stage, it having incorporated the previous ones. The truth also refers to the entire process as a whole, including its revealed teleological potential. The power of a dialectical proof resides in its immanently necessary sequence of deduction: nothing arbitrary or external imposes on it. This is true also, as we have seen, of dialectic in historical reality. An example of a stage in such an analytic proof is Hegel's statement in the *Science of Logic* that the Idea of spirit emerges in the logical exposition from the Idea of life, so that the "Idea of spirit has proved itself to be the truth of the Idea of life".[40] The phrase "reality and power" in Thesis II is specifically Hegelian, occurring in the *Phenomenology*. It refers to the *extent* to which universality has realized itself at a given stage. Hegel says that it is through culture that the individual begins to gain power over his substance, *qua* individuality, without which self-consciousness would be further away from mastery of its world, and powerless and estranged: "The extent of its culture is the measure of its reality and power."[41] The word "*Diesseitigkeit*" in Thesis II means terrestriality, this-worldliness, here-and-now-ness,[42] again underlining Marx's insistence on asserting the exhaustive provenance of thinking in worldly practicality. Interestingly, in his *Prolegomena zur Historiosophie* of 1838, Cieszkowski had claimed in a characteristically Hegelian fashion that in the ancient stage of history the Concept corresponded to objectivity as the "direct *thisness* [*Dieses*] of being, as particularity" when the intellect informed the externality of the world. Whereas the modern period was the "stage of truth" which reversed the correspondence of objectivity to the Concept, so that in the age of the Absolute Knower (which I mentioned earlier) objectivity was "no longer *Dieses*, the thing, etc., but generic reality, essence, the idea". Objectivity had thus come to itself, i.e. in Hegelian terms its universality now explicitly coincided with and informed the intellect.[43] Now the thrust of Marx's critique of the Young Hegelians was effectively to deny Cieszkowski's acceptance of the present historical stage as the realization of truth by suggesting that it mystified the real alienation of truth. He does this by affirming precisely that practical, particular, "*Diesseitigkeit*" of thinking as sole domain of reality: Marx has reversed the Hegelian primacy of the general over the particular. It is thus this human practical historical reality which creates and realizes its own essential nature solely within itself, as a truth or potentiality which continually proves and re-proves itself in that activity. Since the potentialities of a given period change with the level of social development in the historical process as a whole, they have their existence as the potentiality of what men can become given that development only so long as men do not act successfully to realize them. Aside from the relation of his remarks to philosophical definitions of truth[44], it seems that at the most general level Marx's quarrel is with certain kinds of theological interpretations of human history in the name of an Enlightenment commitment to Reason and science to inform the steering of historical processes for the benefit of mankind. Because of the period in which he wrote, his work is a constant implicit dialogue with that kind of thinking. Against the Hegelians he wanted to demonstrate the particular, earthly source of what he saw as their superstitious metaphysics of a transcendent 'universal' reality because this philosophy hindered adequately conceptualizing and thus rationally mastering real circumstances to usher in communism.

But when all is said and done, Marx's 'Theses on Feuerbach' are unpublished jottings and far too cryptic to permit the deduction from them of unequivocal principles about the relations between knowledge and action. My aim here has been, by showing the significance of certain Hegelian terms, at least to guard against some possible misinterpretations. Even so, they remain endemically ambiguous, suggestive rather than definitive and dependent necessarily upon a great deal of careful inference to fathom their intention. Hence, even when something of Marx's 'praxicalised' Hegelianism has been laid bare, one is still left with serious problems. For example, consider one meaning of Thesis II taken together with the famous Thesis XI about "changing" rather than merely "interpreting" the world. Marx seems to be saying that men can act to make "reality" better coincide with "thinking" since such congruence or incongruence is not to be settled solely in theory because it is ongoingly sustained by and thus subject to practical activity. But the undiscriminating terminology involved vitiates understanding the import of these remarks. The woolly philosophical language used ("reality", "thinking", "world", "objective truth", etc.) blocks the way towards distinguishing what could be important *kinds* of correspondences. Nor is there any way of determining the all-important *extent* to which certain relations between 'thought' and 'reality' may remain the same whilst others change, or of suggesting which such relations are more readily subject to being altered by specified forms of practical activity. Furthermore, the Utopian vision of the potentiality of men to create conscious correspondences or congruences in practice between 'reality' and 'thought' is not developed in any systematic way in relation to the various aspects of socially imprinted Nature and social objectivity which I expounded earlier. In short, a great deal could potentially be determined in theory on a number of practical levels which other kinds of practice would not affect.

Another interpretative problem arises over the several connotations attached to the notion of 'proving the truth in practice' which Marx never separated out clearly. Having 'inverted' the Hegelian dialectic to provide the scientifically powerful dialectical necessity of socialism, Marx thereby retains the Hegelian conception of history as a process comprised of various stages, each of which proves the truth of the previous one so that, as in Hegel, the self-developing historical process continually strives to realize what it essentially *is*. But in Marx that essence is the "ensemble of social relations", a truth or potentiality which continually re-posits itself consonant with what the level of social development at any stage makes possible and is subject to being harnessed by real men in practice. In Marx the stress he had to keep on making in his historical context on the exhaustively earthly character of human activity and thought meant that his work in general, and the Theses in particular, became a cry in the name of Reason for the realization by real men of the truth or 'rational' social potentiality possible at the present stage. (And for Marx of course this imperative focused on the fettering of possible development by class interests.) Now, it seems that the verb "must" in the expression 'must prove the truth' probably also connotes the additional overall meaning that man is obliged, almost inevitably condemned, by the exigencies of practical, historical, intergenerational life itself to move beyond, to authenticate and thus to affirm the 'reality and power'of stages of his own self-made history. But notice in addition that Thesis II also plays with the notion of the relation in this process of the "this-sidedness" of "thinking" to practice. Hence the implication is that in the inevitable authentication process of history man exemplifies in practice that the 'reality and power' of ideality or of potentiality in the Hegelian sense is, however, *solely* terrestrial. That is to say, the source of the *idea* of truth (or other 'universal' principles or concepts) lies in the particular unrealized social potentiality of various periods which must at the present time be made *real*, *real*ized in practice; i.e. proving its truth in such a way as also to abolish (transcend) the idea itself.

Following directly from those remarks we must note two further points: first that, as I showed earlier, Marx's practical orientation enables him to envisage, unlike Feuerbach, "practical-critical activity" to make society better accord in practice with what it ought to be or ideally should be, a notion which definitely invests Marx's version of 'proving the truth' with an ethical imperative. It is unlikely that Marx intended a separate ethical meaning since what was ethical was for him written into the imperative to realize the inherently unrealized rational possibilities of the society at whatever stage. For Marx, as for Hegel in a different sense, although its implications and scope are never fully spelled out, the actualization of truth in practice in the sense of social rationality and self-determination, *is* ethical. Second, it seems to me in the light of all the foregoing analysis to be a misunderstanding of the meaning of the phrase 'prove the truth' to conclude, as some have done, that the Theses are intended as an unqualified exhortation to go out and *act*. Moreover, I think it is also a mistake to take their meaning, as some have done, as suggesting in a general and unspecified way that acting to try to change something in the social or natural domains provides the only opportunity of reaching the most profound insights into its structure or nature. One may come to believe that this is the case, but my point is that Thesis II cannot plausibly be regarded as asserting it. The general point at issue for Marx here in the context of the 1840s is the post-Hegelian problem of the realization of truth and freedom in practical activity, a problem which assumes a unique significance for Marx because he has reworked the Hegelian dialectic in what he saw as a secular fashion which threw up a different (practical) conception of truth. But (possibly for fear of conservatism) Marx seldom addresses the issue of what can and cannot be changed by practical activity in society conceived within the conception of human history as a developing socio-natural complex to which he is committed.

Finally, like many other commentators I am also not averse to highlighting a tension in Marx's practical orientation which is, however, a direct product of the time in which he wrote and the theoretical vocabulary available to him but which, as we will see later, was to preoccupy later theorists in the tradition. Marx is equivocal as to whether the historical dialectical process should be regarded as what Lukács and Mannheim both called an unbroken series of 'next steps' or stages (as described in the previous paragraphs) or as tending towards the rational end-state or final stage of communism. Marx frequently insisted that the level of development of productive forces proscribes what it is possible to realize in practice at any given time. He also insisted that it is futile to make abstract provisos about the future before any action has taken place. As Marx explained in 1881,

> What should be done at any definite, given moment of the future and done immediately, depends of course entirely on the given historical conditions in which one has to act. This question however is posed in the clouds and therefore is really a phantom problem to which the only answer can be – criticism of the question itself. No equation can be solved unless its terms contain the elements of its solution.[45]

For Marx, as for Hegel, it would have been unthinkable to have posited an underived static Ought-postulate towards which historical men must strive. Marx's notion of 'proving the truth in practice' implies an endless process since each newly authenticated stage of development throws up a different essence or potentiality for practical realization and the truth of the whole process must continually pose and re-pose itself within and through the historical process of realization. By definition he has excluded a final state of truth. So in the framework of Marx's thought practice and praxis should not be conceived of as separate domains but as aspects of a historical process of becoming by which *practice* always carries the potentiality of becoming *praxis*, or rather more praxical. Practical activity for Marx represents the force of reality itself and, as Rotenstreich rightly remarks, in Marx

> The practice that creates reality also creates the correspondence between essence and reality: that is, it is truth.[46]

But the hard-headed realism implied by the very logic of Marx's practical conception of history as an endless ongoing process of reality-transcendence stands unreconciled with the more appealing Utopian promise (expressed in the terms of political economy) of communism as the rational, uncontradictory end-state to an irrational 'pre-history' of mankind towards which the historical process can be scientifically shown to be tending.

Part two

Georg Lukács: theoretician of praxis

Such fullness in that quarter overflows
And falls into the basin of the mind
That man is stricken deaf and dumb and blind,
For intellect no longer knows
Is from the *Ought*, or *Knower* from the *Known* –
That is to say, ascends to Heaven.

W. B. Yeats

3 Lukács in context

To devote several chapters of this study solely to some of the theoretical issues arising from Georg Lukács's *History and Class Consciousness*[1] does not require extensive justification. That the book marks a watershed in Marxist thinking and has exercised a profound influence on so many Marxist and others since 1923 is beyond doubt.[2] And as will become clear later in this study, aspects of the theoretical problematic of *History and Class Consciousness* permeate the early work of Horkheimer, Adorno and Marcuse.[3] It also represents an activistic attack against fatalistic, deterministic Marxism contemporaneous with Gramsci's, and informed by a similar anti-positivism. Therefore, it must form the starting point of our deliberations, for few would challenge Kolakowski's view that the book is "the most important theoretical work of 20th century Marxism".[4] It hardly need be said that on the level of theory the early Lukács, like Karl Korsch, Gramsci and others at the time, was reacting against orthodox vulgar-materialist Marxism, in Lukács's case from a particular standpoint of praxis. The denigration of Lukács and Korsch by the Soviet orthodoxy in the 1920s as 'professors', 'deviationists', 'idealists', etc., as a result of their writings has been well documented. However, Lukács's theoretical reaction to vulgar materialism is treated elsewhere than in this Part. This chapter should therefore be read in conjunction with the first chapter of Part three, which briefly situates Gramsci, Lukács and Korsch in the development of Marxism, with special reference to their polemics against vulgar Marxism, focusing on Gramsci's and Lukács's critiques of Bukharin's *The Theory of Historical Materialism: A Manual of Popular Sociology*. That chapter also mentions and provides notes of studies of the Marxist controversies of the 1920s. Thus a discussion of the early work of Korsch, usually associated with that of the young Lukács, also appears in that chapter rather than here. Korsch is taken up again in Part four on the subject of the role of philosophy in early critical theory and in Marxist theory in general, to which debate he made a special contribution. In Part three Lukács is further discussed in a comparison with Gramsci in the Excursus on the problem of the mobilization of myths and 'arbitrary' ideologies, since, although writing in different socio-political contexts, they were dealing with this same Marxist practical-theoretical problem.

The rest of this chapter is devoted to four tasks: (a) the schematic delineation, for present purposes in the manner of a historian of ideas,[5] of some of the intellectual 'currents' and 'influences' which Lukács brought to Marxism (notably the '*Lebensphilosophie*' and neo-Kantianism) and which inform his early work in social theory; in *History and Class Consciousness* he is often conducting an implicit dialogue with or sometimes a polemic against these ideas and this section should enable us to obtain a fuller understanding of its content; (b) a selective excursion into the socio-political context of the early Lukács for the purpose of bringing out the important simultaneous ethical and political content of Lukács's epistemological theory of class consciousness; (c) a special focus on some aspects of Max Weber's work as perhaps the most important sociological influence on Lukács (and on subsequent Frankfurt 'Critical Theory'), particularly the processes of the rationalization of society and science under capitalism and the famous notion of the institutional 'iron cage' which men have built around themselves;[6] (d) related to the rationalization problematic, and to the influence of the '*Lebensphilosophie*', a short account of Lukács's concept of reification and its relation to Marx's concepts of alienation and fetishism to introduce the further ramifications of Lukács's thought treated in subsequent chapters.

(a) Intellectual currents and influences

At the biographical level it is pertinent to note that Lukács was taught sociology and philosophy by Max Weber, Rickert, Simmel, Windelband and Emil Lask, Marxism initially by Ervin Szabo, and was also active in Hungarian ultra-leftist politics for which he became for a time a leading theoretician.[7] Like Gramsci, Lukács could be said to have been one of many political thinkers who were trying to theorize the spontaneous workers' movements during and after the First World War. His early more Messianic position changes, however, coincident with his involvement with the Communist Party, his study of Lenin and the building of the Soviet State. But on a more general level, however, we can detect a dialogue in Lukács's early Marxism with the declining neo-Kantianism of the Marburg (Cohen and Natorp) and Heidelberg (Windelband and Rickert) Schools. These

Kantians had formed a sharp reaction along with many other writers at the turn of the century to natural-science-based positivism, and this philosophical orientation was also importantly associated with German sociology in Simmel and Weber. Theoretically speaking, these schools (although by no means unified) broadly located sociological theorizing and philosophy between the co-ordinates of facts being distinguished sharply from value-judgments and the abstention from metaphysical speculation in the name of empirical social science, so restricting philosophy to logic and epistemology. (It was left to Lukács's contemporary Emil Lask to reintroduce ontology into philosophy.) In Germany – unlike in France and England – positivism as such never had a very strong hold and the various schools of Kantianism dominated, providing fairly clear-cut boundaries in human science between fact and value, science and ethics, the natural and the social, and philosophically between subject and object.

In addition, Dilthey's *Geisteswissenschaften* hermeneutic enterprise was firmly entrenched in German human science and it, too, was a theoretical reaction against positivism, which was seen as erroneously wanting to explain the social world without understanding it; and against certain tendencies among the neo-Kantians which agnostically denied the possibility of complete insight into the nature of reality. (This was partly the legacy of the Kantian thing-in-itself.) For Dilthey the historian, by an act of intellectual intuition, sought "hermeneutic understanding of the past through an act of imaginative recovery of other men's thoughts"[8] which was to be a spiritual act aiming to reconstruct the creations of the human spirit which had been laid down in its history. This critique of 'scientism' in social science was in general expressed through the familiar neo-Kantian distinction between natural and cultural sciences, each demanding a different methodology, one causal explanation and the other some kind of method of understanding since the latter dealt with the recovery of the meaning of human history.[9] Lukács, however, was probably never a totally committed Kantian although the orientation provided the philosophical sources of what he saw as fundamental theoretical problems to be solved by a radical reinterpretation of Marx. The important methodological principle which Lukács absorbed from the *Geisteswissenschaften* school was that men are able to understand only that which they have made, a view which was common to Hegel and to Marx, except that Lukács was to develop the Marxian position that it is possible to move beyond the mere *post festum* comprehension of the historical process to its conscious creation and continuation.

The reaction to positivism at the turn of the century also produced the opposite of scientific rationalism in the movement of thought usually known as *Lebensphilosophie*, a form of Romantic intuitionism informed by biological vitalism which Lukács absorbed via Simmel, who was influenced greatly by Bergson. The move towards hermeneutics, intuitionism and irrationalism by philosophers and aestheticians and Romantics (e.g. the symbolist poets and the Stefan George circle) at this time represented their genuine fear that the pursuit of scientific generalizations about society threatened the spiritual autonomy of man. According to Lichtheim, Lukács arrived on the European scene before the First World War at a time when it was widely held that if one had rejected religious faith and traditional metaphysics the choice lay between "the positivism of empirical science and the vitalism . . . of irrationalists such as Nietzsche or Bergson".[10] Both the 'science of spirit' and the 'philosophy of life' were treating of the living, moving totality of world history in which the natural-science distinction between subject and passive, lifeless object over and against it was to be refashioned for the study of human history into a reflective dualism with the stress on the *self*-comprehension of the spiritual creations of men. Philosophically unsolved problems of the two trends lay in the field of how metaphysical certitudes could be arrived at from the study of history when this revealed that human perception was conditioned by each culture; and sociologically, particularly in the work of Weber, the problem became one of deriving complex methods of *Verstehen* sociology whereby the subjective meanings of actors could be 'objectively' incorporated into a science of society.

The themes of life versus dead matter, intuition versus science, understanding versus positivism, culture versus civilization, *Gemeinschaft* versus *Gesellschaft* and so on recur, in pre First World War European sociology and philosophy. It was Rickert for example who talked of the limits of conceptualization in the natural sciences in the name of intuition (in the Kantian sense) and the transcendence of the conceptually knowable from which both Heidegger and Lukács were to develop theories of the reifying function of science.[11] The *Kultur* and *Zivilization* antithesis[12] of German philosophy was extrapolated at length by Oswald Spengler[13] and also developed later by the Frankfurt School into a critique of the estrangement of man in technological-industrial society. Weber provides the link in this tradition through his elaboration of the rationalization-charisma-routinization dialectic. Simmel's notion of the 'tragedy of culture' expresses the theme in another way as the solidifying into objective institutions of the finite forms engendered by infinite life which come to constrain life into a repetitive routine. The forms of life become detached from the stream of life in order that the content of life can become real, but this means that men become enslaved by their products – this is the 'tragic fate' of existence. Lukács's work bears the mark of this notion, which was mediated to Simmel via the highly influential philosophy of Henri Bergson, who developed the idea of the 'reification' carried out on life by the intellect. The historical process for Bergson is pervaded by an impulse, the inward life of things, the *élan vital*, that comes "gushing out unceasingly . . . from an immense reservoir of life".[14] The exigencies of society and intersubjective communication falsify or translate the *durée* of experienced time into the discrete terms of externality-spatiality, which means that men never experience time as authentic continuity. This means that our perceptions and sensations are comprehended clearly and precisely, yes, but *impersonally*, through a public language of stable mechanistic categories. The other confused, inexpressible experience we can sympathize with intuitively, but language cannot express it without arresting its flux and mobility. Bergson sought fluid concepts capable of following reality "in all its sinuosities".[15] The preoccupations of European intellectuals before the First World War were finely anticipated by Heinrich Heine two generations earlier:

> Life is neither means nor end. Life is a right. Life desires to validate this right against the claims of petrifying death, against the past. This justification of life is revolution.[16]

So, seen against the philosophical and sociological controversies of his time, Lukács was, to put it briefly, caught up in the anti-positivist revolt of the Romantics, irrationalists and neo-Kantians, which pushed analysis towards hermeneutics and intuition and away from socio-structural science. (We will turn to the Kantian values/facts separation in a moment.) This tendency provoked great debates on the difficult issue of how objectively to incorporate into social science the subjective meanings which conscious human actors bring to social situations. Two unacceptable alternatives had to be avoided: either (1) reifying or devitalizing that subjective social experience through the procedure of categorizing it scientifically; or (2) running into the arms of irrationalism and relativism by trying hermeneutically to recover that lived experience in all its uniqueness. As for many thinkers in his time, for Lukács at this stage of his development scientism and irrationalism formed the twin horns of an intellectual dilemma, the solution to which he sought in a new totalizing perspective with the aid of the philosophy of Hegel. This would also, however, have to provide a political perspective which was based on neither the positivistic scientific socialism of Bernstein, nor the ethical social democracy of the Kantians nor the anti-bourgeois irrationalism of Sorel which tended also to inform the Romantic Right. Much later Lukács said that in 1923 he had sought the fusion of " 'left' ethics and 'right' epistemology (ontology, etc.)".[17] Lichtheim captures well the "spiritual anguish" of the young Lukács:

The truth is that during those years before the First World War Lukács was torn between the neo-Kantianism of Lask, the neo-Hegelianism of Dilthey, the religious irrationalism of Kierkegaard and the aestheticism of the circle around Gundolf and George; while his political thinking reflected the influence of Sorel, who was then philosophically an admirer of Bergson.[18]

(b) The ethical dimension

This section is intended to support the argument of both Kolakowski and Lichtheim[19] that, in addition to simultaneously proferring an all-embracing praxical solution to the philosophical and sociological dilemmas mentioned above, Lukács provided a theory of history intended to solve a moral dilemma posed by the neo-Kantian ethical socialists. An important element of the neo-Kantianism in German philosophy was, as already fore-shadowed above, the separation of judgments of fact from those of value and the concomitant separation of science and ethics. Moral decisions are reached from one's conscience since moral life is free and self-determining unlike the causal order of Nature. There can be no theory of morals because freedom does not belong to the world of appearances and is not causally bound (if this were so, morality could not tell us what we ought to do). But, as Lichtheim points out, in moving towards Hegel and Marx, Lukács was moving towards a philosophy "that raised no insuperable barrier between 'is' and 'ought' ", for the understanding of history as man's *self-creation* meant that in "*describing* the human condition, such a philosophy likewise *prescribed* the ethics proper to man".[20]

More specifically in relation to the political reality of the time, according to Kolakowski the Kautskyist orthodoxy held that Marxism was a scientific theory which described the social laws leading to socialism which included the self-consciousness of the proletariat as a necessary condition. Thus what the people want, as one of the reasons why socialism must happen, is inscribed in the scientific theory as a fact, not a value. The Kantian 'ethical' socialists (Cohen, Vorländer, Adler and Bauer usually taken together despite individual differences) believed, however, that the historical necessity of socialism built into Marxism needed to be supplemented with a normative ethic, since to be convinced of the historical necessity of socialism does not enable one to make the value-judgment that one approves of socialism. The Marxian doctrine therefore required to be supplemented by the Kantian ethical doctrine that may show the socialist society as the only possible fulfilment of the highest moral requirements. Furthermore, Kautsky's position meant that the scientific understanding of socialism necessarily arose in the activity of the scientists of the party, for the working class were in principle unable to produce this consciousness since it would not be science in that form. This theory leant itself well to the famous Leninist vanguard party conception.

Now, Kolakowski says that Lukács was the first to show that the controversy between "determinist versus ethical interpretations of socialism is meaningless"[21] because the movement of the objective process of history cannot be separated from its perception in the minds of the actors. In Lukács the growth of consciousness of the working class is not simply scientific knowledge, not mere information to be supplemented by the practical or moral attitude. For Lukács the two sides of the controversy are un-Marxian, since the knowledge of the working class about its own social situation is the self-knowledge of society – the famous Lukácsian coincidence of the historical subject and object in the process of knowing. (We can note the similarity here with Gramsci's rejection of Bukharin's 'external' scientific stance *vis-à-vis* society in favour of the practical recreation of the object of enquiry itself, i.e. the self-changing of the masses' unconscious routine activity.)[22] In the privileged consciousness of the proletariat no distinction appears between " 'cognitive' and 'normative' elements: the perception of the social reality and the practical act of its transformation involve each other".[23] Thus the working class knows the socio-historical reality as a whole in the very act of knowing itself and of transforming this reality – Marx's "coincidence of changing and self-changing of circumstances". This Marxist reformulation challenged not only Kantian moralism but Nietzschean immoralism as well and, since Lukács stressed the Hegelian notion that the truth of social phenomena had to be mediated to their place in the whole and applied this to proletarian class-consciousness, the piecemeal reformism of the social democrats was also ruled out.

Kolakowski is quick to point out, however, that even though Lukács heretically departed from Lenin's theory of perception and radically from his and Engels's technological interpretation of the concept of praxis, as well as from Engels's mythological dialectics of nature, the epistemological distinction in Lukács between the actual (empirical) and 'imputed' class-consciousness of the proletariat *still* lent itself to the directive Leninist vanguard party conception *in practice*, since the Party was held to embrace that imputed consciousness.[24] A statement such as the following from Lukács in 1923 might lead us to agree that Kolakowski has got a point here:

> because the party aspires to the highest point that is objectively and revolutionarily attainable – and the momentary desires of the masses are often the most important aspect, the most vital symptom of this – it is sometimes forced to adopt a stance

> opposed to that of the masses; it must show them the way by rejecting their immediate wishes. It is forced to rely upon the fact that only *post festum*, only after many bitter experiences will the masses understand the correctness of the party's view.[25]

Kolakowski's view clearly has profound political implications and must qualify the frequent blanket praise that the early Lukács tends to receive along with Karl Korsch as an anti-authoritarian 'heretic' and 'renegade'.[26] But it should not be allowed to detract from the intellectual quality of the theoretical *tour de force* of *History and Class Consciousness*, nor from what we can learn from its main arguments (as I will try to show in subsequent chapters). Nor must that qualification blind us to the widespread influence of the book on thinkers as diverse and culturally important as Horkheimer, Marcuse, Goldmann and Mannheim and its possible inspiration today of political and sociological currents quite hostile to the putative connection of one theoretical aspect of it with elitist Bolshevik practice.

(c) Max Weber's philosophy of history

The principle of rationalization is arguably the most important element in Weber's philosophy of history and one which Lukács was to counter with an activistic Marxian interpretation, purging it of its heroic pessimism and quietism. In Weber the general direction of secular rationalization is measured by the degree to which magical elements of thought are displaced or by the extent to which "ideas gain in systematic coherence and naturalistic consistency".[27] The relentless and apparently inevitable process of rationalization of art, ethics, education, human institutions and everyday life in the society of the occidental bourgeoisie is such that what were originally institutionally established by men as means to satisfy their needs historically turn into their opposite and dominate subsequent generations of men as ends in themselves. According to Karl Löwith's interpretation the Marxian domination of things over men, of products over producers, is in Weber the domination of means over ends, and the compartmentalization of man through his specialized activity. Because of that process the world is experienced by men as hostile, meaningless, incomprehensible, alien – it is the 'disenchanted' product of the "irrationality of the rationalized".[28] Rationalization demystifies the world but instrumentalizes it at the same time by rendering it calculable. In Weber's famous words, men have made, and continue to make and remake, in the "tremendous cosmos of the modern economic order", an "iron cage"[29] of institutions around themselves and there is a trend towards further rationalization of inexorable power in the form of bureaucracies, in a world governed by 'ascetic' rationalism.

In Weber's historical depiction of the genesis of these processes there is not the banal formula that Protestantism 'caused' capitalism, but rather that the mode of life of the occidental bourgeoisie carried a normative ethos, manifested in the 'spirit' of (bourgeois) capitalism as well as that of (bourgeois) Protestantism. There is the formation of an all-pervading rationality of the mode of life which has allowed the formation of the religious attitudes as well as the economic attitudes which inform capitalism. Wherever the definite attitudes of a practical, rational mode of life are missing, then the development of an economically rational mode of life, he says, also "encountered serious internal obstacles".[30]

The comprehension of the apparatization of society and the formation of the iron cage carries for Weber the political intention of restoring the potentialities of the individual in the face of this increasingly rationalizing world. The individual, at least, can oppose rationalization and fight it: it is this opposition which *gives* him his individuality, against the conformity of the rationalization. For Weber, freedom is the ability of the self-responsible individual to choose means towards his ends *within* the rationalized world. Like the Frankfurt School later on, Weber was afraid lest historical development might lead to the total victory of the "technical man" over "cultured man".[31] He sees history as an endless struggle between creative, charismatic eruptions and rationalizing bureaucracy, with the latter always likely to win out because it has every material condition, in Marxian terms, on its side. Implicit in Weber's conception is Nietzsche's call for great men animated by spiritual ideals to rise above the fetters of their time and has a longer-term ancestry in Hegel's 'world-historical individuals' in *The Philosophy of History*. Weber is concerned with the individual at a time when both developed capitalism and nascent socialism were threatening to bury him: "We individualists and partisans of democratic institutions are swimming against the tide of materialist forces."[32] The rationalization-charisma-routinization dialectic has an overall tendency towards bureaucracy and reification which (under all social forms, including socialist) politically had the effect of precluding the exercise of power wholeheartedly, responsibly, with personal commitment, authority, heroism and strength. This is because it tended to produce, as part of the processes of specialization, professional politicians who act out the practice of ruling in an unvocational way as a form of business administration which "can never hope to exceed the limits of the established order".[33] Politics must not be given up to professional politicians who can only conform. Weber thus comes out politically against both anaemic, weak, 'irresponsible' liberalism *and* the "psychic proletarianization in the interests of discipline"[34] which sets in when everyday life has routinized itself after the emotional surge of a socialist revolutionary sequence. In all those cases everyday life and its traditional dominance jells again, which men's strength and nobility must strive to move beyond once more:

> all historical experience confirms the truth – that man would not have attained the possible unless time and again he had reached out for the impossible. But to do that a man must be a leader, and not only a leader but a hero as well, in a very sober sense of the word.[35]

Expressed in terms of Weber's taxonomy of types of legitimate domination, charismatic dominance is dialectically related to traditional dominance, and Wolfgang Mommsen points out that Weber elaborates his typology in the reverse order in order to imply that there is no sort of logical sequence intended or still less a fixed cycle. (These would be metaphysical prejudices.) But Mommsen also says that Weber's analysis of the historical process of the enslavement of man by his institutions is in terms of

> a descent from a predominantly charismatic form, through traditional, to bureaucratic forms of life and dominance, interrupted again and again and directed into new courses by further eruptions of charisma.[36]

Marx too of course talks of the historical bondage of men in their alienation from their own social and institutional products but Engels stressed the two-sided character of the Marxian perception of that process of 'descent': it was in Marx, however, simultaneously an 'ascent', laying the foundation for its collective supersession. Politically, on this view, Engels said that the proletariat must seize the means of production to free those means from the character of capital they have thus far historically borne. This gives their socialized character laid down under the bourgeois mode of production freedom to work itself out. The corresponding sociological process meant that

> Man's own social organization, hitherto confronting him as a necessity imposed by Nature and history, now becomes the result of his own free action . . . Only from that time will man himself, more and more consciously, make his own history – only from that time will the social causes set in movement by him have, in the main and in a constantly growing measure, the results intended by him. It is the ascent of man from the kingdom of necessity to the kingdom of freedom.[37]

In the rationalized and alienated world of men's own forgotten creation, the value-judgment in Weber is what the individual is compelled to carry out in the face of what Hegel would call the 'in-itselfhood' of the 'external', incomprehensible, rationalized social world. The stripping away of magic in the process of the disenchantment of the world through rationalization removed any 'objective' meaning in the world and men needed to enquire anew about objectivity and its meaning, since an independent meaning could no longer be imputed to it. Thus, man is forced to forge his own objective meaning and a meaningful relationship to things on his own, and Weber's 'ideal-type' methodology flows directly from this view of man and history. It is founded in a "specific 'illusionless' man who has been thrown back upon himself alone in a world become objectively meaningless".[38] For Weber this view is a sociological judgment based on an assessment of the compartmentalization of society at higher stages of the division of labour: his philosophy of history is tied to this scientific analysis. The ideal-type emancipates men from metaphysical illusions about the world and from the old religious belief in essences behind appearances which go beyond the scope of empirical knowledge. The construction of the ideal-type brings the characteristic unique elements of *a* particular phenomenon together to substitute a coherence for the incoherence of the experienced rationalized reality. All these judgments are based on ultimate standards present in concrete value-judgments, and science must bring these to consciousness to free men from their thrall. Objectivity for Weber is always "so-called objectivity", about which he remarks:

> so-called objectivity rests exclusively upon the ordering of the given reality according to categories which are subjective in a specific sense, namely in that they present the presuppositions of our knowledge and are based on the presuppositions of the value of those truths which empirical knowledge alone is able to give us.[39]

This objectivity is constitutive of the process of rationalization which carries with it specialization, professionalization, bureaucratization and separation of life spheres, and Weber's science of these processes is intended to move *towards* 'value-freedom'. The aim is to reveal "the '*apriori*' of the determining value ideas in all and each specific individual enquiry".[40]

Freedom in Weber is, as we have seen, the ability of the individual to choose means towards ends and for Weber science cannot tell one what one 'ought' to do, but only what one can consistently do with given means in relation to a preconceived goal. Science, then, for Weber, provides the knowledge of the adequate means in society for pursuing the ultimate ends which arise during the age-long charisma-rationalization dialectic. Weber is not advocating 'value-freedom' in any crass, scientistic sense; rather that in the face of the multiplicity of value-judgments of the reified, disenchanted world one must reflect upon the "extra-scientific standards operative in scientific judgement"[41] instead of taking science on trust. In this way the value ideas are not eliminated nor is this pretence made, but values inherent in scientific enterprises are objectified, made conscious, so that men can have the possibility of distancing themselves from them. What is being advocated, then, is a *process* of distanciation, of freeing from values, (in the special sense used by Weber), not an abstract 'value-free' position. To move towards value-freedom – which is the expression of the separation of life spheres – is to move towards fighting all absolute value claims from any source as superstition. Weber wants to know the meaning of specialized, occidental rationalized science for he realizes that faith in scientific truth as a value is a product of societies. The disclosure of the values inherent in scientific enterprises is to demagicize them. The destruction of absolute value-claims thus serves further to liberate man on the level of theory from the forces which enslave him, just as Weber's appeal to the sovereign individual in the face of the heartless rationalized world is intended to "salvage the human hero".[42]

An example of an absolute, enslaving value claim for Weber was the Marxian concept of objective historical necessity. For Weber, Marx's idea of the 'objective' progressive development of history (mediated for Weber through the deterministic orthodoxy of the German Social Democratic Party of his time) is untenable since it, too, is a mere transcendental prejudice, which went "beyond the workaday prosaicness of a disenchanted world".[43] Weber declared that the Marxian conception of historical necessity appears in history only when

> the need arises to endow the course of humanity's fate, depleted of religiosity, with a this-worldly 'meaning' that is nevertheless objective.[44]

This can be taken as a succinct statement of the issue dividing Marxism and neo-Kantianism on the question of the inherent meaning of social reality. So Weber held that Marxism could not distance itself from a positivistic faith in science to question scientific objectivity. Löwith rightly equates Weber's rationalization with Marx's self-alienation in the sense previously quoted from Engels and sees the crucial difference between them as lying of course along the axis of the understanding of self-alienation *vis-à-vis* changing the alienated world through the self-consciousness of its participants based on that understanding. Marx believes that the historical process is both an ascent as well as a descent, such that the alienating effects of the division of labour and its concomitant ideological illusions can be abolished, and specialist man along with it, since the same process lays the foundation for its transcendence. This is the emancipation of man for the highest classless human community, as envisaged in *The German Ideology*. Whereas for Weber rationalization was seen as inevitably retrenching itself and viewed with a kind of heroic pessimism, so he sought the salvation of the human hero in the face of those social forces and lauded the charismatic moment. Weber wants liberation from superstition and prejudice and the creation of a committed self-responsible political vocation in the face of the inevitably rationalizing world, capitalist or socialist.

For both thinkers, knowledge is the socio-historical self-knowledge of mankind, in that it brings to the consciousness of its participants the patterns of the social institutions their ancestors made and they ongoingly reproduce. In Marx, as in Weber, the point is at least to understand the world. But Marx, as we saw in the last chapter, also does not want to give up the possibility of the quasi-Utopian, Hegelian elimination of forms of social-structural historical bondage and contradiction and hopes for a more total transcendence of alienation.[45] Löwith points out, however, how Weber's individualism is far more profound than the "average individualism", the "philistine freedom of private convenience" which Hegel and Marx fought against; but that

> it is also in extreme contrast to that "freedom" for which Marx wanted to emancipate man "humanly" and which, to him, was a freedom of "highest community". To Weber, this idea of Marx's was utopianism, while to Marx the human hero of Weber probably would have seemed a "conjuration of the dead", an isolated second edition of the heroic age of the bourgeoisie whose "sober reality" is "unheroic" and merely the ghost of its once great past. What for Weber was "ineluctable fate" for Marx was nothing more than the "prehistory" of mankind and that point which, for Marx, would mark the beginning of true history was, for Weber, the beginning of an ethic of irresponsible "conviction".[46]

(d) Fetishism, alienation and reification

Lukacs has a grand conception of the class-conscious proletariat as the identical collective subject-object of the productive history of mankind whose action reveals the secret of commodity fetishism, 'solves the riddle of history' (to paraphrase Marx) and ushers in a reality which no longer requires illusions. This theory is predicated on the idea of the reification of reality at certain stages of the development of capitalism and the part in this process of the consciousness of the proletariat of their role in the capital/labour dialectic. Lukács's theory is developed from Marx's analysis of alienation and the related concept of the fetishism of commodities in *Capital*.

The young Marx, convinced that the Hegelian dialectic saw history as the product of a self-activating Concept and was thus on its head, asked this question in his notebooks of 1845: why do "the ideologists turn everything upside-down"?[47] And his reply was that some of these illusions arose from the relations of individuals in the division of labour, i.e. from the standpoint of their particular sector of it (e.g. that of a judge, a religionist) they came to believe that their own ideas which are developed there are the active driving force of reality. It is thus to the relations of real life that one must turn for an explanation, for example, of the religious consciousness: "Religion is from the outset consciousness of the *transcendental* arising from a *real* necessity."[48] Marx then proceeds in *Capital* to a detailed analysis of commodity fetishism as an example of another mechanism from which certain illusions of the transcendent arise. Commodity production based on exchange endows commodities with enigmatic and mystical qualities: Marx says that as soon as an everyday object "steps forth as a commodity, it is changed into something transcendent".[49] This fetishism, says Marx, has its origin in the social character of human labour which appears to men as an objective character stamped on the product of labour. This is because the relation of the producers to the sum total of their own labour under capitalism is presented to them as a social relation between the actual products of their labour (commodities). The qualities of commodities are not therefore exhausted by their physical properties. The hidden value relation, although not perceptible to the senses as such, is none the less *real* and not of supermundane provenance. Hence a definite social relation between men "assumes in their eyes, the fantastic form of a relation between things"[50] analogous to the pseudo-independence that the deity has in religions.[51] The point of this for Marx is to show the precise earthly roots of the enigmatic, seemingly independent, mystical qualities of commodities and, by extension, the illusory independence of ideas in any form. It enables Marx to speak of real phenomena beyond direct experience without being accused of metaphysics, as well as enabling a more powerful piece of 'true criticism' of the object. In particular, of course, Marx is anxious to expunge from human science, by showing its secular basis, what he saw as the Hegelian notion that in each epoch one looks for a category, the developing representative of the "Idea" as the independent subject of the historical process, the "demiurgos of the real world".[52]

Even though under capitalism the relations between persons in the productive process have taken on the appearance of relations between things, Marx says that the appearance is none the less the real and palpable social reality for the participants of society. In other words, for Marx reality in this respect is *inherently* illusory, or 'ideological' in the broadest sense. In Maurice Godelier's words: "It is not the subject who deceives himself, but *reality* which deceives *him*."[53] This 'real illusion' relates to specific mechanisms of appearance generation under commodity production of which it is the task of a critical social science to grasp the essential relations with a view to promoting action to change them. But the conception is also tied to the place of the bourgeois epoch in Marx's longer-term historical perspective, whereby the spontaneous process of social development systematically mystifies itself as long as the level of social development and class-consciousness are not sufficiently developed to enable a stage to be achieved whereby ideologies are sublated in a condition in which men consciously create history. As George Lichtheim wrote of Marx's philosophy of history:

> Consciousness is ideological because it is powerless. When it becomes the determining factor, it sheds its blinkers along with its dependence on material circumstances. *A rational order is one in which thinking determines being*. Men will be free when they are able to *produce* their own circumstances.[54]

Lukács's concept of reification (*Verdinglichung*) is a characteristically turn-of-the-century theoretical development of the Marxian *Entfremdung*, or estrangement, as the second moment of the self-alienation of men in their social products and of the related notion of the fetishism of commodities. *Entfremdung* in Marx carries the connotation of men being thwarted by a hostile power of their own making.[55] Reification in Lukács is an extreme stage of the loss to consciousness of men's externalizations after their 'initial' objectification or *Entäusserung* when, at higher stages of development, the institutional 'iron cage' in Weber's terms has become an alienated, utterly incomprehensible, hardened and intractable reality which blindly determines men more or less totally outside their conscious control. Reification connotes a harsh thing-like dead character pervading social reality.[56] Lukács fills out the socio-historical genesis and cultural consequences of such a development. His argument is that advanced capitalist society, characterized by commodity production and exchange, produces an "immediate", reified world together with a conceptual apparatus and modes of consciousness which in social science and philosophy produce abstract, formalistic, irresolvably antinomic categories because their mediated origin and genesis in the "real substratum" of bourgeois society (the set of social relations of production) remains untheorized. (Bergson expressed this in a philosophical fashion as the generalized falsification of lived experience by the socialized intellect.) Thus, the true relationship of human subjects and their objects has been inverted, since the immediately ascertainable world of social objects (thing-like relations) only has such an 'objectivity' so long as men are not aware of the real relations that have created it and are ongoingly doing so. Under reified conditions men are virtually completely determined by blind self-made forces both in theory and in practice, constituting the nadir of inhumanity if fulfilled humanness is defined as potential self-determination. Since there can be little truly self-conscious creative activity in this reality, most activity is purely "contemplative".

Lukács stresses that commodity relations are specific to capitalism and that their effects qualitatively penetrate all aspects of the "*total* outer and inner life of society"[57] since the commodity is universal in this society. There are objective and subjective sides to the phenomenon of reification: objectively, says Lukács a "world of objects and relations between things springs into being" and man eventually discovers the laws governing them, although "even so they confront him as invisible forces that generate their own power".[58] Subjectively, a man's activity becomes estranged from himself and becomes inhumanly independent of him, abstract, comparable, measurable with increasing precision according to the time socially necessary for its accomplishment. A commodity society work-process, says Lukács, in Weberian terms anticipating within Marxist theory the Frankfurt School's concept of instrumental rationality, "turns into the objective synthesis of rationalised special systems whose unity is determined by pure calculation and which must therefore seem to be arbitrarily connected with each other".[59] Lukács is maintaining that calculative reasoning has its basis in relations between things on the surface of capitalist society and the measurable comparability of commoditized, quantitized, exchangeable articles, irrespective of their other properties. In Weberian terms, Lukács observes "a continuous trend towards greater rationalization" based on "abstract, rational, specialized operations" and on "what is and *can be calculated*".[60] Unless one can show that the essence of this process comprises human productive relations lost to the consciousness of their participants – and then raise them to a conscious level – then conceptualizations of the reified exterior are bound arbitrarily to generalize and equate under measurable categories what are or were simultaneously qualitative, real relations. Lukács thus locates in commodity fetishism the source of Weber's analysis of the irrationality of the rationalized.

At later stages of capitalist development this process becomes more radically autonomous and mechanized, so that the activity of men becomes paradoxically less and less active. The penetration of reification deeper and deeper into men's consciousness produces in practice a closed system of social laws impervious to human intervention, a closed system which, says Lukács in Bergsonian language, "reduces space and time to a common denominator and degrades time to the dimension of space".[61] In arguments which anticipated Marx's analysis of estranged labour in the Paris manuscripts which were not to see the light of day until a decade later, Lukács develops a conception of the "reification of work" and relates it to the quantification of time, the atomization of the worker, rational calculability and the apparently immutable nature of the produced and reproduced mechanism of capitalist society: what Adorno later called the "administered" reality. Lukács maintains that the "intellectual confrontation of the individual with society"[62] could only take place under commodity production where isolated acts of exchange take place between isolated commodity owners. The self-experience of being an individual in the face of a hostile world outside ("society") is, however, a product of and is embodied in a definite type of social order – one of commodity production which carries with it levels of mystification which produce a reality comprised of arbitrary processes, calculability and isolated, atomized commodity relations. This analysis enables Lukács to locate specific mechanisms of reification under commodity production, a position which expressed more sociologically (although, as we will later argue, not sociologically enough) what Simmel and Bergson saw as an anthropological feature of human social existence itself, i.e. the falsification of lived experiences through their apprehension via mechanistic, spatial and impersonal public categories. For Lukács, however, these theories were products of and expressed the real experiences of men of the fetishized, surface features of the relations between things which characterize capitalist reality. Simmel's 'tragedy of culture', the loss of infinite life to forms of finite social organization, and Weber's routinization of charisma, were not inevitable, but the specific expression of men's experiences of the reifications associated with capitalist commodity exchange and thus potentially changeable by the action of the primary producers within the real capital/labour relation which give rise to the reifications – the proletariat.[63]

When at later stages of development the consciousness of men is thoroughly permeated by reification it determines their theoretical and philosophical deliberations. The rational, calculative transformation of the commodity relation into a ghostly objectivity imprints itself upon the whole consciousness of men and is epitomized by the scientific concept of a law, which formalizes the "unthinking, mundane reality that life seems firmly held together by 'natural laws' ".[64] This statement in its time (1923) struck at the basis of the orthodox Marxist emphasis on inevitable laws of social development, since Lukács was virtually saying that belief in social laws was a product of reified bourgeois thought. At the same time, Lukács was countering the Weberians by showing that their perception of an incomprehensible reality, understandable only in its unique parts, simply articulated the normal, irrational, thing-like relations of the surface of capitalist social reality. Of this everyday reality and its laws Lukács declared:

> it can experience a sudden dislocation because the bonds uniting its various elements and partial systems are a chance affair even at their most normal. So that the pretence that society is regulated by 'eternal, iron' laws which branch off into the different special laws applying to particular areas is finally revealed for what it is: a pretence.[65]

This conception enabled Lukács to agree that society *was* law-like in the way the positivists said it was, but that such theory exemplified reified thought; it was a product of a calculative commodity society in which commodity relations have permeated profoundly into men's consciousness. Although at the same time it actually *accurately* captured the reality of bourgeois society for its participants. (In so saying of course, he unwittingly reinstated positivism: but more on this later.) The connections produced by the social laws were of necessity fortuitous collocations of random instances which are inherently arbitrary or irrational in the reality and therefore pre-eminently amenable to such positivist, natural-science-like explanation. There is no need to see as inevitable the elaboration of nominalistic arbitrary value-judgments in the face of the iron cage of rationalized capitalism, nor to go for a *Verstehen* hermeneutic approach against the intrusion of positivism into social science.[66] Lukács effectively said that the choice between positivism or such anti-positivist strategies was not an important one once the praxis of the proletariat is on the agenda. Lukács historicized these two standpoints into their genesis in a specific mode of production at certain stages of its development as the scientization of the law-amenable regularities of its exchange relations in a "totality ruled by chance"[67] and the subjectivist reaction to that social science's consequent acquiescence in the atomized dehumanization of men.

The hermeneutics of the *Geisteswissenschaften* school rightly feared that scientism in human science threatened the spiritual autonomy of man, but failed to see the mechanism of reification which gave rise to the experience of the surface regularities of society of which the law was the expression, both in its origins and subsequent social applications. A change in the structure of the commodity-based totality was what was required to eliminate the conditions which gave rise to the irrational society in the first place. If Lukács had paraphrased Dilthey he would have said that natural-science laws embraced that part of reality which is independently produced from men's thoughts and that such laws can also embrace the reified social reality as long as this, too, is produced outside men's thoughts, in the sense of their not understanding what they are creating. Thus for Lukács the class-conscious proletariat, whose location is locked into the real relations which produce the fetishes of reality, *can overturn the whole illusion-creating totality from 'within'*. (Failure to see the politics of the matter this way led either to quietism or Weberian individualism.) This would be tantamount to the disenchanted, demagicized objective reality of the Weberians giving *itself* meaning in praxis instead of the problem of objective meaning remaining a question resolvable in terms of liberating men in theory from values and prejudices present in judgments of an inherently incomprehensible reality. The victory of the proletariat also resolved the scientism versus irrationalism dilemma in a self-conscious collective praxis which overturned the social reality which generated them.

By the essentialist dialectical method it could be shown critically that the process of value production is dialectically wedded to surface social relations and the reified forms of consciousness which have so permeated bourgeois thought. Against Weber, Lukács was saying that there *was* a supra-individual objective meaning in the seemingly incomprehensible rationalized and specialized life-spheres of social reality which was not a mere transcendental prejudice. Moreover, not only did one have to look beneath the intensely reified appearance of society for this, but as a corollary one had to embrace the *totality* rather than one of Weber's unique elements. Lukács's analysis of bourgeois thought, to which we will now turn, was an attempt to show that neo-Kantian philosophy and Weberian sociology were the inheritors of an irrationalist and individualistic form of thought which could not overcome the problem of the 'givenness' of the reality of bourgeois society. What these disciplines ironically regarded as the sole source of empirical knowledge, however, was the illusorily transcendent result of the social relations of commodity production developed to a level of concrete reification unsurpassed in the history of mankind.

4 Subject and object in bourgeois philosophy

The phenomenon of the reification of institutions and social relations produced at advanced stages of the development of commodity capitalism also permeates the consciousness of their participants. Lukács argues that the "Modern critical philosophy" (i.e. that of the Kantians) springs from "the reified structure of consciousness"[1] and it is this circumstance which distinguishes its specific problematics from those of previous philosophies. He advances a sketch not of the history of this philosophy, but of the "connection between its fundamental problems . . . and the *basis in existence* from which these problems spring and to which they strive to return by the road of the understanding".[2] This reconstruction of traditional European philosophy and its development in terms of its social basis is directed towards illuminating the significance of the self-imposed limitations of the neo-Kantianism of his contemporaries in a historical perspective – an aim which also had a political meaning since many of the ethical socialists were Kantians. By focusing on what the philosophies dealt with and also pregnantly did *not* deal with, we can reveal in them their "inability to grasp their own societal existence in the present and hence also in history".[3] (Althusser seems not to have noticed Lukács's foreshadowing of the method of studying the absences as much as the presences in a social theory or philosophy and tracing these to its 'conditions of existence'.)[4]

The classical philosophy being discussed by Lukács is roughly European philosophy from Descartes onwards and including, in addition to Kant, the rationalists, the empiricists, Fichte and Hegel, the vast complexity of whose thought Lukács reduces to permutations of the twin problems of: (a) the *content* of the forms and categories which men bring to their objects of cognition, through which they to some extent 'create' the world (and are thus able to know it); and (b) the problem of the ultimate substance of knowledge, i.e. the quality of what extra knowledge is needed to bring partial knowledge up to a system of perfect knowledge of the world. These problems are epitomized in the epistemological debates associated with the Kantian 'categories of the understanding' and the issue of the unknowable 'thing-in-itself'. The notions result, putting it simply, in the view that the subject filters the world of objects through *a priori* categories which he brings to it prior to experience, ever ignorant of the ultimate knowledge of the world's real nature. Lukács has clearly simplified the concerns of the philosophers he is dealing with here, overstressing their epistemological deliberations at the expense of other areas, such as moral and political philosophy or aesthetics (although he could argue that these, too, were caught up in the same limitations deriving from the same basis in existence.) Simplified this way, however, it renders more straightforward the task of presenting the basic problematic of Western philosophy since Descartes as being the relation between subject and object and tracing this to the reified society of abstract commodity relations – thus paving the way for the notion of the proletariat as the identical subject-object of history. (The issue of the legitimacy of Lukács's reduction will be taken up in the next chapter in relation to Hegel.)

Lukács's recurring argument about the insuperable problem of the 'given' perennially facing bourgeois philosophy, and that of Kant in particular, can be seen as the application and reapplication of the following statement by Hegel:

> The critical philosophy . . . like the latter idealism . . . was overawed by the object, and so the logical determinations were given an essentially subjective significance with the result that these philosophies remained burdened with the object they had avoided and were left with the residue of a thing-in-itself, an infinite obstacle, as a beyond.[5]

According to Lukács, Kant could not face that the problem of the content of the forms or categories was not something unproblematic or which could be assumed or left out of consideration. The problem was whether the content of the forms could be taken as given or conceived, too, as the 'product' of reason. It was this problem which classical German philosophy tried to overcome; that is, how to "grasp and hold on to the irrational character of the actual contents of the concepts".[6] So Lukács sees classical philosophy faced with the same apparently insoluble dilemma which he himself found relived in the debates about the irrationality of matter or other aspects of reality among the neo-Kantians of his own time. This dilemma was of either integrating 'irrational' contents into the system of forms by making them universally applicable, in which case the content becomes non-existent in a system of dogmatic rationalism; or of conceding the interpenetration of the contents into the structures of the forms and into the system, which effectively destroys the system since it then becomes a mere register of facts which are inherently unlinked and can therefore not be made systematic even though the forms themselves are rational.[7]

Lukács argues that the systems that mathematics influenced (particularly that of Leibniz) actually thrived on the irrationality of the given world. Mathematics regarded the irrationality of a given content as a challenge and a stimulus to modify and reinterpret its formal system which, by the necessity of its logic, could show such 'given' content to have been 'created'.[8] The given conceptual content of mathematics is, however, of purer origins and qualitatively different in its irrationality from "the irrationality of existence (both as a totality and as the 'ultimate' material substratum underlying the forms)".[9] But this did not deter most of the classical German philosophers from pressing even that material substratum (as well as matter) into the mathematical method. This procedure blinded them to the fact that the continual creation of the content of the categories has quite a different meaning in reference to the "material base of existence" from what it involves in the world of mathematics which is "a wholly constructed world".[10] For the mathematicians, new concepts meant creating new content since the process of creation of the forms and the content were internal and self-referring, so comprehension and formal invention coincided.[11] But rationally comprehending the facts of material existence in formal concepts is only a possibility since the origin of the content or object here is beyond the control or creation of the conceptualizer. It thus has to be left out of account for the purpose of explanation. It remains given, non-created, irrational. Significantly, this object is the historically transitory material substratum of bourgeois society. Faced with the basis of the form-content relationship philosophers tended either to laud the mathematical method as the proper method for philosophy or sought to establish the irrationality of matter as an ultimate fact of existence. In either case, according to Lukács, they by-passed the issue. In so doing they expressed the horizon which delimited the world of the bourgeois class, a class which had—

> Naively equated its own forms of thought, the forms in which it saw the world in accordance with its own existence in society, with reality and with existence as such.[12]

Moreover, the simple recognition, without solution, of the problem of the givenness of a material existence which was assumed to produce itself for rational categorization, led not only to a rejection of ontology but also to the decline of attempts to grasp the totality. Abstract rational systems could be applied to knowledge of isolated specialized areas to which such systems were well suited. This became the epistemological focus of philosophy. But any attempt to achieve a unified grasp of the totality was relegated to the realm of the 'unscientific'.[13] Indeed, regarding the special sciences as independent of each other in all respects assumed that the totality problem was insoluble. Hence, the underlying material substratum of neither individual sciences nor of the totality was ever theorized.

The philosophical consummation of the confrontation of subject and object in a dialectical process "enacted essentially *between the subject and the object*"[14] comes of course with Hegel, who recasts the problems of logical forms by grounding them in the nature of their content at various stages and various grades of *self*-determination. In the Hegelian system of self-mediation and the self-creation of the world, 'subject' and 'object' interpenetrate in a complex totality of levels of self-activating processes, of different grades of objectivity. Lukács's view of Hegel's system of subject-object relations is that his method itself blocked the way to a systematic understanding of the origin and nature of the *real* contents in their evolution. These appear only as obstacles to be overcome in Hegel's processes, not as the "simultaneous result, goal and substratum of the method"[15] which requires us to be able to theorize how the substratum is produced and reproduced *by men*, as their activity (even though it may largely be alienated activity). Although Hegel has an ultimately identical substance-subject, for his 'we' subject (given that he has superseded the subjectivist Kantian standpoint) all he can find is the "World Spirit, or rather, its concrete incarnations . . . of individual peoples".[16] This conception makes deeds transcendent to the doer, rendering any freedom attained as specious freedom. Moreover, in his pursuit of the real producers of reality Hegel was driven into the arms of mythology, into a standpoint "out beyond history".[17] (I will return to this point later.) It was an attempt to break out of the boundaries imposed on "formal and rationalistic (bourgeois, reified) thought" and thereby to restore "a humanity destroyed by that reification".[18] But ultimately the duality of subject-object in Hegel remains contemplative and the content ultimately irrational since actual human praxis is not its basis. Thus the antinomies of the "life-basis" of classical philosophy were taken to their extreme in Hegel, who was unable to resolve them because he would have had to have founded a philosophy that would envisage the end of the society which gave rise to the antinomies. For the only way the real can actually be made rational is through human praxis. So he could only provide a "complete intellectual copy and the *a priori* deduction of bourgeois society".[19] Although the dialectical method remained, which beckoned beyond bourgeois society and was historically destined for its true bearers, *the* 'we' of history, the real collective subject-object: the proletariat.

The foregoing can now be more closely integrated into Lukács's theories of reification and praxis. The rationalizing process of the development of bourgeois capitalism and the growth of the specialized division of labour produces and reproduces a social reality of repeatable, quantitative, calculative relations mediated by measurable, exchangeable commodities which engenders a reified consciousness in men. This consciousness duplicates the situation whereby real relations masquerade as ghostly relations between things. The rationalization of the world has reached extensive proportions when this reification jells, because individuals then know less and less the mechanisms of the world which confronts them. This reality operates beyond their control and all life becomes calculable. The classical philosophers up to Kant naïvely took this world for granted because they partook of this reified consciousness which only saw the given, irrational, empirical social world as reality, isolated from its real "substratum". Because they believed this appearance of irrationality to be indubitable (which to an extent it is) the philosophers created forms of thought and took philosophical stances which were based on a naïve acceptance of that world. Individuals were precluded from a comprehension of the society as a whole because they had absorbed the atomizing capitalist rationality. This rationality encourages that narrow comprehension because in an economic system in which commodity production is universal and a market operates, the system's very foundation and functioning is dependent upon the ability of individual commodity owners calculatively to be able to exploit isolated aspects of the probabilities of its operation for their own ends. The economic laws of the system are indeed the unconscious product of those commodity owners acting independently in that way but, since it is only a limited view of the whole they need, this is what they tend only to develop. This calculative reality fosters competition which would not be feasible if there were an exact, rational systematic mode of functioning for the whole of society "to correspond to the rationality of isolated phenomena".[20] As soon as the overall mechanisms of a competitive economy are known, i.e. known in their true nature, the chances of exploitation and profit would disappear.

Assumed in the absolute terms of philosophical discourse about the subject and the object, form and content, rational and irrational, was a givenness of reality which the philosophers took as a taken-for-granted starting point, and which remained irrationally untheorized and assumed to be beyond human knowledge. This was the actual givenness, however, of a specific social reality at a specific level of development born of the activities and creations of men, but lost to their complete consciousness. It assumed an arbitrary splintered (but unfortunately functional) facticity. Thus the progress of rationalization and specialization of bourgeois society carries with it in analytical bourgeois thought an increasing grasp of its details but a decreasing grasp of its totality. It is in Hegel's philosophy of the dialectical interpenetration of subject and object and the grounding of logical forms in their content as part of a self-mediating totality, that bourgeois thought reached the zenith of the possibility of grasping the totality of its own existence. It was the Marxian project, however, which then sought the praxical *realization* of philosophy at the level of the totality by the proletariat. Thus, after Hegel and Marx bourgeois philosophy collapsed into fragmentation.

Taking his cue from Marx's famous statement that "mankind only sets itself such problems as it can solve", Lukács maintains that because of the underdeveloped stage of societal development at which they stood, the classical German philosophers, particularly Hegel, were able to think the "deepest, most fundamental" problems of the development of bourgeois society through to the very end – but solely on the plane of philosophy, solely in thought. Yet at least the necessity of going beyond this historical stage in mankind's development was seen as a problem; although still uncritical about its own premises, "the grandiose conception that thought can only grasp what it has itself created strove to master the world as a whole by seeing it as self-created". But, as always, philosophical thinking "came up against the unsuperable obstacle of the given".[21] Some philosophers took the road into individual interior consciousness. Others strenuously sought the subject of thought and reality whilst continually warding off falling back into a residue of a '*hiatus irrationalis*' or the agnosticism of the thing-in-itself. Alternatively, the actual acknowledgment of the givenness of reality only resulted in the mere contemplation or intuition of it, or perhaps a reflection on the conditions necessary for thinking about reality. Thus until philosophy realized (in Marx) that the contemplative relation of subject and object could only be truly sublated *in practice*, the irrationality of the given continually re-emerged as untranscended in philosophical thought.

Lukács's analysis is redolent of Marx's 'Theses on Feuerbach'. To put the matter more methodologically, the problem of the relation between form and content, of the irreducibility of the irrationality of matter, of the 'given' to consciousness philosophically, needed, according to Lukács, reformulation through the infusion of the principle of praxis. The essence of this concept at this level consists in annulling in a manner different from Hegel the "indifference of form towards content",[22] an annulment which potentially occurs because simultaneously a conception of form is found which is not simply universally applicable to every content, by an act of rationality. To put it another way, philosophically speaking (as we saw in Chapter 2) the concept of praxis provided the potential for the identification of subject-object, form and content through the real, practical world-changing dialectic of their interpenetration. In this way, the age-old antinomies of opposites and contraries, the mutually exclusive juxtaposition of which reached its highest point in the Kantian antinomies, is now, for Lukács *practically* resolvable. Formal factors, i.e. forms so abstract as to be liberated from all content, are the highest forms reached by pure contemplation because

> Theory and praxis in fact refer to the same objects, for every object exists as an immediate inseparable complex of form and content. However, the diversity of subjective attitudes orientates praxis towards what is qualitatively unique, towards the content and the material substratum of the object concerned . . . theoretical contemplation leads to the neglect of this very factor.[23]

Theoretical contemplation, as the static assumption of subject and object and form and content in a relation of comparison, reaches antinomies held to be mutually exclusive, such as freedom and necessity, cause and effect, etc., because it was stuck fast in immediacy. It fails to see that the object itself is the result of a process of mediations in which the subject and the object are mutually inseparable, inconceivable in isolation and developing against each other. Thus the alternatives are either to assume the irrationality of content, or its indifference (or its partial unknowability) in relation to form, or to seek the solution to the problem of the irrationality of the given in praxis: i.e. to *make* the real 'rational'. To see the object as historically praxically constituted and constituting, leads away from the inherent irrationality and subjectivism of contemplation.

Lukács's analysis is an attempt to explain in a quasi-sociological fashion the divagations of the philosophers about subject and object, irresolvable antinomies and the problem of the irrational givenness of reality, by the increasing process of reification in society. These entanglements are therefore for Lukács "nothing but the logical and systematic formulation of the modern state of society".[24] In the following passage we find a heroic statement of the Marxian perception of the contradiction between the increasing domination of men over nature and over the past social relations which at the same time leads to the enslavement of men by their own further creations. Here Lukács re-introduces the notion (originally in Hegel) of developed social reality as a 'second nature', in tones strongly reminiscent of the closing pages of Weber's *Protestant Ethic* about the 'iron cage' of institutionalized life under capitalism:

> on the one hand, men are constantly smashing, replacing and leaving behind them the 'natural', irrational and actually existing

> bonds, while, on the other hand, they erect around themselves in the reality they have created and 'made', a kind of *second nature* which evolves with exactly the same inexorable necessity as was the case earlier on with irrational forces of nature (more exactly: the social relations which appear in this form).[25]

It is this self-made (but now even more reified) reality that the critical philosophers found so ineluctable. It was the object to which they applied the mathematized positivist ideal of science which had been so successfully applied to the law-like regularities of the 'first nature', but of course such application as a predictive method was only possible so long as that reality became increasingly more predictable, feasible, regular, quantifiable and – most importantly – in need of control. The abstractly conceived philosophical givenness of the world which can be expected to appear and reappear without apparent human intervention was the specific and increasingly rationalizing and reifying institutional world of capitalist society. It was the character of men's experiences of this reified order that enabled the notion of a law to be formulated in all its applications. As Bauman has succintly put it: "positivism is the self-awareness of the alienated society".[26] Employing a notion of human activity which was later to animate the Frankfurt School,[27] Lukács maintains that in the contemplative, law-like reality of the social world the Greek ideal of knowledge being related to self-determining activity has been smothered. It has been substituted by a 'voluntaristic' concept of action as the exploitation of the 'super'-human laws of society by the individual. Human activity is conceptualizable in this way because that is what it has actually become, mainly the manipulation of the quantified, the individual orientation and adaptation to the repeatable; rather than permitting the possibility of orienting praxis towards what is "qualitatively essential and the material substratum of action".[28]

To conclude, the classical philosophers remained formally trying to seek the union of subject and object and form and content without reference to what Lukács repeatedly terms, after the early Marx, a 'material substratum'. Form can only truly coincide with content and subject with object when the subject sees that the object is, to use Hegel's phrase, "rational on its own account".[29] This is the antithesis of the situation in the reified society of capitalism, in which the 'object' is the arbitrary result of blind, irrational social processes. Unless one comprehends the 'material substratum', the reality behind and including the commoditized social relations, then insoluble antinomies arise in conceptualizing those appearances. These either-or antinomies reflect the periodic fluctuations in men's experiences of the phases and elements of determination and self-determination within the cognized appearances of social life described. These dualisms include freedom and necessity, voluntarism and determinism, existence and essence, and so on, all of which are static formalisms irrevocably antinomic outside their unity in the concrete totality.[30] In Marx's programmatic words in the 1844 manuscripts,

> subjectivism and objectivism, spiritualism and materialism, activity and suffering, only lose their antithetical character, and thus their existence, as such antitheses in the social condition; it will be seen how the resolution of the *theoretical* antitheses is *only* possible *in a practical* way, by virtue of the practical energy of men. Their resolution is therefore by no means merely a problem of knowledge, but a *real* problem of life, which *philosophy* could not solve precisely because it conceived this problem as *merely* a theoretical one.[31]

A position which carried, as it did for Lukács, the Utopian corollary that the historical process of the overcoming of bourgeois reality potentially created a situation in which those characteristic antinomies became sublated in a more self-determining reality in which it was no longer appropriate for them to be antagonistic. Marx again:

> Communism [is] the real appropriation of the human essence by and for man; communism therefore [is] the complete return of man to himself as a social (i.e. human) being – a return become conscious, and accomplished within the entire wealth of previous development. This communism . . . is the *genuine* resolution of the conflict between man and nature and between man and man – the true resolution of the strife between existence and essence, between objectification and self-confirmation, between freedom and necessity, between the individual and the species. Communism is the riddle of history solved, and it knows itself to be this solution.[32]

5 From Lukács to Hegel and back

We saw in the last chapter how in locating the 'basis in existence' of traditional European philosophy, Lukács sought to show how it failed to solve the problem of the irrational content of its forms, i.e. the givenness of reality was taken as read and its mechanism of self-production left untheorized. This was because it was the reified thought of commodity fetishism. Seeing this philosophy as basically revolving around the subject-object problematic, and in particular the problem of the irrationality of the given, led Lukács to interpreting Hegel as the highest (speculative) point in this trajectory. Hegel rightly grounded the object and the content of the categories in a constituting dialectic between an ultimately identical subject and object, but never dealt with real contents – the world as created in practice by real men. Thus in Hegel's philosophy 'we' experience could only be mythologically subsumed under the Spirit of a people and it could similarly deal with its own existence and the necessity of moving beyond the present stage of human history in thought only. He was forced 'beyond' history. It was Marx who sought the praxical realization of philosophy at the level of the totality by the genuine majority 'we' of capitalism – the proletariat – whose action would consciously create 'the given' in a truly collective dereified society in which productive forces ceased to have the character of capital. The object and subject would thus coincide in practice since the planned, conscious organization of society meant that the ideal did not stand over and against the givenness of an arbitrary and blindly developing reality.

As I indicated in the previous chapter, we may feel that in *History and Class Consciousness* Lukács has at least unjustifiably reduced the concerns of classical European philosophy to the problems of subject and object and the givenness of reality. That is quite apart from his failure to engage empirical material of the actual social contexts and processes involved. Lukács's analysis of European philosophy's "basis in existence" is not strictly speaking historical or sociological but social-ontological. Lukács is talking about levels of social being under the reifications of commodity capitalism and how this leads to contemplation. This view philosophically generalizes across the many different social contexts and stages of development from which the philosophies emerged. It is Lukács's method which enables him to advocate and justify the identical subject-object achievable by the proletariat's praxis as the real solution at the level of the totality (in whatever particular society) to the philosophers' epistemological problem and one which they could not face because it brought their philosophizing to the *threshold of praxis* – the self-changing of the world. And traditional philosophy is interpreted by Lukács through this imperative. The philosophers are seen as falling back continually into individualistic applications of philosophy to local problems or into regarding the problem of the irrationality of reality as unsolvable, or, as in Hegel, resorting to conceptual mythology in order to grasp the self-creation of the object.

The present chapter will begin to pose the question of the extent to which Lukács can be seen also as ironically having erected a mythology in the notion of the proletariat as the authentic subject-object of history in order to solve the problems posed philosophically and politically in his time. But, for the moment, our main concern will be to throw some doubt on to the adequacy of Lukács's depiction of the basic problematic of bourgeois philosophy as outlined in the previous chapter on the level of validity *vis-à-vis* the philosophers' actual work, with special reference to Hegel. Considering, as an example, to what extent Lukács's critique of Hegel's mythological subject-object as an attempt to get over the problem of the self-creation of the object actually engages Hegel, is selective, or is a valid interpretation, would be seen by a Lukácsian as missing the point. It would be held that the basis in existence of all philosophy was and will always remain the same as long as commodity capitalism, its reifications and systematic denial of self-determination survives. Irrespective of the particular conceptual dress of philosophies or theories which come along they are inevitably, like their predecessors, tied to this basis in existence which will tacitly circumscribe and structure their deliberations towards antinomic contemplation or irrationalism. Only the inclusion of praxis will lead away from these positions, since in practice the co-ordinates of enquiry are fused and subject to change.

My reply to this would be, first, to see this approach in the light of Lukács's overwhelming commitment to proletarian political praxis as a device for encompassing a universal solution to the age-old as well as present philosophical problems in a proletarian praxis. It justified and gave a mighty significance to the perceived necessity to act in a specific context and was also a political broadside against the ethical socialists in philosophical terms. That is, informed by the standpoint of this study, Lukács's theory of 'social ontology' can be seen as a historically specific product. Second, to bring together using an argument from an ontological basis philosophies as diverse as those of Descartes, Hegel and Rickert from such vastly different social contexts is surely to stultify their significance within their particular societies at whatever stage of development they had attained. Even if the various philosophers were operating in what could be called a social "basis in existence" this was in each case still *historical.* Third, if the adducing of evidence either internally from the texts of the philosophers, or 'externally' from society, in order to undermine Lukács's depiction of their philosophy is held ultimately not to impinge on the general theory of the "basis in existence" and its implications for proletarian praxis, then this seems to me to be dogmatic and obscurantist. Fourth, the activistic Lukácsian could claim of course that my previous three points are still seeking to settle or qualify in theory what are practical questions; thus, like the theoretical efforts of all the preceding philosophers discussed, serve merely to reproduce the disjunction between thought and reality which characterizes the reified society of capitalism. In practice only the victory of the proletariat can secure the coincidence of the object of enquiry – social circumstances – with the subjects who ongoingly constitute them. The question is, however, what moral and political significance is to be attached to what *can* be settled in theory. As I said in Chapter 2 in relation to Marx, the Utopian vision of the total correspondence in praxis of 'reality' and 'thought' leaves out of account potentially crucial practical aspects of the socio-natural complex which cannot be changed or which persist unaffected by certain kinds of practice. When one begins to make these kinds of qualifications the undiscriminating, totalizing, millenarian sweep of Lukács's position begins to move out of focus.

Lukács's whole advocacy of the significance and need for a proletarian praxis and its epistemological ramifications is based on his reconstruction of bourgeois philosophy, which, like Korsch, he sees as requiring to be realized in science-informed praxis. So it is important that we critically assess this reconstruction both within Lukács's own terms (and by implication from a more sociological standpoint) since Lukács builds a very large political imperative and a radically activistic conception of social science upon it. However, fully to assess the adequacy of Lukács's analysis of European philosophy since Descartes and its relation to the complex social processes in which it was embedded is a task beyond my scope here. But what I can do, first, in this chapter is to offer a few observations at least on Lukács's interpretation of Hegel out of all the philosophers he covers in relation to their basis in existence, in order to show its particular stresses and selectivity which hark back to Marx's similar interpretation, also politically selective. This exercise can serve to inform an understanding of Lukács's particular philosophical and political purposes in 1923 and suggest that the same procedure could profitably be carried out on the other philosophers dealt with. My second aim in this chapter is to extend the discussion of Lukács's Hegel to a demonstration of the further mechanisms of selectivity, and in this case also of dogmatism, present in some contemporary orthodox interpretaions of the early Lukács which, also largely for political reasons, quite wrongly regard Lukács's *History and Class Consciousness* as an 'idealist', 'Hegelian', etc., text, positions which he specificallycom batted.

Clearly all three of these theoretical clusters (Marx-Hegel, Lukács-Korsch and contemporary neo-Marxism) are crying out for a sociological analysis of their contexts, their emergence at different stages of social development, their place in the development of Marxism, their political import, and so on. But my aim here is the more modest one of showing on the level of theory that various exclusions, emphases and uncritical assumptions were applied and this procedure is in order to establish that a strong *prima facie* case exists for analysing further the developing social processes which are directing the selectivity and in which its complete significance lies. But to attempt this in either Lukacsian or orthodox Marxist terms would be self-fulfilling: one must step outside these positions. To clear up some possible misunderstandings: because I contend that Lukács's Hegel and the orthodox Marxists' critique of Lukács are particularly selective and flawed critiques motivated largely by political considerations in given contexts, does not mean that I see them therefore as vulgar, shabby or low-calibre. Nor do I see my position as the pure critique, unsullied by interests. No interpretation is absolutely pure or correct; all are partial, selective and interest-laden, mine included. (Although certain evaluations *vis-à-vis* evidence for example can develop an 'independent' legitimacy over time.) Nor should my remarks be taken as the protest of an outraged Hegelian dismayed by the barbarous critiques of the Master by Marx and Lukács. I am not arguing from a Hegelian standpoint but simply saying that they did not engage him adequately and asking what they omitted and for hinting at why. All I claim is that although the theoretical debates discussed in this chapter had an overt political character, this does not exhaust their significance. A more adequate view of them is possible from a higher stage of social development and from a different level of detachment, without implying subscription to absolute 'value-freedom'. The idea that one's position in scholarly work must fall on one side of the absolute dichotomy of either revolution-committed or bourgeois-detached is abstract and chimerical.

(a) Lukács's Hegel

1 Lukács appeals many times to a "substratum" of society, a material social basis created by men to which the concepts and ideas of the philosophers (including Hegel) had to be referred, but which their contemplative, reified thought could not address because it meant questioning the horizons of the alienated bourgeois world and facing the practical changing of the object. They thus sidestepped the issue of the givenness of reality. Lukács is here effectively generalizing to all bourgeois philosophy Marx's critique of Hegel. As we saw in Part one, however, Marx's general critique of Hegel is by no means definitive and was a particular set of stresses and systematic exclusions elaborated for the purpose of political critique in very specific circumstances. One reason for Lukács's uncritical acceptance of this aspect of Marx's critique of Hegel (the appeal to a substratum) is that within Marxism Lukács partakes of what Raymond Williams calls a "selective tradition"[1] whereby a whole set of emphases, omissions and exclusions within the practice passes as *the* tradition or *the* significant past. Within this Marxist tradition Lukács takes it as read that we can accept and work in sociological theory with a conception of a 'material' base or substratum juxtaposed to a realm of ideas, a conception stemming from the erroneous Feuerbachian/Marxian inversion of the Hegelian dialectic. The tenacity of this model of society in the tradition lies in the power of the call to action which it enables through pointing out that to change ideas is not enough. The social conditions require to be overthrown, and the 'economic base' can be analysed with scientific precision for this purpose. But this dualistic view is more a rallying cry than a theoretical statement since ideas and consciousness permeate every nook and corner of social reality, on every level: as I suggested in Part one, the inversion is of a non-existent, static, Platonized Hegel who never required to be turned upside down in order that the Marxian dialectic of the real world could be salvaged from Hegel's mystifications of it. The very core of Hegel's mediations, the pith and marrow of his whole philosophy, is that it is embodied in and articulates the self-changing world and its historical development. This point cannot be too strongly emphasized.

Furthermore, Lukács also uncritically accepts Marx's erroneous and simplistic depiction in the 1873 Afterword to *Capital* that the motor of the Hegelian historical dialectic is the self-absorbing "Idea", the "demiurgos of the real world", which interpretation makes no sense in relation to Hegel. The Idea in Hegel is not a disembodied spirit-subject but is a methodological conception, referring to an active universal embodied in the world containing within itself the results, represented categorially, of the development of the dialectic in its various determinations up to the point in the logical development in Hegel's system where it appears (although always presupposed at the start): the "proof" that the Idea is the truth, i.e. the absolute unity of the developing process of the Notion (the active substance element) and objectivity is contained in the whole deduction up to that point.[2] Like Marx, Lukács assumes that the Hegelian dialectic is ultimately a dialectic of concepts, of thought over and against the world, which is a quite erroneous separation of their developing unity in Hegel. Methodologically, the category of the Idea contains categorially the extent to which it has developed itself out of itself as an overall process embodied in the world in a myriad of co-present lower order stages of development. Hegel warns:

> Because it has no *existence* for starting-point and *point d'appui*, the Idea is frequently treated as a mere logical form. Such a view must be abandoned to those theories which ascribe so-called reality and genuine actuality to the existent thing and all the other categories which have not yet penetrated as far as the Idea. It is no less false to imagine the Idea to be mere abstraction. It is abstract certainly, in so far as everything untrue is consumed in it: but in its own self it is essentially concrete, because it is the free notion giving character to itself, and that character, reality.[3]

And as if to drive the point home Hegel adds:

> When we hear the Idea spoken of, we need not imagine something far away beyond this mortal sphere. The idea is rather what is completely present: and it is found, however confused and degenerated, in every consciousness.[4]

2 Lukács talks a great deal about *history* but hardly at all about its relationship to *development*, a basic and crucial distinction in Hegel and Marx.[5] As a category of the Notion, development deals with self-realizing processes which can be seen as having an immanent dialectic even though their individual stages and components may not fall contiguously in a historical sequence. Marx's "progressive epochs" in the economic formation of society (the Asiatic, the ancient, the feudal and the modern bourgeois modes of production) form such a development even though they may not fall *seriatim* in history. Hegel is well aware, as was Marx, that the order of exposition of historical material should reflect the inner logic of history, its development, rather than its actual sequential history, and the importance of this to Hegel and Marx is evidenced by their both devoting a great deal of space to explaining their methods and undertaking enormous labour to present their theoretical work in elaborately wrought dialectical sequences. In such a presentation, however, in both Hegel and

Marx, the abstractions presented (in their progress towards concretion) can appear to be unrelated to real historical events or structures, but in both cases the real world and its development is presupposed at the start of the work and the work is designed to *construct* that end-product from abstract determinations *without leaving out any element*, i.e. to avoid arbitrariness. Thus when employing the dialectical method even the most empirical work can appear as though it is aloof from real history and in a world of concepts, when in fact the presentation conceptually mirrors the development itself (i.e. it moves from the abstract to the concrete) and the real world is present as a presupposition and as a result in the study. It might be tempting, and indeed this is what Marx appears to have assumed and Lukács accepted at a later stage within the selective tradition, to regard a work like Hegel's *The Philosophy of Right* as not dealing with the world but writing it off as a mere product of the Idea. And then in reaction lauding the scientific possibilities of looking at real history, at the "substratum" of society. But in Hegel this substratum is already presupposed in the study and the individual stages or moments of the presentation are *already* reality-laden, so to mistake the presented categorial development for history or as a statement about the history of empirical reality is to misunderstand the inner logic being constructed.

Thus, when Lukács accuses Hegel of blocking an understanding of the "real" nature and origin of "real" contents, produced by the activity of "real" men and not the concrete incarnations of the mythical Spirit active in history, he implies that stupid old Hegel does not realize that men make history, which is just not the case. Lukács says that Hegel's conception makes deeds transcendent to the doer, rendering freedom specious freedom. Not only a materialism of the substratum but real praxis too is already encompassed by Hegel in the conception of the co-present levels and moments of realization in a given totality, i.e. Hegel is already talking about action in the world. Lukács, like Marx, has failed to distinguish between *presentation of development* and real history in Hegel. Willed action for Hegel is *simultaneously* of 'universal' and 'particular' significance, i.e. at one and the same time of a particular, finite significance *and* 'transcendent to the doer'. Hegel merely claimed that action was explicable in terms of its historical configuration, interests, etc., but that the significance it had over and above that was necessarily cognized or dimly cognized by the actors and discernible *post festum* from a higher stage by those who perceive the process. And this is presented in analysis as a development which relates to vastly long periods of history. The Universal significance is not an *a priori* assumption but only has its existence in and through the discernible, real, open-ended moments of history.

It is quite compatible with Hegel's philosophy to advocate praxis (as Bakunin, Cieszkowski and Michelet realized) in order to further the development of finite reality by human will since such will exemplifies its revealed further significance to the observer, even if not totally to its alienated participants, at the same time. The unity in praxis of the epistemological moments of subjective consciousness and the objective block of natural reality in Marx were already present in Hegel. The practical moment in Hegel is the "finite teleological standpoint", about which he remarks:

> In man's *practical* approach to Nature, the latter is, for him, something immediate and external; and he himself is an external and therefore sensuous individual.[6]

This experience represents for Hegel a stage in a development even though perfectly real to the participants and co-present with other standpoints at this stage of history. One occasion when Hegel appears to dwell above the real sensuous world is in the Introduction to the *Science of Logic* when outlining the purpose behind the study:

> The system of logic is the realm of shadows, the world of simple essentialities freed from all sensuous concreteness . . . In logic consciousness is busy with something remote from sensuous intuitions . . . thought acquires thereby self-reliance and independence. It becomes at home in abstractions and in progressing by means of Notions free from sensuous substrata . . .[7]

But even the exposition of the dialectical logical deduction of the categories here remote from the substratum presupposes the developing content which has given them form. Hegel considers the categories in themselves instead of uncritically taking them for granted and presents them in a necessary sequence of dialectical overcoming in order to avoid presenting them arbitrarily, as he believes the previous systems of metaphysics did. But the sequence presented may not be the order in which the categories were discovered or elaborated in history. Hegel hopes to supersede the previous metaphysics by considering the categories in relation to their "specific content" (as determinate in varying degrees) rather than merely in their abstract epistemological validity as *a priori* or *a posteriori*.[8] For Hegel the latter procedures would constitute subjective idealism.

Having argued that Hegel's philosophy adopts a position just about as firmly embodied in the world as it could be, what can one make of Lukács's assertion that having failed to discover the "identical subject-object in history" Hegel was forced to "go out beyond history" to a point from which "to establish the empire of reason which has discovered itself"?[9] This view runs counter to the very basis of Hegel's conception of the concrete Universal. There can *never* be a standpoint beyond history in Hegel: it is the very stuff of his philosophy. The answer to that question lies in Lukács's desire, within the selective tradition in which he was operating, to construct a total explanation to unite past, present and to-be-created future in one totalizing praxical scheme; to leave no philosophical, political or ethical stone unturned which could block the absolute imperative to seek the urgent victory of the proletariat.

3 Let us now turn specifically to the subject-object conception in Hegel in relation to the previous remarks. Leaving aside the validity of Lukács's assertion of this as the most crucial and essential epistemological task attributable to the labours of classical European philosophy in general (implicitly or explicitly), some doubt can be cast as to its central importance to Hegel, at least in the form presented by Lukács. Again, Lukács's stress highlights his insistence on seeking a totalizing perspective to prove that all roads *must* lead to the proletarian praxis without which there can be no further creativity, no economic, social, political or philosophical solutions which do not simply permutate the routine, calculable, reified reality either in practice or in theory. Lukács endows the victory of the proletariat with such far-reaching world-historical significance that all history, economics, social theory, science and European philosophy must be appropriated, somehow unified and fed into the politics of the proletarian movement on whose victory further progress depends.

Lukács rightly sees Hegel as inheriting the Kantian heritage of the thing-in-itself, the agnosticism of which Hegel indeed relentlessly combats in his work, which dilemma he sees as the inevitable and untenable residue of an ultimately subjectivist starting point which cannot grasp the logic of the object itself. However, too rigid a construal of the aim and intention of the Hegelian project and the resulting system as being the consummation of the subject and object problem of classical philosophy through positing their ultimate alienated identity, over-generalizes and formalizes Hegel's mediations. I will suggest (a) that Hegel proceeds far more from an intention to reconcile the problematic of *substance* and subject rather than subject and object; and (b) that to facilitate the run-up to his argument about the possibilities and historical imperative of proletarian praxis, Lukács fudges over the complexity of Hegel's conception of the unconditioned Absolute as also *potentially* capable of unifying itself as subject and substance through its conditioned mediations. The subject-object formalism also further stultifies the rich organicity of the Hegelian totality. It would be far more correct and appropriate to speak of subject*s* and object*s* and of subjec*tivity* and objec*tivity* in

Hegel. In the same way that the infamous triad of thesis-antithesis-synthesis plays no part whatsoever in Hegel's philosophy despite the persistence of this legend,[10] Hegel also rarely refers to the notion of identical subject-object in his work.[11] He far more commonly talks about "substance qua subject", "consciousness knowing the object as itself", "subject as negative self-relation", etc. Subject-object for Hegel would have implied subjectivism and formalism.

On (a), Nathan Rotenstreich has usefully pointed out[12] that substance and subject have etymologically the same meaning, being renderings of the Greek '*hypokeimenon*': substance or '*substantia*' is that which subsists independently, while '*subjectus*' is that which underlies, which is underneath, so that both terms have the broad meaning of foundation. Later a separation between the two terms occurred, such that subject became identified with consciousness, perceptions, images, feelings, while substance retained its original meaning of that which underlies. Now, as Rotenstreich says, Hegel's system is an attempt to reconcile substance and subject, but "retaining substance as essence and subject as consciousness or cognition".[13] For Hegel the separation of substance and subject is a diremption to be redeemed through philosophy, the truth of their identity being authenticated through a dialectical sequence of argumentation at the categorial level. This comprehension is not arbitrary since it is the self-understanding, i.e. truth, of the substance-as-subject attained as part of a system (categorially) and at the same time includes what Marx would call the real praxis of the world. Thus the return of the substance (which is a multi-faceted entity comprising the infinite totality of historically developed and developing alienations of the socio-natural totality) to itself is for Hegel an "infinite self-return".[14] This is because the particular finite mediations of its variously moving, evolving self-identity are simultaneously general and infinite; the self-return, the generation of conscious infinitude and human life being the *same* process. And that infinitude as Absolute only has its existence once it is comprehended as a "result", as a determination philosophically delineable as a determination of the Idea as an embodied universal and not as an abstract beginning. Thus history and its consciousness coincide but they do not always know it. Hegel summarizes the methodological significance of the Idea as the master conceptualization of the self-realizing identity of substance as a subject in the *Encyclopaedia*:

> The Idea may be described in many ways. It may be called reason (and this is the proper philosophical signification of reason); subject-object; the unity of the ideal and the real, of the finite and the infinite, of soul and body; the possibility which has its actuality in its own self; that of which the nature can be

> thought only as existent, etc. All these descriptions apply, because the Idea contains all the relations of understanding, but contains them in their infinite self-return and self-identity.[15]

In this passage we see that the subject-object identity is only an aspect at best of what the Idea can be said to define at that stage in the proof in the *Encyclopaedia*: a particular and relatively formal, rough-and-ready dualism contained within a vastly organic self-mediating substance. Indeed Hegel is implying here that this formalism is a product of the old metaphysics and superseded by the rigour of the proof of the Idea. This is why Hegel does not give the conception any more centrality in his system.

With regard to point (b) about potentiality, Lukács's statement that having failed to discover the identical subject-object in history Hegel's philosophy was forced "to go out beyond history" not only misconstrues Hegel's monism, as we have seen, but also more particularly staticizes his dynamic and potential-oriented conception of the self-mediating substance and its subjective active element which moves via contradiction. It was not that Hegel failed to find the identical subject-object in history, but rather that history had failed totally to find the identical subject-object. Hegel's substance is the partly particular, partly universal actual totality endowed with thought at a given stage of development, categorially represented in its development in various fields and sectors of the totality, e.g. natural right, consciousness, logic, nature. *Qua* Idea within such dialectical proofs, that conceptualization of universality is not the arbitrary representation of the totality in its development, but is proved, as the result of dialectic. The active unity of identity and non-identity, between particularity and universality, subject and substance is a theoretical result which presupposes the previous history from which that development has been constructed. Thus at any point the total identical subject-object is never found *in toto* nor is it found today in actuality in all its determinations (in so far as it is synonymous with the Idea) since history has left all the lower stages towards the identity co-present. Thus in many of its determinations, and thus as a whole as well, the totality as realized and realizing self-activating substance always contains on various levels a *potential*; it is never merely 'found' complete as a stage in history, never posited, but *self-active*. "Truth", says Hegel, "lies in the coincidence of the object with itself, with its Notion";[16] i.e. truth is realized progressively as a process of identity of reality and thinking; that is, as the *extent* in various determinations to which the active Notion has rendered substance self-identical. But the identity of substance and subject as a systematic deduction, categorially, of a given content is a statement of development, not of history. It thus necessarily does not totally coincide with the various grades of processing non-identity in the totality at a given stage of development. The self-identical subject-substance in Hegel is variously self-identical in various sectors and on various levels of reality, it is partly achieved and partly a potentiality, even though *categorially* its total potential identity has been proved.

Feuerbach and Marx argued that Hegel separated thought and the other than thought, but did so at the start of the *Phenomenology* solely as the thought-of-the-other-than-thought, thus remaining in thought. In other words, that Hegel reduced ontology to epistemology. But this view, as we have seen, ignores the processes of authentication in Hegel in which the real world is the presupposed starting point as well as conclusion of his studies. The criticism has failed to see the concrete nature of categories in Hegel and their reality-laden character which, as a categorial development, do not stand over against the world. Lukács uncritically absorbs this critique from Marx, which leads to his own position on Hegel. Subject-object, however, is actually one relatively formal way of talking on the categorial level about the Idea and Hegel certainly never therefore tried to search for the identical subject-object in history. It was not an issue for him. Lukács has, then, passed over the difference between the levels of development towards self-identity present in the totality and their potential total identity deducible categorially and existing on a number of levels potentially in the reality. For Hegel the Absolute as total identity only existed in so far as it continued to reproduce itself on its various particular, alienated levels.

Aside from the political motivation behind Lukacs in 1923, immanently we can see that he has uncritically absorbed Marx's misleading view in the *Critique of Hegel's 'Philosophy of Right'* that in Hegel contradictions in reality are reconciled in a supermundane sphere of the Absolute which Lukács says is "outside history". Both Marx and Lukács assumed this because they sought a specific praxis at a specific time in the real world and backed up their theory by criticizing Hegel. But in saying this they only selectively engaged Hegel, who had already anticipated that argument in his polemic against Kant:

> It shows an excessive tenderness for the world to remove contradiction from it and then to transfer the contradiction to spirit, to reason, where it is allowed to remain unresolved. But the so-called world . . . is never and nowhere without contradiction, but it is unable to endure it and is, therefore, subject to coming-to-be and ceasing-to-be.[17]

(b) Georg Lukács – idealist?

To what extent is the frequent charge from within Marxism against the young Lukács justified that the conception of the historical identical subject-object to be achieved by the praxis of the class-conscious proletariat and Lukács's overall theoretical position, constitute 'idealism'? Does he "dissolve the materialist dialectic into an idealist dialectic" (Connerton)?[18] Is the " 'base' etherealized virtually out of existence" and the proletariat's abolition of society its "final interiorization" (Stedman Jones)?[19] What are the implications of Lukács's so-called "pre-Leninist Hegelianism" (Watnick)?[20] We would do well to be guided in our thoughts on this matter by the words of Stanislaw Ossowski:

> Marxists use the term 'idealism' as an offensive weapon in discussions with their adversaries, and do not always trouble over much about its meaning in concrete contexts.[21]

Indeed, idealism is often used vaguely in Marxist debate to cover a whole range of intellectual activities, from elaborating ideal-types, model-building and creating typologies to the study of ideologies, attitudes, beliefs, etc. without reference to their so-called material basis. In Marxist discourse it is often taken as an assumption or as a self-evident truth that idealism is either fallacious or undesirable in some way. Hence, simply to apply the label is seen as being a sufficient indictment in itself. Furthermore, the labelling procedure mentioned by Ossowski often also means failing to give tolerant credence to the fact that idealists of whatever persuasion may be sincerely convinced by the arguments for idealism, which means that the actual arguments are seldom engaged. In answering my first question, then, we can say initially that it depends on what is meant by idealism, who is "charging" Lukács with this and why it is seen as a charge.

We saw in the preceding section how Lukács funnels the rich mediations of Hegel's self-activating and self-realizing substance into the narrow subject-object formula and then falsely pushes Hegel beyond history. This selective procedure was part of a philosophical reconstruction of the basis in social existence of the problems of European philosophy to inform the pursuit of the urgent necessity of proletarian praxis, seen as the practical solution to all those problems and those of society in general. This view, however, wrongly sees Hegel's thought as being ideally above the sensuous world. In this case Lukács has absorbed and employed against Hegel the dubious Feuerbachian/Marxian inversion to inform the all-important proletarian praxis. But on the other hand, as we will see shortly, for similar reasons his position in other respects follows Hegel in order to be able to theorize the profound epistemology of the process of the acquisition of class consciousness by the proletariat. For Lukács this involves reality, through that process, effectively overthrowing its own objectivity in practice and thus becoming social knowledge in action. However in this case, theoretically speaking, Lukács plays on the 'this-worldliness' of Hegel's dialectical idealism and its affinity with the Marxian praxical project, again in order to demonstrate the profound, world-historical significance and absolute imperative of furthering the victory of the proletariat, but which import would not be theorizable in metaphysical materialist terms. It is this circumstance which makes it possible to defend Lukács against the orthodox Marxist charge of idealism as well as at the same time to argue against his uncritical deployment of the standard Marxian critique of Hegel. In other words, the orthodoxy do not seem to grasp the nature of Hegel's dialectical thought and its affinity with Marx's, and Lukács, who apparently does, only selectively follows it through. I will leave for the reader's interpolation the political significance of these positions.

Idealism refers to the great variety of specifically philosophical epistemological doctrines of which there are many types – subjective, objective, immanent, transcendental, and so on, the debates within which revolve around (a) the basic assertion that ultimately knowing depends upon the experience of the mind, and (b) the problem of the nature of matter. The content of idealist philosophy is rich indeed,[22] such that the term idealism, unless used in a very discriminating way (as is seldom the case in Marxist discourse) can be so vague as to be practically meaningless. Moreover, the issue is further complicated in relation to the dialectical positions of Hegel and Marx. Hegel's idealism and Marx's "new materialism" both make the real world ultimately consciousness-dependent, seen developmentally, even though, from the standpoint of the individual, in both cases the natural-social complex of phenomena can be said to exist independently of his consciousness. This is Dick Howard's terse statement of the relationship:

> I would assert that any dialectical philosophy is idealist in the broad sense insofar as it does not accept the brute positivity of matter but introduces a subjective element of becoming into a material world which is inherently social, praxical . . . The Marxian dialectic is not mechanistic, and makes sense only in a social world constituted, and continually reconstituted, by social human praxis.[23]

Following the anti-Machist defence of epistemological materialism by Lenin in *Materialism and Empirio-Criticism*, it has become common for orthodox Marxists to set great store in locating their enemies in terms of the extent to which they deviate from materialism, when, theoretically speaking, it can be argued, as we saw in Chapter 2, that Marx had transcended debate in terms of these epistemological categories anyway. He understood materialism in a praxical, sociological sense as a stress on the study of the human relations which men enter into to satisfy their practical needs in the face of nature as being the secular point of departure for understanding human society, thought, politics and culture in their historical development.

Lukács, then, has been accused of idealism by this orthodoxy who follow Lenin when it can be more convincingly shown that materialism in Marx's thought is not the metaphysical materialism fought for (politically, ideologically) by those Marxists. Marx is not an ontological materialist in the sense that he did not allow consciousness or Nature to ossify into a final metaphysical principle.[24] In social praxis the moment of perception of reality and the existence of the cognized object coincide to constitute each other, which Marx sees as the practical transcendence of the idealism/materialism dichotomy. Keeping for the moment within this discourse, Hegel and Marx are brought close together because both relate 'subject' and 'object' as interpenetrating and mutually constituting themselves actively on many mediating levels. So within this philosophical discourse at any rate they seem to constitute both sides of the same coin. Thus, *neither* Hegel *nor* Marx were idealists or materialists in a static metaphysical sense, an affinity which Lukács grasped and brought to bear in his theory of the overthrowing of social objectivity. It is therefore misleading to believe that a critique of Lukács amounts to "exorcising its metaphysical spook"[25] of Hegelianism, which as we have seen in this chapter is inapplicable to Hegel anyway, let alone to Lukács. But in any case Marx had moved into a realm of sociological discourse in which debate in terms of abstract epistemological standpoints was transcended in favour of an appropriation of the inherently socialized and humanized nature of all perception and knowledge.[26] But, because of the tradition within orthodox Marxism, interpretations of Lukács still tend to get filtered through the metaphysical, materialist set of assumptions, which naturally find his work idealist. Now my procedure is to defend Lukács against the charge of idealism in the latter sense, simply because such a critique irrelevantly brings to bear on his thought a pre-Hegelian, pre-Marxian separation of thought and being, consciousness and reality, subject and object, let alone not making the Marxian sociological transition. Now I would want to object to Lukács's theory of the proletariat as identical subject-object of the historical process on other grounds, notably that it is mythological and stuck in an archaic superseded philosophical standpoint. But to do so I feel it is necessary first to actually engage what he is saying, which the orthodox accusation of idealism (falling back behind Lukács's post-Hegelian, post-Marxian standpoint) does not.

So, in the light of the preceding remarks, the judgments mentioned earlier that society is "interiorized" in Lukács's proletarian victory or the material base "etherealized" must be considered carefully. Lukács says for example that the proletariat's ability to move beyond the reified immediacy of commodity society to remoter factors "means the transformation of the objective nature of the objects of action",[27] which is in Lukács a *process* of transformation not the elimination of objectivity *per se*. Keeping to the level of the theory of consciousness in Lukács, the objection that he is talking purely about consciousness as opposed to the material base is to impose a dualism of thought and matter on to what in Lukács is a relationship of consciousness and its objects which holds, following Hegel, that consciousness is always consciousness *of* something, since in cognitive activity the object is constituted by and embodies the categories. This was the basis of the Hegelian revolution against classical metaphysics and carried on into Marx's conception of the praxical embodiment of the categories in the social world. The nature of mediations in Hegel and Lukács means that it is not a question of an absolute distinction of 'thought' over here and 'matter' over there. Rather we have a conception of a totality of processes whereby the objectivity given to praxical consciousness, and which that consciousness also thereby constitutes as object, is a unity in practice. And it is comprised in a vast totality of processes and grades of awareness in various stages of self-development. Speaking of the integration in Hegel of lower stages of dialectical advances into a more concrete and comprehensive totality, Lukács avers:

> When Marx makes dialectics the essence of history, the movement of thought also becomes just a part of the overall movement of history. History becomes the history of the objective forms from which man's environment and inner world are constructed and which he strives to master in thought, action and art, etc.[28]

Changes in consciousness and changes in social objectivity are *in practice*, bearing in mind the different levels, potentially the same thing as social relations (which presuppose consciousness) change. The objects of society itself become aspects of the development of the society since they and the subjects mutually constitute each other, although, through alienation and the reifications associated with commodity fetishism, the precise nature of this constituting dialectic is not clearly and completely present to the consciousness of the subjects of the process.

To begin to concretize the arguments more, the long historical process of the accumulating loss to men of awareness that the social world around them is their own creation, a process related to the division of labour and to rationalization, is heightened with the reifications of commodity capitalism. But the historical process permits a process of the regaining of awareness and control by men over their social productions, by the level of its development, which harnessing is mediated by the process of bondage itself. Now, the dynamic nature of Lukács's conception means that such a 'recovery' by the proletariat is not to be regarded either as a blinding single moment of change nor as the *actus purus* of consciousness. Stedman Jones erroneously asserts for example that in Lukács "the leap from the realm of necessity to that of freedom is given no material content".[29] Rather we are dealing with a *process* of historical self-comprehension which means that at no point along the road is the process reducible to thought, at no point is consciousness on its many levels and its objectivity not in social praxis mutually constituting. It is a question of the relationship between consciousness and its objects progressively changing. At a higher level of abstraction, the process of self-comprehension of the objective nature of society as being the alienated product of its subjects is historically mediated by its relative uncomprehension, and vice versa, since both are aspects of the same process. In Lukács and in Hegel comprehension is not merely necessarily comprehension-in-thought, since in the concrete process thought and being form on various levels a discrepant unity. As Hegel declares:

> existence and self-consciousness are the same being, the same not as a matter of comparison, but really and truly in and for themselves. It is only a one-sided, unsound idealism which lets this unity again appear on one side as consciousness, with a reality *per se* over against it on the other.[30]

To paraphrase Hegel, it is only an *unsound materialism* which lets the material base metaphysically stand over on one side with consciousness *per se* over against it on the other.

And now to relate these remarks more specifically to commodity fetishism in Lukács and to the concrete capitalist commodity totality. Under this mode of production relations between men become progressively more ossified and experienced in the immediacy of thinghood, of being nature-like. And these relations mask the real relations of society: "beneath the quantifying crust there was a qualitative, living core".[31] The objectivity of society is a function of its not being understood, comprehended as a human artefact by those who mainly actually produce its products, but whose surplus labour power is accumulated as capital over and against them: the proletariat. Thus, a praxis which envisages a genuine transformation of these relations (which in their totality constitute the whole of the forms of social life) as opposed to merely changing the personnel involved in them, cannot, says Lukács, "be divorced from knowledge".[32] The process of the development of capital and its relations has an immanent logic which inevitably includes the life-giving and meaning-endowing consciousness of its participants. But this is, under the quantified, calculative social relations of commodity capitalism, *un*conscious of its real human basis.

The way in which Lukács locates this process of growing self-consciousness within the commodity fetishes of capitalist social relations, and the possibilities of social reality being objectively changed by it, is neither understood nor defeated by the abstract demand for reference to 'material conditions' or 'material content' or seeing Lukács's conception as 'idealist', "spiritual", or even "thaumaturgical".[33] These views fail to see the *process* nature of Lukács's thought as well as assume that changes in consciousness are no more than just that, both in themselves on all levels and cumulatively as elements of long-term social processes. Lukacs says that the addition of self-consciousness to the commodity structure provides a new element which is different from consciousness "of" other situations. Once the worker knows that his appropriated labour power lies at the root of the exchanged commodities, then this knowledge is, in its process of acquisition, *practical* because it brings about "*an objective structural change in the object of knowledge*".[34] That is, in grasping the labour process for what it really is, the workers have themselves become aware of reified social reality as it were *from within*. Consciousness here is not just knowledge of an opposed object. Society as an object comprises reifications supported by a core of appropriated labour power in the capital/labour relation. This structure is normally sustained as an indubitable practical reality by the proletariat's lack of awareness of its constitutive role in the process. But once the class begins to become aware of society's true nature in this way then that total societal object qualitatively changes.

There are two elements to be distinguished: (a) the standpoint of the worker who now grasps that the surface reified mystifications of commodity relations are not the total reality; that is, objectivity has changed for him; and (b) the standpoint of the observer or scientist from which the reality has qualitatively changed with the infusion of what is essentially the growing self-knowledge of the productive society. So now the true subject of the mysterious, anonymous, reified social process begins to see why he fails to impinge on the reified "second nature" of bourgeois society and, from standpoint (b), this knowledge can be seen as having structurally changed the objective character of society (seen in its total historical development). All social objectivity consists in a conscious, practical, constituting element, and in this case consciousness beginning to change in the essential reality-creating sector gives the growing consciousness of the proletariat a great importance for Lukács. The social nature of labour, its use-value, now "awakens and becomes *social reality*".[35] There is an interaction of the "awakening consciousness and the objects from which it is born and of which it is the consciousness";[36] i.e. the core value relation which is of remote, more mediated existence. This gradual process of the social configuration qualitatively changing means that the objects of action, the reified, quantified commodity relations, and (now) the real relations, "become fluid"[37] and the whole structural transformation gets under way. Thus, from a beginning in the immediacy of reified commodity relations, their foundations in the real relations of men are discovered and given objectivity through that consciousness, in the sense described. They, too, begin to take on a determining role as existents alongside the reifications. The forms of immediacy confronting men, of which they can become aware and which they can abolish are, says Lukács, "by no means merely modes of thought",[38] but are rather the forms in which contemporary bourgeois society is objectified.

Lukács is aware of the delicate relationship between the proletariat becoming aware of the nature of commodity fetishism and the practical overthrow of the relations as a whole as part of the overall historical process. The nature of the consciousness possible and its origins lie in the long-term historical rhythm of contradictions producing themselves relatively automatically. Acts of awareness of a certain kind – notably those involved in workers becoming aware of the nature of commodity fetishism – have a great significance since here the core of capitalist production is revealed, and this is needed to further the historical process towards socialism. Of the abolition of the reifications of bourgeois society he says:

> Their abolition, if it is to be a true abolition, cannot simply be the result of thought alone, it must also amount to their *practical* abolition as the *actual forms of social life*.[39]

(Remembering always that "abolition" here is a *process* of transcendence, overcoming, an "*aufhebung*", not a sharply conceived leap.) Consciousness of the worker of commodity relations crucially forms the *beginning* of the consummation of a total historical process of long-term contradictions of capitalism being overcome. Thus individual acts of overcoming immediacy have a world-historical import and are thrown up by the wider total contradictions working generally uncognized in history. Echoing Marx's methodological remarks in the Introduction to the *Grundrisse*, Lukács points out that

> The category of totality begins to have an effect long before the whole multiplicity of objects can be illuminated by it.[40]

It is the transition of accumulated consciousness into deed which is important and in the following passage Lukács describes that praxis and its processual interplay of consciousness and objects within the commodity structure itself which, in normal conditions, depends for its successful functioning on the unconsciousness of its participants. Of the historically developing contradictions of capitalism he says:

> But as a mere contradiction is raised to a consciously dialectical contradiction, as the act of becoming conscious turns into a *point of transition in practice*, we see once more in greater concreteness the character of proletarian dialectics . . . namely, since consciousness here is not the knowledge of an opposed object but is the self-consciousness of the object *the act of consciousness* overthrows *the objective form of its object*.[41]

From that last quotation one could easily be misled into thinking that Lukács, if not an idealist of some kind, certainly seems to be envisaging the elimination of all opposed objectivity by the act of consciousness of the proletariat in their revolutionary praxis to create an unimaginable 'reality' in which *all* sciences were deprived of their 'objects'. But there is a difference-in-unity in Lukács between objectivity *qua* natural objects (first nature) and the extreme form of nature-like objectivity taken on by social institutions at high stages of reification (second nature). Lukács would not, like Hegel and Marx, deny the reality or palpability of natural objects. The reifications formed by the commodity relations of bourgeois society permeate consciousness and also institutions, which become "forms of social life"[42] possessing effectively a hard objectivity since they are lost to the consciousness of their participants at higher stages of the division of labour and rationalization. Natural-science practice in this framework constitutes a special kind of subject-object relation. But Stedman Jones, setting out determined to write Lukács off as a Romantic, anti-science, idealist polluter of Marxist science, is affronted by Lukács's audacity in suggesting that scientific experiment is "contemplation at its purest",[43] which is interpreted as part of a Romantic reaction against all science and industry in the name of bourgeois sensibility.

The context of Lukács's remark, however, is a comparison of Marx's conception of praxis as relating to the process whereby through activity men come consciously to change the world of objects of which they are as yet unaware they are the creators, with Engels's view that the behaviour of industry and scientific experiment constitutes praxis in that sense. Lukács claims that this equation is erroneous. Scientific experiment is "contemplation" because it creates an artificial milieu of controlled experiment through which merely to *observe* the workings of laws, eliminating all "irrational factors both of the subject and the object".[44] However, to say that natural science is contemplation is not necessarily a denial or rejection of science or a pejorative judgment, but a comparison of the natural-science method with the object-changing potential of self-determining human praxis.[45] Lukács goes on to compare this natural science activity with social science and to make the juxtaposition, in the fashion of the *Geisteswissenschaften*, that in the latter the 'objects' are the creations of men, such that natural-science's contemplative attitude *if applied to social science* has anti-humanistic and *status quo* justifying implications, since the object is assumed not to be impinged upon by the subject. He quotes therefore, approvingly, Engels's assertion that capitalist society is based on "a natural law that is founded on the unconsciousness of those involved in it",[46] implying that it must be changed to abolish the conditions which make those laws possible. We may not agree with those views, but at least we should get them right.

Stedman Jones, however, because he is determined to locate Lukács as a deviationist from Marxist science, strives to prove that Lukács is against science *per se*, when Lukács's only point here is a condemnation of scientism in social science. Stedman Jones stands in a long tradition of scientistic Marxism which both Lukács and Gramsci criticized, an example of which we will see in Gramsci's critique of Bukharin's 'sociology of the proletariat' in Part three below.[47] Having got the early Lukács firmly located in the anti-science Romantic tradition, Stedman Jones then doggedly refuses to engage Lukács's actual arguments, often misrepresenting his thought. For example, Lukács had argued that the reified, commoditized, thing-like relations of bourgeois society provided the experience of randomness and irrationality which lent itself to the growth of the scientific concept of the law, which then had both natural and social-science-applications, the latter application being condemned by Lukács as above. But on this question and in the name of Marxist science Stedman Jones wildly careers off into the following about Lukács's theory:

> the methodology and findings of natural science are demoted to the status of being a particular form of expression of the world vision of the bourgeoisie. Like the rest of the bourgeois conception of the world, natural science is partial: it is a necessarily false consciousness which will be dialectically transcended by the totalizing standpoint of the proletariat, the last and only true claimant to the universal.[48]

This imputation does not follow from Lukács's position, which is (rightly or wrongly) about the overthrowing of the objective reified forms of capitalist society from within, in so far as they are forms of objectified social life. The natural-science laws, even though genetically linked to the reifications of the previous order, must continue to account for the natural world, which remains a 'realm of necessity' in the process of the overcoming of capitalist society. Lukács admitted later that in 1923 he blurred the role of labour as the mediator of metabolic interplay between society and Nature whilst Nature remained 'in-itself';[49] but its law-amenable autonomous role in human affairs must always remain, *on his own original argument*, since the alternative would be to assume that the objectivity of Nature also would be abolished with the particular elimination of social reification. The unity of the natural and the social in Lukács's work precludes that interpretation.

Finally, then, let us look at that last issue of the extent of the elimination of objectivity in Lukács's conception of the overthrow of commodity capitalism. This subject reveals some possible interesting nuances in Lukács's changing theoretical stances as well as throws light on the general problem of alienation and its elimination.[50] Lukács envisages a process of the transcendence of the reified forms of social life which coagulate as institutions and as reified thought under commoditized and quantified social relations. Once these relations have been transcended there is no reason, on Lukács's argument in *History of Class Consciousness*, why the reified forms of life should not be supplanted by open, self-directing, more rational and transparent social institutions which correspond with the actual collective productive relations and the greater self-determination of men. And these would possess an 'objectivity'. Lukács said in 1967 that the "ontological objectivity" of Nature was not made a centrepiece of his earlier analysis,[51] but his mode of approach then, as we saw earlier, is not solely operative on the level of consciousness, since the social/natural mediation complex is *presupposed* in the forms within the theory and, at the level of the analysis of reifications, Nature is present also, even though necessarily as a relatively remote determinant. But even so, in his self-criticism of 1967 Lukács said that in 1923 he made the crude error of equating alienation and objectification, thereby enjoining the Hegelian abolition of *all* objectivity under communism, which would mean the "end of objective reality and thus of any reality at all".[52]

But one cannot take Lukács's self-critique at its face-value, bearing in mind the many changes and apparent changes of theoretical and political stance he adopted over the years. There is reason for doubt here because the conclusion of Hegel's voyage of the experience of consciousness which forms the *Phenomenology of Mind*, contrary to Lukács's statement, by no means entails a projected total abolition of alienation, which a Hegelian scholar like Lukács would presumably know. Complete or total mutual self-recognition of objectivity and subjectivity implies its Other (i.e. some grade of objectivity) in order to have existence at all, *qua* complete self-recognition or Absolute

Knowledge. Far from leading to a position of an end-state of harmonious elimination of contradiction, the category of Recollection (*Erinnerung*) in the final chapter of the *Phenomenology* would imply a cyclical rather than a finalist view of history and would be consistent with Hegel's view of the dialectical method being a "*circle* returning upon itself, the end being wound back into the beginning".[53] The point is that the inherent logic of dialectics forced Hegel into placing in the dialectical proof a new authenticating mode of existence of Spirit as truth, rather than positing a simplistic, Utopian end-state of non-contradictory harmony which for Hegel would be arbitrarily to oppose an abstract Ought over and against Is. The new mode of existence of Spirit was necessary, otherwise no dialectical characterization of Absolute Knowledge was possible. In a famous phrase in the *Phenomenology* Hegel castigated an abstract conception of an Absolute as being like "the night in which . . . all cows are black";[54] i.e. one which was unenvisageable since it contained nothing determinate, no opposition, contingency, aberrant finitude or particularity. This image recurs in the final chapter on Absolute Knowledge when Hegel says that at that stage "Spirit is engulfed in the night of its own self-consciousness".[55] But this Absolute cannot exist as it were blandly, as a realized universal, as the end-product of a total process of concretization, as a state in which all is one, without determinations, otherwise it would imply no existence at all. It must dialectically imply its Other, i.e. an opposition to consciousness in some determination or other, in order to have existence. Hence, for Hegel it is a necessity that "a new world, and a new embodiment or mode of Spirit" is "born anew".[56] An abstract conception of the Absolute which resolved all differences and distinctions was contemptuously rejected by Hegel as a "monochrome formalism" which hurled distinction and determinateness into the "abyss of vacuity"[57] (a position which assuredly gives the lie to received views of Hegel's pan-logism and manic rationalism).

In Lukács's case, however, his self-defined more 'secularized' portrayal of the process of the abolition (overcoming) of reified forms of objectified life under communism, for similar reasons could not, within the dialectical universe of discourse, imply, as Lukács said in his later disclaimer, "no reality at all". The nature of dialectics makes this position problematic since a tension must always exist between subjectivity and objectivity. Even though Lukács's remarks in 1967 about his previous underestimation of the autonomous role of Nature and his later acceptance of Marx's position in 1844 that alienation is a special variant of active objectivity operative under specific social conditions,[58] do indeed usefully supplement his earlier position. But they are only a supplement and are by no means *necessary* for supporting an argument for the retention of objective reality under communism. Its total abolition was never on the agenda. Either Lukács still remained trapped in the Marxian interpretation of Hegel which we saw at work earlier or, as a Hegelian scholar, deliberately tilted the 1967 Preface for other reasons towards a renunciation of the 'Messianic', 'idealist', 'deviationist' text of 1923. Overturning the commodity system overturns the self-objectivity of a reified social world, the particular forms of life under reified commodity conditions, not all objectivity *per se*. In Hegel and Marx, to see oneself in the world one creates, to be self-determining in a comprehensible, rational world, is to acknowledge a situation of *comprehended* (and thus benign) necessity, objectivity or otherness, not its total abolition.

6 Towards conscious mediations

As a philosopher, Lukács assailed the neo-Kantians of his time by going back to Hegel's critique of Kant, particularly Hegel's attack on what he saw as Kant's ultimately subjectivistic and agnostic theory of the categorial conditions of knowledge. But Lukács additionally spelled out what that critique would look like in Marxian terms once one had carried out Marx's inversion of the Hegelian dialectic and theory of alienation; and then he exploited its resultant social and political implications. Lukács perceived that the power of the Hegelian system also lay in the 'truth as the whole' postulate which purged arbitrariness, caprice and relativistic values in a dialectic of necessity, both methodologically and historically. As both Hegel and Marx averred: the dialectic 'lets nothing impose on it', i.e. nothing external or arbitrary. For Lukács, too, the historical dialectic of necessity is one which totalizes all other perspectives. Lukács implicitly polemizes against the neo-Kantians who grappled with the problem of trying to find an Archimedean point among a welter of value-judgments, all of which attempts failed because they foundered on variations of the basic dilemma of bourgeois thought: the belief that evaluations, conceptualizations or categorizations of immediate social reality are merely a subjective picture of an aspect of the given social world which is assumed (irrationally) to produce itself.

For Lukács, subjectivity, as for Hegel,[1] is immanent in the facts of reification (alienation) and the process of growing proletarian class-consciousness is subjectivity and objectivity progressively finding they are only apparently alien to each other. The proletariat for Lukács is historically and sociologically uniquely capable of de-objectifying the immediate facticity of the reified social relations of capitalism *really* and at the level of the totality. This conception is elaborated against the limited view of 'de-objectification' on the methodological level of single partial historical phenomena sociologically selected by way of (ultimately) arbitrary value-positions by the individual or within social science. Against the Kantians Lukács argues that

> For the 'facts' of history must remain – notwithstanding their 'value-attributes' – in a state of crude, uncomprehended facticity as to every path to, or real understanding of them, of their real meaning, their real function in the historical process has been blocked *systematically* by methodically abandoning any claim to a knowledge of the totality.[2]

But for Lukács, on the contrary, the becoming self-conscious of the proletariat within the structure of commodity fetishism – i.e. their awareness of the social nature of labour, the core value-creating social relation beneath commodity relations – begins the process of the total practical overthrow of the forms of reified social life of the entire bourgeois society. This is the beginning of the consummation of a long-term process of transition of historically developing contradictions into conscious dialectical contradictions through the practice of the class whose appropriated labour power reproduces under capitalist wage labour the fetishes which constitute the objectified forms of reality. This historical process of growing proletarian class-consciousness eventually issues in the true identical subject-object of history sought by the philosophers, since the producers of reality see themselves in the reified world they have produced once the fetishes of the commodity production are transcended.

History and Class Consciousness was a remarkable synthesis of the social, political, theoretical and ethical problems of its time. The Weberian question of how to reconcile an understanding of men's social action with an objective social science is absorbed in the practical sublation of its assumed passive subject-object dualism. In practice the social world becomes transparent to itself and rational, and thus positive science or hermeneutic understanding are no longer appropriate modes of enquiry. The appearance and essence of society would coincide in human praxis.[3] The ethical socialists' and the determinist socialists' standpoints are transcended since in the victory of the proletariat its self-knowledge is at the same time total knowledge of the nature of society: the perception of reality and the act of its transformation coincide. Irrationalism proves to be individually based and related to the random and meaningless reified husk of a commoditized society and thus sublatable in the overall rationalizing historical process towards socialism. Bergson and Simmel's theories of the falsification and deadening of lived experience or infinite life by the spatial categories of socialized man prove to be a conservative eternalization into a tragic condition of human existence of what is historically the specific experience of men of the reifications of the rationalized bourgeois world. Instead of seeking merely the pessimistic salvage of the human hero in Weber's iron cage of heartless rationalized institutions and advocating responsible vocational politics in the face of it, a true collective overthrow of the very objectified nature of that cage from within is possible by the proletariat's act of becoming conscious of its role in commodity production. And this act is also the practical solution to the antinomies of bourgeois thought thrown up by the nature of the givenness of an irrational, calculable reality. And finally the victory of the proletariat ends the confrontation and antagonism of the individual and society, the self-experience of which was a product of atomized, isolated commodity-owners facing the hostile, irrational surface thing-like relations of a commodity society against which the individual must calculatively adjust himself. In one sweep of dazzling ingenuity *History and Class Consciousness* accomplished a historical and praxical solution to the characteristic philosophical and sociological dilemmas of its time. It simultaneously gave hope for an end to the crises of capitalism which had produced the carnage of the First World War and the accompanying economic dislocation in the same proletarian victory, to which end the book was an apocalyptic and all-uniting call for action. It was an extraordinary *tour de force.*

In deploying Hegel's critique of Kantian subjectivism in his analysis of the problem of the given in bourgeois philosophy, Lukács rightly drew attention to the individualistic, subject-centred character of bourgeois philosophy since Descartes (which, as we shall see in Part four, is taken up by Horkheimer). It is this legacy which pervades the often implicitly subjective starting point of much philosophizing today and is tacitly present, for example, in the phenomenologists' preoccupation with *inter*-subjectivity. This tradition has bequeathed the philosophical question of the epistemological status of the self as the consciousness that knows it knows, typically presented in terms of the conception of the sovereign ego, the I-Thou duality and arguments about how the individual can be convinced of the indubitable character of his knowledge. The revolt of the individual started, of course, much earlier, and is notably epitomized in the writings of Kierkegaard and Max Stirner who reacted in the name of individual subjectivity against what was regarded as the levelling of individual existence in the universality of world-historical processes in Hegel's system.[4] (Marx the scientist subsumed the individual into a different world-historical process.)[5] The individualist tradition is typified by Stirner's defiance:

> I, therefore, am the kernel that is to be freed from the husk – free from all confining shells. What remains when I have been freed from everything that is not I? Only I and nothing but I.[6]

Now, Lukács tries to root the subject-object problematic in a quasi-sociological fashion in the reified thought and self-experience of commodity owners in a differentiated, fragmented commodity capitalism. This reality atomizes people, who face the reified institutional world as individual sellers of their labour power in a free labour market. They inevitably perceive the world from an individual standpoint, as revolving around the subject who has to adjust to the blind processes of that reality and for whom, under bourgeois conditions, morality, conscience and religious belief are individual matters. And, as Horkheimer puts it, this process generally subjectivizes reason so that finally ends and outcomes cannot be judged as reasonable in themselves.[7] Against Weber, Lukács says that " 'inner freedom' presupposes that the world cannot be changed"[8] and the individual can only make subjective responses of recognition or rejection in relation to the reified world, whereas politically "only the class can relate to the whole of reality in a practical revolutionary way".[9] Furthermore, the "cleavage of the ego into 'is' and 'ought' ", into the empirical and intelligible ego, cannot for Lukács serve as the foundation for a dialectical process of becoming even for the individual. This is because there is no interaction between the former (grounded psychologically and physiologically in deterministic laws) and the latter, which thus takes on a separate existence as an ideal to be realized or as a transcendental idea. The result is mysticism.[10] Notice that Lukács does not address the so-called epistemological problem about indubitable personal knowledge but locates its origin in the self-experience of commodity owners and seeks its solution in the "we of the genesis" of the conscious proletariat which discovers within itself, on the basis of its life-experience, "the identical subject-object, the subject of action".[11] Lukács sociologizes the genesis of the conditions which render the problem an issue in the first place and projects its solution into a future collective social condition to be created in practice. But leaving aside objections to his sociological analysis, it could be argued, however, that it only engages the epistemological issue itself[12] if one is satisfied with genetic explanation and the projected collective overcoming of the problem in a true community. However, if like Weber one rejects that as Utopian, then what other processes of collectivization, if any, are tending towards transforming the atomizing social conditions upon which the existence of the self-experience and thus the epistemological issue depend?

To return to the various political and theoretical standpoints which Lukács sought to absorb and to transcend in the totalizing praxical sweep of *History and Class Consciousness*, we will see that, like Gramsci, Lukács is also sceptical about "contemplative" sociology in the name of the advocacy of a mass praxis which can falsify social science knowledge. Steeped in the brute givenness of the present, sociology, like traditional philosophy, will not theorize the production of its object. (Horkheimer's division between traditional and critical theory and contempt for the apotheosization of 'facts' in social science have their direct roots here.)[13] Both Gramsci and Lukács, emerging from anti-positivist milieux intellectually similar at least, appealed to creativity and action against the stultifying deadness of predictive social science which, for both writers, enshrined routine social passivity and, for Gramsci in particular, was "frivolous" unless directly political.[14] Lukács approaches his criticism of 'bourgeois sociology', argues for the necessity of moving in theory to the remoter domains of the social formation, frames his theory of how the proletariat perceives reality and exhorts the creative continuity of historical tendencies, by developing the Hegelian concept of mediation (*Vermittlung*).[15]

Lukács argues that bourgeois sociology fails to move beyond the immediacy of given facts because of the reified habits of thought born of the experience of objectivity as primary, fixed, immutable, objective. To go beyond this immediacy in theory one must, in Hegelian fashion, move towards greater concreteness, which is to move towards making connections with the totality in which the truth of the abstract immediacies lies, and towards their mediated genesis. For Lukács, in their process of becoming conscious of the basis of commodity relations, the proletariat makes those mediating moves in praxis, in reality and at the level of the totality, thus consciously *continuing* the historical mediating process heralded by its grasp in theory. There is only one way to avoid merely illustrating typologies with examples from history, which cannot "surpass the purely factual nature of historical facts".[16] This is by the "genesis, the 'creation' of the object" which assumes that

> the forms of mediation in and through which it becomes possible to go beyond the immediate existence of objects as they are given, can be shown to be *the structural principles and the real tendencies of the objects themselves* . . . intellectual genesis must be identical in principle with historical genesis.[17]

Methodologically speaking, the ancestry of Lukács's position (which he infuses with a stronger emphasis on mass creativity and action) lies in Hegel's critique in the name of Reason of the critical philosophy and of empiricism;[18] as mediated through Marx's critique of the drawbacks of the "analytical method" of classical political economy which was, however, a necessary pre-requisite for his "genetical presentation" of the formative process of social development in its various phases;[19] and in Engels's critique of the "metaphysical mode of thought" in 'Socialism: Utopian and Scientific'.[20] The idea that the logic of the method and the logic of history must in principle follow each other's contours in order to avoid arbitrary reality-attenuating impositions of categories in a nominalistic fashion is very fundamental to the dialectical tradition.[21] Lukács is saying in effect that the methods of factual sociology are doomed to an inadequate treatment of reality because they contemplatively cannot surpass it nor deal with its spontaneous creation and potentially more conscious continuation, *not* that such a sociology is impossible. (He is postively hostile to some sociologists, though, when he remarks of typology only relying on chance connections with reality that: "This may take the form of a naive 'sociology' in search of 'laws' (of the Comte/Spencer variety) in which the insolubility of the task is reflected in the absurdity of the results."[22] Although this is hardly a serious critique.) In the same way that for Hegel the analytical Understanding is a useful and necessary clarifying prerequisite to critical Reason, so too for Lukács (and as we will see later for Horkheimer as well) analytical, factual social science and a genetico-critical appropriation of reality mutually presuppose each other. They exist as moments in the whole historical process, feeding on the reified forms of life and their "human core" and its potentialities.

Bourgeois thought has tended to pull apart intellectual genesis and historical genesis through the application of formal laws. Even though moving beyond the immediately given and being thus apparently critical, this approach still ultimately returns to the given immediacy of reality since this is "made permanent and acquires a justification . . . as being a necessary 'precondition of the possibility' "[23] of the perspective itself. For Lukács, the only solution to contemplation, in this sense of the perception of immediacy of the given object, is ultimately praxis, i.e. the truly critical *real creation* of the object which in practice eliminates the givenness. And of course under capitalism the collective subject which can potentially accomplish this self-creation of the object at the totality level is the proletariat.

The central Hegelian idea in *History and Class Consciousness* that immediacy is a process of mediation not conscious of itself, not only provides the underpinning of Lukács's portrayal of the perennial problem of bourgeois thought being the nature of the givenness of reality, but also enables a theoretician to look beyond facts towards a whole historical process determined not only by the past, but in a special sense by the future as well. (This was to become a major preoccupation of the Frankfurt School and also informs Lukács's 'standpoint of the proletariat'.) Hegel deals with the category of mediation (defined as the principle of dialectical self-change by movement towards Other, essential to the existence of finitude) extensively in the *Lectures on the Philosophy of Religion*. Lukács makes a great deal of Hegel's argument there that what appears as indubitable, immediate reality is the mediated result of vast sequences of dialectical processes even if men are unaware of them. Hegel says:

> 'Immediate knowledge' exists where we have not the consciousness of mediation; all the same, it *is* mediated.[24]

Probably in order to counter a sociology of facts which would appeal to evidence to refute, say, claims about the development of working-class consciousness, Lukács has mustered the Hegelian notion of finitude as a moment of a necessity in which what *is* is determined not only by what *was* but by its necessary *Other*, i.e. mediated also by its beyond, such that it is in a double sense misleading to regard facts as exhausting reality. Hegel explains:

> Immediate knowledge discards all differentiations; it puts away these modes of connection, and has only what is simple, one mode of connection, one knowledge, the subjective form, and then, 'it is' . . . This standpoint is, that what is empirical only is to be regarded as valid, that man is not to go beyond what he finds in consciousness. It is not asked why it is found, or how it is necessary.[25]

In methodological practice, the knowledge of mediations is a raising to consciousness of the genesis of historical processes and the category of mediation applied to the development of the proletariat is itself an expression of what Marx called the "real movement which abolishes the present state of things".[26] Against the Weberians' and Kantians' claims that historical necessity or a tendency in reality is a metaphysical prejudice, Lukács sees the category of mediation as born of that movement itself. To drive the point home, Lukács rejects variants on the value-judgment theme by Rickert which purported to have achieved objectivity as foundering in arbitrariness, subjectivism or an abstract Utopian Ought.[27] (The parallel with Marx's insistence, against Stirner's egoism and against Utopian thinking, that historical law-like tendencies are moving towards socialism is striking.) Lukács stresses therefore the need for the practical creation of *conscious* mediations to realize in practice at the level of the concrete totality the historical tendency whose mediations have become conscious in theory. As Mészáros[28] rightly says, the Lukácsian programme is essentially a struggle against the suppression of mediations through 'practical-critical' activity which dissolves immediacy.

The standpoint of the proletariat is in Lukácsian terms no mere option to support the disprivileged class, nor a value-judgment about reality, nor an ethical judgment justified on the basis of knowledge of historical facts, nor is its realized guise of full class-consciousness a necessary factual condition for socialism; but it is a theoretical standpoint existing as an abstract potentiality and held to be theorized as such by intellectuals since at the present stage of development it is not yet able to become full class-consciousness and thus has not become fully concretized. To make the point again, Lukács's concept of historical necessity ran counter to the Weberian view that it is a metaphysical prejudice to endow an objective meaning to a meaningless reality depleted of religiosity. Lukács does this by asserting one such meaning and then claiming it to be realizable, provable, *in practice*. For Lukács the long-term historical tendencies embraced a dialectic of contradictions (expressible in its tendency as the polarizing of classes) the negating progressive aspect of which was the proletariat. The concepts of historical necessity and mediation were expressions of this tendency, and thus aspects of the developing reality, although its necessity required a conscious element for its furtherance. Thus, for Lukács, the invocation of the Hegelian category of mediation-to-Other provided a theory of the totality which ultimately comprised the historical process in its entirety, including the empirical contradictory development which revealed the emergence of the proletariat up to the present as well as its 'ideal' theoretical continuity in the tendency towards communism. The latter was thus present as an abstract potentiality, a determining Other within the overall movement and expressible in theory as the standpoint of the proletariat at the present stage of development. The mere sociological delineation of immediacy, of facts of reality, would fail to take account of this overall mediated process, including its potentiality, hence "the developing tendencies of history constitute a higher reality than the empirical 'facts' ".[29]

The present concretely unrealized standpoint of the proletariat would in the future communist society constitute the new perspective on reality at present provided in bourgeois society by the bourgeoisie, but in the former case a truly communistic, democratic, collectivist world view based in a society less determined by blind necessity and archaic social-class relations, which thereby prove themselves to have been a transitory phase in human history. To espouse the standpoint of the proletariat as a theoretical perspective existing in an abstract, relatively unconcretized state, *in potentia*, was for Lukács also to have overcome sociological relativism.[30] That position was statically caught up in the immediate and not geared to a historically necessary 'absolute' social process of mediation which had *yet* to fulfil itself, but which needed to be consciously aided to become realized in practice. Hence to take the stance of the proletariat in this sense provided an absolute theoretical, epistemological, ethical and sociological certitude as well as a positive and certain spur towards political commitment. In its period this probably seemed a most solid, scientific, all-explaining and definitive position amidst the many competing ideologies and the potentially limitless welter of value-judgments. Lukács's theory carried the apparently unbeatable claim that the standpoint of the proletariat was in his extraordinary words "on a higher scientific plane objectively".[31] This was because it was capable of rising above the mire of immediacy in theory, which only expressed a historical tendency which in its fulfilment by the class-conscious proletariat really mediated that immediacy to the totality. As Morris Watnick rightly says, Lukács's theory of the two types of class-consciousness ("actual" and "imputed") embedded in the historical dialectic of conflict between the bourgeoisie and the proletariat seems to have been "a sociological version of the concept of 'two truths', derived from the Hegelian distinction between the actual and the real or rational worlds",[32] so that proletarian class-consciousness was necessarily on a potentially higher plane. Their perception of reality and the act of its transformation would coincide. In what would be, in analogous Hegelian terms, a stage beyond the Sceptical Consciousness and the Unhappy Consciousness to a further level of concretization where, as Reason, consciousness "discovers the world as its own new and real world".[33]

To summarize: for Lukács, the structure of the historical development of the struggle of classes is to be grasped genetically, and created in analysis in the sense of reconstructing the mediated movement itself by appropriating the categories which have actually come to be embodied in human practice. This critical reclamation of the past presuppositions of the historical development of the real tendencies of history brings to consciousness (together with penetrating the present reification springing from the commodity structure) knowledge of the social institutions of men which they do not realize are their own. The movement of history and its critical-theoretical appropriation into consciousness as genetical method thus coincide and history better comprehends itself. But to avoid remaining in the thrall of theorizing mere immediacy, the act of theoretical 'creation' (appropriation) of the past mediations must carry over into the real conscious creation of those processes in reality.[34] In Lukács, therefore, genetic method, past, present, future, subject and object, science, politics and morality are ultimately a unity in theory in the standpoint of the proletariat. This he believed was a non-arbitrary absolute historical standpoint, capable of visualization because it is embedded in the real development and tendencies in history and capable of realization in praxis, if mediated to and harnessed by the proletariat. Lukács states:

> the fact that it is possible to go beyond the given, the fact that this consciousness is so great and so profound is itself a product of history. But what is historically possible cannot be achieved simply by a straightforward progression of the immediately given

(with its 'laws'), but only by a consciousness of the whole of society acquired through manifold mediations, and by a clear aspiration to realise the dialectical tendencies of history . . . And the series of mediations must be a movement of mediations advancing from the present to the future.[35]

7 Sociology and mythology in Lukács

In the last chapter we saw how the Lukácsian concept of mediation treated of a socio-genesis which needed not only to be critically and creatively appropriated in analysis, but also continued into the future in order to avoid the tendency of bourgeois thought to become contemplatively stuck in immediacy unable to move beyond the facts: immediacy was a process of mediation not conscious of itself. This practical-critical perspective was based on the Hegelian notion that the facts, i.e. what *is*, carry a higher meaning both in their mediation to the whole and to its genesis as well as its determinacy by its Other in the sense of the 'universal' goal the historical process acquires and tends towards. From this conception it follows for Lukacs that the standpoint of the proletariat is on a higher scientific plane since it at present embraces the abstract potentiality of a form of consciousness which history is preparing more fully to concretize in the proletarian victory. Lukács's philosophy of history and his theory of class-consciousness were essentially the same thing. In its time this conception carried an absolute sociological certitude expressed in the celebrated concepts of the "empirically given" (psychologically describable) ideas which men form and the "imputed" consciousness of a class, "the appropriate and rational reactions 'imputed' to a particular typical position in the process of production".[1] For Lukács, this perspective transcended pure description to yield methodologically "the category of objective possibility",[2] a position which was, in its future-orientation, not directly subject to challenge from empirical reference or falsification. It would be proved in practice.

Inherent in Lukács's position was the epistemological view that the facts of social existence were merely experiential, merely a transitory way station on the road to the proletariat's victory, so that to remain stuck in the mire of immediacy (which would include the present beliefs and attitudes of the working class) would be to espouse an inferior order of truth. To be geared to the higher potential stage of truth revealed in the present avoids psychologism, empiricism and relativism and provides a motivating theory for working towards the concretization of the standpoint of the proletariat by trying to transform long-term historical contradictions into dialectical contradictions. This makes true, in dialectical terms 'proves', the standpoint by mediating it in praxis to its Absolute Other, which it in effect already *is*. For Lukács, even though he advocated urgent conscious action (which could fail) to realize historical tendencies in order to prevent capitalism from drifting into the "abyss",[3] there was nevertheless ultimately only one outcome of the historical process – the victory of the proletariat.[4] This had to be so in the dialectical perspective to avoid the irrationalism, arbitrariness and psychologism of perspectives which theorized only immediacy. At the same time it claimed adherence to a higher truth which was none the less objective. Lukács's position was essentially Hegel's critique of Kant rewritten as the historical development of proletarian class-consciousness. Lukács would thus have agreed with Hegel that

> What is universally valid is also universally effective: what *ought to be*, as a matter of fact, *is* too; and what merely *should* be, and is *not*, has no real truth.[5]

This chapter follows up the sociological implications of the postulate that the world of facts does not exhaust reality which, in its historical tendencies, contains a higher reality to which all immediacy must be shown to be mediated and which must be ultimately concretized through conscious historical praxis. We shall explore that as an aspect of Lukacs's philosophical position and its relationship to social science, a position that Watnick has rightly called Lukács's "self-validating scholasticism".[6] For Lukács, during the period of the pre-history of mankind leading up to the victory of the proletariat, actual proletarian thought is "merely a *theory of praxis* which only gradually . . . transforms itself into a *practical theory* that overturns the real world".[7] In theory this consciousness, in the possession of the theoretician today, is identical with that of its future concretization by the proletariat but in an abstract less mediated form. Lukács's philosophy of history was redolent with a Hegelian belief in the higher order of truth embraced in a tendential totality leading towards itself through a world-historical process of progressive disalienation, a belief which effectively pruned Marxian social science down to its philosophical core, which would remain intact no matter what occurred in the imperfect temporal world. In a famous statement, Lukács saw Marxist orthodoxy as referring "exclusively to *method*"[8] (meaning the scientific appropriation of the structure of historical processes by the dialectical method) and sought to develop and build on its founders' contributions. But this position still made the unassailable assumption that the core philosophical assumptions (praxis as mediation between active idealism and passive materialism, praxis rendering congruent 'reality' and 'thought', etc.) remained, irrespective of whatever sociological evidence could be cited about the nature of social processes. His polemics against facts are, like those of Horkheimer, predicated on the assumption of a higher tendential historical reality existing over and above the facts of immediacy which orthodox social science patiently delineates. This latter enterprise must remain contemplative and regard its object as passively immutable. Of sociological evidence and Marxist philosophy Lukács writes:

> Let us assume for the sake of argument that recent research had disproved once and for all every one of Marx's individual theses. Even if this were to be proved, every serious 'orthodox' Marxist would still be able to accept all such modern findings without reservation and hence dismiss all of Marx's theses *in toto* – without having to renounce his orthodoxy for a single moment.[9]

It is an irony that many of the main disciples and most influential expositors of the almost wholly social-scientific teachings of Karl Marx have been philosophers, who, one would have thought, by the nature of Marx's project of the realization of philosophy in practice, would find the least number of congenial insights in his work. This chapter contains an early adumbration of the theme of the role of philosophy in Marxist theory and in sociology in general which comes up throughout this study.[10] From its inception Marxian human science was an attempt to unite philosophy and science through seeking the realization of philosophical wisdom based on a scientific analysis of society which revealed its fettered rationality. Human science had overcome philosophy as the competent discipline for scientifically analysing society but was thus in the Marxian case burdened with it in its very essence. Marx kept the two enterprises closely united by attempting a critical analysis of bourgeois society using inherently genetico-critical conceptualizations which attempted to theorize how society ought (rationally) to be organized, by showing its presuppositions as being human products and not eternal. (This aspect of Marx is taken up in Part four below.)

Now, in Lukács, however, in the call to recognize the autonomy of Marxist theory as method, we have the elaboration of a theory which very largely consists of a set of philosophical assumptions more divorced than in the case of Marx's theories from their linkage with empirical reality, concepts or knowledge. It is this philosophical cast which gives Lukács's work its particular character and it will be my contention that his main arguments are a highly inventive project to deal a death-blow to all forms of philosophical and social-theoretical enterprise which are not geared to a framework for proletarian action, but that this position, since it had to be abstractly social-philosophical in order to accomplish such a task, flickers uneasily between philosophy and sociology and veers towards mythology. When reading Lukács we *think* we are reading about social processes and their development but we are in fact talking in a universe of discourse attenuated from them by several levels. And it is this character which makes his position self-validating and apparently unassailable. For present purposes in this chapter I will argue sociologically against Lukács's philosophical presentation, for reasons which will become clear later on in the study. Lukács's arguments are more or less held not to be subject to empirical refutation or modification because of their future-orientation and assumption about the higher reality over and above the facts towards which society is tending. Furthermore, the misgiving that reality does not seem to be tending in the direction suggested or the mustering of findings to disprove the Marxian hypothesis are of no avail according to Lukács because the universality of his position is capable potentially of creatively being proved *in practice*, which would absolutize his relative position, which is then revealed for the truth that it *is*.

This is a difficult aspect of Lukács to deal with since for him the domination of the ruling class and the overwhelming positivity of the established order were only guaranteed as long as action did not occur to overthrow them. Error in the theory was only up to a point a theoretical question. Put this way, it is difficult to oppose his position by any of the common kinds of argument and evidence. Within Lukács's terms, at any rate, there is no way of cutting through the tightly co-ordinated conceptual matrix which revolves around the concepts of mediation, immediacy, contemplation, praxis, passivity versus activity, givenness of reality, etc. Indeed it seems that it is only by retreat into a philosophy of praxis that Lukács was able to hold on to Marxism as *the* truth amidst a welter of competing ideologies and the clamourings of empirical evidence. The only effective way of critically appraising his position must be to move outside his realm of discourse and outside that of his intra-Marxist detractors as well. To argue against Lukács from within Marxism would be only to excommunicate him on the grounds of not being a good historical materialist or for being an 'idealist', a 'deviationist',[11] and to criticize him on his own terms would be to acquiesce in his categories and remain trapped within their circle. It is far better to try to transcend the co-ordinates in which the debate is usually conducted, to question the presuppositions of the argument – this is the essence of critique.

In view of Marx's insistence, against the Utopians and moralizers, that his theory articulated the historical development of the contradictions of bourgeois society towards their higher resolution and provided the conscious ideology of the proletariat for its world-historical mission of organizing society in the interests of all men, his theory was always subject to the charge of being self-referential and irrefutable. But in the case of Lukács, having effectively pared Marx's theory down to a philosophy of history, this unassailability became particularly exacerbated. Lukács's sophisticated theory claimed that in Lukács himself (and in the consciousness of any others who also embraced the potential consciousness of the proletariat before its full concretization in praxis) history was effectively conscious of itself. This feature made Lukács's theory resemble closely, and be subject to similar problems as, the Left Hegelian theory of the 1840s. It is this element which not only gives Lukács's theory its self-validating character and leads to the dangerously elitist position that the small clique of the *cognoscenti* embrace a higher form of truth, a higher scientific level than what can be discerned empirically in people's beliefs about the world, but also, I will argue, ironically falls back behind the Hegelians into nihilism and despair.

Let us divert briefly to the origins of the practical-critical perspective. August von Cieszkowski's advocacy of creating the further mediations towards the filling-out of Absolute Knowledge through human praxis, now that it had been completed in man, was an eminently Hegelian task already implicit in the tensions of the Hegelian system. Having traversed the trajectory of contradictions and grades of experience which constitute the standpoints in the *Phenomenology* or stages in the *Encyclopaedia*, one is enabled to think the whole since the contradictions of the Understanding were now overcome, transformed into Reason and authenticated. The whole had been constructed in thought, leaving out nothing. Having reached this stage of Absolute Knowledge the Hegelian sage is capable of speculative thought, which unites the abstract antinomies of the Understanding: speculative thought thus has no pejorative connotation in Hegel. Practice is assimilated into theory for the speculative thinker, and Cieszkowski's project involved praxis finding its own theory, as it were, because it *was* theory (and vice versa) although still enshrined in the speculative thinker who embodied the historical completion of theory as a whole in human practice. Further practice was the only road leading from the complete fulfilment of philosophy. Michelet, never a radical Hegelian, had seen that Hegel's Absolute Knowledge had to be translated into conscious practice as early as 1837:

> As far as thought is concerned, the reconciliation is completed. It only remains for reality to elevate itself from all sides toward rationality too . . . As philosophy teaches us, truth, in order to

> become ours, has too become our own activity; and by means of truth transformed into activity, we shall reach freedom.[12]

Cieszkowski, still within Hegelianism, accordingly advocated "post-theoretical practice"[13] in the sphere of society in order to pervade reality with Absolute Knowledge in self-conscious practice, the highest synthesis of thought and being achieved in the praxis of the Absolute Knower. Cieszkowski saw himself as furthering Hegel and the activity was not for him mere finite activity (or "dirty Jewish practice", in Marx's terms) but was incarnated Absolute Knowledge, "thought which has again become being",[14] an assertion which kept Cieszkowski within Hegelianism since in a theological vein he was able to unite universality and particularity as self-conscious activity and thus not allow temporal concerns to vainly place themselves above the Godhead. (This was something that did not bother Marx.) Armed with our post-Marxian concept of ideology we would automatically interpret Michelet's and Cieszkowski's deliberations on the temporalization of eternity in the praxis of the Absolute Knower as an ideology which provided a set of rationalizations for acting in the real, finite world while at the same time retaining religious faith. Indeed, it is precisely on such a commitment to the primacy of finite, earthly, human practice that, as we saw in Chapter 2, Marx took his stand and upon which he built a social science.

But the Absolute Knowers of the 1840s, who believed that they themselves had achieved Absolute Knowledge of the dynamic of history (the world having, as it were, revealed its secret to them) faced a dilemma. This was whether to try to continue the realization of the Absolute into further sectors of the world in practice or whether to adopt a quietistic stance and await the self-fulfilment of the Absolute of its own accord. (A striking analogy with the activistic versus deterministic interpretations of Marxism.) But in both the Hegelian and the Marxian–Lukácsian theory, there was no doubt of the actual achievement of the total knowledge by respectively the sage or the socialist. The self-validating character, latent elitism and projected universality of Lukács's 'two truths' theory have their roots here. Hence, on its own (philosophical) ground Lukács's position is unassailable because he can argue that embodied in him is the consciousness of the proletariat which the contradictory historical development has brought to a head and made possible by its progress, such that his view of the potentialities of the proletariat for changing the commoditized objectivity of the world is only the expression of the real development and movement as a whole, including its consummation in the future through the class becoming conscious of itself.[15] Like the Young Hegelians he effectively embodies the most advanced consciousness possible in the epoch in which he stands, as an expression of the level of development of the society of that epoch. It is thus a question of allying oneself with the real tendencies working themselves out and providing them with the total 'ideal' consciousness which they do not as yet possess. But by claiming an ultimate truth at another time, 'over there', a fulfilment in the future to be realized in practice, Lukács created a closed system. Any other stance, therefore, if it does not represent this putative real tendency, must be, methodologically, say Utopian (just placing an abstract Ought up against reality), pseudo-detached, and above the real class antagonisms (Moses Hess),[16] a moralizing critique of existing reality (social democracy, neo-Kantians) or a subjectivistic egoism (Stirnerites).

Now Cieszkowski, like many of the Young Hegelians, as Lukács himself points out,[17] tried to continue Hegel's dialectic into the future through praxis and never tried to transcend it. Whereas others, such as Lassalle or Hess, did try although they remained either trapped within it or (influenced by Feuerbach's unmediated sensualism) regressed to Kantian and Fichtean positions. They failed to make Marx's move of accepting conceptual realism while making the methodological switch to a praxical materialism of mediation.[18] By the same token, however, Lukács tries to transcend the philosophers' entanglements but also remains trapped in them. He tries to transcend the subject and object problem by sociologizing it into its rootedness in the commoditized structure of social relations and men's self-experience as isolated commodity owners in an arbitrary market reality which works with a randomness to which the individual must adjust himself calculatively. In this effort Lukács adumbrated a collective praxical overcoming of the subject-object dualism in the victory of the revolutionary proletariat which created a situation in which the givenness of the object and its subjects within the commodity relations coincided in praxis, thus solving the philosophical hiatus of the production of the object *in reality*. But in doing this he uncritically retained the concepts of subject and object as relevant explanatory concepts, so remaining on that philosophical terrain, the culmination of which he exalts as Marx's philosophy of praxis. He approaches the sociology of the problem through the prior Marxian methodological precept of praxis as the constituting medium of active consciousness and passive objectivity, between subject and object, i.e. the notion of praxis as the subject seeing himself in the world he creates. Couple this assumption with Lukács's belief in 1923 in the absolute imperative of proletarian action and commitment to the Marxian theory of the nature of commodity fetishism, and we see him rewrite the history of European philosophy in terms of that theory of praxis to show that the philosophy was inherently incapable of solving its subject-object dualism. The missing theory of praxis is foisted on to European philosophy and the development of commodity capitalism in order that the proletariat could emerge at the end of it as the one collective agent capable of resolving the philosophical divagations of the classical philosophers. To regard subject and object as mutually constituting and interpenetrating each other in praxis and then to attribute the 'failures' of the whole of European philosophy to their lack of this insight and inability to theorize the nature of the given reality of bourgeois society, leaves the individualistic subject and object concepts uncritically intact. They then permeate Lukács's objectivist reasoning and inevitably drive him into the arms of mythology – the *collective* identical subject-object of history which really sees itself in the world it creates.

It is ironically by stressing the philosophical layer embedded in Marxism that Lukács is driven in exactly the opposite direction from that intended by Marx, i.e. towards mythology. And yet Marx (although not himself free from mythology) took his stand on a social scientific appraisal of the social conditions which have led to and continue to perpetuate inequality and productive irrationality and which sustain ideological illusions. The Marxian project was at least an attempt scientifically to understand the world in terms of the actual social relations into which men enter in order to live. Marx in his time had to stress that the mundane, interest-laden, real social relations of men alone carried the key to understanding the 'universalistic', philosophical, religious, etc., ways in which men try to understand the world. And this project involved appropriating the actual historical structures of human societies, to treat of thought categories in terms of their emergence from and reference to definite societies at definite stages of development. Marx repeats that injunction almost *ad nauseam*. But Lukács's analysis of the nature of classical philosophy falls back behind Marx's project by unjustifiably and non-empirically pushing that philosophy selectively into the subject-object mould which, as we saw, at least in Hegel's case is less than accurate. In arguing from the philosophy of praxis Lukács deploys not sociological but social-ontological categories to theorize the levels of experience arising from the commodity structure of capitalist society. This is simply assumed to have resulted in the basic individualizing, randomized, quantified social life to which a philosophy corresponded characterized by an inability to theorize the production of the object – bourgeois society. With this type of theory the 'endemic' structure of philosophy and kinds of political position can be read off from any given stage of societal development within the mediation-praxis, immediacy-contemplation co-ordinates.

Lukács also generally remains uncritically in the terminology of the philosophers, employing as a matter of course, in addition to subject and object, concepts such as form and content, material substratum, man, freedom, mediation, etc., his orientation being epitomized by the following statement:

> Man himself is the objective foundation of the historical dialectic and the subject-object lying at its roots, and as such he is decisively involved in the dialectical process. To formulate it in the initial abstract categories of dialectics: *he both is and at the same time is not.*[19]

The problem is that very seldom does Lukács move beyond those "initial abstract categories" and, despite Marx's strenuous rejections on many occasions of the concept of 'man' as being theological and abstract in favour of a sociological analysis of specific men in given societies,[20] Lukács applies and reapplies it in Marx's name to history as part of his aim to "restore humanity destroyed by reification" (Lukács's phrase). Lukács's perspective was undoubtedly born of the mood of cultural despair of the post-First World War world. In a telling and prophetic passage which sums up that mood well, Lukács, echoing Rosa Luxemburg, says the following of the opportunities for the working class in 1923, in an "age of the dissolution of capitalism":

> on the one hand, there is the increasing undermining of the forms of reification – one might describe it as the cracking of the crust because of the inner emptiness – their growing inability to do justice to the phenomena, even as isolated phenomena, even as the objects of reflection and calculation. On the other hand, we find the quantitative increase of the forms of reification, their empty extension to cover the whole surface of manifest phenomena . . . As the antagonism becomes more acute two possibilities open up for the proletariat. It is given the opportunity to substitute its own positive contents for the emptied and bursting husks. But it is exposed to the danger that for a time at least it might adapt itself ideologically to conform to these, the emptiest and most decadent forms of bourgeois culture.[21]

Lukács assails social science in terms of a philosophy of praxis operating in effect to delimit through assertions about "man" the range of what can be empirically appropriated from social reality. Again continuing a critique to this philosophy in the name of social science, we can see that informed by the assumptions in the following statement all empirical investigations of stages of development of bourgeois society can reveal nothing that would either produce a new concept of man or affect the extent to which this ideal picture of man had been realized in a given society. Quoting Ernst Bloch, Lukács declares:

> As long as man concentrates his interest contemplatively upon the past *or* the future, both ossify into an alien existence. And between the subject and the object lies the unbridgeable "pernicious chasm" of the present. Man must be able to comprehend the present as a becoming. He can do this by seeing in it the tendencies out of whose dialectical opposition he can *make* the future.[22]

Although we can identify in general with the appeal here to reality as historical reality and with the notion of dereification in the most general sense, this passage contains much of what is abstract and mythological in Lukács – "Man", "subject and object", "alien existence". These do not purport to deal with real human societies and real specific men but, being philosophical categories several steps removed from societies, they attenuate a given reality through their very applicability to any reality. Similarly, Lukács's analysis of "bourgeois thought" is categorially of a similar character. It has a very undiscriminating abstract meaning compared with, say, culture, cultural artefacts, symbolic representations or thought styles, etc., which would have far more specific, empirical, sociological reference. Bourgeois thought is again tackled ontologically, in relation to how it coped with the "givenness" or "immediacy" of the "material substratum" of the world abstractly undifferentiated and assumed to be the experience of all men. The notion that the antinomies of philosophical and social categories lose their antinomic character in the flux of the social condition is a valuable insight, but that they will be resolved in the revolutionary praxis of the proletariat is a mythological projection.

The style, vocabulary, type of abstraction and self-validating character of Lukács's theory, then, makes it unassailable in its own terms. Outside its circle, however, we can ask, for example: what exactly does Lukács's statement mean in relation to "contemplative" bourgeois thought that it ends up by returning to the "same immediacy that faces the ordinary man of bourgeois society in his everyday life"?[23] Put this way, we have no way of checking this statement, for which "ordinary man" are we talking about, of what social class, of which society, at which stage of development? What does the Hegelian concept of immediacy, put in this way, tell us about how any particular empirical groups or individuals concretely perceive social reality? Lukács conceptualizes society in such sociologically naïve terms and is subject to those kinds of critical questions from a social science standpoint clearly because of his chosen philosophical-methodological emphasis. Leaving aside for the moment the problem of the complex relation of the theory to the circumstances of the Weimar Republic in which Lukács saw himself fighting for a totalizing socialist perspective against competing ideologies and political philosophies, let us examine the steps by which Lukacs arrives theoretically at the kind of abstract position we have been discussing and then its consequences.

In his article 'Moses Hess and the Problems of Idealist Dialectics' (1926)[24] Lukács tries to show how the social critique of the Young Hegelians (especially those of Hess and Lassalle) were ineffective because they could not, unlike Marx and Engels, trace and demonstrate the underlying mediated social causes of a problem and the social prerequisites of a solution. Marx and Engels alone saw that

> in the social being of the proletariat itself the process whose real dialectics has only to be made conscious in order to become the theory of revolutionary practice.[25]

And yet it is here too that Lukács, in further interpretations of Hegel, confirms the view that although Lukács appears to be attempting to theorize sociologically (in this case in what became called the sociology of knowledge) the result is an arbitrary historicalized philosophical anthropology. He cites a passage from Hegel's *Phenomenology* about the category of Utility which appears there in the section 'Enlightenment'. This section contains the stages of self-certainty as Spirit in social consciousness and culture struggling to overcome opposition to its self-knowledge. At the stage of Utility, "insight qua object finds expression in the useful, the profitable",[26] and an earlier more abstract stage of pure insight is brought up to consciousness of itself as objectivity. Hegel states:

> What is thus wanting is reached in the fact of utility so far as pure insight secures positive objectivity there; pure insight is thereby a concrete actual consciousness satisfied within itself. This objectivity now constitutes its world, and is become the final and true outcome of the entire previous world, ideal as well as real.[27]

Now Lukács says that by "world" here Hegel 'really' means "This world, the world of bourgeois society translated into thought", Hegel's objectivity here being a confronted "legitimate world".[28] And he goes on to suggest that Hegel's argument constitutes the highest point attainable by bourgeois thought, since Hegel had comprehended mythologically the real objective forms of bourgeois society in their contradictoriness as immediate, but simultaneously as moments in a mediated process stretching from the past through the present and beckoning to the sublation of the contradictions in the future, in a process of self-overcoming. But this position founders also in immediacy, says Lukács, since Hegel cannot conceive of the practical-critical *continuation* of the process beyond the present. He elaborates the contradictions purely in thought in a society not ripe for their practical abolition.

But in absorbing Marx's critique of Hegel and being determined in the 1920s to stress the necessary active collective carrying through of the tendencies of history in practice, Lukács has executed a sleight-of-hand in relation to Hegel by which he retreats from dealing with what is really problematic in Hegel's thought and becomes mythological. Lukács has again confused history and development in Hegel – the dialectical stages of experience of self-certainty (as Spirit) in the sections of the *Phenomenology* he is talking about are movements of Spirit (experience at a certain stage of self-awareness) struggling to find itself against opposition, and each qualitative and active stage of experience "finds expression in", as Hegel puts it, various institutions, attitudes and types of experience such as discipline, the pursuit of wealth, belief, etc. The historical material employed by Hegel in these arguments stretches across several different historical epochs and he draws examples from widely separated periods (including the French Revolution), which he claims embody principles of spiritual development fundamentally alike. The operative words used by Hegel here, and throughout the *Phenomenology* are, therefore, "finds expression in", which describes the types of experience (in this case) which may occur in a different historical order from their presentation or in various social locations. Thus, the important premise which Lukács sidesteps by the arbitrary importation into the analysis of the notion of what objectivity Hegel 'really' means and its revolutionary significance, is that Hegel has already appropriated the material from the real, finite, corporeal human societies, and institutions, states, social classes, cultures, etc., etc., but is saying that the types of experience arising within them constitute an immanent necessary development simultaneous with their occurrence in their particular historical situation. The developmental sequence endeavours to prove this without any arbitrary criteria imposing on it and the stage of Utility and the "world" referred to is but a stage which incorporates the previous ones and beckons beyond itself by its immanent dialectic.

However, pursuing the Marxian inversion of Hegel, Lukács simply arbitrarily says that the process of overcoming by consciousness of the experience of strangeness and nullity being dealt with by Hegel here as the "objectivity constituting its world" *is* a perception in a mystified way of the real experience of strangeness of men in the face of the legitimized bourgeois world, but at least showed the antagonistic character of the world and its process of self-overcoming tending towards sublation. This argument is undialectically informed by an extraneous criterion brought in from the standpoint of seeking the overthrow of what were seen as the reified forms of life under capitalism by the proletariat in an attempt to show that, although Hegel's theory saw the ultimate working out of all contradictions towards the identical subject-object instead of positing a Utopian ought,[29] it still foundered in immediacy because it never specified an agent, a real active subject which could carry it out. This argument erroneously foists on to Hegel a finalism which he is said to have perceived in a mystified manner, in order to retrieve in the act of demystification another finalism – the proletarian historical dialectic issuing in socialism. It could be argued, however, that Hegel is working at a different (categorial) level, i.e. that of the method of assessing the significance of the historical process, which would be valid through whatever conscious willed activity directed it towards further concretization. As long as there is finitude and contingency (which dialectically there must be) Hegel's method applies. The extraneous concern forces Lukács into a needless reconstruction of the dialectical logic of the Marx/Hegel relation in order to show Hegel as incapable of solving the contradictions which the proletariat can and, in 1923 *must*, carry out. A dialectical pedigree is apparently established, without a dent being made in Hegel, but at the expense of creating the historical mythology of the proletarian identical subject-object.

Let us put what is also an important general point in another way, in order to extend the argument further. By assuming that consciousness and objectivity at this particular point in Hegel's *Phenomenology* were 'really' the *actual* mystified experience of men of the pseudo-objectivity of a commodity-based reified capitalist society which can be overcome by the proletariat, (and this is Lukács's basic argument as a whole), he thus remains on the terrain of philosophy and emerges from the interplay *still bearing the imprint of what was inverted.* From a perspective at a higher stage of development, however, we can see that Lukács thus creates another philosophical definition of a human historical dialectic of subject-object constituted in praxis which Hegel was 'really' trying to grasp. But once one makes this switch, one is forced (as was Marx) into the position of assuming that reality is *still* (but in the new sense) estranged, mystified, tending towards rationality and thought the reified consciousness of a reality lost to its producers. This is because Hegel is regarded as having conceived of this alienated reality in the mystified way that he did because he was misled as a result of its *real* alienating nature and effects. This general theory is then held up as a *methodological postulate.* From this the rest of Lukács's position follows, which definitionally locates all theoretical and political positions abstractly as one-sided elements of its total unyielding perspective, within the praxis-contemplation co-ordinates. As I suggested earlier, nothing can impinge on this schema of man, praxis, contemplation and becoming since one just reads off from the history of social thought and societies examples which must all inherently fail to cross the threshold of praxis. The measure of a thinker's greatness becomes the extent to which he grasps and faces the historical horizons of the bourgeois world and perceives the "tragedy of the bourgeoisie" in the dialectics of history by which it is

> cursed . . . with the tragic fate of developing an insoluble contradiction at the very zenith of its powers.[30]

As a sociology of knowledge, Lukács's theory is predicated on a mythological, undifferentiated, future subject-object in which, in self-determining praxis, knowledge and the objects of knowledge coincide, towards which the present alienated forms of social life are an imperfect way-station, and against which total world-historical process all perspectives must be related. All moral and sociological standpoints or postulates other than the one totalizing standpoint of the proletariat which is mediated-to-Other (its concrete fulfilment) are relative or arbitrary. All value-judgments are psychologistic and ultimately irrational because they cannot accept the inner logic of their object. The Lukácsian can still argue, however, that for all that the perspective is still *provable in practice* and in any case is merely expressing the real dialectic of history. Hence challenges against it in terms of its mythology or from evidence, are anti-proletariat and detract from the need to consciously promote the fulfilment of the dialectic of history. They would be the perspectives of those who do not act towards that end. This criticism is, however, still predicated on an assumed dialectic of historical necessity which Marxists like Lukács cannot jettison, otherwise socialism potentially becomes just another empty Ought, or a value-judgment, potentially equi-pollent with others. However, reject this historically necessary dialectic tending towards the conditions for greater rationality, and the argument that Lukács's philosophy is subject to proof in practice, then becomes potentially applicable to *all* other philosophies too, and thus collapses into truism.[31] As a social philosophy dealing with questions about the quality and significance of social life in human societies, however, it has not been elaborated in sufficiently close contact with the findings of the social sciences about men's social lives, to which enterprise such philosophy is necessarily wed. Instead, it has taken on an autonomous life of its own as a philosophy which is then foisted on to all societies.

Now my criticisms of Lukács from a social science position are not to be taken as presupposing a standpoint of pure unsullied value-freedom and I am cognisant of the charge of arguing from a standpoint which does not theorize itself. As I have remarked similarly before in relation to the intra-Marxist critiques of Lukács, the only successful way in which the self-validating Lukácsian position can be overcome is to move beyond the realm of the discourse, to transcend the terms and arena of the debate, critically to appropriate the presuppositions of the positions, which is what I have attempted to do above. Lukács's problem was that his social philosophy dominated his sociology, so it is initially to the latter that we must turn for answering empirically questions about society and its development to which Lukács, locked in his historicalized philosophical anthropology, has barred the way by assuming that he has answered them.

The sociological significance of traditional philosophy in general and of Hegelian philosophy in particular in their social contexts and the nature of Marx's thought in relation to them cannot be adequately sought in Marxian terms since the inversion-based Marxian social science forms a scholastic closed system which can only confirm and reconfirm its own significance and pedigree and, in Lukács's case, assume the unassailable two truths perspective. Assume this and there is no point in bothering with investigating social reality sociologically. The sociological standpoint articulated in this study (from which its critique is mounted) is rendered possible because it is elaborated at a later stage of social development than that at which either Marx or Lukács stood. The later stage potentially enables us to bring out the further significance of the Marx-Hegel configuration which could not have been perceived at that time. Marx undoubtedly made a methodological switch in the Hegelian dialectic in order to gear it to a communistic critique, retaining the historical necessity of socialism against Utopian, egoistic and gradualist camps. The historical dialectic of necessity gave Marx an unassailable socialism, the science of emancipation which was a social science of the process whereby history was contradictorily processing towards the conditions for human freedom. But to remain today in this theoretical structure, elaborated at a specific stage of social development, is to remain in a self-validating system which forces social and political issues to be posed in a certain form (e.g. the advocacy of revolution versus reform).

This position implies, first, that Marx's theoretical overcoming of Hegel, which he believed linked his new position *necessarily* with communism, was definitively the only overcoming of Hegel possible. The foregoing discussion in Chapters 2 and 5 indicated that this is doubtful. Second, it implies that the putative coincidence of the epistemological and the political in Marx still holds today. However, the particular stage of social differentiation and social and political development at which Marx stood spawned historically specific political positions which Marx sought socio-scientifically to unify with the traditional epistemological categories handed down to him. Marx's dialectical synthesizing perspective provided the close unity of these positions (i.e. as materialism-Utopianism, objective idealism-conservatism, psychologism-egoism-liberalism, praxical materialism-communism) which were one-sided 'isms' incorporated in a Hegelian style into a developing concrete totality. Marx's position was the crowning standpoint, the truth of the other standpoints, logically as well as world-historically. Today, however, we are historically distanced from Marx's period, and from the stage at which the Enlightenment philosophers deliberated about society and politics in terms of sense perception. It is possible now to realize that the connections between traditional epistemological positions thus grounded and the great ideologies of the nineteenth century made by Marx can no longer in that form be relevantly made.

Lukács has, however, inherited this Marxian perspective of dialectical necessity as the totalizer of one-sidedness and has applied it to society uncritically in its archaic formulation, cleansed of contact with the developing social process whose structure he has given up all hope of ever grasping due to his ontological version of necessity based in a "mode of existence" analysis. He still operates with Marx's historically specific praxical solution to the simultaneous epistemological-political positions of his time, which formulation in Lukács's case uncritically informs a purely philosophical theory of praxis which is foisted on to the world. This position thus takes the Marx-Hegel interplay at its face-value and perpetuates it in its own terms, irrespective of its possible appraisal from a higher stage of social development with sociological tools of analysis available from that stage which may be potentially more illuminative of the previous Marxian stage. Lukács's categories are archaic and meta-historical, not historical. Adorno's words apropos of Heidegger are applicable also to Lukács:

> when history is transposed into the *existentiale* of historicality, the salt of the historical will lose its savor . . . historicality immobilises history in the unhistorical realm, heedless of the historical conditions that govern the inner composition and constellation of subject and object.[32]

To conclude, we can turn to another aspect of the Lukácsian perspective which concerns the nature of the emancipation of 'man' envisaged and the relation between mythology and nihilism which I raised at the beginning of this chapter. It was in fact the young Jozsef Revai[33] who as long ago as 1924 first pointed out that the Lukácsian identical subject-object was a mythology. It contained the immanent flaw that the proletariat as subject was not present at the beginning of history but was only the product of a specific phase of it – capitalist commodity production. It thus could not be the subject-object of the whole of history. In fairness to Lukács, however, this criticism is, within the terms of his theory, in error although it highlights an important issue.

Lukács says that only when the consciousness of the proletariat has awakened to the objective dialectics of history and its tendency,

> *only then* will the proletariat become the identical subject-object of history whose praxis will change reality.[34]

And again in relation to ethical questions involved in the total process by which class-consciousness becomes real in practice Lukács says that this part of the process

> gives a more concrete form to the proposition that the proletariat is the identical subject-object of the historical process, i.e. the first subject in history that is (objectively) capable of an adequate social consciousness.[35]

It can be seen, therefore, that Revai failed to see both the *process* character of Lukács's thought as well as the crucial element that the identical subject-object is a conscious postulate made theoretically possible at a stage of history when the socialization of production makes possible the perception of objectivity as being a product of the activity of men at the level of the totality. And the deed of the proletariat authenticates the truth of the *entire* historical process incorporated into itself, including that part in which the proletariat did not exist, the significance of which as a presupposition of its own deed is then fully and adequately grasped by the class. The proletariat 'proves the truth' of the entire historical process. Although Revai's critique is thus insufficient and constitutes a formalistic misconception of Lukács's position, it does not mean to say that he was not right to accuse Lukács of mythology. As we have seen, Lukács's identical subject-object is mythological on other grounds (e.g. it assumed a historical dialectic of necessity involving the Manichean tragic curse of the proletariat on the bourgeoisie and fell back into a philosophical self-validating scholasticism unamenable to empirical reference), even though Revai's reason for saying so does not hold up.

But in making the point about the proletariat not being present for all history even though it is held to be its potential subject-object, Revai did raise a problem within Marxist theory. The theory conceives of a stage of social development issuing in socialism as part of a tendency-become-conscious which liberates all humanity, when the actual event of revolution would inevitably be carried through by a specific class of particular men at a specific time. These men, even though they are held to be the conscious leading edge of age-long historical processes, *in the event* only liberate *themselves* from the accumulated institutional and economic alienation which their ancestors toiled and laboured to bequeath to them during the "prehistory of human society". Moreover, there is no reason to believe that knowledge of the blind historical processes which have thrown them forth will move men to action and still further little pay-off in the present in the knowledge that the revolution has been made possible by the blind sacrifices of one's ancestors.

The perception of these processes in their world-historical significance and structure lies with the theoretician and it is from the consciousness and social experience of the high-culture intellectuals that such a conception of history arises. It is only from that standpoint that the theoretical principle is grasped that it is only in relation to a historically necessary process which can scientifically be discerned as tending towards the conditions necessary for socialism and only requiring the conscious harnessing of the blind contradictions, that socialism can be justified as more than just a Utopian ought or a value-judgment for a better society. Again, it is only a certain kind of high-culture theoretician who sees that to jettison the historical tendency argument and advocate socialism from the present situation drops into relativism and begins to compete more closely with other ideologies also seeking to mobilize the proletariat (e.g. fascism). Until that proletarian victory, so urgently needed, there is a strong motif of pessimism and even nihilism in Lukacs, because until the revolution the theorist can know no peace, he cannot be reconciled to present reality or feel fulfilled within it, even though he grasps its rational tendency.

Now, the Young Hegelian Absolute Knowers also believed they had individually achieved a consciousness of the general dynamic of history, as did Lukács. In the case of the Young Hegelians they had achieved the level of the wisdom of speculation, of the Absolute thinking itself, embodied in them and achieved after the historical completion of theory in human practice. For the Hegelians this achievement meant that eternity was present in them in their very temporality. As a contemporary Hegelian scholar has elegantly expressed it,

> by achieving the level of speculation, man identifies himself with God, or dwells in eternity, but in an eternity which includes temporality. To this extent, Hegel's eternity is *temporalized.* Individual men (and sages) continue to be born and to die, but the reconciliation of eternity and temporality is accessible to the human race for so long as its sages possess and understand the Hegelian teaching . . . this wisdom cannot be dependent upon the preservation of the Prussian monarchy, or any other version of the rational regime. Having achieved his reconciliation with temporality, or "completed" history by understanding it, the sage finds his satisfaction even in corrupt regimes, knowing that each man finds satisfaction only as a citizen of his own time. This satisfaction is not impaired for him by local defects,

> because he knows their necessity (or the necessity of contingency) and does not seek to repair them in a heavenly "Beyond" or utopia.[36]

Lukács's 'two truths' theory of class-consciousness effectively meant that the abstract potentiality of proletarian class-consciousness as part of the developing historical dialectic was incarnated in him and others (in the party) of similar belief until its full concrete realization in the praxis of the proletariat: in the same way that the Young Hegelians embraced perfection, rationality and eternity in themselves and either sought, like Cieszkowski or Hess, to extend Absolute Knowledge in practice or, in the case of others, quietistically to wait for the Absolute completely to work itself out. In either case (irrespective of the correctness of their metaphysics) the decision for the Hegelians *in practice* was a positive one since they had achieved knowledge of eternity – they were reconciled to the world, at peace in it. But in Lukács's case, until socialism, social life within the reifications of capitalism is the unreal, calculative, repetitive and decadent permutation and rehearsal of its own commoditized nothingness, a situation in which reification has utterly penetrated and dehumanized life to the extent that men are existing completely determined rather than self-determining. Even a limited reconciliation is out of the question because it implies quietism, but without the active proletarian victory there is only the abyss. Within this perspective, particularly in its extreme hortatory form, it is not possible to be reconciled to society because happiness and fulfilment are always defined in the deferred terms of their greater extent as 'over there', in the future (socialist) time, not in the crippled present. As we will see in Part four, in relation to Marcuse, if the Marxian scenario seems to fail to work itself out, the result for the post-Lukácsian theoretician is a needless nihilism and despair, since in the world of the bourgeoisie social life has become a quantified, instrumental and worthless sham and alternatives to it unenvisageable.

Part three

Antonio Gramsci: practical theoretician

Commonplace thinking often has the impression that force holds the state together, but in fact its only bond is the fundamental sense of order which everybody possesses.

Hegel

8 Gramsci in context

This chapter is intended to provide a brief introduction to the general character of Gramsci's ideas on theory and practice and their place in the development of Marxist theory, prior to a closer scrutiny of his specific concepts, such as hegemony, later on. In this chapter, then, Gramsci's characteristic concepts will be employed more or less undefined. I think it is fruitful to consider a thinker's theoretical work dialogically, i.e. in relation to what positions he conceived himself as developing his theories, or as reacting against, agreeing with, extending or moving beyond. (It is a paradoxical result of Gramsci's practical-critical perspective, as we shall see, that he objects to Bukharin elaborating an axiomatized position at all.) It is a commonplace that, like Lukács and Korsch in the 1920s, Gramsci too can be seen from the standpoint of theory as reacting against orthodox, 'vulgar' materialist Marxism. A significant comparison that has not been made as far as I know in this historical theoretical configuration is that between Lukács's and Gramsci's parallel criticisms of the theoretical framework of Bukharin as an exemplar of that orthodox tradition. Initially then we shall examine Gramsci's perspective through the sharp focus of his specific criticisms of Nikolai Bukharin's *The Theory of Historical Materialism: A Manual of Popular Sociology*, published in 1921[1] compared with Lukács's contemporary comments on the same book.[2]

Gramsci's criticisms of Bukharin's *Manual* are of double significance for an understanding of post-Lukácsian Marxist theory and its relationship then and now to sociology. First, both Gramsci and Lukács unbeknown to each other and in different social contexts subjected Bukharin's book (which was intended as a textbook in Marxism-Leninism for higher party cadres to complement the earlier *ABC of Communism* written in collaboration with Evgenii Preobrazhenski as a primer expressly for workers and rank-and-file members of the party) to remarkably similar technical criticisms. These arguments thus significantly demonstrate the autarky of theoretical issues. Moreover, in and through the methodological level, we also find focused in the critique of Bukharin as issues of doctrinal, theoretical dispute, an expression of the growing general historical separation between the orthodox Marxist practice of the nascent Russian State and its revolutionizing critics. Furthermore, the very notion of a *textbook* or primer of popularized Marxism written by intellectuals for the masses was an anathema to Gramsci, since it sought to bring to ordinary people a kind of philosophy alien to their commonsense world views or, in its use by party workers, confronted those people as an alien force. It was a style of theorizing which lent itself to a definite kind of political practice. Gramsci's writings are fragmentary but, as Nowell-Smith rightly says, it is in his critique of Bukharin's vulgar materialism that Gramsci "comes closer than anywhere else to a systematic exposé of the principles underlying his own approach to the problems of Marxist theory".[3] Second, Bukharin had digested a great deal of the then contemporary sociology and sought to incorporate it into the *Manual*. His espousal of historical materialism as the sociology of the proletariat, prediction in social science, and Gramsci's and Lukács's criticisms of them as examples of positivistic, vulgar materialism have their echo today. That the orthodox Soviet historical materialism, as a proletarian *Weltanschauung*, reduced the organic critical dialectical method to a dogmatic Party-held set of principles or laws of application to any society at the expense of proletarian self-emancipation (which was essentially the force of the critiques by Lukács, Korsch and Gramsci), has become a perennial criticism of orthodox theory from within Marxism.[4]

Gramsci declares that since Bukharin's *Manual* was destined for a community of readers "who are not professional intellectuals" it thus made the initial mistake of not orienting itself to "folklore philosophy" and the philosophy of common-sense.[5] It at first appears that this statement misunderstands that the book was, as I said before, intended for higher party schools who are by the usual criteria more nearly intellectuals than the masses. It was only a 'popular' manual in the sense of being a clearly set out, accessible textbook of basic ideas of communism. But Gramsci's attitude stems from his commitment to a distinction between traditional, professional, academic intellectuals and "organic" intellectuals who articulate the ideas and interests associated with historically basic social classes, such that on Gramsci's view *all* men since they possess intellects are intellectuals. So against Bukharin Gramsci maintains that the *Popular Manual* is a system of philosophy (the principles of historical materialism) conceived by intellectuals embracing high culture, a way of thinking unknown to the masses and thus confronting them as an "external political force"[6] because these systems of thought form part of the cohesive cultural force or *hegemony* exercised by the ruling classes. The critique of these systems should not be neglected but should be secondary to a starting point of common sense, the "spontaneous philosophy of the multitude".[7] For Gramsci this philosophy is much more intimately linked with religion in the mass consciousness than the high-cultural philosophical systems of the intellectuals. (Interestingly, Lukács does not draw out these kinds of democratic-cultural points against Bukharin's assumptions but mainly enumerates various theoretical and methodological deficiencies in the book and actually praises the project of producing a systematic, popular handbook, which purpose the book "admirably fulfils".)[8]

We must, however, be careful to do justice to Bukharin. Even though it is true that the *Manual* does not actually start from a critique of common sense but does, as Gramsci says, largely criticize systematic bourgeois social science in the name of a proletarian sociology, it is not true to say that the level of commonsense views of the world and of everyday life is left in abeyance or assumed to be unimportant. On the contrary, under the rubric of "social psychology" Bukharin devotes a substantial part of his analysis of the workings of bourgeois society to the place in the "equilibrium of social elements" of norms, customs, feelings, prejudices and "non-systematized" knowledge in general. These fragmentary feelings, tastes, wishes are sometimes called a "folk soul", a "popular mood" or a "*Zeitgeist*" and Bukharin maintains that their importance should not be underestimated.[9] In Bukharin the difference between social psychology (which is more or less common to all individuals of whatever class in a given society) and social ideology is the degree of systematization: "ideologies are a coagulated social psychology".[10] At certain stages of social development the general social psychology and the psychology of the ruling class may not coincide, whereas at later stages the prevailing social psychology is that of the ruling class. Bukharin makes the changes in the social psychology dependent upon the social mode of production and the economic structure of life, in a characteristic 'in the last instance' causal analysis. But in so far as he is aware of the development of commonsense views of the world and ideologies as being part of a total integrated social formation and related to the ruling class, he can be said, I think, to have been at least aware of what Gramsci stressed as social hegemony. He explains this in a passage which, bearing in mind Gramsci's remarks, gives a surprising weight to the autonomous existence and influence of popular consciousness:

> It is sometimes difficult to draw the line sharply; the actual process is a slow solidification, consolidation, crystallization of

> the social ideology out of the social psychology. A change in the social psychology will of course result in a corresponding change in the social ideology . . . The social psychology is constantly changing, simultaneously with the alterations in the economic conditions from which they grow . . .[11]

The point to be made, however, is that while not denying that the mass of the people live by a commonsense view of social order and even going some way towards showing how such "social psychology" may change with overall transformations of society, Bukharin, unlike Gramsci, does not make popular beliefs his starting point nor accord them an equal status with social science. Instead he regards them as quaint, superstitious, "freakish", and as "ordinary, everyday thought", distinguished from "scientific thought".[12] He says that only when such material has been subjected to the keen scrutiny of criticism and stripped of its contradictions "do we begin to approach science".[13] There is in Bukharin the optimistic, rationalistic Marxist assumption that once Marx's 'condition which requires illusions' is dissolved so will the illusions be. In Bukharin's case he is not concerned to stress the social psychology and the ideology since his equilibrating model[14] of a society continually producing and reproducing itself governed by fluctuations in the development of productive forces, remains focused on the reciprocal action of legal and property aspects of the superstructure in such transformations.[15] He seems to assume that what Gramsci calls common sense would simply change along with the changing other levels of the social formation. The *Manual* confidently states:

> It is obvious that the psychology and ideology of the classes *will change, depending on the alterations in the "social being"* of the corresponding classes . . .[16]

Gramsci, on the other hand, makes popular beliefs his initial focus and maintains that Marx many times stressed that popular beliefs have a solidity and an imperative character when they produce norms of conduct. (I would have thought this was an exaggeration, however, an emphasis Gramsci gives Marx to back up his critique of Bukharin.) He says that there was always implicit in Marx's comments

> an assertion of the necessity for new popular beliefs, that is to say a new common sense and with it a new culture and a new philosophy which will be rooted in the popular consciousness with the same solidity and imperative quality as traditional beliefs.[17]

Gramsci draws an analogy between the strategy for teaching a student about past philosophy, and developing a starting point for a liberative theory of society. When teaching the student one takes as one's starting point what the student already knows, a presupposed average intellectual and cultural level of a fragmentary kind, and then works up this common sense via a discussion of religion to consideration of the philosophical systems of the traditional intellectual groups. This shows the student that he is, qualitatively speaking, already a philosopher. Because of this organic conception of philosophy, Gramsci castigates the *Manual* for assuming that the "*true* philosophy is philosophical materialism"[18] and believes that the preferable order of questions is on the nature of philosophy and particularly on the relationships between "ideologies, conceptions of the world and philosophies".[19] Gramsci is right about Bukharin's acceptance of a materialist epistemological standpoint[20] and we can add that he has in addition a characteristically postivistic view of the status of philosophy as a meditation, a generalization, a systematization of the findings of the individual sciences which, he says, imparts to them "their 'common point of view', their 'method' ".[21]

What is at stake on the level of theory between Gramsci and Bukharin concerns ultimately the nature of philosophy. It is the difference between Bukharin seeing it as a technical, clarifying second-order mode of analysis, dependent upon the progress of the natural sciences, as against Gramsci's view of philosophy as an entire conception of the world, as a general methodology of history, relating together fact and value, scientific knowledge and human practical aspirations in one total scheme.[22] Bukharin sees Marxism scientistically solely as a social science and views philosophy as a technical-logical discipline separate from it. Gramsci sees philosophy organically as interpretations of the world applied to reality by various groups in the form of common sense or traditional, high-cultural philosophy by intellectuals. More profoundly and importantly, however, Gramsci puts the will (which he says in the end comes down to practical political activity) at the base of philosophy conceived in his way. The will must be

> a rational, not an arbitrary will, which is realised in so far as it corresponds to objective historical necessities, or in so far as it is universal history itself in the moment of its progressive actualisation.[23]

Like Lukács, Gramsci sees a unitary historical process in which the objective bearers of tendencies carry with them philosophies (in the case of the proletariat it is Marxism) which express such tendencies and which cannot be arbitrarily separated from them. Gramsci takes Bukharin to task for separating out this philosophy and regarding Marxism as a sociology, as a positivistic "science of social facts"[24] providing a description of political and social facts based on 'external' criteria.[25]

Gramsci's critique of the *Manual* as scientistic proletarian sociology, as a mechanistic enterprise divorced from the real concerns of active human life expressed as philosophy, bears the marks of Benedetto Croce's critique of the "science of economy" in the name of the "philosophy of economy" in his *The Philosophy of the Practical: Economic and Ethic.*[26] Croce writes:

> And owing precisely to this mechanizing process of economic Science, it is ingenuous to ask oneself why ethical, logical or aesthetic facts are not included in Economy, and in what way they can be included. Economic science is the sum of abstractive operations effected upon the concept of Will or Action, which is thus *quantified.*[27]

and:

> Economic Science, then, is a mathematic applied to the concept of human action and to its sub-species. It does not inquire what human action is.[28]

Gramsci's argument is also closely akin to Lukács's accusation that a science of society, aloof from theorizing itself as part of a real tendency moving from the past through the historical present to its conscious praxical consummation in the future, must be purely "contemplative". Gramsci does not deny that concrete knowledge is required in this process, but stresses, as Lukács did in his emphasis on the future-creativity of 'practical-critical' activity that

> the philosophy of praxis [Marxism] is realised through the concrete study of past history and *through present activity to construct new history.*[29]

Any other approach to human science which ignores this creative dialectic, Gramsci maintains, lapses into "nominalism" and into the futile attempt to schematize dialectics outside its concrete embodiment in historical experience.[30] Philosophy, says Gramsci, is not expressed purely in concrete historical essays and works, as Bukharin says it is, but is embodied in the practice of groups in real societies (as common sense and in the philosophy of intellectuals and in "ideology as an intermediate phase between philosophy and day-to-day practice")[31] in an immediate, real political and social order.

It is here, in contrast to Bukharin's position on the nature of philosophy, that we can see sharply focused the profound pivot of what a traditional Marxist has called Gramsci's "daringly novel, sometimes even eccentric"[32] thought. For Gramsci, to quote one of his most celebrated aphorisms, statistical laws can be employed in the "science of art and politics",

> only so long as the great masses of the population remain (or at least are reputed to remain) essentially passive.[33]

Political action on the other hand "tends precisely to rouse the masses from passivity".[34] Gramsci was again apparently following Croce, who wrote: "Statistics prove the determinism of human actions, which always reappear in the same way and in the same quantity whenever certain actual circumstances appear."[35] Like Lukács, who put the issue more philosophically in terms of the subject-object problematic, and the progressive recovery of social objectivity to men, Gramsci is saying that if the very stuff of social science is the practice of ordinary people who possess a commonsense philosophy of the world in an integrated society with other intellectuals who also pursue a (different) philosophy, then the nature of that 'object', considered as the organic whole of its practical embodiment in human beings, is perennially subject to changes resulting from qualitatively changing levels of awareness within it and at any level. The extension of mass parties and their "organic coalescence" with economic and productive life means that the random and contingent process of the standardization of popular beliefs can become "conscious and critical".[36] Thus Gramsci puts on the agenda the *creation* of the object of sociological enquiry in the conscious reconstitution of practical life itself, which *is* that object and its subjects. (Marx's coincidence of 'thought' and 'reality' in practice.) Bukharin's picture would be the rather more mechanical one of a change in productive forces 'causing' a change in social psychology and then a change in class psychology, a process analysable and predictable in theory (a "rational and intellectual way" of looking at it, says Gramsci),[37] whereas Gramsci visualizes an organic ongoing qualitative change of the whole collective social organism. In the course of this process of the harnessing of practical-political life itself

> a close link is formed between great mass, party and leading group; and the whole complex, thus articulated, can move together as "collective man".[38]

Gramsci and Lukács, both schooled in historical philosophies of total mediation (those of Croce and Hegel), are not surprisingly in agreement on a critique of other detailed methodological areas of Bukharin's *Manual.*

1 Bukharin's reduction of productive forces to technology or pure technique misses the "*spirit* of dialectical materialism" (Lukacs)[39] which would see technology as a moment of the social productive forces, not as constituting them. Similarly, of this "completely

mistaken"[40] notion Gramsci says that scientific advance cannot be reduced to a one-sided technological perfecting process since seen as a totality one has to take account of the intellectual, political and methodological order such that " 'intellectual instruments' . . . are not innate in man, but are acquired, have developed and are developing historically".[41]

2 Both draw attention to Bukharin's neglect of dialectic. (Alfred Meyer[42] quotes Lenin's last judgment on Bukharin as that he "had never quite understood the dialectic".) As we have seen, the point here is that Bukharin is a contemplative materialist, so by extension a scientistic sociologist, who takes an external stance on historical development, outrageously divorcing theory from practice. Gramsci, echoing Rickert,[43] makes a great deal of Bukharin's position as "metaphysics" and "idealism upside down"[44] and Lukacs also says that Bukharin's position is "completely in harmony with contemplative materialism".[45] Gramsci sees Marxist dialectical method as the "concrete historicisation of philosophy and its identification with history"[46] and Lukács in a similar vein says that our knowledge of directions or tendencies (rather than statistical predictions) is not a result of the difference between what we actually know and what there is to be known, but "*of the objective, qualitative difference in the object itself*".[47]

3 And finally Gramsci and Lukács both highlight Bukharin's scientistic statement that, as in the natural sciences, prediction is possible also in the social sciences, which is juxtaposed against the conception of the 'unity of theory and practice' in the practical dialectical method discussed above. Paradoxically for a declared historicist Gramsci asks the Popperian question:

> And how could prediction be an act of knowledge? One knows what has been and what is, not what will be, which is something "non-existent" and therefore unknowable by definition.[48]

In reply Gramsci invokes the 'Theses on Feuerbach' to argue that the continuous contradictory historical movement as a process is never reducible to fixed quantities (which would be amenable to prediction through extrapolation) since within these quantity is continually becoming quality. Thus, in reality, one can "foresee" to the extent that one acts, since that voluntary effort contributes to the concrete result "foreseen":

> Prediction reveals itself thus not as a scientific act of knowledge, but as the abstract expression of the effort made, the practical way of creating a collective will.[49]

We can begin to see now how activity plays such an important part in Gramsci's thinking. He sees the only valid social science to be political science predicated on the possibilities of activity and knowledge coinciding in praxis, as against the assumed passivity of the masses implied in orthodox contemplative social science, or positivism. In Leonardo Salamini's words, Gramsci held that

> positivism, by elevating sociological concepts to the status of scientific concepts, perpetuates the historical passivity of the masses.[50]

It is this kind of philosophy which underlies both 'bourgeois' sociology and the 'Marxist sociology' of Bukharin. It was with delight therefore that Gramsci was able to turn pre-Leninist deterministic Marxist theory against itself in 1917, in welcoming the Bolsheviks' voluntaristic victory as an event which "exploded", when within orthodox historical materialist theory it should have "unfolded":

> If the Bolsheviks have denied certain predictions made in 'Capital', they have not thereby denied what is living and immanent in it. They have shown that they are not 'Marxists', nothing more; they have not turned the master's works into an empty compilation of dogmatic axioms. They are living out Marxist thought, the part of it which cannot die, *that part which is the continuation of German and Italian idealism*, and which in Marx himself became contaminated by positivistic and naturalistic encrustations.[51]

This passage exemplifies Gramsci's commitment to a viewpoint which held that social science could not (and by implication should not be able to) predict the outcome of conflicts in society which were dependent upon the fluctuations of the organized collective will of men. This was in contradistinction to a mechanical fatalism which is identified with the "moral resistance", and "patient, and obstinate perseverance" of one who comes to believe that everything will work out well eventually since "the tide of history is working for me in the long term".[52] In this departure from deterministic Marxism (which was not so much a departure, but, as in the case of Lukacs, arguably a re-emphasis of the suppressed active side of a dialectical unity in Marx of theorization and its embodiment in a historical tendency pointing towards realization in praxis) Gramsci substituted for human passivity "*conscious critical activity*, the only force capable of breaking up the laws or pseudo-laws of social science".[53]

Gramsci's scepticism about prediction in the social sciences (which implied, as it did for Lukács, not that the operation was technically impossible but that a certain kind of passive, repetitive, unconscious 'quantitative' social activity deleteriously allowed it to be possible) was, then, part of his commitment to the creative potential of the human will against an iron fatalism. In this conviction he was not of course alone in his time. The anti-positivist activism he brought to bear on Marxism and social science in general is characteristic of European cultural milieux of the period before the First World War, exemplified by Croce and Sorel and the generalized influence of Bergson's vitalism.[54] On the biographical level Gramsci himself, a Sardinian, it is said possessed, for various personal, biographical reasons springing "from the deeper pent-up grudge of the islander unable to open out except in action",[55] a practical, activistic bent from early on. Annibale Pastore, Gramsci's philosophy professor at Turin in 1915, said of him that he was concerned above all else with the "practical significance of theoretical life" and in understanding "how ideas become practical forces".[56]

Without going extensively into the influence on Gramsci of the philosophy of Croce that I have already foreshadowed, it will be enough for present purposes to say that Gramsci's stress on the importance of the will and the inseparability of the theoretical and the practical (which we will discuss in more detail later on) were probably developed from Croce. Croce elaborated a neo-Hegelian formulation of the dialectical mediation of will and knowledge, in which the two terms theoretical and practical formed an "Absolute unity".[57] In talking about questions of theory and practice Croce advocated that

> we must in the first place declare the thesis that *the practical activity presupposes the theoretical.* Will is impossible without knowledge; as is knowledge, so is will.[58]

That Gramsci took such a unity for granted is obvious in many places in his writings, but typically here, when discussing in the Prison Notebooks the concepts of quantity and quality:

> Since there cannot exist quantity without quality or quality without quantity (economy without culture, practical activity without the intelligence and vice-versa) any opposition of the two terms is, rationally, a nonsense.[59]

Another salient feature of Croce's philosophy, put very briefly, was that the world was the objective embodiment of imagination, emotion, moral and aesthetic values and as such had intrinsic value, human activity being therefore an inherently value-creating activity, tending in its particularity towards those pure forms, or universals. Croce wrote of the 'universal' significance of human practical activity:

> in order to be purely theoretical, it is necessary to be at the same time in some degree practical; the energy of pure fancy and of pure thought springs from the trunk of volition. Hence the importance of the will for the aesthetic and intellectual life; the will is not theory, nor is it the force that makes grain to grow

> or guides the course of rivers, but as it assists the culture of grain or restrains the force of fancy and of thought, causing them to act in the best way, that is, to be as they really ought to be, namely, fancy and thought in their purest manifestation. The practical activity, therefore, acts in this way, as it drags the man of science from his study and the artist from his studio . . . [60]

Theoretically speaking, Gramsci stands to Croce as Marx stands to Hegel. For Marxists it is generally important to demonstrate that the main innovators within Marxism have defined their theoretical position as having rejected any trace of idealism. In relation to Gramsci, John Merrington for example follows this tradition closely, being at pains to claim that Gramsci made a "complete break" with his early Crocean idealism.[61] To accept such a view, however, would blind us to the subtleties of Gramsci's views about human praxis and imposes on Gramsci's relation to Croce's work an inaccurate semblance of total rejection, or of a fissure or gulf. This view could only regard as an idealistic pollution of Marxism, for example, the following activistic Crocean-inspired declaration, made by the young Gramsci in 1917, whilst politically active in Turin.[62] Gramsci said of the principle of the integral fulfilment of the whole human personality:

> This is not Utopian. It is a concrete universal, it can be willed into existence. It is the principle of true order, socialist order.[63]

I will discuss shortly Gramsci's views on realizing in practice such 'universal' principles, but right away it must be stressed that from the standpoint of mass praxis, it is largely irrelevant whether Gramsci's statement – in so far as it potentially might inspire action at any level – is philosophically speaking idealist or not. The significance of such a statement at a certain point in time lies in its potentiality to mobilize people to act: the question then becomes who is mobilized, and the extent and quality of their activity. The origin of this activity in a conflict of hegemonies in a particular "historical bloc", in Gramsci's terms,[64] is a matter of politico-sociological theorizing, not of philosophizing. Furthermore, the idealists could easily claim that the activity so observed and experienced was in any case an exemplification of their idealist metaphysics, even though it is explicable simultaneously in sociological terms. The philosophical, epistemological categorization is of consequence for certain Marxists, however, as a label for locating the theoretical inspiration of organized political activity, which they regard as 'incorrect' activity, which of course in no way wishes away the reality of the activity itself, nor necessarily grasps its significance, nor renders any more likely the success of other differently labelled political practice.

Those sorts of comments by contemporary Marxists interestingly exemplify the latter-day perpetuation of the theoretical division between Bukharin and Gramsci which we have been looking at in this chapter. John Merrington again, also imputes to Gramsci the view that the critique of ideology and culture in order to reveal its universality, which is at present expressed in "distorted metaphysical terms", is for Gramsci a process of "demystification on the intellectual level".[65] As will become clearer in my later remarks about hegemony and intellectuals, this view misses the importance in Gramsci of the practical, organic generation of a universal, hegemonic cultural cohesion within the present ethico-political social relations which would *make real* what was at the present stage of development articulated as "concrete universal", which has a reality as an abstract potentiality in and through its particular social embodiment. Gramsci says that when society has become classless one could *truly* talk of the "Spirit", which would then be a reality.[66] There is no demystification in Gramsci in the usual Marxist sense of a relatively static intellectual act of removing ideological veils (in the manner, as we shall see, of Bukharin on religion). Because of the unity-distinction of theory and practice in Gramsci's work, such demystification would form part of a practical-theoretical process, in which social reality effectively becomes known to itself, with theory (*qua* demystification) only a moment in the process. Hegel's dictum about the rationality of the actual and the actuality of the rational becomes a project of practical proof in Gramsci:

> The identification of theory and practice is a critical act, through which practice is demonstrated rational and necessary, and theory realistic and rational.[67]

Another example of these Marxist tendencies of criticism occurs when Hoare and Nowell-Smith take up some aspects of these well-known sentences in which Gramsci conceives of the historical passage to socialism as a "catharsis":

> The term "catharsis" can be employed to indicate the passage from the purely economic (or egoistic-passional) to the ethico-political moment, that is the superior elaboration of the structure into superstructure in the minds of men. This also means the passage from "objective to subjective" and from "necessity to freedom". Structure ceases to be an external force which crushes man, assimilates him to itself and makes him passive; and is transformed into a means of freedom, an instrument to create a new ethico-political form and a source of new initiatives. To

> establish the "cathartic" moment becomes therefore, it seems to me, the starting-point for all the philosophy of praxis [Marxism], and the carthartic process coincides with the chain of syntheses which have resulted from the evolution of the dialectic.[68]

They say that here Gramsci characterizes the passage from freedom to necessity in terms of the "free movement of thought" untrammelled by "either tendentious ideology" or by the need for "thought to take as its basis contradictions engendered in the world of material production".[69] And in order to eliminate Gramsci's idealism they declare that he here only makes "instrumental use" of Crocean terms.[70] But Hoare and Nowell-Smith are caught up in a static, unmediated metaphysical polarity between 'thought' and 'materiality' (an example of the kind of thinking Hegel called ratiocination, or the Understanding) which exactly characterizes the orthodox historical materialism which Gramsci was criticizing and which is quite alien to his thought.[71] This view misses the dynamic conception of theory and practice in Gramsci as well as the notion of the anticipatory universalizing of the socialist cultural condition in the present as an abstract potential prior to, but as part of the same praxical process, its realization completely in practice. In the same way that the economic and the ethical form an inseparable unity in Croce, so in Gramsci structure, and culture, base and superstructure, at this level of abstraction categorially mutually presuppose each other and in practice form an organic and discrepant ensemble of social relations.[72] Gramsci is establishing the cathartic moment as a practical goal to be realized as a *process*, whereas Hoare and Nowell-Smith have taken Gramsci's remarks as meaning an abstract, isolated one-off passage to socialism. Structure "ceases to be an external force" and is "transformed into a means of freedom" says Gramsci, which does not mean that it would suddenly cease to exist but only that it would processually cease to exist *as a coercive force.*

As Gramsci says elsewhere in the Notebooks, "material forces are the content and ideologies are the form",[73] i.e. inconceivable without each other. On the dialectical view, seen concretely – that is, more at the level of the totality – the *process* of catharsis enunciated by Gramsci here conceives of form and content, ideology and material forces, 'thought' and 'materiality' as inseparable, changes in one simultaneously entailing changes in the other on various levels. Hoare and Nowell-Smith have formalistically and metaphysically torn this unity apart and wrongly imputed to Gramsci a view of the passage to socialism as being purely in the realms of the free movement of thought; whereas for Gramsci the passage from freedom to necessity is conceived here as the Hegelian (and perhaps Crocean) notion of freedom as the cognition of necessity, in so far as each moment implies the other for its existence and each ongoingly develops against the other. In Gramsci, as in Hegel and Marx, consciousness is always consciousness *of* something. Moreover, it is clear elsewhere in the Notebooks[74] that the use of Crocean terms by Gramsci is by no means instrumental or subsidiary to Marxist ones, a meaning which Hoare and Nowell-Smith want to foist on to them. As I have already shown, Gramsci assumes as legitimate the elaboration of 'universalist' socialist principles in that form before their realization is possible, practice ultimately fulfilling that role as a process. For Gramsci, the idealists are only expressing and have always expressed what the level of development of society only enables men to express as *in potentia*. It is real historical development which may tend towards it or be harnessed to realize it, a view which is perfectly compatible with a secular dynamic sociology of praxis. So Gramsci's theory of praxis means that Crocean terms are employed not merely instrumentally, but organically.

Gramsci is, then, far more tolerant towards idealism than many Marxists. Because he says, to repeat the previous argument with a specific quotation, in the historical passage to socialism,

> many idealist conceptions, or at least certain aspects of them, which are utopian during the reign of necessity, could become "truth" after the passage.[75]

The critical act is the willing into existence of that which is posed philosophically, such that the process of acting is simultaneously a process of knowing to what extent the particularity of the new situation more approximates to its 'universality', which universality has its life *in and through* the particular acted-out situations. When Gramsci does come out against Croce it is on the ground, for example, that the latter's *History as the Story of Liberty*[76] sees history as the self-development of the *concept* of liberty, thus confusing liberty *qua* concept with liberty *qua ideology* (although, we must realize, he is still talking about 'liberty'!); whereas the history of the nineteenth century for Gramsci is seen in the more sociological terms of the "self-knowledge of liberty" being a real and relative matter, i.e. being under the guise of religion throughout the intellectual strata and as supersitition among the masses. All feel their liberty in real forms, and the masses feel

> conscious of participating in a political bloc of which the intellectuals are priests and standard bearers.[77]

To recapitulate thus far: like Lukács, Gramsci maintains that the neglect of dialectic cuts Bukharin off from what is specific in the tradition of Marxism, i.e. the critical reclamation of the development of a historical dialectic of human organization as a whole as developed in the face of the necessity of nature. During the course of this development a stage is reached which enables the emergence of a system of thought (the philosophy of praxis) which represents the practical possibilities of that stage and expresses the whole processs as developed to that point. This enables men's conceptions of the history they are making to be raised to a point of consciousness where they can actively move to harness the blind development and its achievements to the conscious rational advantage of socialized men by shedding the fettering, archaic private social relations. For Gramsci, as for Korsch at this time, this whole picture of the historical humanizing of nature to men's productive ends in society and the potential conscious practical direction of that society into the future through theory-informed political practice, was a unified philosophical project, embracing the "organic unity" of the specialized sciences.[78] During the course of this overall process, historical materialism is itself (as both Korsch and Lukács said) seen to be historically transitory like all other systems of philosophy, in this case changing as part of the dialectical process and finally being superseded as it is realized in practice. But Bukharin had eternalized this historical theoretical result to inform Bolshevik practice. Bukharin's scientistic 'sociology of the proletariat', with its technical view of philosophy, its reduction of productive forces to pure technique and its schematization of dialectics, erroneously denied the connection of the standpoint of the proletariat to the dialectic which it is expounding and endeavouring to harness, took a position of "mechanical exteriority" to the dialectical method and tried to "manualize"[79] it: historical materialism ironically thus became an eternalized coercive power.[80]

Gramsci's call for the reinstatement of the practical-critical and philosophical dimensions of Marxism were also classically formulated by Karl Korsch, in his *Marxism and Philosophy* (1923),[81] which contains many similar themes to those found in Lukács and Gramsci. Korsch's central argument was that, 'applying' historical materialism to itself, it could be seen that at the stage of development of the dialectic of society reached by the time of the Second International the various components of the total scope of the theory (economy, politics, economics) became, incompatibly with their original unity, separated out as sets of purely scientific observation without any immediate connection with the dialectic in which they were embedded and their original practical, *philosophical* revolutionary intention. Marxist theory for Korsch had become an abstract enterprise, ironically akin to the "normal positivist science of bourgeois society"[82] which draws a sharp division between consciousness and its object. But what brings Korsch close to Gramsci is on the subject of the status of philosophy in the orthodox position and on the stress to be placed on ideologies as realities. Korsch argued dialectically that the abolition of philosophy by Marx and Engels in their early writings did not mean its simple rejection, but that in the founding of the materialist conception of history, whose "theory comprehended the totality of society and history, and whose practice overthrew it",[83] the new theory was, in the total historical process, burdened with it as the carrying into practice of the philosophical critique by changing the world. Thus, says Korsch, dialectically speaking, Thesis XI on Feuerbach about changing the world does not, "as the epigones imagine", mean that all philosophy "is shown to be mere fantasy". Rather, he says, affirming again the unity of theorization and the self-changing of objectivity in practice as part of a historical dialectic, its meaning is that

> It only expresses a categorical rejection of all theory, philosophical or scientific, that is not *at the same time* practice – real, terrestrial, immanent, human and sensuous practice . . . Theoretical criticism and practical overthrow are here inseparable activities, not in any abstract sense but as a concrete and real alteration of the concrete and real world of bourgeois society.[84]

The error of vulgar Marxism is for Korsch that it simply regards philosophy and other ideological systems in the way we have seen Bukharin did, i.e. as fantasies and superstitions destined to fade away when the material interests of the ruling class in their preservation have been abolished,[85] whereas, for Korsch, as for Gramsci, these systems of beliefs must be grasped as *realities*, not as empty fantasies, and treated in practice as such. To abolish them in thought by decree is not enough since this was by implication a scientism which left their existence, as Gramsci would have put it, as cultural realities, unproblematic and intact. So for Korsch the reinstatement of philosophy is the reinstatement of a total world-changing materialist stance to carry out in practice the transcendence of philosophy as a reality, a position which in its faithfulness to Marx and Engels also entails regarding ideologies as realities. He avers that

> it never occurred to Marx and Engels to describe social consciousness and intellectual life *merely* as ideology. Ideology is only a false consciousness, in particular one that mistakenly attributes an autonomous character to a partial phenomena [sic] of social life.[86]

To regard the critique of ideologies as pure critical philosophy, as impartial science, is for Korsch an example of bourgeois consciousness which imagines itself above society, whereas, like Gramsci, he wishes to carry out such criticism in practice too, both *before* the transition to socialism as well as after, when the proletariat "must accomplish definite revolutionary tasks in the ideological field, not less than in the political and economic fields".[87]

Although expressed in different language, with Korsch far more unoriginally Marxist-Leninist in his terminology than Gramsci and without the latter's detailed concepts of cultural integration, sociologically speaking both thinkers can be seen as responding to the same social reality. Through the universe of discourse of Marxism and the desire to return to an authentic union of theory and practice, they were articulating the opposition to the social reality of a static official Party ideology of power jelling in the Soviet Union under the banner of Marxism. The renegades were making the epigones dance to their own tune (methodologically speaking at least), by showing their theory to be outrageously undialectical, schematized, metaphysical, static, compartmentalized, scientistic, un-Marxian and even abstractly bourgeois, which was how they expressed their (Marxist) opposition to processes of institutionalization and rationalization going on under their eyes. And the epigones could only reply that the early Lukács, Korsch, Gramsci and company were 'deviationists', 'idealists', 'petit-bourgeois', 'professors', etc.,[88] which labels can be seen sociologically as the ideological dress of the political necessity, as conceived by the victorious Bolsheviks, of consolidating their power in practice. The theoretical, methodological, doctrinal issues themselves, in the realities of power, were secondary to their ideological function. The proletarian *Weltanschauung* lent itself well to the central elite rule for speeding capital accumulation, legitimized a relatively static society and ensured passivity. To interpret these events from within the Marxist categories of either side of the confrontation, however, rather than from a standpoint which critically appropriates both positions from a later stage is to remain trapped in one of two self-confirming universes of discourse instead of appropriating more nearly the actual structure of that reality. The orthodox description of those events is typically of the crushing of the idealist left-wing enemies of the proletarian revolution in the interests of its consolidation; and the contemporary New Left position which has developed from the renegades' critique is that (with variants) the early Lukács, Korsch and Gramsci were the standard-bearers of the authentic Marxism, shamelessly distorted by the Soviet theoreticians as they betrayed the proletarian revolution.[89] Theoretically we find either the dogmatism of schematized dialectics or a potentially new dogmatism of claiming to be the bearers of authentic Marxism.

My exposition of the Bukharin-Gramsci confrontation should not then be taken as a commitment to either Gramsci's side or Bukharin's, nor to the apparently only alternative of 'bourgeois' sociology. We must reject these alternatives posed this way as absolutist chimeras. In the neo-Marxists' critical revolutionary dialectic (which has its antecedents in Gramsci, Lukács and Korsch) the current stage of the development of the class struggle is seen to have entered a phase of cultural oppression and mystification so that its creative harnessability faces that obstacle as well as the abstract, highly differentiated detached bourgeois social sciences which give us no grasp of the totality. But this position does not, by virtue of its historically structured horizons within a Marxian scenario, critically theorize its own presuppositions and is, I will argue again later, neither adequate, *critical* nor historically progressive, but tends towards mythology. For example, this approach still presupposes as indubitable the eschatological world-historical mission of the proletariat and then looks for cultural mechanisms whereby its class-consciousness is systematically dismantled. Both this variant of Marxism and the orthodoxy remain deleteriously trapped in such mythological assumptions, the transcendence of which beckons but is ideologically and institutionally blocked. Such a transcending sociological standpoint potentially enables a more adequate analysis of the reality of the conflict, together with its participants' self-descriptions which we are talking about here as well as its later development, although it in no way implies embracing the banal, ahistorical, metaphysical, law-like scientistic sociology which Gramsci so rightly criticized. On the contrary, it is exactly the very innovatory dialectical discoveries of Hegel and Marx which necessitate moving beyond them towards a higher sociological standpoint which carries even further the potentiality for liberation from hypostatized forces, but which standpoint is neither Marxian *nor* 'value-free', such dichotomy emerging as a false dualism. And it is from this standpoint that this study proceeds. I thus argue against the Marxists in a sociological fashion and against the sociologists in a Marxist fashion.

To conclude, the methodological criticisms of both Gramsci and Lukács against Bukharin (mechanism, vulgar materialism, scientism, etc.) have, then, the further significance that they were the weapons by which a battle was being fought against the social reality of the routinization, the jelling into a Marxist orthodoxy, an ideology of established power, of what was in its "spirit"[90] an enlightened, dereifying critique, which process can potentially be more adequately understood from outside and beyond the standpoints of the protagonists, so avoiding scholastic debate. Korsch and Gramsci both called for what was in effect a moral, cultural, regeneration of Marxism, a new philosophy in the widest sense (expressed as a return to Marxian authenticity), as a counter-weight in theory to the political practice informed by the old philosophy. This renewal was referred to by Gramsci when he remarked in 1932 that Croce had been out-of-date even when he *started* in the early part of the century to criticize the old economistic Marxism. Whilst Croce was still working out his "liquidation" of the old "economic-juridical" history in the name of his "ethico-political history" (which Gramsci accepts as valid provided it is not "speculative"), the greatest post-Leninist Marxists

> were doing the job of shaping a much more efficient instrument; they were engaged on a systematic revaluation of the concept of the moment of "hegemony" or cultural direction in opposition to the mechanistic and fatalistic conceptions of "economism". Indeed it has been asserted that the essential characteristic of the most modern philosophy of praxis consists precisely in the historico-political concept of "hegemony".[91]

For Gramsci the spirit of Marxism could best be kept alive in the latest epoch by the elaboration of what Gramsci might have called the cultural structures of passivity, encapsulated in the concepts of hegemony and civil society.

9 Hegemony and civil society

It is significant that neither of the two hoary old concepts of the Marxist tradition, demystification and false consciousness, is systematically employed in theoretical analysis by Gramsci (at least in the English translations from his prison notebooks, correspondence and early journalism so far published). The reasons for this lie I think in (a) Gramsci's conception of the organic integration in various groups in civil society of different interpretations of the world, including common sense, religion and philosophy, all of which have unique developments and traditions and are welded together in a complex cultural formation; and (b) his insistence on the need to shed a solely 'external', scientistic standpoint with regard to popular beliefs. The integrated types of world interpretation form a progressive developmental sequence from relatively mythological representations of the world up to the fuller comprehension of philosophy which ultimately sublates into political activity when theory and mass practice coincide. Each is a legitimate and autonomous system of interpretation and co-present in society embodied in real groups of people, even though the lower levels of interpretation may constitute an inadequate grasp of the whole of society. The Engelsian concept of false consciousness and the programmatic notion of demystification, abstractly advocated, would be symptomatic for Gramsci of the scientific stance of the high-culture Marxist who judges all inferior lower levels of belief *tout court* from an enlightened scientific standpoint without seeing them as the real remnants of lower stages of social development and embodied in practical activity. As we saw in the previous chapter, Gramsci was suspicious of Bukharin's failure to take as his starting point the beliefs of ordinary people, instead reducing Marxist theory to a detached Party-based positivistic sociology of the proletariat which could analyse and predict social processes so long as the masses remained in their routine passivity. Because Bukharin took such a position *vis-à-vis* socio-historical processes he was in danger of losing sympathy with popular beliefs and those who hold them. In the same vein Gramsci also effectively criticizes Bukharin for purely negative judgments in the name of social science on past high-culture philosophies which he saw as "irrational and monstrous".[1] It might perhaps be illuminating to compare respectively Bukharin's attitude towards religious believers and the Church with Gramsci's, to epitomize the two contrasting attitudes towards unscientific popular beliefs:

> The Orthodox faith which is defended by the priests aims at an alliance with the monarchy. This is why Soviet power finds it necessary to engage at this juncture in widespread anti-religious propaganda. Our aims can be secured by the delivery of special lectures, by the holding of debates, and by the publication of suitable literature; also by the general diffusion of scientific knowledge, which slowly but surely undermines the authority of religion [Bukharin].

> All they ever teach you here is a stupid anti-clericalism, quite misguided intellectually and politically. I don't go to church either, because I'm not a believer. But we must recognise that the majority of people are believers. If we carry on ignoring everyone but the atheists, we'll always be in a minority. There are plenty of bourgeois atheists who make fun of priests and never go to church, yet they are anti-socialist, interventionist, and wage war on us [Gramsci].[2]

Gramsci's perception that Bukharin's attitude towards popular beliefs had to be supplemented by showing them to be a qualitatively different kind of philosophy of the masses in their own right which contributed to the consensual cohesion of society and which could be transcended, was one of a number of post-Leninist Marxist responses to (a) the problem of the apathy of the masses and (b) the dangers of Party elitism. The latter danger had deep roots. At its inception Marx's scientific socialism was the transformation of the Hegelian notion of Absolute Knowledge enshrined in the Absolute Knowers into the self-knowledge of the real dynamic dialectic of history in the possession of those bourgeois ideologists who, Marx said, had "raised themselves to the level of comprehending theoretically the historical movement as a whole".[3] Marxist theory was then always incarnated in a small band of *cognoscenti* facing the very large band of the masses comprising various levels of ignorance and indifference, an asymmetry which even built into its epistemology. The 'standpoint of the proletariat' carried the unique certitude of being the only non-arbitrary philosophical position since it embraced now in a particular mode the consciousness of the negation of a necessary historical process which would be totally realized in its full universality in practice with the proletariat's victory, all moments of which constituted one complete practical-theoretical process. But the problem of the passivity of the masses, their inertia in fulfilling their historical mission as perceived by the theorists, prompted a number of different theoretical explanations at various stages of social development. Lenin, for example, following Kautsky, propounded the celebrated notion that the workers would tend towards instrumental 'trade union consciousness' and could only therefore acquire class-consciousness from outside their economic relationship with employers. He added at a later stage the again classical formulation of the labour aristocracy which forms itself at the highest, imperialist, stage of capitalism. This group, by its example, provides a wages yardstick for all workers to aspire to, thus pushing them more towards making further economic demands rather than developing a revolutionary consciousness. All Western Marxism since Lukács can be seen as trying to answer the question why hasn't the working-class revolution occurred? Or, if it apparently has, why did it reproduce the same alienation it attempted to supplant? But it was Gramsci who was the first Marxist systematically to formulate – through his concept of hegemony – that one reason for the solidity of Western societies against the inroads of socialism was the rule by consent of the ruling class achieved by its having historically attained ideological, cultural hegemony throughout the society: its legitimacy to carry out the 'universal' goals of the society was assumed by the mass of the people.

Before considering hegemony and its sister concept of civil society in more detail, it may be instructive to draw out some of the antecedents of the notion within the Marxian tradition, both as term and as the conception itself. Within the modern Marxist tradition the term hegemony was used to mean political leadership by Lenin, Plekhanov, Axelrod and Lukács.[4] But it is in the *obiter dicta* of the founders of German dialectical theory that we find an awareness, even if not developed and conceptualized as the hegemony of a given class, of the unconscious consenting inertia of everyday life. It was only later, when such hegemony had become a more concrete reality, that it could be conceptualized by Gramsci and be seen to have developed historically. Hegel's remark in the *Philosophy of Right* (the motto for this part of this study) is apposite here:

> Commonplace thinking often has the impression that force holds the state together, but in fact its only bond is the fundamental sense of order which everybody possesses.[5]

While Marx, too, realized that where consent exists force is not required. Writing in *Capital* about workers being compelled to sell their labour power, he says that the whole process of production produces conditions which the workers regard as though they were "self-evident laws of Nature", the capital/labour process being one in which

> The dull compulsion of economic relations completes the subjection of the labourer to the capitalist. Direct force, outside economic conditions, is of course still used, but only exceptionally. In the ordinary run of things, the labourer can be left to the "natural laws of production", i.e. to his dependence on capital, a dependence springing from, and guaranteed in perpetuity by, the conditions of production themselves.[6]

But it does not apparently occur to Marx to refine this insight into a theory of cultural, normative or moral consensus and integration as part of a class hegemony on the Gramsci model. Zygmunt Bauman says that Marx was "unaware of the cultural dimension" and therefore of the "culture shock" involved in the transition to industrial society from feudalism because, in common with the nineteenth century's faith in the "clearly superior rationality of industrial modernity", he assumed that people would opt for the new type of living without hesitation.[7] Marx may well have had such a faith but by the time he was writing his analysis of capitalism, industrial society was in any case a historical *fait accompli.* At the historical stage at which he stood Marx could only theorize the spontaneous development of society through the most developed social science at his disposal – political economy, which he harnessed to Hegelian dialectics – with the aid of which he felt he could demonstrate "with the precision of natural science"[8] transformations of the economic conditions of production. He was concerned to describe in this way the development of capitalism out of feudalism as a largely spontaneous process with a tendency, such that the cultural dislocation of the uprooted rural workers (an understanding of that process only made possible at a much later stage) would not and *could not* have been his direct concern in the analysis, *qua* scientific political economy. The comprehension of those processes takes on a different character depending on the stage of development at which the investigation occurs.

The quotation from *Capital* above shows at least an awareness of the cultural dimension of society, the interesting sociological question being why Marx did not systematically develop it. The answer lies in the fuller hegemony in Gramsci's terms of a ruling class being only in earlier stages of formation in Marx's time, so that he could only perceive hegemony in a 'potential' state. And it is only a later stage of the concrete development of such hegemony that enables its past gestation to be grasped and appropriated. Bauman also maintains that not only did Marx assume that people would opt for the new type of living without hesitation, but that, quite rightly, it was not until Max Weber that attention was drawn to the impoverished peasants and artisans not automatically being "reborn in the new industrial roles", but having been subject to "ruthless discipline to extirpate their restless and migratory spirit".[9] We must take care, however, not to proceed from an ahistorical moralizing standpoint and implicitly and unjustly to assign *blame* to Marx for not systematically developing the cultural dimension or for not having dealt with the ways in which rural workers can now be seen as having been socialized and/or forced into new industrial roles. At the specific stage of societal development in which he was theorizing, however, and with the analytical tools at his disposal created by men to deal with the unique changes being experienced and observed, it is unlikely that he could have done otherwise.

To return more specifically to Gramsci's concepts of hegemony and civil society, we can say immediately that the latter concept does not carry the same meaning for Gramsci as it did for Marx. For Marx civil society denoted the socio-economic structure of relations of production (the "anatomy" of which was to be sought in political economy)[10] which in some way 'determine' political and other elements of the superstructure. In Gramsci, however, civil society is part of the superstructure. The editors of the English translation of Gramsci's prison notebooks are right to point out the confusing use of the terminology 'civil society', 'political society' and 'the State'[11] in Gramsci's fragmentary writings on these matters. But there is a basic consistency which I think runs as follows.

For Gramsci the Marxian superstructure is divided into two major qualitatively different institutional levels: *civil society* and the *State* (sometimes Gramsci conforms to a usage common in his time and earlier and makes the latter synonymous with *political society*). Civil society comprises the private institutions of society where the intellectuals mostly operate. It is "the ensemble of organisms commonly called 'private' "[12] and includes at least the Churches, schools, municipalities and trade unions. This sphere embraces the only location of what is truly ethical in society even though it functions to maintain the hegemony of the dominant group in society through the ongoing, routine consent of the masses to the "general direction imposed on social life".[13] Civil society constitutes the consensual living out by the people in everyday life of the hegemony of that dominant group in society; this hegemony having been achieved over a long period to culminate at a point where a particular class interest in society masquerades as the universal one of the society as a whole. The *State* on the other hand comprises the institutions of society which are public, e.g. the legislature, judiciary and bureaucracy, and this organ acts to conform civil society to the economic substructure of society, that is to say for example it induces via legislation the appropriate mode of commonsense economic behaviour in civil society. This ensures that social life will ongoingly carry on contributing to the working out of the consenting mechanism of society as a whole in the interests of the ruling social class, which has its power basis ultimately in the relations of production in the economic base. The correct content of this inducement is achieved by representatives of the economic structure getting in control of the State *qua* legislature and administration. In addition, the State has a *coercive arm* (i.e. institutions of police, armed forces) which Gramsci says is often what 'political society' in narrowly taken to mean. But Gramsci's message is: *don't identify all power or all politics solely with State coercion.* It is the ongoing conformity of civil society to the economic structure by the State-as-legislature in the power interests of a ruling class mentioned above which mainly gives the State its political character, because it covertly ensures social compliance with ruling-class interests. The apparatus of coercion exists, however, only in the anticipation of the failure of spontaneous consent to enforce discipline upon subaltern (subordinate) classes *if necessary.* Some confusion can arise however, reading Gramsci, because he sometimes uses 'State' also to mean nation-State or total society, country, i.e. the institutional State (public) plus civil society (private) taken together as two political elements of the superstructure dependent upon the economic base.

At one point in a letter from prison Gramsci apparently contradictorily says that the State exists as "an equilibrium between 'political society' and 'civil society' ".[14] But I think that here he means the institutional State. This statement is in the context of playing down the 'political' function of the institutional State as being *solely* coercive. The institutional State can constitute such a balance if we see 'political society' as referring to that part of society's *activity* which is related to power considerations, not as some have done as a separate thing.[15] In Gramsci all activity, particularly when subject to incumbents becoming aware of their social position, is ultimately political. In this sense, then, the conforming of civil society to the economic base, in Gramsci's terms achieved by the activity of the institutional State-as-legislature backed up by the potentiality for force by the State-as-coercion, is an inherently political activity since the interests of a ruling class are dependent upon its success even if such conformity is indirect and mediated by the total fabric of society and its history. In other words there exists the institutional State whose activity (in the interests of the ruling class) in inducing the economic conformity of civil society is political even if it is not overtly coercive. In the quotation above the single quotation marks round the words 'political society' (a concept often identified solely with State-as-coercion) indicate that Gramsci is shifting the focus and definition of politics away from State coercion into civil society. The institutional State thus keeps a balance between 'the political' and 'the civil' by never allowing 'the civil' (civil society) to realize its actual political function. Clearly the stability of society is subject to inroads via undermining the mechanisms of consent and common sense within civil society: and this for Gramsci is political activity.

Gramsci thus distinguishes between "social hegemony" and "State domination"[16] corresponding to a distribution of institutions and functions throughout the society to which all intellectual activity of the society, from the highest (science, the arts, philosophy) to the most humble (folklore, everyday philosophy) corresponds.[17] The historical phase of development of a society at which a class has achieved hegemony over the whole society is what Gramsci calls, after Sorel, a "historical bloc", which comprises "the complex, contradictory and discordant *ensemble* of the superstructure",[18] and it is the analysis of the play of forces within this bloc (and their historical development) that the key to the revolutionary transformation of the social whole lies.[19]

The dialectical unity of "force" and "consent", or between "liberty" and "authority",[20] in Gramsci expresses at its most abstract the complex play of forces embodied institutionally in a given concretely developed historical bloc. Gwyn A. Williams says of these distinctions in Gramsci's writings that

> It is in the sphere of *dominio* that change in the structure becomes immediately effective and *dominio* is always associated with coercion, state power, the 'moment of force'. *Egemonia*, on the other hand, is always associated with equilibrium, persuasion, consent, and consolidation.[21]

The analysis of this dialectic Gramsci claims, against the idea that "immediate economic crises of themselves produce fundamental historical events"[22] (economic well-being or hardship being a "partial aspect") can only culminate in "the *sphere of hegemony and ethico-political relations*".[23] These statements demarcate Gramsci clearly from total economic determinism. Once historically developed and achieved over the total society, hegemony permeates the entire social order, is the very stuff of the social process embodied in the voluntary, everyday, commonsensical practice of living men (intellectuals) who make up civil society, which activity Gramsci calls "spontaneous consent".[24] At later stages of development, therefore, the moment of *dominio*, although present as a presupposition, is seldom exercised in concrete terms as State coercion. According to Thomas R. Bates, Gramsci's conceptions of civil society and the State correspond roughly to Croce's view of the "Church" as "the formation of moral institutions in the largest sense, including the religious institutions and revolutionary sects, including the sentiments and customs and fantasies and myths of a practical tendency and content" as distinguished from the institutional State, which for Croce cannot have ethical content. Gramsci's intellectuals who inhabit civil society correspond to Croce's "political geniuses".[25] Gramsci illustrates the relationship between State and civil society through a comparison of Russia and the West, in relation to the revolutionary movements of 1917 and 1919 respectively. He says that the aspects of civil society represent elements of a "trench and fortress" behind the "outer ditch" of the State. Whereas in Russia

> the State was everything, civil society was primordial and gelatinous; in the West, there was a proper relation between State and civil society, and when the State trembled a sturdy structure of civil society was at once revealed.[26]

Put another way, at advanced stages of social development, hegemony embraces all the particular instances in society of the ongoing consenting activity of individuals and groups which exemplifies Hegel's "fundamental sense of order which everybody possesses", and which thus *constitutes* social reality for its participants. Gramsci maintains that a single, or a combination, of ideologies "tends to prevail, to gain the upper hand, to propagate itself throughout the society"[27] and brings about not only a unity of economic and political aims but also "intellectual and moral unity", posing questions on a "universal plane"[28] creating the hegemony of the ruling class. (I will outline Gramsci's delineation of the historical stages of this process in the next chapter.)

This developed hegemony embraces the effective working reality for people in society but the tension between coercion and consent ensures that the limits of action seldom transcend a point which would result in a situation which was anything but the unconscious reproduction of the hegemonic reality. Gramsci would have agreed with Hegel that customary life was "the watch wound up and going on of itself".[29] Indeed, in so far as Gramsci's conception of hegemony treats of an all-embracing dominant ethos, ambience, basic style or cast of the culture of a society which pervades its whole practical fabric at higher stages of development, it is analogous to Hegel's Spirit in the mode of the "Spirit of a People" in *The Philosophy of History*. (Although Gramsci's concept is tied more closely to the historical development of social classes and how the structure of culture perpetuates a specific social order; as against Hegel's metaphysical stress on the simultaneous 'universal' and ontological significance of particular historical customs and culture.) Hegel says that the Spirit in general is inherently active, producing and reproducing, through finite human practice, conceptions of itself as an objective existence, through which it continually makes itself through its own deeds:

> Thus is it with the Spirit of a people: it is a Spirit having strictly defined characteristics, which erects itself into an objective world that exists and persists in a particular religious form of worship, customs, constitution, and political laws – in the whole complex of its institutions – in the events and transactions that make up its history. That is its work – that is what this particular Nation *is*. Nations are what their deeds are.[30]

For Hegel, it is in relation to the Spirit of a people that the particular individual has his significance, which enables him "to be *something*", for he finds in that people to which he belongs "an already established firm world – objectively present to him with which he has to incorporate himself";[31] although the Spirit of a nation must eventually exhaust the potentialities inherent in it through its own activity of self-discovery. It is in the twilight of a nation that, having realized its grand objects, having attained its desires as objectively present to itself, having all but removed the contradiction between its potentiality and its actuality, activity becomes merely the reproduction of the conditions thus reached, drained of zest and vitality. Having no further need of its institutions, because the need for them is satisfied, Hegel says that life in the nation evinces a "political nullity and tedium".[32] Like Gramsci, as we will shortly see, Hegel looks for a rejuvenating new principle, which arises in Hegel's case because the Spirit of a people carries within it its own negation:

> In order that a truly universal interest may arise, the Spirit of a People must advance to the adoption of some new purpose; but whence can this new purpose originate? It would be a higher, more comprehensive conception of itself – a transcending of its principles – but this very act would involve a principle of a new order, a new National Spirit.[33]

Now Gramsci's attitude towards this kind of thinking (for him epitomized by Croce) is extremely interesting. (a) He maintains that the cultural unification of the human race will remain unfulfilled so long as the conditions of conflict and contradiction which characterize class societies prevail.[34] This means that transient, partial and fallacious ideologies will continue to be born, which are "not concretely universal",[35] i.e. which are not objective knowledge for all men at the level of the totality (the natural sciences, he says, having taken this universalizing process furthest). In conceptualizing this "struggle for objectivity", which constitutes the process of cultural unification Gramsci notes that

> What the idealiste call "spirit" is not a point of departure but a point of arrival, it is the *ensemble* of the superstructures moving towards concrete and objectively universal unification and it is not a unitary presupposition.[36]

And again, employing the characteristic Marxian inversion, Gramsci writes:

> The unity of history (what the idealists call unity of the spirit) is not a presupposition, but a continuously developing process. Identity in concrete reality determines identity of thought, and not vice versa.[37]

Gramsci does not, then, simply reject the notion of Spirit, but is claiming that it has historically been a way of expressing the potential cultural unification of men, which in the current epoch can be explained as constituting the tendency towards unification of the discrepant contradictory ensemble of the institutions of the superstructure (civil society and the State). The closer society develops towards the real socio-economic possibility of ending irrationality, scarcity and conflict and the real founding of a truly human community, the clearer becomes the perception of past mythological attempts to express this possibility in terms of the unity of history, Spirit, God, etc. But now it is possible consciously to mobilize men to end their dispossession and to make that unity a reality. A class society will always generate fallacious, partial ideologies in relation to itself which often masquerade as of universal import, i.e. as being expressions of the truth of an objective reality but actually being the illusory expressions of a particular class interest. Gramsci's "struggle for objectivity" is therefore a struggle for definitions of the aims and interests of the society as a whole epitomized in its organization in the proletariat's interests, against prevalent spurious ones. Moreover, within civil society a sedimented ruling-class hegemony constitutes the practical reality of men and Gramsci advocates (as we will develop later) the creation of a working-class hegemony, a rival principle to employ in a battle for hegemony, via a party organization, to be realized as the real unity of men as the social conditions which would enable such a realization fully mature in the existing society.

(b) The creation of a new hegemony expressing a *truly* universal intent was of far-reaching significance for Gramsci, not just culturally, nor just for the end of inequality, but simultaneously epistemologically, since it is under a social hegemony that the practical life of men in civil society constitutes a reality at all. There are two inseperable elements in this epistemology. First, the creation of a society governed by a new truly universal hegemony which would constitute the true Utopian unity of men actually lived out in reality, so changing the whole character and institutional fabric of the social world in novel ways. Society would have in Hegel's words "a higher, more comprehensive conception of itself".[38] It would create a new conception of social life, and open up undreamt of possibilities for fulfilment and creativity untrammelled by the dissimulations of partial ideologies stemming from the irrationalities of a fettered productive system (although always wedded to an "economic moment", in Gramsci's terms). Gramsci brings this mighty vision of the infinite possibilities of a new hegemony created by self-knowing human praxis to the fore in relation to Croce's parallel formulation of the necessity of creating a new morality:

> that men acquire consciousness of structural conflicts on the level of ideologies should be considered as an affirmation of epistemological and not simply psychological and moral value. From this, it follows that the theoretical-practical principle of hegemony has also epistemological significance . . . The realisation of a hegemonic apparatus, in so far as it creates a new ideological terrain, determines a reform of consciousness and of methods of knowledge: it is a fact of knowledge, a philosophical fact. In Crocean terms: when one succeeds in introducing a new morality in conformity with a new conception of the world, one finishes by introducing the conception as well; in other words, one determines a reform of the whole of philosophy.[39]

The second epistemological, implication of Gramsci's conceptions of hegemony and realized counter-hegemony lies in the sphere of knowledge of the natural world. Gramsci subscribes to the Marxian epistemological principle that "objective always means 'humanly objective' ";[40] that is, the notion that the level of social development determines men's always humanized and to some extent anthropomorphic knowledge of Nature. The agency of human societized labour in Marx qualitatively continues in practice the history of Nature at a higher level since socialized men and women are also part of Nature even though they also confront it as external to them.[41] Higher stages of social development potentially enable greater and deeper knowledge of 'external' Nature by its most self-conscious element – mankind. It would I think legitimately supplement and consistently extend Gramsci's remarks to claim that for him revolutionary praxis could potentially provide a new horizon of natural as well as social objectivity. A fuller harnessing of human potential unfettered by the inefficiencies and irrationalities of class-mediated production would free enormous productive forces in science as well as lay social-cognitive foundations of such a different order that qualitatively new scientific theories would be possible. What has so far been achieved by the "pre-history" of mankind would appear puny indeed. Such a revolutionary praxis can be said to have, therefore, as Alfred Schmidt has put it, "a cosmic as well as a social significance".[42]

(c) Assuming Gramsci's remarks about idealists and about the Spirit as intended to be applicable to Hegel, it is paradoxical that even an argument of the subtlety of Gramsci's about realizing in praxis what the idealists called the unity of man does not engage Hegel adequately. Gramsci says that the superstructures can be seen as having been historically "moving towards" unification and, as we shall demonstrate in a later chapter, Gramsci had a democratic practical programme for helping history towards this goal. This concerned the activity of the party (conceived as an entity absorbing intellectuals from various strata and extending its hegemony over the society) which was part of that "organic" developing process of unification owing its existence to a fundamental social group in that process, whose self-conscious action was needed to bring it about, to make it a complete reality. Hegel rhetorically posed the need for a new principle of universal interest as the old world grew old and, on his formulation, the new principle produces a new Spirit from out of itself through negation carried within it, thereby destroying the determinate form of its being. It thus gains a "comprehension of the universal element which it involves", which alters the national Spirit and gives rise to another, higher principle.[43] One might be tempted to say that the crucial difference between Hegel's and Gramsci's conceptions of the sublation of one hegemonic social order into another is that Hegel advocated just sitting back and watching the new principle of integration (Spirit of the People) fulfil itself and develop out of the old order; whilst Gramsci, believing that 'idealistic' formulations of human unity could *become* reality after the passage to socialism, held that the new hegemony as a concrete universal could be willed into existence through the mass praxis of men, via its progressive embodiment and diffusion over the entire society by the party. That is indeed what Gramsci apparently thought.

It would indeed follow from a refined activistic Marxian conception of the relation between idealist and Marxist accounts of historical social reality, i.e. that although some ontological and epistemological parity between them can be conceded the crucial difference between Hegelian idealism and Marxian materialism lies in their relationship towards praxis. Hegel's analysis was *post festum* and only understood historical processes *after* they had occurred, whereas Marx advocated praxis by the key class to make true the tendencies revealed by that analysis. But the problem is that this formulation is a misunderstanding of the nature of Hegel's thought or perhaps a selective interpretation used later to back up intended political action. One aspect of Hegel which Marx never came to terms with, and which Lukács and Gramsci simply assume as having been solved by Marx, is that for Hegel the 'universal', the principle embodied in the age, in history, in the life of all things developing and changing itself into higher and higher levels of overcome stages, does so *in and through the ordinary finite consciousness and affairs of men*, through which action *alone* such an Absolute has its existence. It is at higher stages that it constitutes itself as Spirit and becomes aware of the process and sees itself in the other stages and can be analysed categorially. This conception is not therefore refuted by either an appeal to materialism for the source of the notion of Spirit nor by an abstract appeal to mass praxis to will or create a new world principle in a reality materially capable of embracing it. Such materialism and praxis are already encompassed by Hegel in the conception of the co-present levels of self-consciousness in the active totality from sense-certainty to complete self-certainty, so Hegel's system, as I have said in Chapter 5, is already in the world. And any activity which is willed consciously by men (individually or collectively) is for Hegel even in that finite volitional immediacy, *simultaneously* exemplifying its 'universal' significance thereby. The identity of thought as Spirit which Gramsci talks of as being 'determined' by concrete reality *already* forms a developing self-moving identity with it in Hegel: it is constitutive of the concrete reality, not separate from it and determined by it as Gramsci, following Marx's 'inversion', maintains.

10 Analysing the historical bloc

In Gramsci's social thought the Marxian base of forces and social relations of production remains as the "*economic-corporate*" or "*ego-istic-passional*"[1] moment in analysis and as the foundation of the superstructure in reality. Within the historical bloc, the level of civil society comprises, as we have seen, a complex of institutions, intellectuals and functionaries, who are the carriers of ideologies, folklore, religion, common sense and philosophy. Of the latter, Gramsci says, "Philosophy in general does not in fact exist. Various philosophies or conceptions of the world exist,"[2] which reflects his insistence that in civil society "All men are intellectuals" in so far as "there are varying degrees of specific intellectual activity".[3] The real activity of each man in civil society, at whatever level, carries with it a conception of the world, whether of high culture or as a popular belief. The material forces of a social formation and its ideologies mutually presuppose each other, related as content and form:

> material forces are the content and ideologies are the form, though this distinction between form and content has purely didactic value, since the material forces would be inconceivable historically without form and the ideologies would be individual fancies without the material forces.[4]

Gramsci further distinguishes between (a) historically "organic" ideologies which are "necessary" to a given structure in its development and which are valid as the psychological organizing cognitive vocabulary of the masses, as the conscious "terrain on which men move" and acquire knowledge of their position; and (b) in a Sorelian vein, those "arbitrary" ideologies that dialectically contrast with these and thus form together a unity. Gramsci calls the ideologies "arbitrary, rationalistic, or 'willed' " and these create "individual 'movements', polemics".[5] Gramsci argues against a purely fatalistic interpretation of Marxism which would give precedence to a determinism of the 'base' over the 'epiphenomenal' superstructure. (He in fact polemizes again and again in the Prison Notebooks against this passive conception.) He therefore concludes that:

> only a totalitarian [i.e. unified, all absorbing] system of ideologies gives a rational reflection of the contradiction of the structure and represents the existence of the objective conditions for the revolutionising of praxis. If a social group is formed which is one hundred per cent homogeneous on the level of ideology, this means that the premises exist one hundred per cent for this revolutionising: that is the "rational" is actively and actually real.[6]

The dialectical unity between developmentally necessary ideologies and arbitrary created ideologies helps Gramsci to articulate the complex social matrix of potentialities at various points on the road towards what Marx in the 'Theses on Feuerbach' called the "coincidence of the changing of circumstances and of self-changing". That is to say that at any given point within that unity lies somewhere a grasp of the beginnings of the process of transition from social practice to social praxis. In a given formation says Gramsci, the levels and moments of the relationship between superstructure and structure must be carefully analysed in order not to pose, but to ultimately *resolve in practice* "the forces which are active"[7] in it, i.e. to determine the play of forces which can be actively moved towards realizing historical tendencies in practice.

In such an analysis of a social formation Gramsci distinguishes methodologically (in coincidence with the two types of ideology) between "organic movements" and, in a Leninist fashion, "conjunctural movements".[8] Organic movements are the historically long-term social processes, the perennial indirect ones which determine ideological conflicts by the stage of development of the basic contradiction between forces and relations of production (if pursued exclusively in analysis, this is "economism"). Conjunctural movements, on the other hand, are the "occasional, immediate, almost accidental"[9] phenomena which give rise to far-reaching political criticism which actually expresses the organic movements and involves public figures, leaders, etc. (pursued exclusively this can lead to an excess of "ideologism"). The organic movements are the subject of much wider social groupings. These two levels of analysis in their dialectical nexus must not be confused since they are of great importance for longer-term political strategy in the case of organic movements and for more immediate politics, agitation and tactics in the case of conjunctural analysis.[10]

Gramsci distinguishes between three moments in the relation of forces in a social formation which are co-present but which in their theoretical articulation represent stages in the developmental process of a fundamental class towards total *hegemony* in society. The three moments are the economic, the political and the politico-military:

1 Gramsci subscribes to the Marxist principle that classes and their emergence is to be traced to the historical location of groups in their economic linkage to the relations of production and the corresponding levels of the development of the forces of production which provides the fundamental economic data for deciding whether there exists in a given society the "necessary and sufficient conditions for its transformation".[11] The level of this development determines the quantity and quality of the transformation possible. It is against this base that the claims, hopes and degree of realism of the various ideologies of the social formation can be assessed, although not, as the vulgar materialists would, in a mechanical manner, for the context of conflict takes us way beyond purely economic determination:

> economic crises . . . create a terrain more favourable to the dissemination of certain modes of thought, and certain ways of posing and resolving questions involving the entire subsequent development of national life . . . [in] 1789 . . . the rupture of the equilibrium of forces did not occur as the result of direct mechanical causes . . . it occurred in the context of conflicts on a higher plane than the immediate world of the economy.[12]

2 The political moment refers to the various elements of collective political consciousness developed up to the present time, divided into at least three levels: (a) the economic-corporate level of, say, the consciousness of solidarity of tradesmen, manufacturers or professionals; (b) a second level of class-consciousness, still solely in the "purely economic field", although at this stage the State may intercede between groups and reform may be granted within the existing structures; and (c) the third most important level, that of becoming aware that "one's own corporate interests, in their present and future development *transcend the corporate limits* of the purely economic class",[13] and thus embrace those interests of other subordinate groups. Following Marx's remarks in the 1859 Preface closely, Gramsci says that this phase is crucial since here the decisive conflicts of the emerged class which determine its social outcome are being fought out in ideologies in the sphere of the superstructure. At higher levels of social development the sphere of the superstructure takes on a decisive importance as the new class begins to gain a consciousness of itself. It is a time of "confrontation and conflict", until one group or class tends to prevail, to propagate itself throughout the society not only on a corporate plane, but on a "universal" plane, thus "creating the *hegemony* of a fundamental social group over a

series of subordinate groups".[14] (Gramsci's term "fundamental social group" is a code word employed against prison censorship and connotes the Marxist conceptions of the bourgeoisie and the proletariat as the most important and successively historically progressive social classes in modern history.)

3 Gramsci adds that historical development is characterized by a third moment, the relation of military forces, which is from time to time "directly decisive"[15] and historical development indeed "oscillates continually between the first and the third moment with the mediation of the second".[16] He explains that the military level contains military in the strict technical sense as well as the level of the politico-military which encompasses threat, counter-threat, and tactical disposition to equalize unequal forces where class independence cannot be won by simple fire-power. Thus for Gramsci the dynamic of history is the dialectic between force and the continual reassertion of the political problem of a rising fundamental class in a society.

The analysis of the relations of forces therefore carries three separable although unified meanings: (a) it is a reconstruction of the development of the European bourgeois classes to societal hegemony; (b) it comprises a conceptualization in terms of "moments" (which in dialectical thought are elements in a given configuration *as well as* importantly formative stages within a process through which that configuration has passed) of the play of forces (historically remote or more immediate) in a given developed social formation which determine the development of a class; in this analysis the "economic moment" is only a minor determinant since its relatively stunted presence as a determinant at the current stage of development is a remnant of its important presence at an earlier stage as representing the sphere which throws forth fundamental classes based in the relations of production; (c) it connotes the trajectory by the active, to-be-created future development of the proletariat (already probably at the economic-corporate stage at least) into full hegemony in a given class society and the consequent creation of a new hegemonic bloc. At the present stage of development, moment 2 (c) [discussed on p. 143] is the important one, for it is at this level that the ideological struggle for hegemony between the two fundamental social classes is taking place, made possible by a very extensive development of the productive forces. The struggle of hegemonies will be mainly an ideological conflict of definitions of social goals (although it could also involve high-culture intellectual conflict). It will involve the systematic conflict between those attempting to inculcate in proletarian consciousness a conception of the transcendence in praxis of the corporate limits of the class (defined purely by its historically emergent economic moment) towards a 'universal' interest; and those conservative forces resisting the generation of such a counter-hegemony. Gramsci's whole analysis is in the end based on projecting into the future as a conscious process of created hegemony for the proletariat what he saw as the unconscious historical genesis of the hegemony of the bourgeoisie.

Gramsci's empirical source for this practical-critical theorization is the historical experience of the European bourgeois classes and various groups such as the Jacobins which inspired them. Gramsci mainly uses the example of the Italian Risorgimento and the Action Party's failure to pose a clear policy for the masses and its defeat by what amounted to the development of Moderate hegemony, in which analysis he elicits the phenomenon of transformism (*trasformismo*). (This term was used in post-Risorgimento Italy popularly to describe the fact that the more governments changed, the more they remained the same. In a more theoretical vein it also refers to the general process of convergence of policy and programme by the Left and Right parties in Italy from the 1880s onwards.)[17] Gramsci maintains that such transformism was only the parliamentary expression of the continuing growth of "intellectual, moral and political hegemony"[18] already established by the Moderates by the absorption of their enemies' élites, thus establishing their hegemony. Importantly, the Moderates were victorious because they had established intellectual and moral leadership before actually coming to power. Gramsci distinguishes in the Italian case between the period of "molecular transformism" – i.e. the incorporation of individual political figures into the Moderate camp – and "group transformism", the going over to the Moderate camp of entire groups of leftists. Seen historically, says Gramsci, the entire State life of Italy from 1848 onwards was characterized by transformism, the "formation of an ever more extensive ruling class, within the framework established by the Moderates after 1848".[19] The authoritarian State-dominated character of Russia and Italy was due to the partial and weak character of hegemony developed within the civil societies in each case.

It is important to note in Gramsci's analysis of transformism in the development of the hegemony of a dominant group in society its practical-critical character. It is intended also to inform a programme for the development of proletarian hegemony into practice by encouraging transformism in the proletarian cause. The development to societal hegemony of the bourgeois classes, exemplified by the establishment of hegemony by the Moderates, shows that

> there can, and indeed must, be hegemonic activity even before the rise to power, and that one should not count only on the material force which power gives in order to exercise an effective leadership.[20]

Gramsci always emphasizes, like Lukács and Korsch, that to avoid contemplation analysis must be genetic, show the development of hegemonic groups over time, incorporate the present social structures and then 'carry over' into the future through the active, creative furtherance and extension through praxis of tendencies revealed by the genetic empirical appropriation. For Gramsci, sociology must be a political sociology since the essential subject matter of such a science under a ruling-class hegemony can only be the complex of practical and theoretical activities by which such a class consciously and unconsciously maintains its dominance: "If there is a residue," Gramsci adds, "this can only be made up of false problems, i.e. frivolous problems."[21] (I will argue against this view later on.) Social science cannot be merely the study of the laws of social development because this leaves out of account the "will and initiative of men"[22] and in any case the discovery of previously unknown realities on the social level must be of political consequence since bringing forth such knowledge potentially transforms men and "enlarges their concept of life".[23] Gramsci's declaration articulates and renders more explicitly political the basic Hegelian-Marxian notion that men can become aware of (and thus in practice sublate) the nature of the 'laws' which their ongoing activity constitutes, but of which they are unconscious. In a passage which resonates Romantic anti-positivism and historicist rationalism, Gramsci declares:

> And does the concept of science as "creation" not then mean that it too is "politics"? Everything depends on seeing whether the creation involved is "arbitrary", or whether it is rational – i.e. "useful" to men in that it enlarges their concept of life, and raises to a higher level (develops) life itself.[24]

To summarize: the theoretical appropriation of the characteristics of the relations of forces in a given historical bloc must, through the methodological, historiographical strategies discussed, serve the possibility of transforming social relations in order to preserve the progressive elements, i.e. the "organic movements" or what is "rational" in the development up to the present time.[25] Such theoretical appropriation leads to the conclusion that the most recent progressive class defined in relation to its historical emergence in the relations of production – the proletariat – as it proceeds on its journey towards hegemony cannot, in Lukács's words "travel unaided".[26] Before attaining power (dominance) it requires to lead, to achieve political hegemony and intellectual and cultural hegemony (as the Moderates did).[27] Gramsci's view that a "fundamental class" can lead the classes which are its allies, and dominate those which are its enemies is an early idea in his writings and takes on an importance when applied to the strategy and tactics of possible proletarian class alliances in the present. Giuseppe Fiori sees the question of class alliances as being the central idea in Gramsci's notebooks in the task of the winning over of other exploited classes, above all the Southern Italian peasants, to the proletarian cause, both for successfully carrying out the socialist revolution and for guaranteeing its stability thereafter. The problem was for Gramsci that the peasantry were locked into a landowner historical bloc permeated by a bourgeois *Weltanschauung* elaborated by middle-class intellectuals which required to be broken by a new stratum of intellectuals.[28]

The analysis of developed social reality points to patterns of intervention in that reality for realizing the tendencies inherent in it revealed by the analysis. For Gramsci the role of high-culture intellectuals and the creation of processes of molecular and group transformism and forming class alliances all play a key part in the struggle to create a new (proletarian) hegemony, since in the practical activity of these individuals and groups rests the current bourgeois hegemony. This creative process is based on past knowledge and prepares for the future, in order, in Marx's phrase, to "lessen the birth pangs" of the new society pregnant in the womb of the old. The prior creation of a proletarian hegemony in civil society not only potentially hastens the socialist order but ensures that the cultural constituency of the post-revolutionary historical bloc has already been primed to become the true hegemony and universality of the proletariat and by extension the unity of mankind. An organized and long-prepared force is, however, required, and the present task is that of

> systematically and patiently ensuring that this force is formed, developed, and rendered ever more homogeneous, compact and self-aware.[29]

EXCURSUS: MYTHS AND THE MASSES

Both Gramsci and Lukács repudiated a fatalistic economic determinist Marxism in favour of a commitment to creative action. Gramsci saw the economic determinist tradition as a hangover of the theory of predestination and grace, a "replacement in the popular consciousness for the cry of "'tis God's will" ".[30] They both substituted the unity of theory and practice in the conscious furtherance of a historical tendency by the progressive class, i.e. the creation of history rather than solely the cognition of its necessity. But they were both aware in their activism of a serious problem. As we have seen in this chapter, Gramsci set about analysing the historical emergence of the bourgeoisie in Europe in the productive relations of society and traced their development from an economic-corporate stage through political phases to the achievement of cultural and ideological hegemony. He distinguishes between organic and conjunctural historical movements which must be related together when working out strategy and tactics for furthering historical tendencies, and he is aware of the need to build up ideological hegemony, credibility and moral leadership on behalf of the newest progressive class, the proletariat, preparatory to the transition to a new hegemonic bloc in socialism. This process was also presented as the creation of an all-embracing unified "organic" ideology which was the rational expression of the historical mission, perceived in its tendency, of the "fundamental" social group and a necessary premise for its "revolutionizing".

Now, Gramsci also noted the existence in the political-ideological moment, or stage, of the second type of "arbitrary", "willed" and "false" ideologies, which are arbitrary for Gramsci since they are not the necessary expression of fundamental socio-economic historical development. To repeat, for Gramsci these ideologies can only produce "individual movements" and "polemics". But we must note that in the hands of other groups of political high-culture intellectuals who may not be geared to 'progressive' historical socialist tendencies, the actual form *in practice* of the process of inculcation of such an arbitrary ideology in the masses by transforming common sense and by molecular transformism can be the same. The theory and practice of fascism and of socialism have both contained a common element: the masses. In practice, and in certain circumstances, the masses can in this way move towards various ideologies and indeed Adolf Hitler based his whole strategy of gaining popular support to save Western civilization from decadence on the volatility of unenlightened mass-consciousness and its consequent proneness to embrace mythology. As Hitler wrote in *Mein Kampf* against Marxists and their social science:

> Since the masses have only a poor acquaintance with abstract ideas, their reactions lie more in the domain of the feelings, where the roots of their positive as well as their negative attitudes are implanted . . . The emotional grounds of their attitude furnish the reason for their extraordinary stability. It is always more difficult to fight against faith than against knowledge. And the driving force which has brought about the most tremendous revolutions on this earth has never been a body of scientific teaching which has gained power over the masses, but always a devotion which has inspired them, and often a kind of hysteria which has urged them into action.[31]

Deeply committed to the potency of the human will to shape its own future, Gramsci was aware that at a certain ideological stage in the emergence of the proletariat there could be contemporaneous attempts to mobilize the masses in various ways by many different political factions and the problem of the possibility of the masses in certain circumstances going for a decidedly counter-progressive ideology. This awareness comes out in a particularly perceptive and revealing passage in the prison notebooks in the section 'Relation between science, religion and commonsense'.[32] Gramsci is talking about his theory of the creation of new intellectuals to develop and modify the "ideological panorama"[33] of the age through the agency of an ideological community. He writes:

> It is evident that this kind of mass creation cannot just happen "arbitrarily", around any ideology, simply because of the formally constructive will of a personality or a group which puts it forward solely on the basis of its own fanatical philosophical religious convictions. Mass adhesion or non-adhesion to an ideology is the real critical test of the rationality and historicity of modes of thinking. Any arbitrary constructions are pretty rapidly eliminated by historical competition, even if sometimes, through a combination of immediately favourable circumstances, they manage to enjoy popularity of a kind; whereas constructions which respond to the demands of a complex organic period of history always impose themselves and prevail in the end, even though they may pass through several intermediary phases during which they manage to affirm themselves only in more or less bizarre and heterogeneous combinations.[34]

The knowledge that this passage was written in an Italian fascist gaol at exactly the time when Hitler was assuming power with mass support in Germany, makes its implications particularly poignant. Gramsci is invoking Marx's notion that the mass adhesion to an ideology turns theory into a "material force". The self-conscious action of the masses creates a situation where social circumstances and the conscious creation of those circumstances by their participants at the level of the totality coincide. In Gramsci this process is the practical realization of political sociology, the elaboration of the structure into the superstructure, the moment of "catharsis", the real, critical test of the historicity and rationality of thinking. Paraphrasing Hegel, Gramsci says of critical activity in general that

> The identification of theory and practice is a critical act, through which practice is demonstrated rational and necessary, and theory realistic and rational.[35]

That is to say, relating this principle to the level of the totality, the complete unity of theory and practice (i.e. the total coincidence of the historically rational and the reality) can only be for Gramsci ultimately the becoming self-conscious of the progressive class in a historically necessary process, which frees the rational, progressive, blind development of productive forces from the privileged social fetters which mediate them. Other mass mobilizations can for Gramsci only be short-lived and 'irrational' in that sense. He is thus unimpressed by the Sorelian theory of the myth as the body of epic images capable of evoking in the proletariat instinctively socialist sentiments thrown up by the class struggle, e.g. the idea of the General Strike being the most important myth for mobilizing the masses. Gramsci says of Sorel's myth that such a collective will would be "rudimentary" and likely to break up into an "infinity of individual wills", and so could not of its nature "have a long-term and organic character". Against this Gramsci places a "new collective will" which is "operative awareness of historical necessity".[36]

In a similar way, he says in the extended passage quoted above that not "any ideology", "any" fanatical conviction, can obtain *lasting* mass-adhesion because the "arbitrary" constructions are eliminated by historical competition, even though they may enjoy brief, fluctuating periods of popularity in various combinations. The arbitrary ideologies in Gramsci, those described as "any" ideology, are neither epiphenomenal nor totally 'irrational' but are the ideological constructions which must dialectically demonstrate the rationality of the "organic" constructions. They are only "any" ideologies against the necessary ones, so are therefore necessarily arbitrary and arbitrarily necessary. However, for all his hostility towards fatalistic, deterministic Marxism as being a secular expression of the idea of reliance on God's will and thus an ideology presupposing mass inaction, he places his faith in those ideological constructions embedded in the "organic" historical development which "always impose themselves and prevail *in the end*" (my italics). And, as we have seen, this organic development is just the comforting, reliable dialectical necessity of the development of forces and relations of production within the *Unterbau* which characterizes fatalistic Marxism. Here we see Gramsci grasp the possibility of the mobilization of 'irrational' ideologies or constructions in the struggle for hegemony within civil society and even grant their temporary sway, but finally come down on the ultimate power of a rational historical movement, the willed ideological concomitant of which will finally triumph over the short-lived reigns of its willed rivals. The theme of historical necessity in this sense is a major motif in Gramsci's writings, expressed in various ways as "spontaneous development", "organic movements", "progressive tendencies", etc. It can be followed through in various contexts in many places in his writings.[37] The irony is that Gramsci's dialectical mind realized that he *must* grant this necessary historical tendency in order to be able scientifically and therefore *necessarily* to show one ideology (socialism) associated with it to be non-arbitrary and thus not equi-pollent with others competing in the hegemonic arena.

Like many of his contemporaries who were trying to theorize about the significance of the working-class social movements during the First World War and immediately after, Gramsci believed early on that only urgent action to hasten the victory of the proletariat could save the material and cultural achievements of capitalism; otherwise inaction would allow capitalism to career towards the 'abyss'. But the pessimistic notion of the abyss was the only way in which, committed to an activistic emphasis on the theory of the dialectics of history, one could conceptualize the *possibility of failure* of the working-class revolution. However, once failure had seemed to have been consummated by the desertion of the appointed class to fascism, despite the conditions for the transition to socialism having seemed apposite, then certain theorists were left only with the belief in the final triumph of the organic historical movement *in the end.* We are reminded of Marcuse's persevering, rationalistic credo written in exile from Nazi Germany at the end of the 1930s: "theory will preserve the truth even if revolutionary practice deviates from its path".[38]

In *History and Class Consciousness* Lukács, like Gramsci, shows an awareness of the problem of the potential mass-mobilizability of various ideologies and also comes down on the side of the ultimate primacy of those associated with long-term historically necessary processes. He argues that the consciousness of the proletariat is history made conscious of itself at a particular stage of development, as its immanent result and, therefore (invoking Marx's famous statement in *The German Ideology*), he declares:

> The proletariat "has no ideals to realise". When its consciousness is put into practice it can only breathe life into the things which the dialectics of history have forced to a crisis; it can never 'in practice' ignore the course of history, forcing on it what are no more than its own desires or knowledge.[39]

Lukács, too, is confident that as part of a total process of historical necessity the proletariat can never force its "own desires or knowledge" on to history *in practice* as a lived reality (as opposed to psychologically holding those beliefs) if they do not correspond to a (socialist-communist) consciousness which is bound up as of necessity to the historical dialectic. There is indeed a strong presumption here, too, that in the long-term proletarian class-consciousness can only be socialist since it forms part of what Gramsci called the "organic movement". But of course for Gramsci and for Lukács once the emergence of the new progressive class has reached an advanced stage then its aims are fought out in the realms of ideology. It is only at this stage that the problem of other than socialist mobilizations occurring becomes problematic, a situation which Marx could not have foreseen.

Commitment to a total process of historical necessity (understood praxically rather than crudely deterministically) leads both Lukács and Gramsci (in an implicit or explicit dialogue with neo-Kantians) to similar stances on Marxian ethics. Lukács generally follows Marx's view as quoted above, but more explicitly states that

> Whether an action is functionally right or wrong is decided ultimately by the evolution of proletarian class consciousness.[40]

Gramsci, too, rooted morality in action geared towards the solution of problems thrown up by the objective necessity of the historical process, "duty" being understood as a decision taken on the basis of the inherent rectitude of the rational solution of those historical problems given that the conditions for their solution exist. Invoking Marx's 1859 Preface once more, he said:

> The scientific base for a morality of historical materialism is to be looked for, in my opinion, in the affirmation that "society does not pose for itself tasks the conditions for whose resolution do not already exist". Where these conditions exist "the solution of the tasks *becomes* 'duty', 'will' *becomes* free". Morality would then become a search for the conditions necessary for the freedom of the will in a certain sense, aimed at a certain end, and the demonstration that these conditions exist.[41]

As in Lukács, in practical terms it is for Gramsci the party (the modern Prince) which is important on questions of morality (although, as we will see later, Gramsci's conception of the party's role is less directive than that of Lukács). The party for Gramsci is the crucible for the development of a new morality since it embodies the potential of the organic historical tendency within itself and therefore historically enshrines moral imperatives. Gramsci writes:

> any given act is seen as useful or harmful, as virtuous or as wicked, only in so far as it has as its point of reference the modern Prince itself, and helps to strengthen or to oppose it. In men's consciences, the Prince takes the place of the divinity or the categorical imperative.[42]

There is another problem which acknowledgment of the possibility of short-lived ideological mobilizations carries with it. (Even though born of a specific context, this problem is arguably a general one.) In the extended passage quoted earlier, Gramsci seems to be having an implicit dialogue with the notion that after any given episode of proletarian activity (accepting the possibility of short-lived mass-mobilizations) there could emerge (within Marxist terms at any rate) doubt as to whether what has occurred is the victory in the class war or just a major battle. Lukács seems to see this dilemma, too, but apparently regards it as an abstract one. He never states it explicitly, coming down in favour of a process view on the question, the defeat of capital being characterized by "an unbroken process of . . . disruptions"[43] of the proletariat's knowledge of the structure of society. This "alternation of outbreaks" ultimately reaches a stage of class-consciousness in which passivity is opposed by a "conscious effort to relate the 'final goal' to the immediate exigencies of the moment"[44] (in Lukács this universality or final goal is embodied in the party, in theory to be superseded by the proletariat which comes consciously to embrace it, transcending the distinction). In Lukács, as in Gramsci, the victory is, then, to be regarded as a process, rather than an unconditioned leap and is to be prepared in advance cumulatively. The movement as a whole may suffer reversals but it always ultimately asserts itself provided appropriate political action continues.[45] Lukács says that the "failure" of the proletariat to become the identical subject-object of history only reproduces the contradictions of capitalism with increased intensity, such is the "objective necessity of history".[46] But this position still seems to assume that once the goal is eventually achieved it will be unequivocally discernible in concrete reality. The problem is particularly sharpened by the declared continuous process nature of the achievement and transcendence of the goal of proletarian hegemony, i.e. there is no end-state implied to be discerned.

Given his commitment to a particular conception of the dialectic and in the socio-economic circumstances of 1923, Lukács concludes that the "blind forces of capitalist economics are driving society towards the abyss", that the "bourgeoisie no longer has the power . . . to break the 'deadlock' brought about by its economic laws",[47] and that the proletariat has the opportunity to turn events towards the "conscious regulation of the productive forces of society".[48] It is this urgent call for action and the nature of the theory of proving the truth in practice invoked to back it up that gives many of Lukács's remarks their particular cast and accounts for our impatience with the ambiguities and omissions in his discussion of the problem of short-term versus long-term mobilizations of the masses. Since he urgently wants to advocate action and repudiates the Utopian view of a realm of freedom existing abstractly and only needing a leap to achieve he always talks of the "next step" *towards* the goal, which achievement may, of course, be subject to reversals:

> The deed of the proletariat can never be more than to take the *next step* in the process. Whether it is 'decisive' or 'episodic' depends on the concrete circumstances . . .[49]

But in this process the nature of the reality of each step could be, in the event, equivocal.

The statement by Lukács above leaves as in principle unanswerable in the abstract two questions: (a) If the proletariat goes for one of Gramsci's "arbitrary" ideologies (Lukács's "desires" of the proletariat) rather than the 'correct', "necessary", "organic" ideology, the question of the longevity of such an arbitrary mobilization: on the Marxian view this is subject to circumstances allowing the proletariat's continuing false consciousness in that respect. (b) Even if an appropriate and necessary *Weltanschauung* is *apparently* mobilized, it may, through circumstances which cannot be totally predicted by their nature, be rendered obsolete as counter-revolution (from within or outside the socialist movement) supplants the new order and the progressive process is set back once more, i.e. the victory proves to have been a battle. The acknowledgment of this possibility by no means provides the wherewithal for recognizing at an initial stage that this has occurred. Within the Marxian practical-critical perspective, however. Lukács and Gramsci probably legitimately felt that such questions are to be regarded as abstract and scholastic, demanding present certainty for future action, when the Marxian theory of praxis entails that action will always involve an uncertain element, the nature of which reveals itself in the newly changed configuration, thus entailing further theory and further action, in a continuing totalizing process of practical authentication. Therefore the abstract question of how we might know whether we have succeeded would be regarded in a self-described "historicist" theoretical perspective such as Gramsci's as at best only a valid enough misgiving.

Gramsci said that the real problem, however, is that of getting people to grasp the historicity of all truths and values, including those upon which action itself is to be based (Marxist theory) without "in so doing shaking the convictions that are necessary for action",[50] i.e. getting people to act at all without absolute certainty of the principles on which they act, let alone of outcomes. The desire for absolute truths, for solid certitudes about society, can result in Marxism deleteriously becoming an ideology for providing eternal verities, deployed by the Party, as dogmatically embodied in Bukharin's *Manual*; or else a fatalistic set of immutable social laws justifying inaction; the dilemma being in a nutshell that the masses are predisposed towards mythology and towards believing in eternalized principles undergirding social life but are at the same time held to be the agent for changing the social order which perpetuates such attitudes.

In addition, Gramsci's philosophers of praxis should not provide such a schematized system of absolute truths in the name of Marxism but show such eternal truths to be relative, historical, human social products which men can master – this being historically the essence of Marxism. For Gramsci, without absolutes the masses will not act; but without their action there is not much likelihood of creating a social order which could relativize those absolutes. Meanwhile, because it shows the provisional historical character of eternal truths, "historicism" becomes decried by the popular mind as leading to "moral scepticism and depravity".[51] Gramsci can only conclude that this dilemma requires to be handled in practice with delicacy and subtlety.

To return to the earlier extended quotation from Gramsci about "arbitrary" ideologies, his affirmation there of the ultimate victory of historically necessary ideologies is not, of course, a rationalization of passivity. It is, as in the case of Lukács's position, an affirmation of the need to act in order to try to ensure such 'necessary victory'. This would prevent capitalism careering further and further towards the abyss unable to solve its inherent contradictions, which fatalistic inaction would fail to do. The victory of the capitalistic enemy in any guise was only guaranteed (subject to Gramsci's strictures about the military's decisive power as a technical force on behalf of the ruling class in certain cases) in so far as collective action did not take place to counter it. Conversely, the victory of the proletariat was only guaranteed, even as part of a necessary process, in so far as action was taken to mobilize the tendency of which it is held to be the bearer. Both aspects were inseparable elements of the historical process of theory-informed action. Like many thinkers in the Marxian tradition from Marx himself onwards, Gramsci was reluctant to enter into abstract speculations about outcomes of action or about future structures of socialist society for the reasons already stated and also because it was the urgent self-conscious creation of the future that was important. Although this future was not regarded as *totally* open-ended. To employ Gianfranco Poggi's terminology from his interpretation of Marx's work,[52] it would be fair to say that for Gramsci (and for Lukács) the future was, dialectically speaking, regarded as neither abstractly 'open-ended' *nor* 'empirically closed' because empirical knowledge only *minimizes* the uncertain element in a process of action – it can never totally eliminate it. Action occurs neither with total knowledge nor totally blindly. In Gramsci's philosophy of praxis the future is only as empirically closed as the extent to which the theory-informed self-conscious action of the proletariat proves it to be. And, conversely, it is simultaneously only as open-ended as the extent to which the self-conscious praxis of the proletariat discovers the previously undiscovered hiatuses of its theory. And so on . . . and on . . . Gramsci explains:

> The historical "automatism" of certain premisses (the existence of certain objective conditions) is potentialised politically by parties and by men of ability: absence or inadaquacy (quantitative and qualitative) of these neutralises the "automatism" itself (which anyway is not really automatic): the premisses exist abstractly, but the consequences are not realised because the human factor is missing.[53]

But at the present stage of social development, the theory of changing the self-made world of men by their self-conscious activity (currently called Marxism) was for Gramsci *more* tied, though not totally, to the Marxian 'realm of necessity' than to the 'realm of freedom', which Gramsci remarks "does not exist and, historically, cannot yet exist".[54] The theory is always subject to sublation as the conditions which render it unnecessary are realized. At the present time, however, and also at no particular time during all phases of action, can the future be more than abstractly outlined. Gramsci remarked:

> [the philosopher of praxis] . . . cannot escape from the present field of contradictions, he cannot affirm, other than generically, a world without contradictions, without immediately creating a utopia.[55]

We will return to the issues discussed in this Excursus in Chapters 15 and 16 in Part four.

11 Towards the ethical State

Gramsci's perception of the need to create a unified cultural hegemony before the transition to socialism was predicated on its generation through cultural and ideological groundwork, initially on the level of individual intellectuals within a party organization. For the countries of the West the problems of the transition to socialism are for Gramsci mainly cultural and ideological since civil society is here the highly developed, routinized part of an integrated historical bloc which works with a remarkable self-equilibrium in the interests of the dominant class requiring little direct force by the coercive arm of the State. At this stage of development the struggle for hegemonies is the key to the transition since the determinacy of the economic moment in the development of the fundamental class, although present, is less decisive. As I have already foreshadowed, in both the creation of a cultural and political hegemony in the working class before the passage to socialism and in the organic generation of the praxis itself, intellectuals play an important role in Gramsci's ideas (as they did in different senses for other thinkers of his time – Alfred Weber, Mannheim, Benda). In more detail, and to bring out how his conception of intellectuals differs from theirs, we can first consider Gramsci's distinction between organic intellectuals and traditional intellectuals.

Every social group which comes into existence on the terrain of the world of economic production (stage 1 of the sequence presented in the previous chapter) creates for itself over long periods of time several strata of intellectuals in the economic, political, social and cultural fields; e.g. capitalists create technicians, political economists, organizers of new culture. These are what Gramsci calls organic intellectuals, since they arise in the course of the development of the fundamental class and correspond to "organic" historical movements. Traditional intellectuals are those still in existence when the new class emerges whose origins were predicated on the previous social order, but who continue to operate in the society dominated by the new class. For example, ecclesiastics under feudalism monopolized many areas of science, religion and learning, but were structurally bound to the landed aristocracy.[1] Because of their traditional status these intellectuals form an autonomous and independent group and Gramsci regards them as of great importance, for example in the Italian case, as being the carriers of idealist philosophy and elaborators of social Utopias. They are particular examples of Gramsci's famous general proposition that "All men are intellectuals".[2] This argument follows from his Crocean view of the inseparability of the theoretical and the practical: all activities require intellection of qualitatively different kinds and all intellection exists in activity. So for Gramsci, it need hardly be said, intellectuals are not just those professional ones of high culture. Therefore he affirms the democratico-political importance of acknowledging that all men consciously sustain in practice various conceptions (philosophies) of the world even if only implicitly. These are real for them, can be tenaciously resilient to enlightenment and are as Gwyn A. Williams says ongoingly activated and made explicit in practice by "the function of intellect".[3]

Historically, Gramsci argues, the bourgeois organic intellectuals have tended to be intellectuals of the urban type since it was in this context that industry grew; whereas the traditional intellectuals are for the most part linked to the "mass of country people" and particularly the small-town *petit-bourgeoisie*,[4] i.e. are of the rural type. The intellectual in the countryside (e.g. priest, lawyer, notary, teacher) has a signal politico-social function among the peasantry since he represents a role model for the peasant to look to for improving his condition or that of his sons. Although the peasant often possesses a contradictory consciousness since he also instinctively experiences envy and anger towards the intellectuals of that kind whom he encounters,[5] in contrast, urban intellectuals (for example technicians) according to Gramsci have passed the stage of development of exercising a similar political function over the instrumental masses; there the political influence is vice versa, i.e. of the organic intellectuals of the masses over the technicians.[6]

Gramsci ties the intellectuals into the historical character of political parties of all kinds but focuses on revolutionary parties with implications for the present proletarian one. The political party is often the organization through which social groups elaborate their own organic intellectuals. Within civil society the political party carries out for all groups the same function as the State carries out on a larger political scale; that is, it is responsible for

> welding together the organic intellectuals of a given group – the dominant one – and the traditional intellectuals.[7]

This function of the political party is a role of clearly paramount importance for the stability of civil society and the changing of the cultural climate of the historical bloc potentially towards the hegemony of the fundamental, rising, but still subaltern, social class: the proletariat. Therefore, within the party in this perspective intellectuals (perhaps of high culture, but of all kinds) joining the party of a particular social group merge with those indigenous, organic intellectuals already in it. The political party modelled in this metabolic fashion accomplishes its function of fusing organic and traditional intellectuals together "more completely and organically than the State".[8] The State cannot absorb and merge intellectuals in this way because unadvisedly many intellectuals in the wider society who enter the State apparatuses come rigidly to believe that they *are* the State, a belief which has important political consequences. Ultimately, for Gramsci, the existing particular ruling-class interests of the State (despite its universal pretensions) must be sublated by its merging with civil society, which process constitutes the transcendence of the particularized State in the 'universalizing' interests of all epitomized in the proletariat's hegemony. The individual's self-government is not then in conflict with political society: universal and particular interests coincide. The belief, however, of certain intellectuals in the wider society that they are the State is clearly inimical to this wider aim, and leads to

> unpleasant complications for the fundamental economic group [the proletariat] which *really* is the State.[9]

At the level of development of the movement of history termed the political moment, in its transcendence (although inclusion) of the economic moment, a political party is possible which enables an emergent socio-economic group (in this case the proletariat) to aspire beyond the economic-corporate, egoistic-passional co-operation permitted by the professional or trade organization towards "more general activities of a national and international character"[10] connected with its organic development. Gramsci also expresses these interests as questions of "intellectual and moral unity" on a "universal plane"[11] in an awareness within the party of "operating for a higher end".[12] The organically conceived party is the "first cell in which there come together germs of a collective will tending to become universal and total".[13] Although the party takes the fundamental social group away from purely economic-corporate interests towards those of a self-determining unified mankind, this aspiration is made possible by the high level of socio-economic development, the economic moment existing as a presupposition both in the analysis and in reality. The theory is not, therefore, *solely* cultural or ideological nor idealist as some have thought. Gramsci is expressing socio-politically what Croce expressed philosophically as the dialectical unity of the economic and the rational-moral wills. Croce wrote:

> To will economically is to *will an end*; to will morally is to *will the rational end*. But whoever wills and acts morally, cannot but will and act usefully (economically). How could he will the rational, unless he willed it also *as his particular end*?[14]

Therefore the assertion by certain commentators which we highlighted in earlier chapters that Gramsci's conception of the passage to socialism is solely in the realms of thought or the frequent accusation that Gramsci's cultural theory is 'cerebral' are mistaken. Both show a basic misunderstanding of the transcendence of the economic moment in Gramsci but its continued presuppositional presence with less determinacy as well as the embodiment of intellection in active individuals and groups.

Gramsci sees the party, comprising itself of various intellectuals from civil society welded together as outlined above, as taking on the task of *becoming* a new universal State, which is ultimately the same process as the rise to social hegemony of the proletariat as well as the creation of the unity of mankind and the overcoming of the present class State. The party accomplishes this universalizing process in practice, cumulatively overcoming the contradiction between universal, rational, human interests at a given historical stage and the particular interests of the ruling class which are covertly embodied in the activity of the present State. The party works from its own foundation, by a process of coalescence of individuals and groups (conscious transformism) to generate the new ethical State organically through the eventual mutual abolition and fusion of party and State in practice. Gramsci believes that this programme can succeed in not simply reimposing another particularized State in practice. This is because

> only the social group that poses the end of the State and its own end as the target to be achieved can create an ethical State – i.e. one which tends to put an end to the internal divisions of the ruled, etc., and to create a technically and morally unitary social organism.[15]

Gramsci, like Croce, held that the sphere of morality is bound up with civil society and not with the State itself, which in its directive function at higher stages of the societal development embodies Croce's economic will by conforming civil society to the economic sphere. In the totalizing task which the party takes on itself, it reacts upon social classes "in order to develop, solidify and universalise them"[16] in a dialectical process which we might perhaps theoretically characterize as the conscious practical achievement of the concrete universal of rational self-government or the fusion of the ethical and the political into one social organism. The project is conceived as no less than a "movement to create a new civilisation"[17] by transcending the archaic antagonistic distinction between civil society and political society which was the product of an earlier class stage of social development, but which exists as a presupposition of the new stage that is to be consciously created. In this process the State must be identified with a new type of man and individuals of the progressive class must become an "element of active culture"[18] to determine the will to construct

> within the husk of political society a complex and well-articulated civil society, in which the individual can govern himself without his self-government thereby entering into conflict with political society – but rather becoming its normal continuation, its organic complement.[19]

Expressed more theoretically this is a process of the making real of human universality by 'working up' its particular abstract social embodiments towards their ideal totality, with which they form a concrete dialectical unity in and through those particular abstract embodiments (notably the party and social groups in this case). But what is remarkable about Gramsci's schema is that he is able to side-step abstract Utopianizing by suggesting immediate steps towards the practical realization of such a theory of a true, ethical State, steps which are organically constitutive of the total process, not simply means towards an end.[20] In practical-critical terms Gramsci not only advocates a political sociology to guide action, but also advocates the ongoing practical creation of the potential rational reality-as-State on the terrain of the organically conceived party, the stages of which creation always create new situations entailing new political-sociological analysis. John Merrington understates but rightly perceives Gramsci's great strength as having "posed these problems in terms which admitted of practical solutions".[21]

How does Gramsci's conception relate to other Marxist theories of the party? Gramsci has a conception of the interpenetration and coalescence of "organic" proletarian intellectuals and traditional intellectuals in a universalizing party whose totalizing praxis generates a truly universal State through the fusion of political and civil society via processes of conscious molecular and group transformism. This theory of the party differs from Lenin's professional vanguard. This was clear even early on in Gramsci's career, when he wrote in 1918:

> The Socialist Party is the anti-State, not a party. Bourgeois groups want to change the State marginally through their parties, merely by giving it one particular direction rather than another. The Socialist Party wants to remould the State not to improve it. It wants to change all of its values. It wants to re-organize it, founding it upon social forces and ethical principles totally different from the present ones.[22]

Later, in the prison notebooks Gramsci sees the party as an "embryonic State structure"[23] and, in the Western conditions of a highly developed civil society, also as a moral force, developing the ethical principles of a new "collective man",[24] because, as we have seen, what is ethical in men cannot reside in the present State, *qua* State. The collective organism of the party, through conscious participation and "compassionality" forms a close organic link between

> great mass, party and leading group; and the whole complex, thus articulated, can move together as "collective man".[25]

For Gramsci the creation and realization of "collective man" is a willed, practical process, in which the historical act which unites dispersed aims and passions is the extension of a previously established " "cultural-social" unity".[26]

It is true of course that in *What Is To Be Done?* Lenin also had a notion of the importance of a total comprehension of life by the proletariat. He said that working-class consciousness cannot be genuinely political unless the workers can apprehend in a "materialist" manner "*all* aspects of the life and activity of *all* classes, strata and groups".[27] But at the same time his position carried the rider that the workers had to be "trained to respond"[28] in this way. This is not the same conception as Gramsci's organic creation of cultural unity through a universalizing process of coalescence and conscious transformism whereby the party becomes the State, thus *constituting* the grasp Lenin wants merely to *teach*. For Gramsci, his practical proposals were intended for advanced stages of the development of civil society where conditions within the social formation as a whole were conducive to the transcendence of the economic-corporate moment. Lenin's more directive professional vanguard conception (which we also find in Lukács) was the product of a very different stage of social development in which a civil society was only embryonic, bourgeois hegemony itself even barely established in a few metropolitan centres and the working class quantitatively minute. Lenin's theory entailed the correspondingly different intention of purely seizing State political power.

It might be instructive briefly to examine what two or three recent commentators have made of Gramsci's conception of "collective

Man", and his ideas on the nature of the revolutionary party in relation to the State in the West compared with those of Lenin. This will serve to throw into relief my own interpretation as well as provide some insight into the way in which current writers of the New Left selectively interpret the works of the classical and venerable names in the most apparently relevant radical tradition of socio-political thinking available to them – Marxism – in order to orientate themselves in a new social context. In the literature there is considerable debate about whether Gramsci's concept of hegemony is synonymous with dictatorship and therefore ultimately totalitarian,[29] and among Marxists in particular on the extent of the later Gramsci's "reformism", apparent departure from Lenin, etc. In short we can discern the beginnings of a young-Gramsci versus mature-Gramsci controversy. This is not the place to enter into this debate at any length, but on the subject of the party I will register my disagreement with Alberto Pozzolini[30] who strings together unannotated quotations from Gramsci in such a way as to convey a picture of him as a militant believer in a rigidly centralized revolutionary communist vanguard party, "a conscious power elite", on the Leninist model. Pozzolini plays down the cultural reflections in the prison notebooks as not fundamental notes on the subject of organization because they were not notes of "the politician in the active struggle".[31] But, as Fiori shows, as early as 1916 during his political activity in Turin Gramsci was talking of the necessity of creating a preparatory culture for the subaltern classes in a polemic against Bordiga's refrain that "socialists are not made by education, but by the real necessities of the class they belong to"[32] and the prison notebooks, as Fiori rightly maintains, represent extended reflections upon this theme.[33] Gramsci returns to Bordiga's dictum implicitly in the prison notebooks when talking about day labourers in agricultural regions: "The essential characteristic of the day-labourers is not their economic situation but their intellectual and moral condition."[34]

Romano Giachetti, on the contrary, says that Gramsci "went beyond Leninism" because it had failed to produce in Russia the "new man", the only entity Gramsci considered essential to "the development of a *true* revolution (which is more than just a change in the structure of the state)".[35] This formulation may be making a valid point about Russia and about revolution in general but in seeking backing from Gramsci it plays down Gramsci's explicit statement in the notebooks that where a new fundamental social group has little independent cultural development of its own "a period of statolatory is necessary and indeed opportune"[36] for the initiation of a new hegemony and a new civil society. Gramsci does warn, however, against fanaticism which could perpetuate the statolatory, but one must not overlook that for Gramsci the nature of the State (and consequently what political and party activity is appropriate) always depends on the stage of social development reached.[37] Finally, Alastair Davidson summarizes the differences between Lenin's and Gramsci's views on the party as lying in its suggested long-term "educatory role", and also seizes on the idea of creating the "new man". He writes:

> Lenin needed only to teach the Russian workers how to conduct a revolution which they already wanted, whereas Gramsci had to convince them that they needed a revolution, and . . . Lenin envisaged the making of the new man after the revolution and for Gramsci it was essentially a case of making him before the revolution.[38]

One must add, though, that the two sides of this statement (the teaching role and the creation of the new man) would not be mutually exclusive but organically related in Gramsci, since the role of the party for him was not solely educative in any propagandizing sense. The teachers and the taught in Davidson's formulation are for Gramsci both comprised of intellectuals and, together in coalescence in the party they *constitute* "new man", in his particular mode, quantitatively and qualitatively expanding and extending towards 'universality' over the society as a whole ultimately to form the new "Ethical State".[39] This is how Gramsci envisages this living process:

> The development of the party into a State reacts upon the party and requires of it a continuous reorganisation and development, just as the development of the party and State into a conception of the world, i.e. into a total and molecular (individual) transformation of ways of thinking and acting, reacts upon the State and the party, compelling them to reorganise continually and confronting them with new and original problems to solve.[40]

Finally, to return to our starting point, Gramsci stresses the fact that on the road to hegemony classes tend to assimilate and to conquer ideologically the traditional intellectuals attached to the previously historically progressive, but now archaic class. This process is facilitated by the creation of their own organic intellectuals by the new class, for whom the traditional intellectuals exist as a historical presupposition and with whom they fuse in the party. Thus, in practical terms, the immediate tactic as far as the proletariat is concerned in the overall practical strategy leading towards a new type of man is the creation of a new stratum of organic intellectuals (both urban and rural), to encourage "the critical elaboration of the intellectual activity that exists in everyone".[41] The new intellectual must not be simply eloquent, but one who takes an active part in practical life, within the party and in civil society, as a "permanent persuader".[42]

But what of the content and types of intellection activated by intellectuals comprising civil society? Gramsci says that "it is not "thought" but what people really think that unites or differentiates mankind"[43] and he always looks at this content normatively and culturally as it is embodied in practical activity. So it is to what people really think, the types of intellection, or types of philosophy in Gramsci's terms, to which we will now turn.

12 The unity of common sense and philosophy

The broad outlines of Gramsci's groupings of types of intellection into a hierarchy of philosophy, religion, commonsense and folklore[1] have already been foreshadowed in antithesis to Bukharin's more 'scientific' and undiscriminating stance *vis-à-vis* popular beliefs as a whole and Gramsci's scepticism about this position. For Gramsci these four groupings are categorially an incorporative developmental sequence as well as comprise levels of cultural integration in civil society each based in its own social stratum. Since he holds that "all men are philosophers"[2] because they realize or embody their world views in practice, he regards all the four categories as philosophy in a broad sense. The first one refers to the high-culture philosophy of professional philosophers and incorporates the other three transcended within it. As we have seen, for Gramsci a sociology which is not a directly political sociology feeds on the apolitical residues of society and is thus frivolous, so not surprisingly sociology does not figure in this schema; unlike economics, however, which he places along with the specialist sciences in general at the highest level along with philosophy.[3] But the notebooks are fragmentary and this aspect of Gramsci's thought is not very systematically worked out. As regards high-culture philosophy, he adds that since previous philosophy has "left stratified deposits in popular philosophy",[4] criticism of past philosophies has the effect of laying bare one's own present conception of the world in which traces of them are sedimented. It is only from the higher stage that these layers can be appropriated and seen to be philosophical. The difference between the professional, technical philosopher and the rest of mankind is not one of quality but one of quantity, i.e. the professional philosopher merely thinks more systematically, with "greater coherence"[5] than the non-professional, who none the less thinks and acts with a conception of the world and is thus also a philosopher.

For Gramsci, the philosophy of an epoch is a general conception of the world, a part of the hegemony achieved by dominant groups over the proceding social reality and is embodied overall in forms of conduct and practical activity. So Gramsci's types of philosophy all correspond to types of real normative social activity within a developed hegemonic bloc, and the history of philosophy is not only the history of high-culture professional philosophy, but also the history of specific classes' attempts to "change, correct or perfect the conception of the world"[6] within the dominant hegemony handed down to them. These conceptions of the world, i.e. of all the philosophers including the masses, form a cultural complex, a combination of elements, which "culminates in an overall trend"[7] which generally permeates the society and becomes a "norm of collective action" (broadly analogous to the "Spirit of the Age" discussed in Chapter 9 but elaborated by Gramsci more sociologically).

The scattered nature of Gramsci's comments on the philosophies and the different contexts in which they appear make a systematic exposition a tricky operation. But nevertheless I do not feel that my interpretation which follows is inconsistent with Gramsci's intentions. Within the "bloc" formed by history and philosophy in general[8] the various levels, as cultural elements and as vestiges of the past, can be characterized in the following descending order of 'rational' comprehension towards mythology. (a) Professional philosophy is "intellectual order" compared with religion and common sense, which can never be so ordered because they cannot be reduced to unity and coherence.[9] Philosophy is the highest, most incorporative form of consciousness because it is "criticism and the superseding of religion and "common sense" ".[10] It thus coincides with "good sense" (as opposed to common sense), which good sense for Gramsci roughly means wisdom, the critical appraisal of aspects of the subordinate forms of consciousness of religion and common sense.[11] (b) Common sense refers to the everyday guiding ideas which inform practical, quotidian social life and includes conceptions underlying commonsense economic behaviour which the institutional State will tend to try to inculcate into civil society via legislation. Together with "good sense" mentioned under (a) above, these two levels will form a strong cultural complex, an "ideological unity between the bottom and the top",[12] because commonsense economic behaviour, for example, can at certain stages acquire the esteem and self-evident wisdom of "good sense" which ensures that members of the subaltern classes go about their business in the belief that their common sense is the highest wisdom. This effectively welds the ends of the social structure together in everyday consenting, legitimized practical activity. (c) Religion is "an element of fragmented common sense"[13] and is also conceived not solely as an illusory form of consciousness or an ideology, but as a world view guiding real practical activity and as a norm of conduct. Illustrating the possible strength of an ideologically unified bloc, Gramsci says that the cultural strength of the Catholic Church in Italy lay in the fact that it was always most vigorous in preventing the rigid formation of two religions, one for the "intellectuals" and the other for the "simple souls".[14] (d) Folklore includes witchcraft, belief in spirits, superstitions, alchemy and magic.[15] These beliefs have "sturdy historical roots and are tenaciously entwined in the psychology of specific popular strata", requiring to be transformed into a "modern mentality",[16] i.e. one which would have transcended these archaisms towards a position which more nearly accords to the rational total comprehension of philosophy.

Gramsci also refers to a common "living" language as a medium of inter-stratum cultural unification in civil society, which language contains "elements of a conception of the world".[17] Great importance is apparently assumed by Gramsci for language in the general cultural problem of the attainment of "cultural-social unity"[18] by the historical act of "collective man",[19] discussed in the last chapter, but he does not develop the point far. Although language tends to be a hegemonic national one which can perpetuate in "metaphorical form the words of previous civilisation and cultures",[20] he acknowledges that even the most radical social change alters mainly the content of language rather than its formal aspects.[21] But, for the present, Gramsci draws attention to dialect as limiting the comprehension of provincials more to "economic-corporate" interests as against the "universal" interests of the Marxist cultural movement,[22] and stresses therefore the importance of the learning of the national language properly by all.

The hierarchy of conceptions of the world embodied in practical activity and language in civil society, as unified aspects of a general dominant conception of the world, is a changing historically continuous configuration. The types of philosophy are not static, closed universes of discourse. For example, a high-culture philosophical current can leave behind "a sedimentation of 'common sense' ", whilst common sense itself is continually transforming itself with "scientific ideas and with philosophical opinions".[23] Gramsci sees folklore as a lower level of popular belief than common sense because it is a lower form of consciousness skewed away from 'rational' self-consciousness or science more towards belief in unknown forces, determinism, fatalism, chance, etc. Common sense exists between folklore and the higher "philosophy, science and economics of the specialists"[24] because it is less dependent on unknown or hypostatized forces. Folklore is present today in popular consciousness as a stunted relic of a past social order in which it was once a dominant motif, but because it is embodied in practical activity it is an important element in civil society. Neither are these general categories intended as a temporal historical sequence of greater clarification towards Reason. They are co-present unified moments (geared to social groups in all cases) kept alive through cultural activity but exhibiting an internal development from the lower forms (folklore) to the higher, more 'universal' comprehension of philosophy which provides a general consciousness of the hegemonic bloc of the particular society or epoch. This development coincides with their existence in various vestigial or dominant forms in civil society today. Methodologically and in reality the hierarchy of forms of consciousness or philosophies stand in the same relationship to one another as do Gramsci's moments in the relation of forces discussed in the previous chapter. They are of the same nature as Marx's conceptual sequence of Asiatic, ancient, feudal and modern bourgeois modes of production as being "progressive epochs" in the economic formation of society, even though they may not occur in that order in the actual historical process. Such developmental sequences are also common in dialectical idealist philosophy which, as we saw in earlier chapters on Lukács and Hegel, also distinguishes between history and development. Gramsci was as we have seen undoubtedly inspired by Italian idealist historicism, from which he has absorbed and creatively utilized the conception of "moments". The point is that without understanding the logic of this approach we could mistakenly assume that the forms of intellection are just a formal typology or conceived in the modern manner as paradigms.

It was this dialectical perspective which gave Gramsci, as we saw in Chapter 8, a methodological starting point for his critique of Bukharin's scientistic "teratological" approach towards popular beliefs. Bukharin failed to see the importance of the fact that the transcended stages of development towards a more scientific appraisal of the social world were still present as vestigial but resilient realities in the practice of life, and were not just ideologies or false consciousness requiring only theoretical demystification. The political implication is clear: since these beliefs are embodied in the practical life of various strata they will form a strong unifying and perhaps conservative bond in practice. Demystification on the level of content in the name of science is not enough because real ways of life are at stake and it is a stance which lends itself to directiveness. Individuals and groups acquire the consciousness of their dependence on mythological representations of reality by ascending from the lower level to the higher and relating this to practical life. This act in itself is political because it alters the conception of the world which people have and upon which they act. The contrast between thoughts and action, between a person's real activity in civil society and his conception of the world, could therefore become disjoined or displaced, but Gramsci points out that such a disjunction "is not simply a product of self-deception",[25] but can reveal a tacit grasp of the reality of the social order. Such changed conceptions can thus await the (socialist) social conditions that they anticipate. From the standpoint of the "life of great masses", these contrasts between thought and action probably signify, Gramsci believes, that there exists an embryonic conception of the world which appears in "flashes" or which has been borrowed from another group, remaining in "normal times"[26] submissive and subordinate. For these reasons, Gramsci maintains that since conceptions of the world are embodied in the practical activity of social groups and competing conceptions of the world are at stake, "a struggle of political "hegemonies" ",[27] or of philosophy in the broadest sense, "cannot be divorced from politics".[28] High-culture radical intellectuals must therefore lead "the simple" to a "higher conception of life"[29] (note the dialectical term higher here). The philosopher of praxis should not just introduce his science externally but should try to

> construct an intellectual-moral bloc which can make politically possible the intellectual progress of the mass and not only of small intellectual groups.[30]

It is not a question of introducing from scratch a scientific form of thought into everyone's individual life, but of "renovating and makin "critical" an already existing activity."[31]

Because civil society is a unity of force and consent within a given ruling-class hegemony, factors serving to perpetuate both consensus and dissensus will be inherently political. In the light of this, Gramsci advocates two procedures: (a) 'working up' people's common-sense beliefs to demonstrate the different kinds of philosophy present in them and to try to build this into a less mythological conception of the world, in the case of civil society entailing an insight into the nature of its hegemony or ultimate social reality; as well as (b) criticism of the philosophy of the high-culture intellectuals itself with which common sense is unified in the activity of the hegemonic bloc. The latter critique reverberates through civil society and helps to lay the foundations for a more enlightened common sense in the future since it is from professional philosophies and sciences that common sense tends to sediment itself. Procedure (a) has the effect of disturbing the self-evident quality of the conceptions of the world at lower levels of the social order, which in turn is also inherently political since it potentially disturbs that order which depends on common-sense conceptions cementing people into their social roles in the perpetuation of a ruling-class hegemony. The relationship between the two kinds of practical-critical activity constitutes a kind of political pincer movement closing from both ends of the cultural bloc, qualitatively changing the stuff of hegemonic reality since the conceptions of the world concerned are embodied in practical activity. For Gramsci it is always the case that

> The relation between common sense and the upper level of philosophy is assured by "politics".[32]

We might add that in putting forward the discrepancies in society between levels of awareness, types of knowledge, and levels of consciousness from archaic hangovers such as folklore to the highest hegemonic philosophy in the way described above, Gramsci saw himself as radically pulling together the two sides of the human science enterprise kept apart by Bukharin and the positivist sociology Gramsci criticized, i.e. subject and object, knower and known, conceived of as comprising social scientists on the one hand and the passive masses (the object) on the other. If the intellectuals of high culture recognize that they are organically related to their object of enquiry through common philosophies and being part of a hegemonic field, then their specialized culture (and they themselves) can remain in contact with "the source of the problems it sets out to study".[33] When men are in conscious control of the forces history has bequeathed to them and are truly rationally acting in the world, science and its objects and knowledge and purposes would be one. The objects of study and the subjects would coincide in practical activity:

> Only by this contact does a philosophy become "historical", purify itself of intellectualistic elements of an individual character and become "life".[34]

Through processes of active critical understanding of their place in a hegemonic field, individuals are, as we saw in the previous chapter, through the agency of the party brought through a series of phases of self-awareness to the level of a more coherent and critical conception of the world – a kind of ideological molecular transformism. This process goes "*beyond common sense*",[35] i.e. beyond purely economic-corporate consciousness. Such an achievement has far-reaching political consequences, even though it would not be regarded as a political action in the accepted sense. Gramsci wrote in *L'Ordine Nuovo*:

> Every mutation of individual consciousness, in so far as it is simultaneously effected throughout the whole popular mass – will this not have unimaginable creative results?[36]

Thus, through the creation of moral and intellectual unity between high-culture intellectuals and the masses, Gramsci hopes to extend such potentially critical awareness to create an "elite of intellectuals"[37] which can extend its circle of influence to other groups in order to win them over, to coalesce, to fuse, into alliance based on the historical experience of the growth of bourgeois hegemony, but in a process of conscious group transformism. Gramsci posits a detailed, practical-cultural formula for actively achieving the 'in-itself-for-itself' sequence of proletarian class-consciousness which Marx spoke of as inherent in the "being" of the working class appropriate to the epoch when the destiny of classes is being fought out in the ideological field. The content, types and function of the philosophies therefore become crucial. Gramsci saw the passing of economistic fatalistic Marxism as a milestone on this road; having played its historical role, it must be buried "with all due honours"[38] as a historically useful and necessary stage.

13 Inequality and the unity of mankind

The Crocean inseparability of thought and action in Gramsci means that ideas are a practical material force in a given configuration of civil society not only when, as Marx said, they "seize the masses" as a whole; indeed Gramsci's work throws into question what at later stages of development a material force might even constitute. The act of becoming aware (as mentioned earlier in regard to conscious molecular transformism within politicizing organizations such as the party) or changing one's world conception is initially enshrined in a practical individual, who is a philosopher, an intellectual, indefinable outside his relations with other men in civil society. And civil society is life itself, since life can only be hegemonic social life in a given historical bloc. Quantitatively multiplied and extended through group coalescence such a change in consciousness becomes a qualitative institutional aspect of the process of reality, embodied in practical activity. And should the conceptions in men's minds become disjoined from their practical activity in the process, this only serves as a necessary condition for a future change in that activity. As part of a cultural movement aimed at replacing old conceptions of the world at all levels in order to create elites of intellectuals (in Gramsci's sense), this activity ultimately gives "personality to the amorphous mass element" which is what "really modifies the 'ideological panorama' of the age."[1]

Gramsci was, as we have seen, well disposed towards the idealists' view that we only know what we do and he wished to bring into existence the unity of man which the idealists had expressed as Spirit. But it would be erroneous to see Gramsci's activistic cultural Marxism as idealist in any Platonic or Berkeleian sense, for he saw consciousness and reality as inseparably unified in practice, not as separate domains.[2] Furthermore, it would also be wrong to argue that Gramsci's aim of modifying the ideological panorama floats above the 'economic base' and is therefore of no avail for changing society, for such a view assumes a crude base/superstructure dualism which Gramsci was trying to move beyond. In so far as the change of ideological horizon is a process (not an unconditioned leap) embodied in acting individuals and groups, then such achievement, in Gramsci's terms, of a higher, critical, conception of the world (on all levels) qualitatively and cumulatively changes the very practical stuff of social reality. And since this reality is a hegemonic one, constituted over time in the image of a ruling class, such acts are political; either in so far as they change activity or in so far as they prepare a foundation of dual consciousness which anticipates and can by its presence in the society hasten the new social reality with which the changed conception of the world will be congruent. The linkage of this process to the "economic moment" is dialectically presupposed, otherwise modifications of the ideological panorama could not exist. (More on this shortly.) This view means, as we have seen, that conceptions of the world and the contest of competing hegemonies are, therefore, in the higher stages of development of Western societies where the development of classes has entered the arena of ideological conflict, an important terrain of political conflict. By moving away from vulgar Marxism Gramsci effectively provided a wider definition of politics which he felt was more appropriate to the stage of development of modern Western societies as well as potentially less amenable to elitist party direction.

This theoretical shift (corresponding to a historical shift) towards conceptualizing the clash of competing conceptions of the world as embodied in practical activity on a number of levels, and away from economic-corporate questions, redefined the political as being about the practice and articulation of everyday life itself and its possible greater rationality. For Gramsci was talking about the total unity of theory and practice, means and ends, the 'rational and the real' in no other possible context than that of all levels of practical social life. This view has interesting consequences for how inequality is to be theorized. Orthodox Marxist analysis tends to root social inequality rather statically in the 'economic base', in the relationship of classes to capital within the relations of production and then theorizes the various correct or false ideological perceptions people are held to have of their structural location so defined. An exemplar of this tendency is Frank Parkin, who claims that "Although there is a factual and material basis to class inequality, there is more than one way in which it can be interpreted",[3] and advances a typology of three meaning systems upon which the working class are said to draw for such interpretations.[4] This kind of analysis is an example of the employment of one of the base/superstructure, infrastructure culture, materiality/thought, material conditions/ideational factors, social being/consciousness arsenal of dualisms in sociological theory stemming from its roots in the traditional philosophy of mind and in particular from the famous Marxian inversion of Hegel, metaphysically interpreted.[5] As we have seen Gramsci, however, theorizes the relative autonomy of the superstructural element of civil society as a level of cultural integration (philosophy, common sense, etc.) the existence of which presupposes a high level of socio-economic development. Since reality for all people is constituted in a given ensemble of social relations, in accordance with their particular world views, the very fabric of practical (hegemonic) social reality is, one could say, 'ultimate reality', there being no external standpoint to it. Raymond Williams has eloquently captured Gramsci's meaning of hegemony as supposing the existence of

> something which is truly total, which is not merely secondary or superstructural, like the weak sense of ideology, but which is lived at such a depth, which saturates the society to such an extent, and which . . . even constitutes the limit of common sense for most people under its sway.[6]

For Gramsci, his view of human society is "the absolute secularisation and earthliness of thought, an absolute humanism of history",[7] so the potent question then becomes why people's lives are not unified, in the sense of their consciousness of what they are doing being at present in apparent discord with their activity when there is no external force which need perpetuate this situation, i.e. why the real is not rational. Paraphrasing the eleventh Thesis on Feuerbach Gramsci says that the "active man-in-the-mass" understands the world in some way in so far as he transforms it, but he has no "clear theoretical consciousness of his practical activity".[8] That is to say he acts relatively passively at a lower level of consciousness with no conception of his dependence on being an element in a historically sedimented hegemonic force. Because thought and activity are intertwined in this way in the hegemonic social fabric which constitutes people's lives, the philosophies or conceptions of the world are potentially subject to politicizing changes of awareness and eventually to their fusion with the people's intentions and actions. Thus for Gramsci

> Everything is political, even philosophy or philosophies . . . and the only "philosophy" is history in action, that is, life itself.[9]

Gramsci also assumes the Marxian view that human nature is the "ensemble of social relations", i.e. that since man becomes there is no man in general but only what men in specific social relations can potentially become given the level of development of productive forces. He says that at a very generalized level conceptions such as

Spirit, Utopia and God can be seen to have been elaborated at various stages in the "continual travail of history"[10] to express the aspirations and unrealized potentialities of the epochs of history, with such 'idealistic' conceptions capable of becoming real with the passage to freedom. Probably because he saw human life in the integrated practical way elaborated here and saw the aim of freedom fused with its practical means in the organic process of realization of a counter hegemony-as-reality, he does not want to pose freedom abstractly as an end-state or as a doctrinaire goal. There is, therefore, probably more than just prison censorship behind the phenomenon of Gramsci's very rare systematic use of the term socialism. Gramsci is sympathetic towards idealist philosophies of history because they have expressed a possible unity of mankind, as yet unrealized or unrealizable during the historical process:

> One could also say that the nature of man is "history" and, in this sense, given history as equal to spirit, that the nature of man is spirit if one gives to history precisely this significance of "becoming" which takes place in a "concordia discors" [discordant concord] which does not start from unity, but contains in itself the reasons for a possible unity.[11]

Following that principle, Gramsci thus interprets the historical significance of the Hegelian system in the same terms that Lukács did, i.e. that it rehearsed in speculative theory the optimistic possibilities of Reason at the beginning of the bourgeois epoch because the conditions for its fuller realization in practice had not matured. He also points out that Croce's "utopistic" dialectic is intended as a purely conceptual one in anticipation of the ending of social contradictions.[12] It is this historical perspective on the development of societies to a point where "Spirit" and Utopia are capable of being made real when the 'realm of necessity' is transcended which enables Gramsci to formulate equality and inequality historically in terms which seem to bring him close to Habermas's notion of the realization of conditions enabling undistorted communication.

A short recapitulation of an argument from the earlier discussion of the relation of forces in the social formation will be advisable to bring this out clearly. For Gramsci, the "economic moment" is only a minor determinant both in analysis and in reality in the epoch in which he is writing since its relatively stunted presence as a determinant at the current stage of social development is a remnant of its more important presence at an earlier stage as the sphere which threw forth fundamental classes based in the relations of production. At the later stage, therefore, conflicts exist on a higher, moral, cultural plane than the merely economic-corporate level since the goals of classes are being fought out in the domain of ideology. To put it another way, the satisfaction of material needs makes possible the shift of significant conflicts and creativity on to the plane of culture, morals, aesthetics and conscience. And the transcendence of the economic-corporate consciousness towards the higher moral interests of a unified mankind is made possible by the level of socio-economic development although the economic moment is always present as a presupposition, but of less determinacy in a unity with, in Croce's terms, the moral will. (In a sense this has always been so to various extents but men have not been conscious of it.) But the orthodox Marxist analysis still roots inequality solely in the material economic base and statically looks for interpretations of this inequality within the superstructure when at later stages the determinacy of the economic moment has been lessened and superstructural elements virtually constitute the hegemonic reality.

Now, in accordance with Marx's dictum that the essence of man is the "ensemble of social relations", it is clear that the stage of development of the social formation in general has always carried with it an extent to which the potentialities for further development of the society are not realized in accordance with the level of development reached. And, coinciding with this, various ways in which such unrealized potential is conceptualized (e.g. Spirit, unity of Man, God, etc.) by high-culture intellectuals and variously interpreted at lower levels in practical activity in common sense, religion, folklore, which orient people and represent their self-understanding of their activity in that epoch. In the current stage, then, social development has satisfied basic human needs such as hunger and survival and so has shifted the terrain upon which men realize their nature as determined by that level of development. In the West it is the ethical-political realm of the highly developed civil societies which increasingly moves to the centre of this realization. Gramsci writes:

> That the objective possibilities exist for people not to die of hunger and that people do die of hunger, has its importance . . . But the existence of objective conditions, of possibilities or of freedom is not yet enough: it is necessary to "know" them, and know how to use them . . . That ethical "improvement" is purely individual is an illusion and an error: the synthesis of the elements constituting individuality is "individual", but it cannot be realised and developed without an activity directed outward, modifying external relations both with nature and, in varying degrees, with other men, in the various social circles in which one lives, up to the greatest relationship of all, which embraces the whole human species.[13]

In such a milieu man's existence remains essentially political although "it is through the activity of transforming and consciously directing other men that man realises his "humanity", his "human nature" ".[14] For Gramsci, the moment of "catharsis", the transition to the realm of freedom, transforms the structure of society into a *means* of life and freedom and a "source of new initiatives"[15] but always with the level of socio-economic development, with the efficient satisfaction of needs, etc., present as a presupposition. In the era of the integrated, highly developed civil society and hegemonic bloc, the extent of the realization of equality is then bound up with the kind of 'human nature' realizable in such a society, which at the current stage is focused into the possibilities of the ethico-political domain. This might include, schematically but I think consistently with Gramsci's intention, elements of moral, spiritual, interactional and communicative life and comprise activity defined by aesthetics, ethics, responsibility, integrity, human self-fulfilment, respect for persons, democracy, community, and so on. Higher stages of social development, of civil society and in particular the ongoing creation and realization of a new counter-hegemony, makes possible the solution of problems in these areas and their creative satisfaction to a high degree of profound fulfilment. (Habermas would express this as the achievement of conditions permitting undistorted communication.) Not only could the orthodox treatment of equality not deal with it in the above terms, but it also has two other flaws: first the general one that the dualistic, metaphysical hangover in the analysis leads to an archaic nineteenth-century assumption that inequality must be analytically rooted in the 'material' base of society, the true solid reality, and in the variable, fallible, fragile interpretations of that reality at the level of consciousness. But this view does not recognize that in the relations between men consciousness plays a part in every aspect as an indispensable prerequisite. Second, assuming 'material' inequality to connote discrepancies among men on the level of the satisfaction of hunger or physical survival, then such a formulation is today an archaic one derived from an earlier stage of social development when those were issues more extensively either actually facing or dividing men on that level. (I will mention shortly the question of other elements which might also be termed 'material', such as the unequal distribution of income, rewards, etc.)

The spiritual unity of man for Gramsci constitutes an overall historical process, stretching from the distant past when, at lower stages of development, it was variously interpreted in its unrealized and unrealizable reality in terms of Spirit or Utopia or as God who was the perfect counterpart of an imperfect world. Thus equality is to be judged today against the historical extent to which the unity of man has been self-consciously realized, seen as the total process of its past elaboration (as an absolute presupposition) sustained in consciousness as history blindly laid the socio-economic and technical foundations for its greater realization as a reality. It was always, Gramsci said, a "possible unity". At the present stage of development the transcendence of the economic moment and its inclusion as an element in the integrated ethico-political terrain of civil society, means that that putative unity of man has spontaneously moved closer towards becoming a reality. It now requires to be consciously moved towards full realization, given that other necessary social conditions have matured sufficiently. Thus equality and inequality are discernible from a higher stage to be two aspects of a historical process moving towards a unity of mankind but shifting the stress of their unity with the level of social development; such that at later stages they become expressible as questions of conscious association, fulfilment and unity within civil society. When people become conscious at whatever level of their conceptions of the world and internalize a new morality then the stuff of social reality is potentially furthered towards the realization of the true, real fusion of civil society with political society. Indeed, the very perception of equality in these historical terms is indicative of a higher stage towards its realization; in the Marxian realm of freedom, and increasingly as its development approaches, equality and inequality and men's experience of their relations with one another on many dimensions move closer. Gramsci writes:

> In history real "equality", that is the degree of "spirituality" reached by the historical process of "human nature" is to be identified in the system of "private and public", "explicit and implicit" associations whose threads are knotted together in the "State" and in the world political system. We are dealing here with "equalities" experienced as such between the members of an association, and "inequalities" experienced between one association and another. These are equalities and inequalities which are valid in so far as people, individually or as a group, are conscious of them.[16]

I would think, therefore, that Gramsci would have agreed with Dahrendorf's remark that "inequalities among men follow from the very concept of societies as moral communities".[17] Although Gramsci would have added that in the realm of freedom society would be likely still to be characterized by unequal distributions of income, wealth, power, skill, etc. But these would not be experienced as inequality with the same moral opprobrium as at present since a truer community would exist with common aims comprised of men who were self-consciously able to realize their individuality in relation to others in a conscious association in which the very definitions of inequality and injustice have changed. At such a stage (of which the present beginnings of growth of the ethico-political realm in the developed civil society is but a precursor) the realization of 'human nature' would be the realization of men's co-operative conscious, responsible "direction of each other" against a presupposition of material satisfaction and consciousness of (and thus mastery of) the remaining *unequal* distributions which would then be experienced rather as *uneven* distributions.

Until the moment of "catharsis" has been willed into existence, its presupposition is the active creation now, but as part of the same world historical process, of the "ideological panorama" I expounded from Gramsci earlier, which in its embodiment in human activity, qualitatively changes the nature of the social configuration of civil society towards the practical realization of the new order. In this programme Gramsci has a place for the high-culture intellectual, who could for Gramsci even achieve the status of a great individual philosopher. He or she would be equivalent in the elaboration of a counter conception of the world appropriate to proletarian hegemony to Croce in the development of the hegemonic bourgeois culture of Italy.[18] Such a philosopher must be capable, however, of "reliving concretely the demands of the massive ideological community"[19] and elaborating a doctrine amenable to collective absorption. Echoing perhaps Marx's famous formulation of the proletariat as the heart and philosophy as the head of the revolution, Gramsci says that the popular element "feels" but does not always know or understand its situation, whilst the high-culture intellectuals know and understand but do not feel the passions of the people. This is why Gramsci insists that the gap between high-culture intellectuals and masses can only remain unbridged if popular feelings are studied simply as "something inert and negligible". The new conception must maintain what we might call a metabolism with the passions of the people to avoid a merely mechanical relationship which would be "bureaucratic and formal". The relationship must be an organic one in which "feeling-passion becomes understanding and thence knowledge" which is the true relationship of representation upon which to realize a genuinely shared life.[20] The kind of dynamic contact with the people Gramsci has in mind is one which "tends continually to raise new strata of the population to a high cultural life", as opposed to, for example, that of the Roman Catholic Church which he says maintains a purely mechanical contact, "an external unity based in particular on the liturgy and on a cult visually imposing to the crowd".[21]

But the new world conception must not remain purely as high culture. Initially it forms the lived culture of a small group, but can at some point through practical initiative make "the passage to the morality appropriate to it" and become "the political action dependent on it".[22] That is, it passes into a new, integrated, 'rationally' consenting hegemony, the unity of the philosophy and of life. The partial conception then comes to "live historically", socially, as a "concrete universal".[23] Gramsci says of the transition from the new generalized philosophy to lived reality that it is the point at which "contemplation" aims rather at modifying the world, connecting itself directly with the self-conscious creative transformation of men's lives and become therefore, in the act of praxis, "rational".[24] This stage constitutes a "single cultural "climate" ".[25] Moreover, Gramsci neither made a complete break with idealist philosophy nor did he fall short of the secular Marxist project through a regression into it, as some Marxist commentators have maintained. As I have shown, he sees the past genesis of this kind of theory and its continuation as related to the hegemonies of various social groups and as the anticipatory elaboration of an unrealized Utopian human community, the blindly developing real conditions for the realization of which can at a certain stage be harnessed and directed in practice. He says that "all critique itself will have its own speculative phase which marks its apogee" when the hegemony of the group of which it is the expression is beginning to disintegrate "molecularly"[26] (as in the Italian case with Croce and Gentile). The question for Gramsci is, therefore, whether this apogee cannot be the "beginning of an historical phase of a new type" when under the realm of freedom an idealist dialectic actually adequately articulates the new rational order.[27] At the current stage of development of Western societies it would seem to be consistent with Gramsci's position *not* to try to make a break with idealism or to turn away from theorizing about the spiritual unity of mankind; but on the contrary positively to encourage such a critique, on the ground that at a higher stage of development even beyond Gramsci the urgency for such an elaboration is even greater, since in Marxist terms surely the hour of the practical elimination of social contradictions and the real possibility for the unity of mankind which such theory putatively articulates draws closer.

As the essential element in the cultural movement, however, Gramsci pleads that high-culture intellectuals should not desert (as did Erasmus the culture of the Reformation) the progressive, absolutely secular, humanist, practical-critical cultural movement of Marxism simply because of the revealed sterility of its vulgar mechanical mode (he has in mind Croce here).[28] No further elements of the philosophy of praxis should be lost to modern (Italian) idealist high culture in that way, but rather intellectuals should aspire to create within its original impulse a "new elixir".[29] In an elegant and heroic passage, Gramsci affirms again this world-historical conception of the creation of the new State and advocates its anticipatory "romantic" articulation in the process of its realization:

> The affirmation that the philosophy is a new, independent and original conception, even though it is also a moment of world historical development, is an affirmation of the independence and originality of a new culture in incubation, which will develop with the development of social relations. What exists at any given time is a variable combination of old and new, a momentary equilibrium of cultural relations corresponding to the equilibrium of social relations. Only after the creation of the new State does the cultural problem impose itself in all its complexity and tend towards a coherent solution. In any case the attitude to be taken up before the formation of the new State can only be critico-polemical, never dogmatic; it must be a romantic attitude, but of a romanticism which is consciously aspiring to its classical synthesis.[30]

If one is concerned with the possibilities of furthering social processes towards a new social order at the present stage of social development, there is a profound lesson to be learned from Gramsci. That is, the need for the continuous "romantic" posing of the ethico-political problem of humanity in 'universal' terms (even 'idealistically') before and as an essential part of the process of creation of the new social order rather than eschewing such critique because such problems seem to be the particularistic mystifications of the bourgeoisie's interests. Gramsci would have maintained that the historical process is progressively moving towards putting the concerns of mankind as a whole on the agenda, so such activity would potentially ensure the realization of the unity of mankind as a concrete totality at a stage when such problems can really be solved in practice because a living culture would have been formed which had already envisaged their solution in theory.

Part four

Early critical theory: the sociology of praxis

The opportunity for relative emancipation from social determination increases proportionately with insight into this determination.

Karl Mannheim

14 Horkheimer in context

Perhaps the classical statement of the nature and aims of 'critical' social theory was made by Max Horkheimer in his often-quoted article 'Traditional and Critical Theory' of 1937,[1] a text which can serve for present purposes as epitomizing the sociological tradition of the Frankfurt School of which Habermas is the heir. Traditional theory for Horkheimer is that type of theory which he says became the dominant mode in the natural sciences, involving the elaboration of a contradiction-free theoretical system amenable to hypothesis formation, mathematization and the gathering of data. As both Lukács and Gramsci also pointed out, in the natural sciences this kind of theory has led to great success and many schools of sociology have scientistically sought to adopt a similar mode of theory in which a stress is placed on the investigation of facts. Horkheimer means what we would refer to as theory conforming to what philosophers term the hypothetico-deductive nomological model of science which is still often advocated for sociology today. In the research practice informed by this ideal

> The phenomenologically oriented sociologist will indeed claim that once an essential law has been ascertained every particular instance will, beyond any doubt, exemplify the law . . . There is always, on the one hand, the conceptually formulated knowledge and, on the other, the facts to be subsumed under it. Such a subsumption or establishing of a relation between the simple perception or verification of a fact and the conceptual structure of our knowing is called its theoretical explanation.[2]

Historically, this kind of theory has its origins in the tasks set by the sciences in the bourgeois period and in the technological advances which took place. It is to be located in the context of real social processes which have occurred in European societies and at a particular stage in the development of the division of labour. Its use has been for the domination and manipulation of nature for various purposes, as in the case of astronomy for use, say, in navigation. When the bourgeois class was forming itself in a feudal society the "purely scientific theory which arose with it tended chiefly to the break-up of the status quo"[3] and this kind of theoretical thinking had the positive social function of transforming older ways of thinking and furthering technical development. But it is this type of theory which, even as societies were transformed, became detached from its original application and became "absolutized", as though it were

> grounded in the inner nature of knowledge as such or justified in some other ahistorical way, and thus it became a reified, ideological category.[4]

For Horkheimer the process of social differentiation which has characterized the growth and expansion of bourgeois society brought with it also the individual experience of consciously having to conduct one's own life morally, responsibly and calculatively in a society which confronted the atomized individual as a massive mechanism outside his control. Horkheimer distinguishes this dualism of individual activity and social passivity at the level of the totality in the Hegelian terms that the activity of "society is blind and concrete, that of individuals abstract and conscious".[5] He maintains therefore that society is, through its individuals, "an active subject, even if a non-conscious one".[6] Echoing Lukács's interpretation that traditional European philosophy ultimately foundered on the problem of the givenness of reality, Horkheimer says that these social processes led to the Kantian interpretation of the nature of knowledge as the result of "passive sensation and active understanding",[7] which articulated the fact that the world of objects is judged by people whose self-experience is that of the monad. The objectivity, the individual experience and the concepts he brings to bear on it are all dialectically produced by an activity that is itself determined by "the very ideas which help the individual to recognise that world and to grasp it conceptually".[8] Again following Lukács, Horkheimer sees the epistemological core of bourgeois thought as being therefore the individualistic subject-object dualism in which "an ego imagines itself to be autonomous".[9] This theoretical tradition stems from the problematic and apparently inexplicable nature-like character of human suffering and wretchedness, despite men's rational intentions, which experience lies at the heart of the alienating effect of human institutions:

> The collaboration of men in society is the mode of existence which reason urges upon them, and so they do apply their

> powers and thus confirm their own rationality. But at the same time their work and its results are alienated from them, and the whole process with all its waste of work-power and human life, and with its wars and all its senseless wretchedness, seems to be an unchangeable force of nature, a fate beyond man's control.[10]

Traditional theory, embedded as it is in this social process, has performed a positive function, however, and Horkheimer affirms that it has a usefulness and is in demand. But in its theoretical construction, and in its elimination of contradictions and hypotheses, it is still "part of general social activity"[11] and must be seen as the product of definite groups in society existing under specific social conditions. The variously conscious levels of activity in the social totality which simultaneously go to make up the subject of comprehension and the object comprehended provide a two-sided dialectic: there is in addition to the traditional attitude, "a human activity which has society itself for its object".[12] This is the "critical attitude" which seeks to question those blind forces which arbitrarily govern individuals rather than merely intending to seek the "better functioning of any element in the structure".[13] Horkheimer says that the attitude informs a "critical theory" which considers

> the overall framework which is conditioned by the blind interaction of individual activities (that is, the existent division of labor and the class distinctions) to be a function which originates in human action and therefore is a possible object of planful decision and rational determination of goals.[14]

It is important to notice that for Horkheimer, since he is developing Marx's position here, the "critical attitude" is not intended only as a value-judgment about how society ought to be organized, but is dialectically implied by the traditional theoretical stance, thus *necessarily* built into a developed and differentiated social totality which operates largely blindly and tends to move beyond itself. Horkheimer is seeking to unite social science and societal indictment in one scheme. So long as society "lacks reason"[15] in the sense mentioned, then the concepts used by men of the critical mind always contain a tension between recognition of the categories of society in their usage in the routine order of society and the realization that they must also be condemned since the structures they represent are not the creations of a "unified, self-conscious will".[16] For the traditional theorist the facts grasped by social scientific conceptual systems are "external to the theoretical thinking", while the critical attitude, *even though* it "as a whole might well be of service in theoretical work carried on within reality as presently ordered",[17] regards objective realities given in perception in a different way. In so far as they are products which in principle should be under human control (and, in the future at least, Horkheimer confidently claims, "will in fact come under it") these realities "lose the character of pure factuality."[18]

Herbert Marcuse's articles from the 1930s also evince similar theoretical and practical preoccupations to those of Horkheimer and he defends a similar structured dualism of critical theory and, in this instance, "positivism", in a dialogue with the logical positivists of that time.[19] In Marcuse's case, the dialectical unity of critical theory and positivism is polemically more sharply etched, centring on their respective methodological attitudes towards the concept of essence. Marcuse emphatically rejects the conflation of appearance and reality in the writings of the positivists because he believes that every theory that attempts to do this makes the "same sacrifice of critical reason"; that is, all facts become "equi-valent" so that we merely recognize facts. This means that there is no tension between the facts and what they could be or ought to be, which can exercise critical reason. Positivism, says Marcuse,

> adheres to the bourgeois ideal of presuppositionless pure theory in which the absence of 'ethical neutrality' or the commitment of taking a position signifies delinquency in rigour.[20]

Marcuse insists on the justificatory nature of all sociological enquiry which takes facts as the final arbiter of truth since the world of facts is dominated by minority powers concerned with its preservation, despite "the already real possibility of another form of reality".[21] Against such a positivism which would take that unequal reality as read, Marcuse opposes a critical theory concerned with the Marxian conception of the essence of man as being "the task of a rational organisation of society to be achieved through practice that alters its present form".[22] In this perspective of commitment to the real fulfilment of human desires (when understood not as solely opinion or value-judgment but as the realizable human potentialities at a given time) the relationship today between existence and essence in this sense is for Marcuse posited as "a historical disproportion"[23] between the real possible potentialities of the epoch and their *un*-realization. The critical theorist gives the *inherent* but unrealized possibilities of a social structure a precise theoretical meaning.

Returning to Horkheimer, he maintained that the critical theorist was opposed both to the ego-centredness of bourgeois philosophy's starting point as well as to the pseudo-collectivist unanimity of nationalist ideologies which exalt a rhetorical "we" illusorily, presenting the individual unproblematically against an apparently constituted but actually internally rent society. Rather, the critical position transcends both in favour of the projected rational organization of society inherent in the present order through the realization of which alone can the opposition of the "individual's purposefulness, spontaneity, and rationality and those of the work process relationships"[24] be transcended. In one Lukacsian passage, Horkheimer focuses on the status of the changeability of the subject and object co-ordinates as being the point around which critical and traditional thinking revolve. He states:

> In reflection on man, subject and object are sundered; their identity lies in the future, not in the present. The method leading to such an identification may be called explanation in Cartesian language, but in genuinely critical thought explanation signifies not only a logical process but a concrete historical one as well. In the course of it both the social structure as a whole and the relation of the theoretician to society are altered, that is both the subject and the role of thought are changed. The acceptance of an essential unchangeableness between subject, theory and object thus distinguishes the Cartesian conception from every kind of dialectical logic.[25]

Horkheimer also implicitly invokes the Lukácsian distinction between the actual and imputed class-consciousness of the proletariat, maintaining that if critical theory were to concentrate on the "feelings and ideas of one class at any given moment" it would be "social psychology"[26] which cannot provide a true picture of the existential tendency and potential of the proletariat's historical situation. It would remain a traditional theory enterprise, i.e. exemplifying the Lukácsian "contemplative" standpoint, theorizing immediacy. Importantly for our concerns in this study Horkheimer says of the critical theorist that "his own thinking should in fact be a critical, *promotive* factor in the development of the masses"[27] and not just passive, external and separated:

> If, however, the theoretician and his specific object are seen as forming a dynamic unity with the oppressed class, so that his presentation of societal contradictions is not merely an expression of the concrete historical situation but also a force within it to stimulate change, then his real function emerges.[28]

It is this idea of theory being an element in a phase of action, an element in either furthering social tendencies revealed in historical research towards new social forms or by bringing to men consciousness of the hypostatized social forces of their own making rather than necessarily any particular set of concepts employed which distinguishes critical from traditional theory for Horkheimer. Given that the concepts employed will be changeable depending on the stage of social development being theorized, then it is the critical attitude informing the analysis which is important. (I will return to the question of which categories might distinguish the two approaches later on.)

In the same way that Hegel (as we saw in Part two) exalts the higher stage of comprehension of the self-mediating totality achieved by Reason (*Vernunft*) over the more formal and lifeless abstractions of the Understanding (*Verstand*), but is dialectically compelled to retain the latter as an indispensable prerequisite in theory and in practice so Horkheimer, more sociologically, sees traditional theory too as necessary (even in future ages), fulfilling a technical, orientating function in society:

> The traditional type of theory, one side of which finds expression in formal logic, is in its present form part of the production process with its division of labour. Since society must come to grips with nature in future ages as well, this intellectual technology will not become irrelevant but on the contrary is to be developed as fully as possible.[29]

This is an important statement since it provides a more realistic and sober judgment from the critical perspective on the status of sociology, both in present society and in a potential socialist society, than is often found in some more extravagant Utopian contemporary Western Marxist statements. Much Marxist theory writes sociology off on various methodological and political grounds as being inevitably metaphysical or conservative, doomed to a historical demise under socialism. This attitude has its theoretical origins in the early Lukacs, for whom sociology was "contemplative", made a fetish of facts, and presupposed an objectivity which could become conscious of itself in the victory of the proletariat, thus absorbing subject and object of enquiry. It is also found in Gramsci, for whom, as we saw in Part three, any sociology that was not political sociology was possible but could only deal with "frivolous" matters and was again irrelevant or transcended in a truly self-determining society.

Hegel and Horkheimer (from their respective standpoints) would appear to have, within dialectics, a consistent position on this issue. In Hegel, the mutual presupposing of Reason and the Understanding, both at the conceptual level and as Reason being a higher developmental stage of experiential awareness of the self-objectivity of objects, was a dialectical necessity built into his system, which was the conceptual result and embodiment of world history. The Understanding constituted methodologically a necessary clarifying prerequisite to an appropriation of reality by Reason. Similarly, Horkheimer has, I think, consistently developed the implication of Marx's observation in *Capital*, Volume III, that Nature would always remain a "realm of necessity",[30] thus continually involving men having to organize in societies (thus creating a social order) in order to satisfy their needs in the face of the exigencies of its domination. This is a logical consequence in view of the wide social co-operation instituted in the bourgeois epoch which socialism would inherit as a presupposition and the endemic dependence of men on that part of Nature external to them. Horkheimer observes the alienating effects of such social structures on subsequent generations and bases critical theory in providing knowledge which would reclaim and demythologize rather than take as read (as traditional theory would) those blindly developed structures and their self-interpretations, so that men can understand and so change the *status quo* they ongoingly unconsciously create and recreate. This position would appear to be dialectically necessary conceptually, *vis-à-vis* traditional theory, as well as socially necessary because of the reality of the established institutional order which perennially mediates the domination of nature and which continually reinstates itself: "Critical thought has a concept of man as in conflict with himself until this opposition is removed."[31] But the removal of that (social) opposition in Frankfurt Marxism is clearly a process *towards* its total removal, never an absolute end-state.

To amplify that argument about the possible extent of disalienation envisioned in the dialectical universe of discourse (particularly as understood by the critical theorists), we can initially divert to Hegel and Lukács. It will be recalled from the discussion of Lukács in Chapter 5, that Lukács said in his own criticism of *History and Class Consciousness* in 1967 that the book made the crude error of equating alienation and objectification. It thereby enjoined a Hegelian abolition of all objectivity under communism which would virtually amount to no reality at all. But as I pointed out there, the conclusion of Hegel's voyage of experience in the *Phenomenology* by no means entails a projected total abolition of alienation, since 'total' self-recognition implies its Other (i.e. some grade of objectivity) in order to have existence *qua* complete self-recognition or Absolute Knowledge. The point is that the inherent logic of dialectics forced Hegel to posit a new mode of existence of Spirit as truth, rather than a simplistic Utopian, harmonious end-state, because otherwise no characterization of Absolute Knowledge was possible. Lukács's more secularized portrayal of the abolition of social reification in communism – the stage of the identical subject-object of history – for similar reasons could not, within the dialectical universe of discourse, imply what Lukács in 1967 claimed, i.e. "no reality at all". Or at least such a condition is theoretically problematic since dialectically speaking a tension must always exist between subjectivity and objectivity.

Horkheimer's commitment to the dialectical necessity of critical theory presupposes the Marxian notion of the practical necessity of societal organization *per se*, which also implies some social reification in order that human social existence can be defined at all. For Horkheimer, men are in conflict with their own institutional creations (what Horkheimer calls their "opposition") so long as they are unenlightened that the nullity and nature-like objectivity they encounter is of their own making. As we saw earlier, Horkheimer's view of the need for the praxical overcoming of that opposition meant an overcoming *towards*, but never reaching, total self-knowledge and self-determination, in the face of the eternal praxical creation and transcendence of human social *status-quo's*. It is of course exactly the all-important *extent* to which that "opposition" or reification can be expected to be mitigated or liberated through reflection or social reorganization in any new social order (always acknowledging that its absolute abolition is never possible) which has preoccupied Marxists since Lukács.[32] Drawing the threads of the argument together, we have seen that Horkheimer recognizes that the "realm of necessity" will continue to exist in human society as a realm of as-yet-unappropriated Nature (which remains in Hegel's terms "in-itself"). This view also connotes the related acknowledgment of that part of men's physical 'naturalness' which is given and determined to a greater or lesser extent outside their conscious control under all modes of social organization. Horkheimer affirms Marx's arguments from 1844 about the necessity of a certain degree of alienation in human life in the double sense of (a) aspects of Nature remaining as externally experienced by men even though they remain a self-conscious part of it; and (b) of an inter-generationally bequeathed institutional order organized to enable the satisfaction of men's needs in the face of Nature. Epistemologically speaking, this processual reified order would sustain inseparably a traditional theory of society as well as a critical one which presupposes 'dead', accumulated, sedimented knowledge produced by traditional theory in its quest to seek genetic knowledge of the reified society in order potentially to 'return' it to its producers. But this acknowledgment of the necessity of reification does not transform our image of man into one which sees men as falsely conscious automata condemned to live in a meaningless, purposeless and arbitrary world. Such a view would be abstract and would overlook the fact that alienation can never be absolute either in its penetration or in its abolition, but always exists as a process, as the *extent* to which men have overcome their own self-externalizations at various levels within the social totality. Horkheimer says of a human subject in such a world:

> If he encounters necessity which is not mastered by man, it takes shape either as that realm of nature which despite the far-reaching conquests still to come will never wholly vanish, or as the weakness of the society of previous ages in carrying on the

struggle with nature in a consciously and purposefully organized way.[33]

In arguing in this way Horkheimer inaugurated the characteristically Frankfurt position on this issue which embraced such a dialectical view of the definition of what it means to be human. Alfred Schmidt's excellent recent study *The Concept of Nature in Marx*,[34] which was originally a doctoral dissertation researched under Horkheimer and Adorno in the late 1950s, expounds the notion of the dialectical unity in Marx between the socially imprinted character of Nature and Nature's autonomous role in human affairs (point (a) above) from Marx's writings. Schmidt also provides textual backing, mainly from the mature texts such as *Capital* and the *Grundrisse* against interpretations of Marx angled towards ontological materialism, philosophical anthropology and a formalistic Engelsian dialectic within Nature as against a practical dialectic between man and Nature, as well as emphasizing the preservation in Marx's historical materialism of philosophy as a layer of critique; all of which are characteristic positions adumbrated by the critical theoreticians of the 1930s. Theodor Adorno, in accordance with reification in the sense (b) above, recently criticized Aldous Huxley's *Brave New World* because it conceived of humanity and reification as incompatible. In so arguing he, too, perceived a positive element of reification as an aspect of a dialectic of creative objectification defining an individual's project:

> Huxley cannot understand the humane promise of civilization because he forgets that humanity includes reification as well as its opposite, not merely as the condition from which liberation is possible but also positively, as the form in which, however brittle and inadequate it may be, subjective impulses are realized, not only by being objectified.[35]

Similarly, Marcuse in the 1960s criticized Norman O. Brown's vision of the restoration of a total unity, a complete fusion between inner self and the outside world, between subject and object, on the grounds that

> such a fusion would be the end of human life, in its instinctual as well as rational, unsublimated as well as sublimated, expressions. The unity of subject and object is a hallmark of absolute idealism; however, even Hegel retained the tension between the two, the distinction.[36]

And in the same critique, Marcuse is in line with Horkheimer's depiction of critical theory as feeding on the tension between a reified *status quo*, the forgotten creation of men, and the continual possibility of bringing those structures to the consciousness of their creators so that they cease less to impose on them, without implying an end-state of total social transparency. The dialectics of this position could perhaps be encapsulated as that the same historical practical process that enslaves men also defines their humanity through their efforts to appropriate and overcome its alienation. Marcuse, following Hegel's *Phenomenology* closely, thus says that Brown

> envisions an Absolute, a Totality, a Whole which swallows up all parts and divisions, all tensions and all needs, that is to say, all life. For such a totality does not exist in any sense or nonsense, and should not even be the vision of the free imagination because it is the negation of all freedom, and of all happiness (at least human happiness).[37]

Horkheimer had years before adumbrated this position, i.e. that the complex of different levels and functions of aspects of the totality, creates the "antagonistic whole of our life".[38] It is this whole which at one and the same time in its alienated objectivity creates and sustains traditional theory, critical theory as Reason and the perennial possibility of greater rational self-determination. Against Brown's absolutism, Marcuse thus allies himself with

> Reason as Freedom. Critical, not absolute vision; a new rationality, not the simple negation of rationality.[39]

There is an important sociological consequence of the general position outlined so far in this chapter. Seen in relation to such a totality and its development as described, it followed for Horkheimer that there inevitably enters into the actual work of the critical theoretician who sets himself up in opposition to society "knowledge and prognosis of relatively isolated facts, scientific judgements . . ."[40] Furthermore, although the generalized application of the traditional kind of thinking to society registers facts, the result of which is the enterprise of "statistics and descriptive sociology", this can, however, be "important for many purposes, even for critical theory".[41] Horkheimer even more emphatically retains traditional theory thus:

> Knowledge . . . is itself a thing which one generation passes on to another; to the extent that men must live, they need it. In this respect, too, then, the traditional scientists can be reassured.[42]

These judgments, to stress this point again, do not simply express an arbitrary option for a critical theory which can utilize handy mainstream sociological facts in a Utopian critique of society, but instead see critical theory as feeding on unrealized possibilities and presupposing accumulated knowledge in its critique:

> Knowledge in this traditional sense, including every type of experience, is preserved in critical theory and practice. But in regard to the essential kind of change at which the critical theory aims, there can be no corresponding concrete perception of it until it actually comes about.[43]

For Horkheimer, as for Weber, it is the higher stages of social development which produce an inherited status quo of an extra-ordinarily high degree of reified solidity. It is the sheer irrational weight of this which tends to submerge the rational critical impulse towards self-determination and, like Marcuse, he claims to be keeping it alive. He traces the hostility to critical theory, even though it is "the most advanced form of thought at present", to its departure from the conventional limitations of "verification and classification" by means of categories which are as "neutral as possible" which characterizes traditional theory; and to the unconscious fear in people's minds that critical thinking in such a reified world might "show their painfully won adaptation to reality to be perverse and unnecessary".[44]

To summarize so far: Horkheimer seeks to establish a logically, historically and sociologically necessary (i.e. not arbitrary) status for a social theory which criticizes the established, reified social reality and furthers its demise in the sense of revealing its pseudo-independence to be dependence on its ongoing unconscious human construction. It is an enterprise which is not at the same time stimulated solely by a value-judgment about a better society. The critical attitude draws upon and indeed presupposes the accumulated facts and knowledge about society gathered by traditional theory, which project is not rejected *tout court* but incorporated and transcended, although granted an autonomous validity in a unity with critical theory. Horkheimer elaborated this position in the 1930s partly in a dialogue with the Mannheimian sociology of knowledge which had gained a certain standing in Germany and was ostensibly dealing with similar problems relating to the social function of social theory and the question of social determination. He is sceptical though, about the famous notion of the stand point of the free-floating intelligentsia which, he claims, is underlain by a "formalistic concept of mind" and corresponds to the "abstract self-awareness typical of the savant", neutrally assuming there is "only one truth".[45] For Horkheimer, the enterprise of research into the social conditioning of knowledge and ideologies by the classical sociology of knowledge is not opposed "either in its aims or in its other ambitions to the usual activities that go on within classificatory science", i.e. it is a type of traditional theory. In the logic of his conception of the unity of traditional and critical theory he gives to the sociology of knowledge the indubitable and valuable status of a "whole field for theoretical work" but, since it is unreflexive in the sense of not promoting change of its objects, of not trying to reduce the tension between the individual's purposes and those of the thwarting social structures, he sees it as a "reaction to critical theory". The sociology of knowledge is a theory in which

> the self-awareness of thought as such is reduced to the discovery of the relationship that exists between intellectual positions and their social location. Yet the structure of the critical attitude, inasmuch as its intentions go beyond prevailing social ways of acting, is no more closely related to social disciplines thus conceived than it is to natural science . . . For men of the critical mind, the facts, as they emerge from the work of society are not extrinsic in the same degree as they are for the savant . . . But in so far as the objective realities given in perception are conceived as products which in principle should be under human control and, in the future at least, will in fact come under it, these realities lose the character of factuality.[46]

Horkheimer adds that the sociological conception of the intelligentsia as having "missionary functions" is an "hypostatization of specialized science" being elaborated in a period when the "forces of freedom in Europe are themselves disoriented" (1937). A concept of an intelligentsia which thus "claims to transcend party lines" is abstract and hides "the decisive questions".[47]

We can make some observations on Horkheimer's view of Mannheim and of sociology in general since this confrontation highlights some of the unique and contentious aspects of critical theory:

1 Horkheimer's last point may or may not have been a realistic political assessment of the practice of certain intellectuals at the time, but it is perhaps an obvious although none the less important point to make that it in no way engages the epistemological implications of the standpoints of classes versus that of the intelligentsia, nor the theory of perspectives in Mannheim.

2 In the terminology of the extended quotation above, critical theorists are surely also "savants". Horkheimer says of the class position of these theorists that the conflict between their insight and that of the proletariat does not have anything to do with "the class to which the theoretician belongs" nor with his income.[48] But it was the *outlook* of Mannheim's intelligentsia which was held to be more likely to be able better to arbitrate between *political* standpoints and they were only said to be a "relatively classless stratum"[49] in this respect, although they had a definite social basis, as is the case with the critical

theoretician. Also, the critical theoretician, as we have seen, proceeds from and his work necessarily contains and presupposes, "facts" and sedimented knowledge. So *in practice* all that seems to distinguish the critical theoretician from the sociologist of knowledge, *qua* traditional theorist, is his attitude. In addition to being a generalized commitment to dereification this is said to be also an undifferentiated commitment to "hasten developments which will lead to a society without injustice",[50] which commitment reflects the basic structure of society and its tendential potential in the way described before. (There are said to be methodological differences, too, according to Horkheimer and Marcuse which we will discuss in the next chapter.) However, when a sociologist of knowledge produces empirically knowledge of social objectivity, as a sociologist he is (like the critical theorist) automatically within the sociological tradition predisposed towards regarding it as related to a non-absolute, secular, man-made and self-sustaining entity – society. If a critical theoretician picks up that same knowledge which he then attempts to use in the same way critically to "promote" the development of the "masses" (Horkheimer never specifies what "promote" may imply, even initially, for practice), then *qua knowledge*, the "facts" involved remain the same. Moreover, merely embracing the attitude that social determination in general is potentially restorable to human control in some way, does not in that act of conception itself remove the character of its objectivity in the experience of the participants of society.[51]

3 Horkheimer is always reluctant to specify in the abstract what he regards as an adequate example of a critical theoretician successfully "furthering" the changing of the objects of social enquiry. This is perhaps a legitimate aspect of the 'proof of the pudding is in the eating'[52] praxical legacy of Marxism, which would imply that action to varying degrees authenticates itself in a new situation which would itself organically incorporate the previous change and imply a different theory for further action, and so on.[53] Horkheimer is thus alive to the limits of what can be stated about future possibilities or general consequences of action in the abstract within a practical-critical perspective. Surprisingly, then, his dichotomy between the pseudo-uncommitted intelligentsia on the one hand, producing neutral knowledge and the critical theoreticians on the other, is a formalistic device out of keeping with his dialectical view of the organic developed totality, which would imply in reality rather less difference between them. Horkheimer crassly and unfairly says at one point that the specialist sociologist's academic interest regards social reality as extrinsic to him and such a sociologist only exercises his interest in changing it through political parties and participation in elections, thus keeping apart the "tension" between the two interests. This is, however, a polemical point not essential for his argument, and which

simply exposes him to the same charge. Critical thinking, on the other hand, is said to be motivated by the effort "really to transcend the tension",[54] and "facts" are not "extrinsic in the same degree"[55] as they are for the sociologists of knowledge. (NB: Although they are still extrinsic!)

4 Against that 'social democratic' caricature of the sociologist's assumed inevitable position *vis-à-vis* changing the object of sociological enquiry, it can be objected that Horkheimer has first, to reiterate, unjustifiably polarized the sociological stance into either detached fact-committed or critical-committed. These are, however simply not real alternatives on his own arguments about the factual content of all social analysis because, seen developmentally, that knowledge has *become* relatively autonomous, i.e. 'factual'. Knowledge never was and can never be totally neutral even though, at higher stages of the development of a scientific specialism, it can appear to be so. By saying that the sociologists of knowledge were pursuing indifferent neutral knowledge when, seen developmentally all knowledge is in various ways partly heteronomous, Horkheimer inadvertently gives credence to the positivists' postulate of abstract, pre-suppositionless pure theory or knowledge. He is caught up for polemical reasons in an idealized mutually exclusive dualism, not heeding the historical social reality of sociology or of other sciences. Second, he has wrongly assumed that only a theory which self-consciously *conceives* of the changeability of its object, or of furthering dereification, does *in practice* actually contribute to a change in that object. He has agreed that the critical social theorist must promote change in his objects of enquiry, having acknowledged them to be reified human products which require to be 'returned' to their producers, but he does not come to terms with the fact that *all* theory has, to use a Hegelian term, a practical moment and thus potentially has practical consequences. By its very presence in some public, communicated form it can qualitatively alter a social configuration and therefore potentially mould future practice, *whether or not it is labelled 'critical'*. Consider Hegel's comment:

> Daily do I get more and more convinced that theoretical work achieves more in the world than practical. Once the realm of ideas is revolutionised, actuality does not hold out.[56]

If this practical principle is acknowledged, then important questions become what kind of knowledge is produced and the extent to which and the mechanisms whereby it is thus effective. Horkheimer is I think wrong, therefore, on at least this count, to assert that the object with which the scientific specialist (in this case the sociologist) deals "is not affected at all by his own theory".[57]

5 Neither does Horkheimer clarify the relationship in his Marxian

framework between (a) bringing to consciousness through critical theory an awareness of men's dependence on hypostatized social forces of their own making (a generalized commitment to dereification) and (b) the furthering, by representing the self-conscious of, historical tendencies understood as historically necessary (as in Lukács). Horkheimer is apparently committed to both but on his presentation the first aspect borders on truism and the other on mythology. The first commitment to the restoration to men's control of their alienated social externalizations taken on its own merits is problematic in critical theory, since how the theory is to be historically promotive in so returning social institutions to their producers is never specified. And this aspect is rendered even more vague by the knowledge that critical theory is not the only kind of historically and socially effective theory in practice. If these two points remain in obscurity, not adequately worked through, then critical theory is left with the rather truistic declaration that social institutions are the non-eternal reified products of human activity, an assumption upon which the secular enterprise of sociology in general thrives. Second, on his own terms within the dialectical universe of discourse, unless he can demonstrate that the critical commitment to the changeableness of subject, theory and object in practice is a commitment to furthering long-term historical tendencies, Horkheimer's position founders in arbitrariness, abstraction, and contemplation. He sees this and, following Engels and Lukács, declares that

> A consciously critical attitude, however, is part of the development of society: the construing of the course of history as the necessary product of an economic mechanism simultaneously contains both a protest against this order of things, a protest generated by the order itself, and the idea of self-determination for the human race, that is the idea of a state of affairs in which man's actions no longer flow from a mechanism but from his own decision. The judgement passed on the necessity inherent in the previous course of events implies here a struggle to change it from a blind to a meaningful necessity.[58]

It is this Marxian idea of theory becoming a "material force" which is important for Horkheimer as a vital hallmark of critical theory. Necessity is seen not merely as referring to an external, Nature-like social process, but as events or processes in society that can be mastered in a self-conscious, rational way.[59] In accepting this notion Horkheimer says that unfortunately the very idea of a transformed society has little widespread acceptance because of the sheer weight of the prevailing reality and its culture so that critical theory faces hostility; to which he adds the obvious need for its constant transmission. (We will see later how for critical theorists philosophy is held to keep the tenuous spark of criticism alight.) The existence of a circle of individuals who can transmit the theory will always be guaranteed by the continual creation in society of a "prevailing injustice"; although they are always spurred on by the knowledge of that injustice which brings its own obligations with it.[60] We have here, then, the classical Marxist putative coincidence of history, social tendency, injustice and moral obligations to remedy that injustice, without resort to an abstract model of the ideal state for man: the continuation of Marx's project set forth in *The German Ideology*. The main difference being that Horkheimer, although in the Marxist tradition, abstains from talking about the actual party organization usually regarded as required in practice consciously to aid furthering important class-based historical tendencies. Within his assumption about historical necessity Horkheimer (in order to avoid as Lukács did irrationalism, moral relativism and arbitrariness) posits the objective unity of the *status quo* with its beckoning, dialectically implied Other, always understood as a higher, better, more just, rational, free, state of affairs. But being within the practical-critical universe of discourse yet not talking specifically enough of practice, he is implicitly forced, however, to make a tacit assumption of the ultimate coincidence of the injustice, the perception of it as part of a tendency and the individuals who are best able to remedy it or who are in a position to do so. This is tantamount to a rationalistic faith in the triumph of Reason. He remarks as follows of the "numerically small groups of men" in whom the "truth" in this world-historical sense resides:

> History teaches us that such groups, hardly noticed even by those opposed to the status quo, outlawed but imperturbable may at the decisive moment become the leaders because of their deeper insight.[61]

A great deal hinges on that word "may". Like Gramsci, Horkheimer cannot conceive of another ideology than socialism being mobilized for very long or with any credibility, for it is assumed that historically necessary tendencies will always in the end be liberative and harnessed by the appropriately enlightened leaders.

On so many counts critical theory on Horkheimer's showing seems to move out of focus. Perhaps the problem lies in his tradition's self-posed weighty project of trying to unite facts and wishes, science and Utopia, sociology and critique simultaneously in one conceptual scheme. As a theoretical task this poses intractable problems since human historical praxis continually transcends and changes the nature of the (unjust, etc.) *status quo* and thus continually alters the range of possibilities which the theory is grappling to encompass. To the critical theoretician, however, the unacceptable alternative to this social science project seems to be *only* the positivist one of a separate morality based on factual knowledge.[62] (I will argue later on that this choice is chimerical.) Like Horkheimer and Marcuse we may for some of the reasons mentioned in this chapter also be pushed towards suggesting methodological features or special concepts as additional hallmarks of critical theory. This search is prompted by the awareness that on the level of knowledge and as located in a complex practical social formation, genetic work in the sociology of knowledge, for example, is, in the act of its public existence, potentially indistinguishable in its assumptions and results from critical theory. (See the quotation from Mannheim as motto to Part four of this study.)[63] Perhaps Horkheimer realized some of these problems when he disarmingly averred: "To transform the critical theory of society into a sociology is, on the whole, an undertaking beset with serious difficulties."[64] We will therefore now turn to some of those conceptual and methodological questions and their relation to the principle within the practical-critical perspective of the unity of the theoretical appropriation of socio-historical reality and its praxical conscious continuation into a more rational future.

15 Praxis and method

Methodologically speaking, Horkheimer claimed that the logical form of both critical and traditional theory was the same, at the level of connections between terms or statements within a theory. Logical necessity was distinguished from real necessity.[1] But in saying this, unlike Hegel, Marx and Marcuse, he did not distinguish between which of the concepts of the critical theory of society related to its appearance and which to its essence, and how this unity of the nominal and the real was to be investigated and analytically presented. Methodologically, Marx on the other hand musters his concepts, as does Hegel, in such a way as to appropriate the totality and construct it as a whole theoretically; in the case of Marx, this is prior to and furthers the real total appropriation of the totality by the proletariat in communism. In the case of the bourgeois capitalist mode of production the concept of essence carries the methodological connotation of relating to the production and expropriation of surplus value from its producers. (The concept of essence in Marx also carries the second connotation of referring to that cognized but presently fully unrealized, shifting social potential for a more rational organization of society made possible by the current level of development of the productive forces of society. But this potential is fettered by the archaic "ensemble of social relations" through which those forces are mediated. The methodological sense of the concept of essence is apparently related to this other general sense, since it is only at a certain stage of the development of society (the bourgeois epoch) that it develops as its essence the process of value production which coincides with the general potential for rational self-determination (its truth) of that stage. The problems in relating the two senses are, however, complex and beyond my present scope, but it is worth noting that in his essay "The Concept of Essence"[2] Marcuse confusingly conflates the two senses of essence mentioned here.)

Marx conceptualizes the essence of the bourgeois capitalist mode of production critically in the following way: commodities have common quality, beyond their physical properties, of being produced by abstract labour, the measure of exchange value. This abstract labour is a fraction of the total labour potential at society's disposal at a given point in time. The labour potential refers to the socially necessary labour for producing the commodity *at a given stage* of the development of the social relations of production, and so is variable.[3] The measure of exchange value in Marx is therefore related to how effectively labour power *could be* ('rationally') utilized in society given the current stage of the development of the forces of production. Since these forces are fettered by various social relations of production (which therefore hinder this *possible* utilization of labour power) then to analyse production in this way is for Marx inherently critical and therefore political, since it highlights the 'irrational' fettering of what is possible. The surface movement of capitalist production (analysable typically in terms of wages, prices and profit), its appearance, exists in a unity with the process of value production, its essence. The young Marcuse maintained that in Marx the first set of concepts (for example wages, prices and profit) focus on how the mode of production is organized, tending to consider its structure as eternal. The second set, on the other hand (relating to value production) critically shows the mode of production as containing the possibility of being organized differently. This is because this set implies surplus value, leading to the concept of expropriation and therefore to the historical class character of bourgeois society. Taken together, says Marcuse, the two sets of concepts form a critical analysis: taken separately, a conservative one.[4]

In Horkheimer's depiction of critical theory, too, we find a methodological orientation towards a (rational) future, towards how society *could be* organized, as well as towards viewing society as a whole, from which that orientation cannot be separated. Concepts which emerge under the influence of critical thought are "critical of the present", such that

> The Marxist categories of class, exploitation, surplus value, profit, pauperisation, and breakdown are elements in a conceptual whole, and the meaning of this whole is to be sought not in the preservation of contemporary society but in its transformation into the right kind of society.[5]

But Horkheimer stresses in addition, on the level of conceptual articulation, that critical and traditional theory differ on the question of the relationship between primary 'universal' propositions in the theory and reality, which difference points to a concomitant differing conception of the relationship between subject and object and eventually between theory and practice. Traditional theory (on the natural-science model) regards facts as examples or embodiments of classes in the theory, but in this system there can be no difference due to time between the unities in the system; and changes made in the theory are made because it is assumed that our earlier knowledge was deficient, or that the changes are a "substitution of some aspects of an object for others" rather than that the relationship to the object or "even the object itself may change without losing its identity".[6] For example, in relation to the evolution of living beings such logic cannot come to grips with the fact that "a person changes and yet is identical with himself".[7] The law-like explanation of traditional theory changes its conceptualization to emphasize different aspects of its object rather than seeing the object as having a changing structure of its own. A critical theory of society also begins with "abstract determinations" (Horkheimer follows Hegel and Marx's methodological terminology), in the case of the present era the Marxian ones of commodity, value, money and an economy based on exchange. However, this kind of theory is not satisfied to "relate concepts to reality by way of hypotheses"[8] as does traditional theory, but shows historically necessary social processes and is committed, as part of them – and this is the important distinction – to change their *blind* necessity into *conscious* necessity.

More specifically in relation to European societies, critical theory outlines the mechanism whereby bourgeois society, having dismantled feudal regulatory mechanisms, survived despite its anarchic principle, such analysis being "guided by concern for the future of the historical process" so delineated. The theory relates facts from concrete reality not by simple deduction of instances from classes, but shows the "inner dynamism"[9] of exchange relations, through a set of "existential judgements" which are not of a hypothetical character.[10] Critical theory draws on men's stored-up knowledge which is then related to the dynamism of the whole socio-historical process to bring out the total movement and tendency brought about by its inherent tensions: for example, the fact that the lowest strata have the most children is related in the theory to how an exchange economy necessarily leads to capitalism's 'industrial reserve army'. As in Lukacs it is in Horkheimer also the unity of the appropriation of past processes in their own objectivity and their furtherance in the present towards fulfilling their tendency in the future which gives critical theory its particular character. But on the level of conceptual articulation the difference between the two types of theorizing (apart from the choice of the concepts of commodity, surplus value, etc.) is chiefly one of an emphasis on existential judgments about society as against hypothetical ones, which emphasis coincides with its praxical orientation: "the critical theory of society is, in its totality, the unfolding of a single existential judgement". This judgment is the Marxian view of the historical development of human powers to a point where further development necessitates a change in fettering social relationships to ensure further more rational development. Horkheimer concedes, however, that isolated parts of the overall critical theory of the totality in motion can be represented hypothetically in traditional-theoretical terms, that the relationship between some propositions of theory to reality is "difficult to determine"[11] and that traditional theories to some degree contain existential judgments.

What Horkheimer is in essence saying here is a development of the Marxian project of the realization of philosophy in practice and is a version of one sense of the principle which became a preoccupation of post-Leninists and has become known in Soviet Marxism under the rubric of the "unity of theory and practice". In Soviet Marxism the phrase can mean the Marxist-Leninist view that the activity of theorizing and practical human action are inseparably bound up together in the proletarian movement (practice without theory being blind and theory without practice being largely purposeless). Or sometimes it connotes the relation between the principles of Marxism-Leninism and their actual application in the Soviet Union.[12] Horkheimer is close to the first sense of the phrase although unlike his Marxist contemporaries he did not in 1937 necessarily see critical theory as concerned solely with the ongoing and potential activity of the proletariat. Like every social stratum they, too, were "corrupted by ideology", so critical theory had "no specific influence on its side" except concern for the abolition of social injustice.[13] Thus Horkheimer's position consists mainly in the methodological side of Marxism, at its most generalized level the Lukácsian view of a genetico-critical scientific analysis of human society in its totality in Marxian socio-economic categories. It is an analysis which brings out society's past genesis (its presuppositions) in terms of the categories which emerged from its own structure (i.e. not more or less arbitrarily imposed by a hypothesis method) in a creative act of appropriation of that socio-genesis by bringing to the level of consciousness today what were partly blind social processes with a view to contributing to furthering those processes consciously in practice as one total process. It also involves coming down on the side of the realists against the nominalists who would deny reality to concepts rather than appropriate the ones which are given life by the activity of the human participants in the reality itself. To put it another way, Horkheimer is, like Lukács, taking a stand upon the nature of the changeability of the subject-object relationship, arguing that it is only if subject and object are kept rigidly apart that the subject is assumed not to impinge upon the object even if he adequately understands it. Traditional social theory presupposes a world in which human beings do not change the reified structures which dominate them – in short it enshrines human *practice* but does not enjoin *praxis*. Horkheimer said that traditional science leaves untouched the question of whether human intervention can alter the character of social processes. If that theory *does* interfere with its object then this is seen merely as a methodological problem, something to be allowed for in analysis:

> Even if it turns out that at a later point in time the objective event is influenced by human intervention, to science this is just another fact. The objective occurrence is independent of the theory, and this independence is part of its necessity: the observer as such can effect no change in the object.[14]

However, theoretically conceiving of society in terms of a single existential judgment, as possessing a degree of unconscious tendency from its past demanding conscious harnessing, Horkheimer is as a matter of course uniting fact, value, history, freedom, necessity and prescription into one scheme, against their separation by traditional theory in its claims to pure knowledge and abstention from evaluative judgments. Such unity comes out clearly in this passage:

> A consciously critical attitude, however, is part of the development of society: the construing of the course of history as the necessary product of an economic mechanism simultaneously contains both a protest against this order of things, a protest generated by the order itself, and the idea of self-determination for the human race, that is the idea of a state of affairs in which man's actions no longer flow from a mechanism but from his own decision.[15]

One would need to hesitate therefore, before accusing Horkheimer not only of conflating fact and value, or 'is' and 'ought' here, but also of paying no heed, say, to the Popperian principle of falsification. For Horkheimer, as for Marcuse, abstract falsificationism would be a product of traditional theorizing which in sociology would laud the importance of falsifying theories against a reified social reality characterized by a tough unchangeable and irrational necessity, which character is perpetuated by such an assumption. Horkheimer would have argued that falsification implies that one simply alters a theory to comply with falsifying facts, while these facts are actually the results of social processes. These relate to an object which comprises the regularities of human activity in a society qualitatively changing in its totality and developing towards certain states tendentially, which processes would be more rationally directable if they were more conscious of themselves. It would thus be to misunderstand Horkheimer to attack him on the ground that his conception of necessity involves a theory of the inevitability of the historical process leading towards socialism, which tendency all knowledge of society can only confirm but never falsify.

This accusation is an abstract one; it would only apply so long as the process was relatively blind and unaffected by its self-knowledge. The appearance of a confirmatory character in all instances of knowledge of the social totality in critical theory as elements in the "single existential judgement" only jars if one assumes falsification to reside purely in theory and its relationship to a random, structureless reality. It may be the case that in critical theory's elaboration of the existential judgment of society as a whole falsification could be said to characterize actual research procedures, i.e. the moments during the sorting out of material in which one is, for example, looking to see if a preliminary statement fits all instances. (Horkheimer conceded this much to "traditional" theorizing.) But this does not affect the final presentation of the findings as a statement of an element in a tendency. If such findings, as confirmatory instances of knowledge of the tendency of the totality, become self-conscious elements of it built into the social configuration they can fulfil themselves in practice as part of the overall fulfilment of the whole tendency of which they are a part. The confirmatory instances are potentially confirmed as true in reality as the result of a praxis which makes them real, thus demonstrating the 'truth' of the whole process (or so the argument runs). Abstract falsificationism for Horkheimer would imply a concept of necessity in which events are anticipated as possible, rather than regarded as events which can be potentially self-consciously mastered.[16] (Although in addition to the limited almost truistic sense of falsification as pragmatic trial-and-error during research, mentioned above, which would have to be admitted into critical theory's actual methodology, we must remember that Horkheimer also conceded that some traditional-theoretical principles could be held to be relevant for research into isolated but complete aspects of the totality and to some elements whose location and function are difficult to determine.)

A moral is beginning to emerge from this discussion, i.e. the danger of applying certain accepted criteria of adequacy to a theory which saw itself as trying to place such assessment in a different moral-political context beyond questions of pure method. One of the positive functions of critical theory was to highlight this tendency. By prevailing standards of theoretical respectability and accomplishment derived from the successful examples of traditional theory in various fields, Horkheimer said that critical theory "has no material accomplishments to show for itself".[17] And its very status as being future-oriented, against the established order and seeming to have, he agrees, much in common with fantasy,[18] can give critical theory a decidedly suspicious, even disreputable cast. Although it at no point proceeds "arbitrarily and in chance fashion", it can *appear* to prevailing modes of thought which contribute to the persistence of the archaic past in the present, to be "subjective and speculative, one-sided and useless . . . biased and unjust".[19] On a more theoretical level, the status of critical theory is, moreover, apparently rendered more precarious when, quite consistently within the practical-critical perspective, Horkheimer says that there also can be no "corresponding concrete perception"[20] of the essential societal change sought by the critical theoretician until the new situation has actually come about, at which time the newly developing situation requires a new theory. Accordingly, Martin Jay has expressed uneasiness about the epistemological basis of early critical theory:

> Dialectics was superb at attacking other systems' pretensions to truth, but when it came to articulating the ground of its own assumptions and values, it fared less well . . . Critical theory had a basically insubstantial concept of reason and truth, rooted in social conditions and yet outside them, connected with *praxis* yet keeping its distance from it.[21]

This statement raises again the important question of the extent to which it is legitimate to make traditional-theoretical demands of critical theory, in this case that it be adequately grounded. But by its very nature its object of enquiry was the relationship between the present order of society in its historically developed state and the continuous possibility of a more rational social order embodied in and realizable by human practice. Horkheimer warned that

> There are no general criteria for judging the critical theory as a whole, for it is always based on the recurrence of events and thus on a self-producing totality.[22]

Thus Jay's judgment implicitly takes a traditional-theoretical standpoint because he unconsciously yearns for grounded 'absolute' certitude, effectively demanding of critical theory to declare its values and assumptions and to show its empirical knowledge to be solid and testable. It is, however, necessary to engage critical theory initially in its own terms. The status of critical theory by those accepted standards was inherently precarious, dependent as it was upon the possibility of a praxis which would prove, in the sense of authenticate as a process, any assumptions and values that could be stated as underpinning it, since they could not be justified solely with reference to the present order. Critical theory maintained that values were inherent in empirically appropriatable historical tendencies of which it was the transitory expression before their conscious realization *in practice*. On Horkheimer's showing, the only criteria of adequacy which could be said to have any kind of fixed or 'absolute' validity for critical theory were those of logical consistency, which he said would apply to the structure of any theory, whether critical or traditional (although even logic itself was a socio-historical conceptual result of the cultural development of human societies). To try to ground critical theory's values or assumptions in the present in any univocal way would be for Horkheimer to bind it to the *status quo*.

Critical theory's central value, if it could be said to have had one, was probably the ideal of a relatively more self-determining society: although even this was not held to be a value-judgment but demonstrable as a developed historical product and potentially more realizable in practice at the present time, the existence of such a universal value always being subject to the extent to which it remained, and always would remain, *unrealized* in particular societies. Similarly, the demand for criteria of theoretical adequacy for empirical correspondence with the rational, possible Other of society which the theory was endeavouring to encompass and promote could only be satisfied when that order came about as the result of human praxis, remembering always that it never *absolutely* comes about . . . At the next stage of development of society such criteria of correspondence could, following Horkheimer's theory through, perhaps have a transitory validity for a short period as traditional theory in a unity with which a new critical theory would be sustained. The latter would take account of and incorporate the new situation and the mobilized theory which accompanied it, in order to promote the always beckoning more rational future. But this period of validity could not be determined in advance.

Two important consequences emerge from this discussion: (a) that all critical social theory, even that which might have constituted itself as the self-conscious mobilization of a past developmental tendency into the future (theory having "become a material force when it seizes the masses") is, irrespective of which social groups in society are important for action in a given epoch, always the theory and practice of what Lukács and Mannheim both termed the "*next step*" in the historical process; and (b) an awareness that our theoretical socialization tends to induce us instinctively to demand that theory be grounded in some semi-permanent and axiomatic way. This precept would appear to conflict with the orientation of critical theory to the inherently moving, changing settings of the historical process and their future possibilities, tending to absolutize a given setting as well as implying a commitment to the elaboration of general categories to produce abstract knowledge applicable to societies of all epochs. But the all-important *extent* to which such a grounding in a given order or such an axiomatization are historically possible in critical theory without it freezing into traditional theory in

Horkheimer's terms or into an eternalizing mythology, remain open for further discussion later on.

Our exposition of critical theory's version of the "unity of theory and practice" in the Marxist tradition needs to be completed by specific consideration of the status of sociologically appropriated knowledge of the past and its relation to human praxis. We can briefly turn to Marx, Collingwood, and the later Sartre for some guidance on this problem, initially in a dialogue with some of Zygmunt Bauman's remarks on this subject. Invoking Piaget's notion of development as "vection", Bauman declares:

> What defies all attempts to apply consistently either deterministic or functionalist approaches to the historical praxis is its essential unpredictability, not necessarily at odds with 'inevitability' . . . Whatever happened, was 'determined' by virtue of the sheer logic of the deterministic analytical framework; but nothing which has not yet occurred, nothing still unaccomplished can be deduced unequivocally from what has already been petrified into a fact, since previous events constrain rather than determine their sequences in processes like biological evolution, growth of knowledge or the totality of human history.[23]

This view is embedded in the post-Marxian tradition which sees the main axis dividing Marx and Hegel as being on the question of the harnessability of history, or of self-consciously changing the world. Hegelian philosophy is seen as always arriving *post festum*, to assess the world-historical significance of events from the standpoint of Absolute Knowledge, and to acknowledge reconciliation between them and the Idea; whereas Marx's orientation was concerned not only with that project, but also with the overall conscious mastery of those now-revealed processes (analysed in such a way as to demystify the Hegelian version) and their creative continuation into the future. Bauman's line of argument operates with an implicit dichotomy between the closed, accomplished past known through petrified facts and the open-ended future,[24] or at least carries a stress on the future as never being totally deducible from knowledge of the past, thus preserving abstractly a domain of human freedom.

The past and the present are not, however, reified, separate domains, but form a living unity. We cannot regard the past as irrevocably and statically simply part of, in Bauman's words, the "already accomplished, sentient, 'empirical' reality" and thus only appropriatable as such.[25] Sequences of events or configurational changes as parts of social processes, as well as their consciously appropriated elements which may have been incorporated into the next stage form, in Sartre's terminology, a totalizing process often towards higher, incorporative stages and not simply a concatenation. I will argue that in a number of ways the past is far from closed, accomplished, or finished in any abstract or final way. Historical facts are indeed as Bauman says, effectively 'culturally created' largely from archives,[26] but they can never, in an organic historical perspective, be the petrified product of only one possible creation, irrespective of the historical stage of societal development at which the interpretation takes place. As Collingwood remarked of the unity of the historical process,

> Because the historical past, unlike the natural past is a living past, kept alive by the act of historical thinking itself, the historical change from one way of thinking to another is not the death of the first, but its survival integrated in a new context involving the development and criticism of its own ideas.[27]

It is not the "sheer logic of the deterministic analytical framework" which 'determines' what happened in history (Bauman), but rather the sheer logic of the historical process itself that 'determines' the analytical framework. If there is a discoverable tendency which can be discerned and appropriated today (i.e. raised to historical consciousness) it should be because it was present in the reality of the historical process itself. Stunted elements of lower stages of this process may be preserved in higher stages of development, including their corresponding socio-economic categories. It is only from the mutual relations of those elements and concepts in the resultant higher stage of development at which the theorist stands which enables him to gain insight into the structure of past social configurations. From the later stage of more profuse concrete development general conceptual abstractions arise which express that stage and provide generalized categories applicable to the previous epochs, too, in which from the later stage those categories can often be discerned as expressing a nascent social reality in a more abstract, 'potential' way. Therefore the categories are, as Marx said in the *Grundrisse*,[28] simultaneously products of specific social conditions as well as valid at a general level for other epochs. But they are only more 'universally' applicable by virtue of their validity in the more concrete stage of development because the remnants of the previous stages are transcended and incorporated in it. As in Hegel, for Marx the universality of categories only has its life in and through their particular embodiment at a given point and usually tends towards more universal, concrete determinacy. Marx makes the paradoxical observation that the reality and effectiveness of a category even from a scientific standpoint "by no means begins at the moment when it is discussed *as such*"[29] (by social scientists) since its complete import is only fully understood when human praxis has at a higher stage further concretized its past abstract potentiality, until which stage that potentiality is not fully known. This is why in Marx's specific concerns, modern bourgeois society was both the presupposed starting point as well as the conclusion of his investigations.

Our comprehension of the past is not therefore irrevocably shackled to petrified facts, as Bauman formalistically states, but is always potentially capable of a better, fuller understanding of it from the higher stages of development with which the past forms a practical unity. The past is not dead. Each new piece of selected evidence about the past is not a pure fact but the bringing to historical consciousness today as part of a total historical process what may not have been fully cognized at the time, although it may have been present in the configuration in a protogenic form. And such a presence only has its total significance in its comprehension at higher stages. A couplet from Goethe's *Faust* springs to mind:

> You come back, wavering shapes, out of the past,
> In which you first appeared to clouded eyes.

Furthermore, the past is obviously always being continually further sedimented as present human practice bites into the future. So what is perceived today as being a past tendency-to-be-mobilized or consciously directed from the present, qualitatively changes with higher stages of social development as the results of praxis are incorporated into a further totalization and history is reinterpreted, reworked and further comprehended from a higher standpoint. (The old cliché that each generation rewrites history from its own perspective is not without a theoretical basis!) Yes, human historical praxis on all levels *is* geared towards the future, and therefore possesses an unconditioned, open-ended element – a point which Sartre makes again and again. Dialectically speaking this could not be other than the case since the alternatives would imply *vis-à-vis* the future either an absolute determinism or an absolute voluntarism. But at the same time such praxis will on any level (e.g. individual, group, class) be more or less informed by appropriated self-knowledge of the past raised to consciousness and thus can contribute also to the *creation and recreation of the past*, which domain *only* has its life as part of that totalizing praxis.

As regards the 'present', a consequence of this organic view is, as Sartre rightly remarks, that

> the rising generations are more capable of *knowing* [*savoir*] – at least formally – what they are doing than the generations which have preceded us.[30]

But too heavy an emphasis (often for short-term political reasons) on the problems of the present, or the rigid methodological separation of the 'closedness' of the past from the abstract open-endedness of the future, will clearly lead in theory to a historically foreshortened vision (although not totally unhistorical, of course, since even our knowledge of the 'present' is to some degree of a past situation the moment we have cognized it.) But the concentration on the 'here and now' and its apparently immediate possibilities as being the most important research concern, divorced from its living unity with the past as a total process with a virtually measurelessly long development, is unlikely to inform successful practice to change society in various ways. This is because the present and its possibilities would have been misunderstood since more of its unconscious dependencies would be present in analysis in variously uncognized and alien forms because their long-term genesis had been inadequately appropriated and raised to consciousness. Practice thus informed is more likely to be caught out by forces it either did not know, was only dimly aware of or knew but did not fully understand. Furthermore, another deleterious consequence could be that in the absence of more adequate knowledge of long-term socio-genesis there would be no standard available by which better to judge the reasons for a possible *failure* of political practice: this could easily lead to disillusionment and cynicism on the part of those involved.

Within the Hegelian-Marxian view of historical development the ever-renewed empirical study of the social processes of vastly long periods of history would appear then to be essential for at least (a) keeping human historical vitality alive, by limiting the extent to which history appears as an alien force, i.e. as the project of genetico-criticism. Without this element theory would not incidentally be "critical" in Marx's sense since it would not involve the appropriation of societal presuppositions. And (b) mandatory also for the related purpose of informing potentially more successful activity to change social institutions in the present, seen as the past's unified continuity. The character of possibilities and potentiality for success in political practice is dependent to some extent upon the all-important nature of the appropriated-tendency-to-be-directed which can only be adequately grasped empirically, not intuitively or dogmatically. On both counts a *principle of permanent research* is therefore implied, since historical tendencies will always qualitatively change with higher stages of development, which can potentially carry with them (although not necessarily inevitably) more inclusive, incisive or generally more 'universally' applicable and retrospective categories. Ironically it is Marxists who often evince a consuming zeal to orient their scholarly work towards the future in order to eschew 'justifying the *status quo*' and/or dogmatically assume that they are *already* in possession of adequate knowledge of an overall historical necessity since they represent its self-consciousness. In either case they have sometimes been led to write off the past, and, as Sartre rightly said, formalistically to consider history to be "the dead transparent object of an immutable knowledge".[31]

Whilst suspending judgment on the existentialist philosophical basis which informs his critique, I think Sartre is right to criticize the tendency of certain "lazy Marxists" merely to "situate" thinkers and philosophies in accordance with a dogmatic *a priori* schema of historical materialism.[32] This kind of analysis for Sartre reduces unique lived experiences and past events to expressions of social structures, relegating the reality of the individual's meanings to the realm of the accidental, contingent or irrational. (Although I am not happy with the absolutism of Sartre's notion that the plurality of meanings of history "at the heart of this polyvalent world" can eventually, through a sequence of praxical totalizations, be unified into *one* meaning at the end of a process of democratization in which men come truly and completely to make history in common.)[33] However, against Marxist dogmatic *a priorism* Sartre stresses the living nature of the past in the sense of the ever-present possibility of regaining for men more complete consciousness of the history which they have made but which appears as an alien force. The point is that for a dogmatic historical materialism all events of the past are by definition closed and finished once-and-for-all since they possess only one *a priori* social-structural scientific significance which, for Sartre, ignores the level of truth of the choosing "good faith" of the participants in a given situation. This can be reclaimed and better understood at a later stage and be vindicated in future action, as in the Kronstadt example quoted in the extended extract below.

Sartre extends this principle into an argument of profound political import. He defends in theory the objectivity of the "individual's signification", i.e. the meaning which the choosing individual places in "good faith" and in good will upon what he does, as well as the objectivity of the individual's social situation which the historical materialists claim to be the sole repository of objectivity. This individual signification is objective because it is part of a totalizing process in which the objectivity of a setting and the subjectivity of the individual are both mutually conditioning objectifications, the externalization of the internality of the subject's "project" appearing continually an objectified subjectivity.[34] This is argued against what he sees as the dangerous Stalinist, "petit-bouregois" view that an act may be seen as objectively blameworthy or traitorous (e.g. by the party) while remaining subjectively genuine. In the course of expounding that view of the act, Sartre draws together, with an existentialist emphasis, some of the arguments about the nature of the past and human action and more generally about the implications of the "unity of theory and practice" which I have been discussing in this chapter. He denounces the view that the historical conjuncture of circumstances exhausts the objective significance of actions because

> an act has many other levels of truth, and these levels do not represent a dull hierarchy, but a complex movement of contradictions which are posited and surpassed; for example, the totalization which appraises the act in its relation to historical *praxis* and to the conjuncture of circumstances is itself denounced as an abstract, incomplete totalization (a *practical* totalization) insofar as it has not turned back to the action to reintegrate it *also* as a uniquely individual attempt. The condemnation of the insurgents at Kronstadt was perhaps inevitable; it was perhaps the judgment of history on this tragic attempt. But at the same time this practical judgment (the only real one) will remain that of an enslaved history so long as it does not include the free interpretation of the revolt in terms of the insurgents themselves and of the contradictions of the moment. This free interpretation, someone may say, is in no way *practical* since the insurgents, as well as their judges are dead. But that is not true. The historian, by consenting to study facts at all levels of reality, liberates future history. This liberation can come about, as a visible and efficacious action, only within the compass of the general movement of democratization; but conversely it cannot fail to accelerate this movement.[35]

16 Sociological facts and mass praxis

For Horkheimer, as we have already seen, traditional theory, however essential and useful for providing technical knowledge, was committed to the accumulation of facts, which was a picture of sociology shared by both Lukács and Gramsci. This fetishism of facts does not permit sociology to see beyond the present to what society ought to be, or is tending to become, assumes the equivalence of qualitatively different elements of society, takes the given *status quo* as read in all its inequality and predicates a social science on a pseudo value-freedom. These postulates were applied and reapplied by the critical theoreticians to other social theory and to philosophies. In these propositions were implicitly embedded the distinction originally made by Hegel, but notably emphasized by Engels, that what appear as *things* in society are actually the results of *processes*,[1] a principle which was given further theoretical elaboration by Lukács in his characterization of "contemplative" social science as remaining stuck fast in "immediacy". For the critical theorists, hostility to the "apotheosis of facts" or an "antinomian empiricism"[2] which could not go beyond the givens of experience became a judge before which schools of philosophy and social thought were to appear: the logical positivists were guilty of a fetishism of facts;[3] Husserl was said to have reified "the given" by a system of categories which simply reproduced that which is;[4] scientific objectivity, argued Marcuse, was no guarantee of truth which spoke "strongly against the facts";[5] pragmatism, like positivism, could also not go beyond the facts;[6] and so on. One could go on multiplying instances of the recurrence of this Hegelian theme from *The Logic* that we must "discard the prejudice that truth must be something tangible"[7] right up to the latest writings of the Frankfurt School. Facts were not of course denied or rejected by the critical theorists either early on or later, but simply put into a wider dynamic perspective which critically appropriated their genesis and sought to 'return' the structures and institutions they expressed to their producers. Adorno, to cite one recent example, said in a survey of German sociology in 1959 that neutrally inclined social research

> by renouncing that comprehensive thinking which surpasses the restrictions of single facts, and is therefore of necessity critical, subserves only too well that constricted condition of consciousness which it registers: the function of social research, however, should be the analysis and sociological derivation of that consciousness.[8]

(Note that Mannheim would have agreed completely with the last statement.) And again in 1967 Adorno considered "matters of fact" to be

> not mere fact, unreflected and thinglike, but rather processes of infinite mediation, never to be taken simply at face-value. [I] cannot accept the usual mode of thought which is content to register facts and prepare them for subsequent classification. [My] essential effort is to illuminate the realm of facticity – without which there can be no true knowledge – with reflections of a different type, one which diverges radically from the generally accepted canon of scientific validity.[9]

But as I have already argued (a) critical theory necessarily presupposed and included 'dead', sedimented knowledge of the developed, 'accomplished' social order, i.e. facts, in its deliberations (acknowledged above by Adorno); (b) in practice all publicly communicated theory (including the non-critical) can to some degree potentially promote changes in its object, i.e. aspects of society; and (c) dialectically speaking access to the 'accomplished' historical reality is by no means restricted to dead facts. All these points were either acknowledged by the critical theorists or were derivable from or assumed in their historical perspective. So one wonders why the facts theme was given such emphasis and why the early critical theory thus overstated and caricatured the reality of sociological culture and procedure and judged all philosophies in the manner of the Lukácsian critique of classical German philosophy, i.e. in terms of its failure to extricate itself from assuming 'the given' as unproblematic. Adorno's analysis of German sociology in 1959 carries on this traditional Frankfurt concern and makes selections from the then contemporary German sociology and interprets them through a preconceived philosophical scheme as pursuing "non-philosophical . . . descriptions and systematizations of whatever is the case".[10] Even accepting the inherently precarious status of the future-oriented mode of critical theory and the illegitimacy of demanding "traditional" criteria of adequacy for it, one could have expected a closer examination of the nature of 'the given' or of the 'facts' which articulated it in the light of the kind of dynamic considerations about our knowledge of the past which I raised when talking about Sartre in the previous chapter.

My view is that the undiscriminating reiteration of the facts theme had the character of a perennial polemic, an automatic response, an exaggeration, to serve as a talisman to keep alive in the relentlessly persistent instances of its application a denial of the present unjust, reified world and the possibility of a more rational society when the appointed class in Marxist terms (the proletariat) had seemed to have deserted its historical mission for fascism. The pursuit of sociological research would therefore appear to the post-Lukácsian critical theoretician as the pursuit of empirical knowledge of a monstrously irrational society careering towards barbarism, an enterprise hopelessly out of tune with and therefore serving to obscure, the real issues facing humanity. Understandable though this position was in its time and given the assumptions of the particular strand of the Marxist tradition in which the critical theorists were embedded, the static, abstract and philosophized picture of the socio-historical development and function of sociology and other sciences which went with it was ironically unfaithful to the very dialectical principles of organic social development upon which they otherwise put such store.

The critical theorists imputed to sociology the highly abstract idealized structure of scientism,[11] holding that it pursued neutral knowledge and facts about society and based itself on the model of the "natural sciences". Even though some sociologists have advocated for sociology the positivists' unitary method for the sciences irrespective of the level of integration (physical, biological, social, etc.) of the universe with which the particular science is concerned,[12] not all of them have. What the methods and practice of sociology were or have come to be, are empirical questions. Moreover, the traditional-theoretical model which the critical theorists casually said was derived from and was successful in the "natural sciences", was perhaps applicable to the early stage of the development of physics, but inapplicable in say biology, geology or modern astronomy, which dropped the pursuit of laws long ago. Thus, the critical theorists' hostility towards fact-finding social science was based on an archaic ideal of scientific procedure not on its reality, on a preconceived *philosophical* scheme about the nature and import of *science*, not a generalization about the social reality of *sciences*. This ideal was then applied uncritically to sociology which only to a limited extent ever exhibited or professed it. If one sees philosophy partly as the moral-political rumination upon the rational possibilities inherent in a given society then one must make such assessments from an adequate analysis of reality.

Instead of appropriating what Marx called "the proper logic of the proper object"[13] with regard to the social reality of sciences they imposed an underived idealized Newtonian schema on to it. But seen developmentally, various values, including the important scientific one of detachment which informs the more dispassionate observation of phenomena as they are rather than as men would want them to be, did not fall from the skies but developed in various fields and *became* what they are. No science was or is *absolutely* detached or neutral of social-interest connections if one sees the development of sciences in a long-term perspective. At later stages certain scientific evaluations (as for example the one of detachment) can *appear* to be 'absolute' and knowledge in natural science can become relatively autonomous of its original producers and their interests.[14]

The post-Lukácsian Marxist position committed critical theory to regarding the present state of society more or less as an unreal tissue of reifications, totally permeated by inequality, illusion and cultural decadence, whose social and economic problems were insoluble this side of communism, which was postponed only by temporary crisis-solving economic panaceas. So the apparent failure of the Marxian scenario to work itself out successfully left them in a void because without the revolution the world remained depraved and insane. In this situation exhortation and polemical exaggeration became inevitable as they searched for the mechanisms of cultural integration which held back human liberation via the working class. Their picture of positivistic dominative sociology was the over-generalized product of a drastically foreshortened historical perspective which thrust sociology and critical theory into a philosophical dualism, but it provided one such mechanism. Horkheimer was less Manichean in his depiction of this dualism than was Marcuse, acknowledging far more the complex historical interweavings of interests in the scientific process and giving, like Hegel, due credence to 'analytical' rationality. But in general this complexity was disregarded or smoothed over by the critical theorists to allow a simplified scientistic, fact-gathering model to survive for the purpose of moralizing polemic, which sometimes bordered on an anti-science stance. Like Lukács, Gramsci, Korsch and so many other writers in this tradition, they could ultimately see no alternative to critical social science than the value-free, scientistic model which could only inform the domination and control of men as the natural sciences had aided the domination of nature. One could not perhaps expect them to have questioned this basic position which was firmly embedded in the thought style of the critical theory community. But even if the thought that the philosophical unity in their own teaching between traditional and critical theory could profitably be tilted towards the former had even flickered at the back of their minds, it would have been repressed. Within their set of assumptions it would be an emphasis inevitably associated with positivism, the pursuit of the static facts of the dehumanizing reified structures in which men unconsciously dwell upon which "traditional" sociological theory, in its mute unphilosophical unreflexivity, thrives and so perpetuates. In short, drop the philosophical commitment and social science will run into the arms of domination.

The erroneous characterization of natural science as unproblematically positivistic (which produced the traditional theory model) is then compounded by its polemical projection on to the development and inevitable nature of social science. Jürgen Habermas has drawn attention to the illusion of neutrality and objectivism which characterizes the self-understanding of natural scientific practice and maintains that this "false consciousness" has a protective function which can guard against the freaks of "national" (Nazi) physics and Soviet Marxist genetics.[15] But the earlier critical theorists took this self-understanding at its face-value. Peter Sedgwick makes a similar point when arguing that the recent *avant garde* of interactionist and social-experiential theoreticians of mental illness (Laing, Cooper, Szasz) in their polemics against organicist traditional psychiatry naively assumed that physical illness was not *also* as socially defined as they claimed mental illness solely to be.[16] They assumed definitions of physical illness in medical practice to be unproblematic and 'objectivistic'. There was of course justification in the early critical theorists railing against the scientistic model absolutized into applicability across the scientific board including for the analysis of society. To have highlighted this tendency was a valuable contribution, but this was a legitimate critique only in so far as scientism actually characterized the social reality of sciences in general or of sociology in particular or was contemplated or championed for it.

The more deep-seated reasons for the character of the critical theorists' polemics here lay in two tendencies in their theorizing. The first of these was the domination of their reasoning by specific traditional philosophical concepts such as man, consciousness, alienation, subject and object and self-determination in praxis. As a set of philosophical categories used as a moral measuring rod of scientific practice and social life it did not matter that they were not produced as generalizations empirically from the socio-historical reality: the philosophical concepts stood underived, their presuppositions unanalysed, and were doggedly asserted. Second, they had absorbed the post-Lukácsian perspective with its preoccupation with the potentialities of praxis, which tended therefore to exaggerate the import of the inevitably still, 'frozen' moments in theory and social reality. That exaggeration became expressed as the "contemplative" model of theorizing, which was held to separate object from subject in a rigid and irrecoverable way. (Notice that this view is not only undiscriminatingly abstract but also uncritically accepted the individualistic 'subject' and 'object' co-ordinates.) Despair at the political circumstances in Europe in the 1930s led them to activate principles from those two sets of assumptions in such a way that the pursuit of the "facts" became a symbol for the self-perpetuation of the hypostatized social forces which ongoingly held back the full realization of the potentialities of the epoch. It was an emblem of one of the many ideological reifications which blocked human liberation. At the present stage of development, however, it is possible to see the historical specificity of the particular emphases of the early critical theory project and guard against its more black-and-white philosophical posturings as tending towards mythology.

Let us examine that latter tendency in the light of the Marxist notion of practice providing the arbitration of certain theoretical questions. Within the practical-critical perspective it would be possible to come back here with the argument that it did not matter to the critical theoreticians whether the pursuit of facts did or did not characterize actual sociology; nor that their own theory presupposed factuality and its knowledge; nor that scientism either did not apply to much sociology or only marginally ever characterized it or now characterizes all natural sciences. The point was, it would be argued, that to pose human life in the philosophical terms of the ever-present societal potential for self-knowledge and self-determination in the light of knowledge of social reality was the heritage of traditional philosophy embodied in critical theory. It is a philosophical position which can serve to promote the possibilities of the practical fulfilment of its Ought-questions through politics in accordance with the level of development of the forces of production in order to create a society in which Is and Ought are sublated in a self-determining reality and philosophy is transcended. Thus it does not matter whether the critical theorists' characterization of sciences or of sociology was wholly accurate, since they were *philosophizing*, embracing the ever-present negative critique which always had the social reality of the *status quo* to criticize in the name of Reason and traditional theory and ideology to criticize immanently, thus continually proving itself *in practice*. My critique above would thus appear to be a purely theoretical critique of philosophy in the name of science rather than their more desirable humanistic critique of science in the name of philosophy. But within philosophy as such in the above sense are there not philosoph*ies* which, in the form of ideologies in the hands of political groups, can at various times be promoted in practice and thus potentially also determine the future?

Within dialectics it is the conception of the "unity of theory and practice" discussed earlier, in which fact and value, is and ought, tendency and practice are putatively united, which embraces a praxical totalizing framework which might absorb these rival philosophies and provide cognitive and/or practical criteria for their discrimination. So, in looking at that question perhaps the most fruitful line of discussion is to return to the problem of the mass-mobilization in practice of belief systems other than socialism, an issue I raised in the Excursus to Part three when discussing Gramsci's distinction between "organic" and "conjunctural" movements. In so far as the critical theorist is committed to mobilizing by raising to consciousness the genesis of long-term fundamental historical tendencies and contributing to carrying them into fruition in praxis, then dialectically speaking he is theoretically secure from arbitrariness, in so far as theoretical criteria are applicable, since he is located as a self-conscious part of a necessary tendency realizing itself. (An objection which could be made here, to which I will return in Chapter 18, would be the methodological one that due to, say, dogmatic archaic presuppositions research into the past by the critical theorist has selected certain material or projected assumptions on to history instead of more nearly appropriating its endemic structures, has therefore falsified the reality and is thus trying to continue in practice a non-existent or theoretically distorted tendency, which would probably result more or less in the failure of practice.) However, the critical theoretician may be dubious about the empirical existence of one important necessary historical tendency or "organic movement" on the post-Weberian grounds of it being a metaphysical prejudice or a mythology; or reject its directive political implications when wielded by the *avant-garde* party. Or, in his philosophical enthusiasm, he might fail adequately to take account of the social science evidence of sociogenesis to which his philosophical critique is dialectically bound. In any of these cases he falls back on to philosophy, which may be comprised of principles elaborated in the circumstances of an earlier, superseded period of history and formulated in the characteristically attenuated abstractions. There is a crucial sense in which it matters a great deal whether the picture of reality underpinning and unified with critique is informed by a more adequate appropriation of sociohistorical reality. In the language of critical theory, before acting to actualize what Ought to be one must adequately know what Is, since this conditions what Ought to be. The rational possibilities present in a given order change with the level of social development which can only be adequately grasped empirically to avoid subjectivism, caprice or mere opinion. And the social science informing this investigation has, like natural science, a historically developed validity. If one argues that as long as the philosophy is a negative critique in the name of self-determination and its fulfilment in practice can always be promoted then it does not matter whether its depiction of reality is completely adequate, i.e. if evidence is seen as secondary; then *methodologically* nothing gives the philosophical content of critical theory any more credence than fascist philosophy, which also seeks to fulfil itself in practice through an appropriation of social reality and through the mobilization of the masses. The stress which we find in critical theory is more on philosophy as the watchdog of society and of science rather than science more as the empirical check on or governing determinant of philosophy. This tends to reinforce the fudging over of facts or evidence in the name of the unrealized historical 'truth', as we have seen in Horkheimer's philosophical depiction of science, and thus pushes theory more towards arbitrariness and mythology. This is because in this case philosophy as critique, divorcing itself from facing more adequate scientific knowledge of the appropriate developed stage of socio-historical reality, becomes *in practice* equivalent to other philosophies which in any case less adequately do this, thus trying to promote the mobilization of the masses in an ironically unenlightened manner. Moreover, satisfaction of the Marxian praxical criterion, i.e. the assertion that exactitude in empirical social scientific matters is, beyond certain limits "scholastic", being continually subject to fulfilment in practice which changes the social formation necessitating further theories, would not reduce the irrationalism of the critical position *vis-à-vis* evidence.

One might at this point resort to the quasi-Sorelian position which asserts the interchangeability in principle of mobilizable ideologies, which is where one ends up by giving philosophy its head at the expense of empirical historical reclamation. But this position is relativistic and therefore also irrational despite its possible satisfaction of the praxical criterion. This is because the abstract assumption of the potential utility of "any" myth, disregards the possibility of the more 'rational', empirical, scientific appropriation of the socio-historical conditions which would enable such a mobilization to take place. The myth itself is only "any" myth or as arbitrary as the extent to which we do not know its origins and understand its power to mobilize people at any time. The 'any myth will suffice so long as it mobilizes' position asserts that the efficacy or validity of such a myth merely depends upon its realization in practice, but this does not remove the implicit assumption of arbitrariness, unconditionality or even epiphenomenality in relation to the provenance of the myth. More precisely: this position ascribes to historical praxis the provision of its own arbitration as reality upon what the moral philosophers' pursuit of abstract criteria of choice between values for a better society or course of action is trying to solve in theory. Even from the point of view of the masses no ideology is totally 'irrational', but some are from their perspective more appropriate to their experiences than others and from the sociologist's standpoint some are less mythological than others. It is only either a formalist or an irrationalist conception which respectively sees all ideologies as potentially equivalent or holds the absolute position that "any" ideology is potentially mobilizable. None of them fall from the sky and which of them 'seizes the masses' at which time and under which conditions can be empirically investigated: it is not, as Hitler believed, *entirely* a mysterious affair.

The question is how better to reduce the element of the unknown involved in any theory-informed phase of action, since it clearly cannot be removed entirely. Minimization of the irrational presents itself as a problem in two empirical areas: (a) in accounting for the particular conditions under which certain ideologies become mobilizable and through which social forces; and (b) in relation to the ever-present element of uncertainty in possible practice in general on various levels. The best strategy for solving this problem on both counts is more adequate long-term socio-genetic empirical analysis. I hope not to be misunderstood here. I am not saying that social science gives us total predictive knowledge of society or of revolutions. Neither am I offering a sociological paradigm which inevitably lends itself to use by bureaucratic elites for the manipulation of the populace as a whole. Nor am I arguing from a solely intellectualistic standpoint, trying to discover within the safety of theory what intellectuals are afraid is beyond their scientific control in the potential praxis of the masses. The first view is an untenable sociological absolutism, the second a New Left chimera and the third a post-Lukácsian Marxist jibe. My point is only that certain kinds of socio-genetic empirical analysis are more likely to varying degrees to provide knowledge which can *minimize* the uncertainty of the outcomes of social processes and action, but can never totally eliminate that uncertainty. Without this kind of work not only is action more blind, but also society is always potentially more alien, opaque, mysterious and 'arbitrary', without implying that its processes can ever become totally transparent to men, either in theory or in practice.

The familiar Marxist "unity of theory and practice" in the proletarian revolution seen in the quasi-determinist mode of contradictions within capitalism resolving themselves into a higher stage of development through their human social class bearers, involving the process of the proletariat's concomitant class-consciousness, is dialectically non-arbitrary since it is held to express a harnessed historical necessity. Both Lukács and Gramsci, as we have seen, believed that the existence of this long-term rhythm of a "fundamental" historical tendency ultimately held sway against the short-term freakish mobilizations of the masses. But the truth of even this position could be proved only as long as its advanced self-consciousness (represented by Marxist theory and its organized bearers) continued to work in theory and in practice to achieve it. Although even this dialectically consistent position in the hands of a small political group does not necessarily carry more of a guarantee of greater liberation than the mobilization of an 'irrational' ideology. Moreover, a falsely conceived historical process could be masqueraded as the real process. Even a 'correct' appraisal of the reality is open *in practice* to the arbitrary denial of greater self-determination in the imposition and direction of social life by the *avant-garde* of the 'enlightened' in the party who may be its bearers. (A Marxist could object here that if this were indeed so, i.e. that the historical process as a whole had been correctly appraised, then the conditions for socialism would be present and the theory sublated in practice. But I would claim that *even so* to assume that the 'new' reality would *necessarily* be liberative is a Utopian faith.) There is further danger, too, when the vanguard come to believe themselves as enshrining the most advanced historically necessary consciousness prior to its fully seizing the masses. Indeed, Lukács for example, can be seen as having provided, wittingly or unwittingly, in his theory of the party as possessing the imputed class-consciousness of the proletariat, a sophisticated epistemological justification for just such directive practice. This telling passage (which I have quoted before) was written in 1923:

> because the party aspires to the highest point that is objectively and revolutionarily attainable – and the momentary desires of the masses are often the most important aspect, the most vital symptom of this – it is sometimes forced to adopt a stance opposed to that of the masses; it must show them the way by rejecting their immediate wishes. It is forced to rely upon the fact that only *post festum*, only after many bitter experiences will the masses understand the correctness of the party's view.[17]

In rejecting this kind of orthodox party-oriented bureaucratic Marxism as well as the iron laws of history approach of the evolutionists and social democrats as either dogmatically directive or fatalistically mythological, the early critical theorists were drawn towards the alternative of general radical cultural dissemination and ideological critique. In this project, however, they seemed implicitly to discern a lurking irrationalism because of the possibility in their terms of arbitrary ideologies seizing the masses as the result of such dissemination also being carried out by others. The untiring reiteration of their own philosophical critique against all-comers reflected the hope that other theories, myths, or ideologies would only be as generally mobilizable as the extent to which they were culturally *allowed* to become so. That was implied also in the process of appropriation and mobilization of the 'necessary' historical movement, given that even the master process required to be "willed" into a reality. But come what may, in Marcuse's words again "theory will preserve the truth even if revolutionary practice deviates from its path".[18]

To conclude, the polemics in the name of an older philosophy against a scientism in social science which advocated the pursuit of facts, drove the critical theorists away from the empirical reclamation of socio-historical reality and the consequent *reformulation* of the philosophical project in a different form which that would have made possible. This ironically blocked a better appraisal of the possibilities for practical change at the current stage because being tilted away from empirical findings their analysis became more and more archaic, dogmatic and mythological. The polemics served to dramatize the perceived ever-present need to pose a constant reminder (in a necessarily highly generalized fashion) that social forces were always potentially more recoverable and amenable to greater self-determination at a time when this was manifestly being denied in Germany and Russia. It was a case of preserving at all cost philosophy as critique because in Adorno's famous words, "the moment to realize it was missed".[19] Since the critical theorists acknowledged that some fact sustaining reification would always be dialectically implied in any future stage of human social organization, facts would on their argument therefore remain appropriatable from social experience since the social world could never be totally transparent. They would presumably have become benign facts of benign reification?

EXCURSUS: HISTORICAL INVARIANTS

Critical theory aimed to be genetico-critical, historical and scientific in the sense of embracing the potentially liberative, demythologizing, rational elements immanent in science when applied to conscious human fulfilment in a more self-determined human social existence. It was the enemy of all superstition or mythology which would impose or surreptitiously reimpose itself into men's lives as an external force. This position carried with it, therefore, the obligation of combating on the level of critique philosophies and ideologies whose content seemed to place mankind in the thrall of seemingly immutable hypostatized forces or eternal co-ordinates which could not potentially be changed through self-conscious praxis or mastered through self-awareness in specific socio-historical circumstances. For example, in his essay 'Materialism and Metaphysics' (1933)[20] Horkheimer declared that the modern metaphysics of "pure Being" (meaning the philosophy of Heidegger) had clothed everything that had human, historical purposes with the appearance of eternity and related them to "a reality which is not subject to historical change and is therefore unconditioned".[21] This was a philosophical procedure which would ultimately make nought of, or severely limit, the possibilities and outcomes of praxis. Both Adorno and Marcuse said that the yearning for eternal essences in the phenomenology of Husserl and Scheler was a source of self-delusion.[22] Martin Jay's account of the genesis of critical theory[23] shows how this position was elaborated by the early critical theorists in critiques of the philosophies of Kierkegaard, Husserl, Heidegger, the early Sartre, Bergson and Nietszche amongst others. As well as maintaining a scepticism about philosophies of Being, they would also brook neither the related reductive claims about '*la condition humaine*', nor the eternal sovereign ego nor any notion of an immutable human nature.

In his early writings as a pupil of Heidegger Marcuse had limited sympathy for ontological speculation since it at least raised in the highly abstract language of "historicity", "authentic being" and "decisiveness" (Heidegger) what constitutes a bad, untrue status of man and the need to act to achieve authentic "being-in-the-world".[24] Horkheimer, however, said there was no "being" as such, but rather a "manifold of beings in the world".[25] And later on, in *Negative Dialectics*, Adorno continued the immanent critique of the formalistic ontologization of the category of Being and the fetishization of the categories of Historicity and Time by Heidegger. This procedure potentially rendered as extraneous, inessential and therefore secondary, the real practical historical processes of human society which sociology was able to delineate. We have here the curiosity of Adorno deploying sociology against philosophy in order to demythologize it. In this case, however, the target is not philosophy *per se*, nor philosophy as critique, but a philosophy of Being which has, through a process, of attenuated abstraction from the historical process, widened the gap between theory and practice to a point where to apprehend the world through its categories cuts analysis off from men's real history and reality and thus from the possibility of becoming conscious of that history and mastering it. Adorno's message was: reified historical categories immobilize real history:

> On the one hand, when history is transposed into the *existentiale* of historicality, the salt of the historical will lose its savor. By this transposition the claim of all *prima philosophia* to be a doctrine of invariants is extended to the variables: historicality immobilises history in the unhistorical realm, heedless of the historical conditions that govern the inner composition and constellation of subject and object. This, then, permits the verdict about sociology. As happened to psychology before, under Husserl, sociology is distorted into a relativism extraneous to the thing itself and held to injure the solid world of thinking –

> as if real history were not stored up in the core of each possible object of cognition; as if every cognition that seriously resists reification did not bring the petrified things in flux and precisely thus make us aware of history.[26]

For both Horkheimer and Adorno, lost in the fetishisms of the philosophy of Being with its language of ontology was the real concrete human social totality at a given stage of development of men's relation to external nature and to one another, with its endemic class antagonisms.[27] That philosophy therefore *cannot mount a critique of that given reality*. This is because, Horkheimer said, it tries

> to obscure the separation between man and nature and to uphold a theoretical harmony that is given the lie on every hand by the cries of the miserable and disinherited.[28]

The tangible situation of real men living in real unequal historical conditions inherently carried with it real practical possibilities for a better, more authentic society through, in Marxist terms, the radical deed of the proletariat. (One could of course accept Horkheimer's sociological critique of the philosophy of Being without accepting that the key to real human liberation lay in the revolutionary victory of the proletariat.)

In general the critical theorists relentlessly combated any claims in theory to the ontological primacy of either being or consciousness materiality or thought in an unmediated way. This task was for them concomitantly political since a static reduction to either pole denigrated *practice* as the constituting mediation which unified them in activity. Such a reduction would by extension shackle the possibility of praxis having any significant bearing on the social relations assumed to be embraced within the absolutized status of the moment to which active human cognition had been reduced. It was this stress on activity which set the early critical theorists against reflective philosophical materialism, seen as a naïve form of unmediated metaphysics, and thus against orthodox Marxist interpretations of materialism deriving from Lenin's *Materialism and Empirio-Criticism.* Marcuse remarked that the old question what has objective priority, what was 'first there', spirit or matter, consciousness or being "cannot be decided . . . and is always meaningless as it is posed".[29] More recently Alfred Schmidt has expounded the practico-social character of Marx's materialism, in a non-ontological interpretation firmly in the anti-Leninist tradition of critical theory. He argues that in Marx the "stuff of nature" is at once extra-human as well as being constitutive of men, so that broadly speaking Nature is the whole of reality: but that in Marx

> This concept of nature as the whole of reality did not result in an

> ultimate *Weltanschauung* or a dogmatic metaphysics but simply circumscribed the horizon of thought within which the new materialism moved . . . [it] was 'dogmatic' enough to exclude from the theoretical construction anything Marx called mysticism or ideology; at the same time it was conceived undogmatically broadmindedly enough to prevent nature itself from receiving a metaphysical consecration or indeed ossifying into a final ontological principle.[30]

The critical theoreticians were in general also sceptical of the attempts by philosophical anthropology to derive a basic model of the nature of man since this also was a generalization of the results of historical analysis of societies into a set of trans-temporal categories implicitly or explicitly regarded as constant. Horkheimer believed Scheler's efforts to discover a constant human nature to be a desperate search for absolute meaning in a relativist world.[31] Philosophical anthropology, which was for the critical theorists a close bed-fellow of philosophical ontology, ran counter to the future orientation of critical theory because it automatically put men in the eternal thrall of an essential nature even before they acted. Horkheimer, quoting *The German Ideology*, maintained that if in practice

> men change not only nature but themselves and all their relationships, then philosophical ontology and anthropology are replaced by "a summing-up of the most general results, abstractions which arise from the observation of the historical development of men". The possibility of using these results in order to grasp developmental tendencies which point beyond the immediate present does not justify transposing that summing-up into the future. Every metaphysics strives for insight into an essential nature, with the idea that the nucleus of the future is already contained in it; what metaphysics discovers must underlie not only the past but the future as well.[32]

17 Philosophical sociology and sociological philosophy

As the early Frankfurt School saw it, the difference between critical and traditional theory, as theory, ultimately came down to the status each accorded to philosophy. The purpose here is to extend the earlier foreshadowings of this theme in previous chapters. Critical theory operated with the presupposition that what the prevailing social reality could be or ought to be was inherently present negatively in the overwhelming 'positivity' of the present and the theory was geared to this inherent potentiality (as appropriated in its historical continuity) and to its possible realization in practice. The critical theorists interpreted their Marxian inheritance as the continuation of Marx's project of the fusing of philosophy and science through the realizing in practice of philosophical ethical imperatives based on a scientific analysis of society which revealed its fettered rationality. The realization of philosophy in this sense carried with it the abolition of philosophy since it would be sublated in a truly self-determining society in which the ideal no longer stood over and against the real. As Marcuse later affirmed: "by virtue of its historical position Marxian theory is in its very substance philosophy".[1] Such a conception of philosophy differs from either of the two typical views of philosophy as an independent exact science or as a subsidiary and auxiliary synthesis of the significance or logicality of the various specialist sciences.[2] The conception of philosophy in critical theory was mediated by Lukács's and Korsch's critique of vulgar Marxism and resembles also Gramsci's position elaborated against Bukharin. Vulgar Marxism saw philosophy as a technical enterprise and had no truck with philosophy as critique because it ideologically claimed that philosophy in that sense had already been realized in the nascent socialism of the Soviet State. Whereas the critical theorists wanted to keep alive the post-Korschian revival of Marxian theory as social science burdened with philosophy and sought to preserve the unity of philosophy and science, purpose and knowledge, and theory and practice which they saw both advanced capitalism *and* bureaucratic socialism as instrumentally keeping apart.

In the previous chapter we saw, however, the danger of veering towards irrationalism or mythology if the unity of philosophy and science in critical theory is allowed to move more towards philosophy and away from a scientific appraisal of socio-historical reality. It was the stress on philosophy which gave critical theory its element of fantasy at the current stage of social development. And as theor y it was the presence within it of philosophy as critique of the extent to which a specific society is ongoingly minimizing greater human self-determination which also constituted by established standards the element of precariousness in critical theory. In the age of unrealized social potential, Horkheimer maintained, the social function of philosophy as critique inevitably meant that the practice of social life "offers no criterion for philosophy; philosophy can point to no successes".[3] The opposition of philosophy to reality arises directly from its principles because

> Philosophy insists that the actions and aims of man must not be the product of blind necessity. . . . Philosophy has set itself against mere tradition and resignation in the decisive problems of existence, and it has shouldered the unpleasant task of throwing the light of consciousness even upon those human relations and modes of reaction which have become so deeply rooted that they seem natural, immutable, and eternal.[4]

The critical theorists' position on the relationship between philosophy and social science was played out in the recurring advocacy of critical reason against the almost total hegemony of what Husserl called "Galilean" rationality in the administered world of developed capitalism. It is at this stage that philosophy as critique particularly needs to be kept alive. For the critical theoreticians instrumental-technical rationality – that is, the informing of ends by technical means using detached knowledge – is a degenerate form of critical Reason, i.e. the notion of human self-determination, of seeing the world as the rational product of one's actions. The distinction between instrumental and critical reason had its forerunner in Hegel's *Verstand* and *Vernunft* and was also expressed by Horkheimer as subjective and objective reason.[5] Similarly, both Marcuse and Habermas have recently identified with the "unity of theory and practice" which is critical reason, by invoking the Greek conception of Reason as "*theoria*".[6] This conception embodies the idea of human beings determining themselves and their world by virtue of their intellectual faculties and implies that men are capable of both comprehending and transforming the world since it is a rational system and therefore accessible to knowledge and change. Against this, Marcuse juxtaposes the calculative, abstract, technical rationality of the positive sciences which is geared not to transforming reality to make it rational, that is as conforming to men's desires, but merely to the control and technological conquest of Nature.[7] (All these characterizations of the two types of rationality hinge on the extent of the unity/disunity of theory and practice and subject and object involved.)

Horkheimer said that both types of reason had been present from the outset in history and, following Weber, that the predominance of subjective, instrumental reason had been achieved in the course of a long historical process. The original faculty of *logos* or *ratio* was the subjective faculty of speech which was the critical agent which dissolved superstition and mythology, but this form of rationality developed an objectivity and a dynamic of its own beyond, although related to, thinking. Concepts became emptied of their content and formalized to the point where, devoid of content, they were incapable of perceiving any particular reality as reasonable *per se*. Such rationality cannot be of any help in determining the desirability of any goal in itself, but only means;[8] whereas objective reason for Horkheimer has two unified aspects: (i) the essence of a structure inherent in reality which calls for a specific mode of behaviour and (ii) the effort of reflecting on this order.[9] This view of philosophical systems was opposed to the nominalistic limitation of reason to mere classification of chaotic data as exhausting the objective basis of our insight about the world. Since the critical position holds that the world has a rational developed structure accessible to men, it progressively aspires to "replace traditional religion with methodical philosophical thought and insight"[10] and to attack all mythology in the name of the objective truth of reality appropriatable in the name of men. Once formalized and having become generalized and unrelated to the objective content emphasized, however, reason became purely instrumental, operational, a tool for further domination of nature *and eventually of society*. Formalized reason, the instrumental detachment of theorizing from specific world-changing, world-moulding projects, has divorced philosophy (in the above broad ethical sense and as embracing the notion of objective Reason) and science, so that the purposes for which knowledge is sought become divorced from the means of its acquisition. The unity of philosophy and science is critical theory, their disunity traditional theory.

A profound problem for the critical theorists was that within the administered world instrumental reason had gained the status of a self-evident immutable form of rationality to the point where its hegemony was even lauded as liberation itself, as the true unity of knowledge and purpose. Thus the consummation of the historical process towards greater demythologization in theory and more self-determination in practice became simply *unenvisageable* as alienation masqueraded as freedom. To put the matter more precisely, modern bureaucratic problem-solving was the use of neutral knowledge for the deployment of means towards ends separated from the self-conscious purposes of most men and was effectively employed for controlling and predicting aspects of a social order which was, however, the forgotten creation and re-creation of its participants. This rationality became synonymous with self-fulfilment and autonomy which thus perpetuated human alienation in a grotesquely degenerate form. Horkheimer declared that in this milieu philosophy and social science rivalled each other "as far as tedium and banality are concerned".[11] But the rub was that the more the administered, instrumentalized, rationalized reality penetrates, dominates and banalizes philosophy, so the more doggedly the dialectically negating layer of philosophy as critique asserts itself (in the shape of critical theory) presaging a more socialized humanity:

> the whole historical dynamic has placed philosophy in the center of social actuality, and social actuality in the center of philosophy.[12]

The debt to Weber in the foregoing exposition is obvious and Horkheimer acknowledged that his conceptions of objective and subjective reason resembled Weber's substantive and functional rationality as well as the great illumination that the work of Weber and his followers had provided into the processes of bureaucratization and monopolization of knowledge and into the social aspect of the transition from objective to subjective reason.[13] (One might add that Horkheimer's reasoning continued Marx's analysis of the historical transition from classical critical, political economy to vulgar justificatory, political economy as the expression of the consolidation of the bourgeoisie's power within developing capitalism.) The unity of the two types of reason in Horkheimer was intended as the philosophical summing-up of the results of that concrete historical process from a later stage, a theoretical result expressing its philosophical significance through social science. It also enabled Horkheimer to mount a critique of both advanced capitalism and bureaucratic socialism as examples of functional rationalization. But Weber's sociology of the historical processes concerned was for Horkheimer ultimately subjectivistic since he conceived of drives and intentions of men in society as *a priori* irrational, which meant that he had no way of discriminating one end from another.[14] He therefore individualized out of existence the possible social realization of philosophy. Neither Horkheimer nor Marcuse would capitulate in the face of the rationalized and reified world and be satisfied with the irrationalist implications of individualistic value-judgments. The insistent stress on the concept of objective reason attempted to circumvent that position. The *leit-motif* of critical theory in this period was that the social reality itself objectively contained the truth, irreducible solely to that reality that society could potentially be more rationally organized, less alien to its producers, less thwarting of their desires. A social stage could be attained which would enable "the rationality of thought to proceed from the rationality of social existence".[15] Only then could what Marcuse regarded as the progressive bourgeois project of the foundation of knowledge on the autonomy of the individual be fully realized. At present, in the period of the 'pre-history' of mankind, this autonomy is only expressible in theory as the individualized philosophy of responsibility, reconciliation and personal morality under relatively unfree irrational bourgeois conditions. Only when such conditions had been abolished could such a project be fully realized in practice under the collective planful, rational regulation of men's lives in accordance with their needs. In other words, true individuality presupposes true collectivism.

To return more specifically to the role of philosophy within critical theory, it is in relation to Althusser that we can see that philosophy does not always play the same part in Marxist theory. Indeed, we might say that there is within Marxism a difference between, to use Horkheimer's terms, traditional and critical Marxism. The recent critique of Horkheimer and the rest of the Frankfurt School by the Althusserian Göran Therborn[16] exemplifies well just how far Althusserian Marxism continues the orthodox Marxist separation of fact and value and particularly of science and philosophy. It would be tedious to elaborate the complete catalogue of wilful simplifications, logical sleights-of-hand, underived assertions and imputations of guilt by association with 'bourgeois' theorists which Therborn brings to bear in his analysis. But the central point of his critique is relevant here since it involves the status of philosophy in critical theory and Therborn's failure to grasp the dialectical relationship of philosophy and social science in critical theory serves to highlight the fetishistic character of Althusserian categories in general. My own experience confronting Althusser's work or that of some of his followers such as Therborn was paralleled and captured finely by Horkheimer when he described his reaction to Sartre's *Being and Nothingness*:

> The dialectical finesse and complexity of thought has been turned into a glittering machinery of metal. Words . . . function as kinds of pistons. The fetishistic handling of categories appears even in the form of printing, with its enervating and intolerable use of italics.[17]

Therborn claims that the critical theorists *reduced* social science to philosophy instead of following what he sees as Marx's lead and making a complete *break* with it to found a science of social formations. But this is to equate philosophy (following the orthodox Marxist framework) solely with *method*. Moreover, Therborn selectively employs some of the terminology of dialectics ("contradiction", "moment") but no dialectician would fall into his either-or trap of philosophy *or* science which he derives from Althusser and foists *a priori* on to Marx's development and on to Horkheimer instead of engaging more nearly the actual theoretical efforts of the two theoreticians in their respective contexts. Therborn does not engage the notion of the historical unity of social science and philosophy in Marx and Horkheimer, the conception of theory burdened with critique as the transcendence of philosophy but guided by it to achieve its aims in practice. Nor that Marx's 'scientific' concepts were intended to be inherently philosophical in the sense that they methodologically tried to embrace how social reality failed to encompass the extent to which it could at the present level of development potentially be more rationally organized by more self-determining men (as we saw in Chapter 15). Historically, the Althusserian position is an orthodox retrenchment against the Korschian and critical theory positions as revived in recent years. Therborn argues for Marx's consummation of a break with philosophy to found an autonomous science and the Frankfurt theorists' failure to make this break is said to condemn them to criticism of bourgeois science "from outside", in the name of philosophy.[18] But this view only makes sense if one accepts a total separation of social science and philosophy and their respective corollaries such as theory and practice, fact and value and is and ought. This implies a denial that these can be mutally conditioning and thus a denial of dialectical social development which can in various ways transcend, overcome and incorporate elements of previous stages in later ones, a position which would, however, seem to run counter to historical evidence of specific processes. Althusser's view of history is dogmatically caesural and ultimately relativistic.

Leaving aside for the moment the validity of the critical theory/traditional theory dichotomy, for the critical theorists (to recapitulate) traditional theory, epitomized in positive science, in seeking knowledge for mastery and control keeps apart fact and value, morality and knowledge, theory and practice, subject and object, immediacy and mediation, means and ends, knowledge and purpose and science and philosophy. The latter is usually seen as the separate logical watchdog of science or as an independent discipline assessing the significance of sciences. But traditional theory, as Habermas has said, generally does not know that its protective belief of being free from interests is illusory. Therborn's position exemplifies traditional theory's separations in every detail except that he *knows* his commitment to a certain kind of 'Marxist science' is interest-laden and culpably foists a simplified 'historicist' schema on to the historical theoretical configuration of critical theory instead of appropriating its structure and precise premises. It is just this important commitment to appropriating the inherent structure of social reality with honesty and humility that characterizes Marx's method as well as the best 'traditional' science and which Therborn's Althusserian critique flaunts. It has the same kind of "bad conscience and the evil intent of apologetic" that Marx saw in the work of the vulgar political economists.[19]

To take up again the question of self-determination and objective critique having become virtually unenvisageable under conditions of total instrumental rationality, Horkheimer saw the inability of men to visualize Reason objectively as a theoretical aspect of the process whereby the bourgeois class threw off the practical and theoretical fetters of feudalism. The destruction in this process of religion and superstition in the name of science had a progressive function, but this enlightenment turned round on itself, gained a dynamic of its own, detached itself from specific concerns to gain ascendancy as technical rationality which, in the social sphere, meant its use for the domination of men as it had been used to dominate Nature. When the Enlightenment philosophers attacked religion in the name of reason "in the end what they killed was not the church but metaphysics and the objective concept of reason itself".[20] In Weber's terms the world became disenchanted and objectively meaningless. Historically, theory and practice became disunited and instrumental rationality came to dominate to such an extent that the older ideas of justice, liberty, equality and so forth lost their intellectual roots as aims and ends in themselves for the triumphant bourgeoisie because there was then no rational agency to link them with objective reality. The result of the atrophy of objective Reason was, *inter alia*, a quagmire of relativism and meaninglessness which was the breeding ground of irrationalism. Viewed from the immanence of critical theory's assumptions, it was for the latter reason that the critical theoreticians saw the preservation of philosophy as critique as the crucial function of critical theory. (Extrinsically, we can suggest that it was the experience of working-class acquiescence in National Socialism that activated this stress.) The critical theorists saw themselves as doggedly fighting against the weight of prevailing definitions of what was possible in society. Critical theory was the seemingly impossible unity of science and Utopia, fact and desire, practice and theory in a social world which *structured* the separation of those domains and erected separate individualized moralities on the basis of factual knowledge.

In the face of this pressure, said Horkheimer and Marcuse, philosophy had to be obstinate. The social function of philosophy was not to be the handmaiden of sciences nor to see itself as a specialist discipline to rival them, for such an attitude is a confession that thought "which transcends the horizon of contemporary society is impossible".[21] Such an obsequious attitude would see questions such as whether the social organization in which tasks set for science by government and industry were the correct ones for mankind as matters for personal decision and subjective evaluation because it operated without a conception of objective reason. Horkheimer declared that "Sociology is not sufficient. We must have a comprehensive theory of history" in order to be able to assess the *objective* consequences for men of the knowledge of the reality which they live out. Swiping at Mannheim again, Horkheimer said that the stereotyped application of the concept of ideology to thought patterns is tantamount to an admission that there is "no truth at all for humanity":[22] philosophy is not *only* related to a specific social stratum, which location exhausts its historical significance. Moreover, neither is the real social function of philosophy just a fault-finding criticism, but rather

> to prevent mankind from losing itself in those ideas and activities which the existing organization of society instills into its members. Man must be made to see the relationship between his activities and what is achieved thereby, between his particular existence and the general life of society, between his everyday projects and the great ideas which he acknowledges. Philosophy exposes the contradiction in which man is entangled in so far as he must attach himself to isolated ideas and concepts in everyday life.[23]

That function was controversial not only because it attempted to bring Reason into the world, but also doubly so in the age of intensified rationalization when philosophy was "inconvenient, obstinate . . . of no immediate use – in fact it is a source of annoyance".[24] To stress the distance of critical theory from the inherently individualizing tendency of bourgeois theory which presupposed the monadic subject facing unchangeable passive reality, Marcuse claimed that the critical concepts were not *reducible* solely to philosophical ones which could compete with other philosophies for a foot in a chaotic reality. On the contrary, they were directly *educible* from the economic conditions as expressions of the unrealized, rational, *objective* possibilities for a different order of society present in the reality.[25] In philosophy conceived in this way, Horkheimer echoed,

> Logic . . . is the logic of the object as well as of the subject; it is a comprehensive theory of the basic categories and relations of society, nature, and history.[26]

To conclude: in effect the critical theorists, rightly in my view, saw that social science had indeed historically overcome philosophy in the *methodological* sense of constituting the new scientific procedure more competent systematically to appropriate the differentiated socio-historical reality of human society and contribute to the historical process of demythologization. They added that in that process of overcoming philosophy Marxian social science was burdened, i.e. determined, by it. Thus the historical intention and role of *philosophy as wisdom*, as the fulcrum between the self-conscious desires of men and the possibilities of their fulfilment, as the repository for problems bearing on the potentialities of mankind, was preserved in critical theory in a cancelled, negated state. And it sought a theory-informed praxis that would realize philosophy in practical reality. Critical theory therefore saw itself as historically the unity of sociology and philosophy. These were kept apart in the conventional social science of the epoch of increasing rationalization in which in general the obverse of critical reason, i.e. the separation of means and ends, the instrumental disunity of theory and practice, held sway. The trajectory of the critical theorists' reasoning took up from the awareness that the philosophical enunciation of perfect political and social forms was inadequate in itself since more than psychological and moral conditions were involved as enabling conditions for their realization. A scientific description of concrete social relationships and tendencies (Horkheimer's "single existential judgement") supplanted but retained philosophy, since at a certain stage of social development questions of human happiness and morality could be seen as no longer accommodatable by reconciling men to reality purely at the level of the conscience or satisfaction of the bourgeois individual, but became *social* questions. Thus reason could not ultimately be restricted simply to questions of individual, subjective thought and will. If reason was about shaping life according to men's free decision on the basis of their knowledge, Marcuse said, then

> the demand for reason henceforth means the creation of a social organization in which individuals can collectively regulate their lives in accordance with their needs. With the realization of reason in such a society, philosophy would disappear.[27]

In the Conclusion we will take up among other things the question of the importance of the more adequate analysis of the 'objective' social reality in the determination of the 'philosophical' questions about collective fulfilment and self-determination characteristically posed by the Frankfurt School. What is educed, in Marcuse's terms, from the objective reality as its unrealized objective possibilities (seen as simultaneously ethical imperatives) depends crucially on the adequacy of, and the assumptions underpinning, the empirical analysis of that reality. If this appropriation is inadequate or archaic then such ethical social questions are more likely to be posed in a fashion that renders the chances of their realization in practice less probable. Extending the adumbrations of this theme in earlier chapters, we will programmatically suggest a strategy, demanded by the present stage of development, for moving beyond the post-Lukacsian critical theory standpoint whilst preserving through a necessary reformulation both its 'philosophical' and sociological moments. In the course of this procedure the validity of the whole philosophized distinction between traditional and critical theory is thrown into question.

18 Conclusion: The cunning of praxis

1 The essence of the Marxian project was that it uniquely tried to be a social science of the objective process of human emancipation. It was a historically specific attempt to bring together into one practical-theoretical scheme the scientific comprehension of social reality and the movement of that reality into what it ought to be. That is to say, it sought the closure of the discrepancy between the organization of society and its 'rational' potentiality in the movement of history tending towards the realization of the conditions necessary for socialism in practice. Marx saw his theory as seeking the conscious harnessing of this tendency of which it was the theoretical expression. He therefore did not need to pose proletarian universality as an abstract Ought-postulate over and against the class inequality of his time, since for him the proletarian victory was written into the dynamic of the contradictory historical dialectic, i.e. into the very "being' of the proletariat under capitalism. In short, he strove to demonstrate that a scientific appraisal of social reality revealed its necessary tendency towards the conditions needed for socialism.

2 Marx's writings are not a totally consistent, infallible monolith but contain, like the writings of any other pioneer of social theory, various blind spots, omissions, errors and tensions. An example of the latter is that the logic of regarding history as a potentially endless process of ongoing practical transcendence stands unreconciled with the expected Utopian end-state of communism (as outlined in Chapter 2 of this study). But we must not be tempted to regard such contradictions, or other dilemmas which have been highlighted, as Marx's profound perception of fundamental universal tensions of the 'human condition' in general when they stem from historically specific theoretical and political preoccupations relating to the context and stage of social development at which he stood. From within the Marxian perspective the proletarian victory in the working out of the contra-

dictions of capitalism into a newer, higher social order of which all that has historically gone before has been the irrational, social class cursed, "pre-history of human society" is perfectly consistent with materialist dialectics. Accept that scenario today and arguments must then revolve around matters such as the nature of the passage to socialism, strategies for raising the class-consciousness of the proletariat as the historically progressive class, party organization to that end, social incorporation of the class and how to undermine it, etc., and evidence and interpretations of texts will be so geared. Marx was, like every other thinker, a creature of his time who appraised the stage of development of the industrial societies of Europe of his period and, like many others, perceived the plight of the proletariat in the social changes he was observing in Europe. He then projected with the aid of an 'inverted' Hegelian dialectic phases of these processes into a final end to social antagonisms, in particular to the immediate class-conflicts of his time and saw that end as inherent in the movement of history. To Marxists, the location of Marx firmly in his period seems to miss the point. That Marx articulated the level of social development of his time seems to them to be one of the strongest elements of the Marxian doctrine – an aspect of the 'unity of theory and practice'. But that Hegelian insight rebounded on Marx as he mythologically connected it with the non-arbitrary self-awareness of the level of social development embodied in himself and the various historical incarnations of the party projected into a socialist future. Methodologically Marx's erroneous but fashionable materialist 'inversion' of Hegel's dialectic was one way within the assumptions of the post-Hegelian dialectical philosophy and early economic and political theory available to him that Marx could, he believed, consistently and non-arbitrarily overcome Hegel. And this at the same time was a politically important project because it enabled him to totalize politics and epistemology into the historical process. But Marx came out of the interplay with Hegel's philosophy bearing the imprint of what he had 'inverted'. Once embarked upon this line of argument Marx was forced automatically also to regard social reality as alienated and mystified, as well as tending towards greater 'rationality' in his new, more 'secular' sense since Hegel, he thought, had expressed this real alienated reality only in estranged, coded terms. However, at a later stage of development of the general historical process of demythologization which Marx none the less moved relatively further forward, we can now bring to bear a different scientific perspective on the inevitably partial Marxian theory and see its genesis in other, potentially more adequate and incorporative terms. Today we can appropriate its wider historical significance in that process rather than remaining trapped in its local historically specific theoretical divagations, the perpetuation of which debates within Marxism relate to the need perceived by later Marxists to establish a theoretical pedigree and purity.

3 The sociologization of the Hegelian dialectic most importantly provided Marx with a conception of historical necessity, embracing the "real movement" of the social process towards communism. This gave Marxian socialism the power over others of being not just an abstract Utopia, not just an arbitrary value-judgment about the good society, but the ultimate result of social development which could be delineated in its tendency with the prestigious "precision of natural science" (Marx, 1859). Marx yoked together the twin passions of radical intellectuals caught up in the social changes of post-Enlightenment Europe: science as the liberation from obscurantism, and communism as the hope for the rational end to social inequality and the real inauguration of justice and freedom. As social science Marx's theory thus overtly tried to deal with society not only as it was but as it could be: it was social science in the subjunctive mood. This interpretation does not mean that this project was not historically specific, nor that social science in general which does not aspire to this superior aim is degraded, inferior, pseudo-neutral or enshrines human bondage. That absolute dichotomy is a chimera, the product of later post-Lukácsian theory. At the present later stage of social development and differentiation the close unity between science and Utopia and between the traditional epistemological positions and the great ideologies of the nineteenth century which Marx saw cannot be relevantly posited. The advocacy today of a social science more detached from relatively extraneous concerns such as Utopian dreams and wish fulfilment is perfectly feasible without running into the arms of positivism, value neutrality, justification of the *status quo*, inhumanity, etc. The apparent choice between a science of freedom or a science of social bondage stems from a needless and false dilemma, a coercive product of the perpetuation today in the Western Marxist tradition of an archaic mode of *fin de siècle* anti-positivist thinking.

4 Lukács, later in the Marxist tradition, remains locked into these propositions of the Marxian legacy which revolve around the basic bourgeoisie/proletariat dialectic. In order to combat and totalize a variety of sociological and epistemological positions which were also for him associated with non-revolutionary political positions very much as they were for Marx eighty years before, Lukács effectively pares the mainly social–scientific Marxian theory down to a philosophy of praxis. Lukács's sweeping, all-embracing *tour de force* achieved its power by tracing European philosophy to its "basis in existence", social-ontologically rather than sociologically. This analysis brought out well the individualizing tendency of subject-centred bourgeois philosophy but by pushing it too harshly into the pursuit of the reconciled subject-object (dubious at least in relation to Hegel)

it generalized across societies and social contexts at various stages of development. This procedure enabled Lukács to show, via Hegel and Marx's insight about the ongoing co-existence of theoretical antinomies in the practical concrete totality, that it is only in the social reality of communism that they can be completely resolved. The analysis was selective towards the goal of showing that all theoretical (as well as political and economic) roads lead to the proletarian praxis. It is this absolute imperative of proletarian revolution in the mood of urgency and despair after the First World War that inspires Lukács's every word, as a similar imperative inspired the special selectivity and emphasis of Marx's work in another context before him. (This statement does not denigrate either for their politics or assume a pure, 'correct' position, but attests to a later standpoint which asserts that such political interest can be seen as not to exhaust their historical significance.) Lukács's 'two-truths' theory of class-consciousness simultaneously offered a solution to the then contemporary preoccupation with sociological relativism and founded the later neo-Marxist and Frankfurt School stress on the empirical facts as not exhausting reality since there was a higher tendential reality over and above them. The 'two-truths' theory was also a sophisticated epistemological gloss of what was already implicit in Marx's theory of class-consciousness because of its Hegelian origins, a gloss also which dovetailed into the directive Leninist Party practice of the time. Bolshevik practice found its own theory.

5 In attempting a sociology of the epistemological deliberations of the classical European philosophers on subject and object but in not, however, fully embracing a sociological standpoint, Lukács was led into perpetuating uncritically the individualistic concepts of subject and object which he injected into the matrix defined by the polarization of mediation-praxis and immediacy-contemplation. This rendered the theoretical position that in so far as a social science assumed not impingement on its object of enquiry it remained contemplative and stuck fast in immediacy, unable to envisage any other standpoint than that of the scientist regarding his object as immutable. But that 'object' was for Lukács actually the reified surface of bourgeois commodity society which could be overthrown in its very objectivity from within by the becoming-conscious of the proletariat in praxis. However, the reduction of Marxian theory from its originally more social scientific character to a philosophy of history effectively made Lukács's position scholastically unassailable by empirical evidence since all systems of European thought could be read off from the scheme as wanting the infusion of praxis to consciously mediate subject and object. And the imputation of perennial failure to the classical philosophers for not rationally solving the problem of the relationship between them since they could not face the

"givenness" of bourgeois reality, leads in analysis inexorably to the proletariat as the agent which can provide the total *real* resolution of the problem *collectively* in practice instead of in a mythological Hegelian 'we' of the Spirit. But this theory implies an all-or-nothing apocalyptic vision in which all human subjects come totally to see themselves in the world they create. Implausible dialectically anyway (since some alienation must remain), this position whilst accusing Hegel of mythology makes its own mythological collective projection in order to inform the advocacy of proletarian praxis. The reduction of Marxian social science to a philosophy effectively put Lukács back behind the historical Marxian project which had at least the aim of explaining the philosophical, religious, 'universalistic' ways in which men try to understand the world by reference to the level of development of the real and specific human social relations in which men are interdependent. Lukács's regression to an earlier stage in the historical development of sociology is exemplified by his uncritical employment of concepts such as 'Man', 'subject', 'object', 'freedom', 'givenness', 'immediacy', already transcended implicitly or explicitly by Marx in favour of more empirically adequate concepts for analysis of specific men in specific societies. Furthermore, Lukacs created a self-validating 'two-truths' theory of class-consciousness unamenable to empirical refutation and assumed a historical dialectic of necessity involving the Manichean tragic 'curse' of the proletariat on the bourgeoisie, also for specific hortatory purposes, in 1923. Thus he merely refined and thus retained, the mythological elements in Marx instead of moving beyond them. By giving the philosophical side of the putative unity of social science and philosophy in Marx a semi-autonomous life of its own, not closely enough related to the social science enterprise with which it was wed, this laid him wide open to the attack from the social science side mounted in Part two above. In doing so he had executed a philosophical regression in relation to the overall historical process of humanistic scientific enlightenment which had undergone an acceleration in the eighteenth century.

6 Gramsci was also embedded in the Marxian tradition of depicting the struggle between the bourgeoisie and the working class within developing capitalism as being a struggle which must issue in socialism, freeing the level of rational development of human powers from the fetters of their archaic social relations. Gramsci adapts the theory to the specific conditions of Italy characterized by the conservatism and inactivity of the passive mass of Southern peasants, as well as stressing the active, "willed" carrying through of the proletarian victory against the more fatalistic interpretations of history of orthodox economic–determinist Marxism. Like Lukács, Gramsci is preoccupied with the need for praxis on all levels against which urgency all theory and effort is measured and assessed. The reality of the

ongoing social consent and recalcitrant folklore beliefs of the masses led him to the analysis of popular beliefs and their place in sustaining a hegemonic reality in the interests of a ruling class. The Gramscian position was epitomized in his critique of Bukharin's 'external' scientistic stance *vis-à-vis* popular beliefs which Gramsci makes his starting point. Gramsci sees the possibility of changing the very objects of social enquiry, assumed as fixed by Bukharin, through 'working up' those beliefs within an organization which effectively constructs a socialized, less particularistic objectivity in practice. Like so many within the Marxist perspective since the 1920s and 1930s, Gramsci was one of the first to begin trying to answer the question of why 'the revolution' had not taken place (or seemed to have failed) when all the socio-economic signs suggested it should have occurred or succeeded. His answer lay in the mechanisms of cultural integration whereby a ruling class historically achieved hegemony over the society as a whole and the consent of the ruled was blindly attained, necessitating progressively less overt State coercion. At later stages in the development of the bourgeois class within the relations of production the determinacy of the "economic moment" became less and the struggle of classes became more played out on the ideological level within civil society. This was highly developed in the West and demanded that the class-consciousness of the proletariat should be generated in practical life by processes of molecular and group transformism within a party and the creation thereby of a counter hegemony. This would ultimately generate in reality the unity of mankind, a universality previously expressed as God, Utopia or Spirit during earlier phases of that overall historical process. Gramsci tried to demonstrate a practical way to realize organically in society what Marx called in *The Holy Family* the "unity of real man and the real human race", which Marx believed had been "metaphysically travestied" by Hegel's notion of the Absolute Spirit.[1] But generalizing the blind historical development of bourgeois hegemony into the conscious project of creating proletarian hegemony kept Gramsci locked into the assumptions of the same mythological Marxian historical dialectic. He perpetuated and generalized Marx's notion that Hegel had travestied the unity of mankind, which could be projected as the *real* outcome of the historical dialectic. Gramsci assumed that that was the historical significance of the many elaborations of the themes of God, Spirit, and Utopia in history and read them as expressing metaphysically a process leading towards the goal to which the real immediate praxis he sought in the *present* was also geared. It was a beautiful and noble vision which gave his exhortations a world-historical significance, but it was a Utopian ideal tilted away from a more adequate sociological appraisal of the tendencies of society which would stand more chance of posing ethical questions in such a way as to render their realization more likely at the current stage; and of combating other less ennobling myths competing in the hegemonic arena.

7 Early critical theory consisted in the methodological, genetico-critical core of the Marxian theory in its Lukácsian mode, minus in theory the characteristic stress on the consciousness of the classical agent for revolutionary transformation – the proletariat; and minus in practice an orientation towards the classical organizational element – the party. Critical theory's audience was any group that would listen to the world- historical truth. The immediate reasons for the excision of the proletariat as the key class for the emanicipation of mankind lay in the disillusioning effects of National Socialism and Soviet Marxism on the critical theoreticians. It meant that the status of critical theory was rendered precarious, geared as it was only to "real possibilities" and the generalized better coincidence of individual purposiveness and circumstances and the conscious, planful organization of society supplanting its blind necessity. The theory claimed to be the self-conscious unity of philosophy and social science preserving the historical truth of potential greater human social self-determination. The theory lauded the salvifically conceived "critical attitude" as exemplifying the continual possibility of critical theory feeding on the beckoning Other implied by a reified *status quo*, which theory was dialectically wedded to a presupposed traditional theory of society. As in Lukács, the theory was informed by a stand upon the nature of the changeability of the subject-object relationship – if these are rigid and separate theory becomes traditional (Lukács's "contemplative" theory) and if it presupposes or is geared to their conscious changeability, it is critical (and philosophical). The corresponding dualism of instrumental-calculative versus critical-objective Reason, which was a basic plank of the Frankfurt platform, was originally Hegelian, and had its sociological continuity in Weber mediated to Horkheimer via Lukács. In practice, however, on the level of the scholarly articulation of the theory and the social location of its adherents, critical theory was virtually indistinguishable from some genetic versions of the sociology of knowledge which also appropriated the presuppositions of a blindly developing social reality. The critical theoreticians were also members of the intelligentsia, like any sociologist, and all publicly existing theory (not just the critical) can potentially contribute to a change in its 'object'. Merely conceiving of social objectivity as humanly produced and potentially 'returnable' to its producers in various degrees is by itself a sociological truism. Furthermore, within the dialectical universe of discourse the generalized commitments to dereification and preserving the 'truth', unless related to a historically necessary process, are also arbitrary. The critical theorists were reluctant to do this because of the

association with orthodox determinist Marxism. So rejecting historical necessity in the orthodox form as well as party organization left them as Marxists only the advocacy of enlightened cultural dissemination once the working class had seemed to have missed the historical opportunity to liberate mankind. This programme had irrational implications since the philosophy of praxis then became *methodologically* compatible with other philosophies (notably that of fascism) which also undertook the task of mobilizing the masses. But once locked into the post-Lukácsian tradition of regarding the world as depraved, reified, totally rationalized, administered, quantified, commoditized and instrumentalized, careering towards "the abyss", the apparent failure of the proletarian revolution in all contexts left the critical theorists with two understandable responses. That is, either polemical cries in the wilderness such as that against the caricatured, banal, scientistic sociology of 'facts', irrespective of its real historical nature or the dogged, martyr-like profession that critical theory embodies world-historical truth come what may.

8 Because of their overwhelming preoccupation with mass praxis and their philosophical anti-positivism, the post-Lukácsian Marxists attacked positivism and scientism wrongly and gave them undue credence for the analysis of the social world. For all of them science had to be like classical physics. The whole Hegelian-Marxian project, however, of moving off in scientific analysis from the apprehension of the "proper logic of the proper object" (Marx) suggests that the social level of integration of the universe (what in the old-fashioned philosophers' language we might call the 'object' of sociology) requires the discovery and elucidation at a later stage of development of the genesis of the categories which its developing structure enabled its incumbents scientifically to apply to it at various stages and which in that application it effectively embodied (socio-genesis creatively appropriated). Put in another way, the level of integration recognized as the social requires concepts adequate to it which more nearly embrace the inherent structure of its development without veering too much towards an attenuating level of abstraction which would push analysis more towards the pole of metaphysics and away from an adequate grasp of real processes. But the Marxists dealt with here erroneously assumed not only that the positivistic pursuit of laws actually *did* mainly characterize science and sociology in particular, but also tacitly assumed that they were potentially appropriate for society so long as reality remained the objectified forms of social life associated with the reifications of commodity capitalism. That is, in Lukácsian terms the randomized, anarchic reality of capitalism which lent itself to law-like representation which became generalized across natural and social phenomena. The argument not only assumed that laws arose in this way (which was simply asserted, particularly by

Lukács, on the basis of generalizing the commodity fetishism argument and invoking economic theory as being based on the random, calculative market reality) but also unwittingly enshrined a natural law type of science as being applicable to the Lukácsian "second nature" reifications of society. These reifications were seen as only a temporary state of affairs, a bus stop on the road to socialism, falsifiable by the supervention of mass praxis. Assume this, though, and the reifying, inhuman nature and function of social science as geared to such mechanisms of 'unfreedom' has been decided in advance, which renders the pursuit of its actual historical character uninteresting or unnecessary. This thus sanctions the advocacy or practice of positivism in social science: an ironically unenlightened procedure. This form of inverted scientism not only flies in the face of the inherent structure of the social level of integration but also philosophically assumes that it either knows what method social science employs or dogmatically decrees that methodologically speaking within the philosophy of praxis that empirical question does not matter. This simplistic, polemical view of science and social science was elaborated by thinkers who saw urgent proletarian praxis as paramount in the age when societal rationalization was monumentally dehumanizing. Seen in a historically long-term perspective, however, this theoretical tendency perpetuated a quasi-theological assumption that the present, merely temporary, unequal, alienated world will be (and/or is simultaneously *in abstracto*) transcended in eternity. When this 'truth' has been realized (under socialism) the self-knowing transparent society will no longer need to sustain social science since its object would be known to itself. Or, if the theoreticians conceded (within this theoretical tradition) the always implied element of reification in *any* social formation, the all-important question of the *extent* to which that reification could be eliminated and the *extent* to which it might or might not be potentially unchangeable or even benign was left unconsidered. This was because it would have seemed to move theory towards justifying quietism and not to have the polemical, exaggerative edge seen as necessary to move men against the *status quo*. Early critical theory thus tended to conceive of social reality and its possibilities in the undiscriminating absolute terms of total determination and un-freedom versus self-determination because it perpetuated a Lukácsian theory which had put human social life in those philosophical terms for short-term political aims. It was ironically uncritical as well as carrying potentially Procrustean or nihilistic political implications.

9 Critical Theory claimed to be the self-conscious unity of philosophy and social science against their separation in traditional theory, and in the era of instrumental reason it was the philosophical substance of critical theory which made it akin to fantasy and

animated the "obstinate" stance *vis-à-vis* the rationalized reality. It was this element that the critical theorists invoked to gear their analysis to the real possibilities for a rational organization of society inherent in the present order. This project argued against Kantians implicitly by appealing to a conception of objective Reason rather than a viewpoint of value-judgment or subjective opinion about the question of what ought to be the organization of society. The critical theorists rightly saw that social science had historically overcome philosophy in the *methodological* sense of constituting the new scientific procedure more competent systematically to appropriate the increasingly differentiated socio-historical reality as well as contributing to the historical process of demythologization and enlightenment. But, they claimed, Marxian social science *qua* theory remained, in the process of overcoming philosophy, burdened, i.e. determined, by it. The historical role of what we might term *philosophy as wisdom*, as the repository for problems bearing on the potentialities of mankind and the significance and meaning of life, was preserved in critical theory and guided its deliberations towards seeking theory-informed praxes which would realize the social-ethical imperatives of philosophy by their transcendence in practice in a society in which the ideal no longer stood over against the real. This is why all the theorists discussed opposed what they saw as the degeneration of philosophy into an independent logical, technical rumination upon scientific method and procedure in the manner of logical positivism. Korsch, Lukács, Gramsci and the critical theorists all embraced the absolute conviction that to separate science and philosophy, to keep apart knowledge and purposes and means and ends was to affirm the pseudo-neutrality of knowledge, its technical applicability for problem-solving and control and to be forced in a Kantian fashion to erect a separate morality for action based on factual knowledge of determined social processes.

10 In order to profit from the dialogue with the post-Lukacsian Marxists the point at which we must start is that of the implications of the nature of the role of philosophy (in the sense of wisdom) in their deliberations and, historically, in social science in general. So far my critique of them has been a critique of philosophy in the name of science. But it would be erroneous to assume that that procedure necessarily drives my arguments once-and-for-all into the arms of scientism or positivism. The earlier remarks indicate quite the contrary since the absolute dichotomies of positivism/criticism, or philosophy-permeated versus unphilosophical science cannot be assumed to characterize the social reality of science. It is a mistaken belief that social science must make the exclusive choice between them. In Lukács, the unity of philosophy and social science, which is another way of talking about the essence of the Marxian project of

realizing philosophy in emancipatory practice informed by theory, was heavily skewed towards philosophy. Indeed in Lukács Marxian social science had become purely a philosophy of praxis, a method, an unassailable philosophy of history working in analysis on a social-ontological level. In Horkheimer and Marcuse, giving philosophy its head at the expense of social science meant that philosophy becomes more the watchdog of science rather than science as the empirical check against and monitor of the ought-ridden deliberations of philosophy. This means, however, that philosophical enthusiasm, often based upon philosophical assumptions about the nature of the historical 'truth' of 'man' elaborated in a previous epoch and related to the stage of development of its knowledge, would tend to encourage the fudging over of evidence. This leads to the proliferation of *ad hoc* sociological theorems in the name of the as yet unrealized historical 'truth' of the proletariat to account for the non-occurrence of the proletarian revolution. This tendency pushes theory more towards mythology because by moving away from the social science to which it is dialectically bound and into a stubborn ahistorical life of its own, philosophy has divorced itself from facing scientific knowledge of developed social formations and becomes *in practice* equivalent to other philosophies and ideologies which are less adequately in touch with social reality anyway (e.g. those of fascism). We might call this tendency *overcritique*. Gramsci is a slightly different case since he seeks to realize philosophy in practice by processes of practical individual and group transformism, although he still falls within this tendency. Philosophy for him is multi-faceted and embodied in all men as "intellectuals", thus constituting hegemonic reality on the various levels of social integration ongoingly in practice. Anti-positivist philosophical assumptions about contemplation and creative praxis to falsify predictions similar to those of Lukács and Horkheimer, however, inform Gramsci's practical reality-creation project against the contemplative deadness and "frivolity" of scientistic social science. But they are underived, merely assumed and placed up against social reality, implicitly as an unchangeable anthropology. The ruling out of 'non-political' social science as frivolous and mechanically detached from social object-changing is not only uncritically based in that contemplation-praxis dualism, but actually blocks more adequate knowledge of the reality in which the action is to take place. This vitiates the possibilities of successful practice. Gramsci's limited view of social science and his theory of the embodiment of philosophy in the processes of social praxis were based in, and weighted towards, a certain philosophical image of man. This was, however, an archaic rationalistic nineteenth-century conception. It was thus divorced from close contact with the developing social sciences with which the overall historical humanistic process of enlightenment (to which Gramsci is otherwise committed) must always be bound.

11 The theoreticians discussed in this book are indeed all ostensibly within that historically progressive, secular, demythologizing, European Enlightenment tradition which regarded science as the vehicle for liberating mankind from superstition and obscurantism. But all failed in varying degrees to push forward that process sufficiently in the social sphere. Unless one appeals more to evidence there is less defence against prejudice, whim, opinion, myth, caprice and irrational, arbitrary ideologies which are further from an adequate appraisal of reality. If one's advocacy of change or 'liberation' is informed in analysis by archaic philosophical concerns greatly divorced from their unity with social science then the critique veers towards mythology and the suggested practice courts failure. What remains historically to be accomplished is to consummate the process of enlightenment or scientification at the present stage because the influential post-Lukácsian Marxists had to greater or lesser extents fallen back to an earlier phase of this process. Their perspectives and those of their more orthodox counterparts provide self-fulfilling, closed philosophical systems capable of locating all other theoretical positions in relation to a necessary proletarian dialectic about the higher mediated-to-Other reality of which 'facts' can tell us little. In order better to comprehend the Hegel-Marx interplay or the nature of Marxism in its various social contexts, however, one needs to step outside the realm of Marxist discourse to avoid theoretical self-celebration and self-fulfilment.

12 The analysis mounted in this study has been a critique in the traditional sense because it is an attempt to expound but also to relocate the theoretical presuppositions of the post-Lukacsian Marxists from such a different perspective, i.e. one which transcends the dualism of Marxism versus positive social science and avoids *both* the scholasticism of intra-Marxist debate *and* shallow, nominalistic scientism where it occurs in conventional social science. As a *first step* in such a strategy one must not allow social philosophy to dominate social science, although dialectically it is retained as a moral or practical imperative in a different form. At the same time the dialectical historical tradition has provided the theoretical lesson that, unless in some way self-referential of the historical process, sociological theories will be abstract, arbitrary, categorial impositions so an alternative sociological position must also be historically demonstrable as moving beyond a previous socio-historical standpoint. The standpoint embraced here can thus be further elaborated: sociologically speaking, Marx's "new materialism" can be appropriated from the present higher stage of social development in another *implicit* significance which it can now more fully be seen also to have

possessed. Marx's position in overcoming Hegel, although *explicitly* linking him with communism, was *implicitly* a stage in the development of a process of scientification in the theory of the level of social integration which is *not reducible* to its historical political character but could not have been cognized as such at that time. In order to inform political practice today Marxists perpetuate only the overt scientifico-political meaning of Marx, their work on the Marx-Hegel interplay only seeking a present praxis-justifying pedigree. But from the higher concretized present stage of the social development of what was only abstractly present in Marx's theories, it is possible to reassess Marx's theoretical configuration and to bring to consciousness what it also implicitly *was*, i.e. a stage in the development of social science. From such a sociological standpoint we can analyse the Marx-Hegel relation from a potentially more adequate position which avoids the scholastic Marxist debates which perpetuate the *particular* historical significance of Marx in the ideologically frozen form of Marxism. Both the Marxian and post-Lukácsian theorizations of their own position as part of the historical process being expounded are only possible as a myth, i.e. that of incarnating the self-consciousness of history in its abstract potentiality as socialism as part of the process of its further concretization in the historical dialectic of the class struggle. This eschatology is a philosophized projection of a specific phase of the development of European societies into a world-historical dialectical process tending towards the liberation of mankind, when there is no evidence that history will tend towards such an end-state.

13 The at least dual significance of the Marxian project (later stages of development may permit the appropriation of more) which only has its life in the re-creation of the past from the present stage of development with which it forms a unity, is in this perspective perceived non-arbitrarily since it is made possible from a higher concrete historical stage which permits the Marxian project to be transcended and incorporated into a higher standpoint. From within the atavistic Marxian perspective, however, analysis remains locked into a particular set of assumptions which guides the questions asked and circumscribes the answers. Once Marx's historically specific elaboration of the dialectical outcome of the class struggle he was witnessing is allowed a generalized life way beyond its period, then the questions inevitably follow: Why has the revolution not taken place? What is holding it back? Was the opportunity missed? What are the mechanisms of cultural integration which systematically dismantle working-class consciousness? Is there a substitute proletariat to be seen? How can the fatalism and economism of the proletariat be undermined? What is preventing the revolution from taking place, given that the level of social development is apposite? Within these assumptions,

the Frankfurt School were forced back on to reiterating that possibilities in society are *real* even if unrealized – as theorists they were not just professing arbitrary value-judgments for a better society. The search then becomes one for the specific cultural mechanisms, e.g. of socialization, of the structured inability to visualize alternatives, of the ongoing consent of the "masses" (itself an undifferentiated conception deriving from the nineteenth century) being secured by common sense, whereby capitalist society is held to produce individuals who, like Byron's prisoner of Chillon, learn to "love their chains".

14 The next question for the post-Lukácsian Marxists locked into these assumptions in their inter-War application, was how can they as high-culture intellectuals promote 'the revolution'? For those who were not Party men for one reason or another the answer lay in cultural dissemination, i.e. the notion that critical interpretations of reality once uttered, circulated and thus sown as cultural seeds will yield the crop of a revolutionary cultural necessary condition for when the historical revolutionary moment arrives, which procedure can also promote its arrival. Until this event occurs, however, and because it is assumed to be waiting in the historical wings, there is in this perspective a strong note of despair since against the rational 'Other' of society which it contains as a potential the social world of the present is crippled and insane, walking on its head, a routine, uncreative celebration of its contemplative, commoditized non-life. For these theoreticians (less so Gramsci) and those like the Situationists who nihilistically took up their mantle in the 1960s, the reified world of capitalism was self-evidently inverted and crazy with capitalist irrationality masquerading as rationality.

15 But 'the revolution' can only be said to have been put off, prevented, diverted, bought off, emasculated by reformism, etc. if it is assumed that it should occur or should have occurred in the first place, the truly *critical* question is never asked – by what theory, by what set of assumptions should the 'victory' of the proletariat be *expected*? For a Marxist this would be an arrantly pointless, if not profane question. The Marxian assumption is generally that a scientific analysis of historical processes shows that the proletarian victory can and must occur because of their "being" in the historical dialectic as the true 'universal' class of history. To restate the point at issue from another angle, in a similar fashion to that whereby Cieszkowski projected what he saw as a Hegelian triadic elaboration of historical epochs into the future, so Marx and many of his followers after him have generalized into a world-historical dialectical succession of class struggles culminating in socialism the specific changes he was observing and theorizing in his period. Thus the proletariat will consciously make a revolution against the bourgeoisie in a similar way as that class can be seen blindly to have done against the feudal classes: but

the proletariat's hidden social universality will make its revolution the final humanity-liberating revolution. Because Marxists believe that their perspective scientifically articulates the leading edge of the various earlier stages of this process and is thus geared to the progressive negation of capitalism, no amount of this kind of historicization of it into its period is usually of any avail in discussion. Moreover, the generally unself-referential pseudo 'value-free' bourgeois sociological alternative to the Marxian theory seems unthinkable. Of course, in reality it is often actually scientistically banal anyway and does not theorize its own location, etc., which, on the level of theory, makes the sociological leap into moving beyond perpetuating the historically local significance of Marx's theory rationally particularly difficult. The notion that social development can and should become liberatively more conscious, less blind and 'irrational' in various respects is a laudable legacy of the Enlightenment provided that the historical tendencies concerned have not been mythologically delineated. If so, then, as in the case of Marx and even more in the case of Lukács, the historical process of scientific enlightenment is ironically more burdened with its opposite – dogmatism, superstition and obscurantism – which vitiates locating more adequately the nature of human societies and the *extent* to which they impose a determinacy on their interdependent members.

16 The element of obscurantism was exemplified in the theorists' anti-positivist hostility towards factual social science in the name of the spiritual autonomy of man and in the demotion of empirical evidence against either the assumed rational tendential potentiality of proletarian society or generalized social possibilities. Horkheimer accepted the findings of empirical research, accepted the historical overcoming of philosophy as the competent discipline for systematically analysing social reality and encouraged a great number of empirical studies, but then philosophically caricatured the social reality of developing social science into the idealized scientistic dominative mould. This was because in grappling with the theoretical tensions of what he believed was the crucial project – the unity of science and critique – the events of the 1930s pushed him, with Adorno and Marcuse, towards obstinate critique alone. Critical theory was the highest point achieved in its time by a social theory which still saw itself as burdened with philosophy, but it was a critique of science in the name of philosophy, whereas the historical development of the secular, demythologizing tendency of which the Marxian sociological heritage was a part, tended towards the reverse. The early critical theoreticians could not fully take the step which we are arguing for partly because they were pole-axed by fascism and Stalinism. To put the principle involved here into the language of critical theory: the pursuit of science, of knowledge of what Is (in its unity with the past)

in a relatively more detached way must at this stage of development inform critique, not the other way round. *In the dialectic of positivism and criticism, of Is and Ought, of science and Utopia in the historical process, the scientific moment must monitor critique to minimize mythology. This must be our methodological oath.* It is the continuation of heroic Enlightenment rationalism, not the absolute capitulation of philosophy or critique to scientism. If this project sounds like a banal plea for empiricism, for having a look at what is there, we most note that as Hegel and Marx showed to appeal to evidence does not make one an empiricist. It is ultimately the only guard in theory against *all* sources of myth, fabrication and obscurantism. Taking enlightenment to its consummation connotes the opposite of capitulation to the dominant groups of the *status quo*, since more adequate knowledge is potentially hostile to *all* vested interests, reaction and superstition.

17 Yearnings about what Ought to be, questions of social morality, the content of philosophy as the wisdom of the significance of human action, can be shown genetically to be related to the various social relations of men at given historical moments. Some values become detached from their historical origins and are later perpetuated and sedimented intergenerationally in different contexts, thus appearing 'absolute' or 'ultimate'. At the present stage the dynamics of this process and the resultant current physiognomy of society can only be reliably known empirically through a genetic investigation. The 'Ought' and social justice questions which early Marxian social science tried gallantly to make scientific in its particular way still remain today pervading its present state *qua* social science, guiding its investigations and inducing its practitioners to look the wrong way. In the language of the tradition, my advocacy of a restressing of the scientific moment of the historical reality of social science as a first step at the present stage of development by no means entails absolutely jettisoning the 'spirit' of philosophy in the above sense in the name of science. The appropriation of the "proper logic of the proper object" enables the more adequate discernment of what needs to be changed in practice and how this can be accomplished. *The knowledge of what Ought to be and the high moral tone of human emancipation redefine themselves in the process of newly discovering what Is, how it developed and what its tendencies are.* We might still want to refer to these questions collectively as 'philosophy' because it has a familiar feel and a noble tradition. But in view of the need at this stage to further the historical process of demythologization and the tendency towards overcritique in critical scholarship, the term must be employed specifically and with historical qualifications, so as not to imply an unlimited autarky to 'philosophical' questions in the above sense.

18 The Marxists, however, operate with an archaic, mythological conception of the process and dialectical tendency of history permeated by an image of man perpetuated from a bygone age. *This* is why 'the revolution' has not occurred (the theory wrongly expected it) and why political practice based on it fails again and again, and why despair and desperation result. But, as Marx taught us, the essence of man is the "ensemble of social relations", i.e. what real men are capable of becoming and achieving at the given level of social development. And to know this state, in order adequately to be able to invoke the notions of "potentiality", "real possibility", more "rational" organization, etc., one must know the nature of developed reality more nearly as it *is* in its unity with the past. The most basic principle for successful action to change social arrangements which is Marx's secular legacy must be taken literally, i.e. that the more adequate one's appropriation of reality the greater is the possibility for successful political practice. Although this need not *necessarily* be the total aim of sociology. The kinds of changes required themselves change, depending on the development of the reality and our knowledge of it, even when that knowledge may have been sought for other purposes. There are many levels and sectors of a social formation, and knowledge in some areas may inspire action and in others it may not. These are abstract questions, the parameters of which can be delimited through empirical research and resolve themselves in practice on their various levels, which the investigation may or may not inform or promote. And this represents a potentially endless process as development bites into the future. So the once-and-for-all Frankfurt School dichotomy of technical, manipulatory knowledge versus "critical", self-knowledge of the alienated institutions of society is illusory. It is a product of a partial, philosophized view of the nature of science and the neo-Marxists' abstract praxis-contemplation antinomy corresponding to the so-called impingement or otherwise of 'subject' on to 'object'. Put like that it is far too undiscriminatingly abstract: particular processes in a complex social formation need to be specified since collectively and individually men to various extents already impinge on their 'objects' and to various extents the reverse is true on many different levels. Moreover, such processes can and are informed by 'dead' knowledge which has become common to *all* of them. Unless freed from the unyielding individualistic 'subject-object' dualism the technical/critical knowledge dichotomy cannot help us very much in directing the investigation of processes of social reality which proceed with relative and changing degrees of consciousness and blindness on various levels. All knowledge discovered about this men-made reality potentially provides some men in some way on some level with consciousness of the world they have made and are ongoingly making and remaking. The extent of this self-knowledge

and the effect it has on the development of the configuration and on which levels must be specified and investigated. Knowledge of men-made social processes and their unintended consequences is inevitably human self-knowledge and is thus by no means the monopoly of "critical" theory. The philosophical notion of man-as-praxis must be supplanted by the sociological conception of men-as-practising.

19 The critical theoreticians' work was implicitly underpinned by the desire to create the Athenian ideal of the civilized, cultivated, self-determining, responsible man, which reflected their intellectuals' standpoint and accounts for some of their aloofness from vulgar, practical concerns. It is the intellectual who has some power, though not as much as the real power holders, who tends to perceive the social order as overpowering. It is the intellectual who sees the world as mad and walking on its head. It is the intellectual who comes to believe that social life is systematically sterile and worthless. It is the intellectual who lauds self-determination when the masses in practice revel in chance, astrology and other forces beyond their control which absolve them of responsibility. To say that men experience "mere immediacy" (Lukács) or that the ordinary man feels weak and oppressed by a sick society is an intellectual's philosophical assumption not a sociologscal finding. Only Gramsci attempted specifically to build a bridge between high-culture intellectuals and, in his terms, other types of intellectuals through a process of the generation of "collective man" in practice. Only Gramsci made this discrepancy the centrepiece of his concerns in this practical way and his work can be seen as a continuous effort to accept the extra edge of comprehension of total historical processes that the high-culture intellectual possesses but not to deify it. For Gramsci, "the active man–in–the–mass" understands the world in some way in so far as he transforms it, but there is no assumption that such understanding is monstrous, shameful, lower, 'incorrect' or 'unscientific', which epithets were for Gramsci symptomatic of intellectualistic scientism in social science, whether from the Marxist or the general social science camp. High-culture intellectuals were to elaborate the romantic, universalistic "new elixir" to further the development of the unity of mankind by laying the cognitive foundations for its fulfilment in reality through processes of transformism.

20 Although potentially cutting through the dangers of scientific elitism implicit in the Leninist-Lukácsian conception of the vanguard party, the crucible in which the molecular and group transformism was to take place for Gramsci was none the less *still* one form of the party (the modern Prince). Gramsci's proposals remained more or less tied to this as the counter hegemony-generating entity because the political experiences of the period in which he lived meant that it was the only vehicle (despite its now revealed unfortunate

omniscient, directive, bureaucratic, potential) he could visualize for this universalizing task. *Hic Rhodus! Hic Saltus!* Moreover, Gramsci assumes the undifferentiated goal of the 'universal' unity of mankind as the liberative aim of political action. This is a notion that stems from and perpetuates Marx's specific arguments from the 1840s about the bourgeoisie's particular class interests mystified as universal interests being sublated under socialism which realized the proletariat's true interests, which were also the true universal interests of mankind. Even though he envisaged a practical way in which to achieve it, against abstract Utopianizing, Gramsci still believed philosophically that, in Sartre's terms, the "polyvalent" world must be and would be transformed into a "univalent" one. He remained a nineteenth-century rationalist who could not envisage that any other historical outcome than the wholly rational reality of socialism was contemplatable. This assumption dominated his thought and action and directed his social science. It is demonstrated by his belief in the long-term triumph of the "organic", necessary historical process.

21 On the level of methodology, the post-Lukácsian Marxists were correct to point out the formalistic weaknesses of the scientistic importation of natural science law-like models into social science, its fetishism of methods and the banality of the rampant proliferation of empirical nodules of knowledge. But they were wrong to associate all social science *per se* with that methodology or with social trends inimical to 'man'. At the current stage of social development the process of the separation out from social science procedure of its wish-fulfilment elements, although not total, is now perhaps more advanced than before towards greater domination by other interests such as the one of more detachment from immediate emotional involvements in the matter in hand. But that does not mean that such social science has or can become *totally* so detached. We can affirm along with some of the Marxists that bourgeois sociology *does* tend to be abstract; does tend nominalistically to attenuate reality; that value-freedom *is* a chimera; that scientistic sociology is ultimately metaphysical; and that it does frequently assume society to be static and eternal. All these criticisms which have come from the Marxist tradition must be mustered against this kind of social science, although to do so does not imply acceptance of other mythological aspects embedded in Marxist social science. Conversely, the sociologists are right to point out that much Marxist analysis does tend to be crudely selective and distortive; is frequently simplistically philistine (e.g. Lenin's *Materialism and Empirio-Criticism*); is self-confirming and unfalsifiable; in its Lukácsian mode does embrace an unassailable two-truths theory of class-consciousness; is perpetuating an intellectual's early-nineteenth-century view of the then emerging proletariat projected into the twentieth; does operate with an *a priori*

schema for locating theoretico-political enemies; and is in the last analysis a secular religion. Marxist analysis, however, is generally, speaking, laudably historical and developmental and intends at least, following Marx, to appropriate empirically the inherent structures of social processes. But its Utopian heritage induces the assumption that that structure is part of a process working itself out towards the conditions necessary for socialism, which all empirical research can only confirm. The sociologists irrationally assume that social reality is structureless and impose their categories upon it, whilst the Marxists dogmatically assume in advance that they know its inherent structure.

22 The sociologists are mistaken to exorcise politics and 'moral' questions from their deliberations and wrong to affirm the absolute position that the analysis of society is one thing and value-judgments another. More adequate knowledge of society gives us a better idea of what needs to be changed in society and potentially influences what we regard as what 'ought' to be. This may not always ensue but the sociologists are wrong to rule it out in principle since it runs counter to social processes we can observe. Their value-neutral stance is self-contradictory since their scientific procedures are permeated by different types of 'values' (e.g. those regarding what constitutes evidence, honesty of presenting findings, etc.) which have developed over time. But the Marxists have allowed one earlier cluster of the values, or the moral, ought-ridden, philosophical, elements which run hand-in-hand with social science in the historical process, to have its head, which has prevented them from developing a new theory and a corresponding new 'philosophy' more appropriate to the present day. Ironically the Marxists (particularly the orthodox strand against which the tradition discussed here has reacted) espousing 'Marxist science' above all else, commit the most heinous scientific crime of all. That is, projecting, for example, into the evidence of the actual beliefs of the working classes, a vision of what they as investigators *want* to find (class-consciousness) and explaining its non-appearance by *ad hoc* theorems such as false consciousness, mystification, reified thought, leadership betrayals, consumerism or ideological diversions.

23 Marxist commentators (notably George Lichtheim) in the Western Marxist tradition have often stressed that it was only Marx of all social theoreticians who tried to embrace social science and human emancipation in one scheme, as the unity of is and ought in science-informed practice which ultimately unifies philosophy and science in a self-determining society in which human purposes, circumstances, self-changing and self-knowledge coincide. But this view as we have seen implicitly assumes that against that absolutely humanistic project any other attempt at social science *must perforce* be banal, shabby and justificatory, keeping values and facts separate.

This view ironically gives credence to the scientistic ideologies of bourgeois (or "proletarian") sociology against which Korsch and Lukács reacted. But by critically appropriating the methodological presuppositions of both positions we can see that both scientistic bourgeois social science *and* various forms of Marxist analysis make erroneous assumptions about the role of philosophy in the sense of wisdom in social science deliberations as being, respectively, either irrelevant or necessarily inherently constitutive. The task, however, is not merely to take the best of one perspective and mix it with the best of the other, purely on the level of method, but rather to carry out what the Marxists (because they believe that they have the monopoly of philosophy-permeated social science) believe is impossible and what the sociologists believe is unnecessary. That is, to argue as this study does dialogically against one in terms of the other to raise them to a higher standpoint, a strategy made possible from a higher stage of social development. To argue against Marxist theory as a sociologist is to appeal to empirical evidence and demand the development of a new reality-adequate, less philosophical theory appropriate to a higher stage of development. And to argue against sociology in the scientistic mould in a Marxist manner is to mount the earlier critique on the level of method and to relate what 'Ought' to be, where necessary, to the newly investigated 'Is' of society after that first (i.e. *next*) empirical step has been taken in what can only be an *unending* socio-scientific process as long as there are men living in societies on the earth. (Thus future generations will inevitably carry out a similar transcending critique of this study itself to incorporate its present concerns and polemics into the overall historical process.)

24 After Lukács, through the young Marcuse to the *Dialectic of Enlightenment* and elements of the New Left the reconciliation of men to social reality has been deemed compatible only with false consciousness and/or conservatism. But once the intimidating mythology of an absolutely pathological, untrue, insane, inverted reality is jettisoned, this problem assumes a different character. In the terms of the dialectical view itself the social world cannot be *totally* 'irrational', sick, manipulated or alienated, so one does not have to be a liberal to affirm that elements of developed societies are already 'rational' and progressive. After Lukács, however, the perceived urgency of proletarian action at that time led to radical intellectuals fudging over what Marx termed the "civilizing aspects of capital",[2] which achievements were conceived purely negatively as concessions gained in spite of the anarchy of bourgeois society. This thought pattern dies hard. But it is by no means politically conservative, based on an adequate analysis of reality, to exalt in the progressive positive achievements of civilization compared with earlier periods which can and should endure: in short, optimistically to exalt in life and human happinesss

here and now instead of espousing the dreary pessimism of sacrifice, renunciation and denial of the possibility of fulfilment now in favour of the deferred deeper fulfilment 'over there' in the better reality of socialism which so characterizes post-Lukácsian Marxism; whilst *at the same time* fighting against dogmatism, irrational blind forces, superstition, inequality, obscurantism, unenlightened action, etc., towards their *greater* removal or appeasement without implying that their *total* Utopian abolition is possible. It is this very belief in the possibility of a final state of human bliss which is potentially a political danger because it tempts and justifies Procrustean action towards it in the present, providing a source for what Weber called an "ethic of ultimate ends".[3] But one is inexorably part of a historical process which continually throws up (both blindly and consciously) complex new social configurations and thus new challenges to fight on various levels. The routinization of charisma must be fought by charismatizing routine if it jells into reification.

25 In the *Dialectic of Enlightenment*,[4] Horkheimer and Adorno are, however, sceptical about the liberating effects of the historical process of enlightenment from superstition, an influential argument which it clearly behoves me to engage. They believe that profoundly inhuman consequences flowed from it and are deeply pessimistic about the possibilities of its furtherance. They see liberation from myth and unknown forces in a Weberian fashion as having become an end in itself, as failing to extirpate itself as a form of enslavement, thus turning into its opposite: a fetish which instrumentalizes all individuality, integrates all human characteristics and repeats in all spheres the rational domination of Nature for which purpose such reason arose in the first place. Individual differences become blocks to the efficiency of administration and organization, a situation upon which, for example, anti-Semitism thrives by branding and stigmatizing difference and thereby further expunging anything that cannot be classified. Through the historical process of rationalization, and exacerbated by the commoditization of all spheres of life, enlightenment turned into blind domination which, in the name of rationality, blindly becomes irrationality: "Enlightenment is totalitarian."[5] Enlightenment tends to level, it turns into the elaboration of repetitive entities and thus dominates what is qualitatively unique through a process of abstraction. At higher stages of the process of enlightenment the terror of the unknown from which enlightenment was intended to liberate men becomes a new terror. It becomes the fear of *anything* inexplicable, of anything that cannot be computed, which leads to reason becoming mere opinion with imposed agreement and force of argument holding sway over what is reasonable *per se*. This lends itself to attempts to impose forms of objective order which can rule over a disenchanted world.

26 This argument was, however, elaborated at a specific historical point at the end of the Second World War after the revelation of Nazi atrocities against the Jews. Any ideal of human emancipation in any way through radical social change or enlightenment was, in the mood of despair of that time, likely to be interpreted as doomed in the long-term to lead to the domination of men. The Horkheimer and Adorno thesis importantly implied that the Marxist socialists' revolutionary culmination of the historical process of necessity as the liberation of men from their blind, 'natural pre-history', was not possible. This was because the same historical process of subjection to the external fate of social alienation, which for Marx laid the foundations for human liberation, also greatly repressed individuals as they acquired self-mastery during the formation of the civilized ego. This was so extensive that in the end there would be no free individual subjects left able to appropriate the promised social wealth of socialism.[6] Their psyches will, like society, have also been permeated by means-ends rationality.

27 This vision, however, demolishes one mythology in terms of another, in a theorization pervaded by what Lukács called the "tragic ideology"[7] in German thought, particularly from Simmel and Weber onwards. For Adorno and Horkheimer, the human organism, in trying to assert itself against its naturalness in developing a self, comes to oppose itself to the natural context in an "unyielding, rigidified sacrificial ritual",[8] a celebration of its consciousness which effectively enthrones it as a means. This kind of deification of means was emphasized by Weber in his studies of rational bourgeois capitalism, but the point made by Horkheimer and Adorno is that it is "already perceptible in the prehistory of subjectivity".[9] That is to say, it is a social-psychological danger built into being 'naturally' human in the first place, for the arrogance of consciousness denies Nature in man in the process of dominating Nature, which leads to the elimination of the individual as a subject since he dominates himself as well as Nature in an irrational, total, technical way. This argument was, however, effectively a pessimistic interpretation of fascist totalitarianism as an example of the tragic flaw in the whole human historical development as part of Nature. Moreover, they assumed that Marxian historical necessity needed to be combated as a real possibility, i.e. they took seriously a mythical notion of the historical bondage of men mediating their emancipation. They then combated it by saying that that same rationalizing process had so stultified the individuals who live permanently under domination in reified societies that the possibilities for liberation historically laid down in socio-technical terms could never be realized since the human subjects have been rendered inherently incapable of harnessing them. An otherwise realistic characterization of what being human means – the

growth of self-controls and self-autonomy – is projected to its logical and idealized conclusion of total, irrational self-domination and consequent inhumanity in practice.

28 But this picture exemplifies absolutist thinking, for the formation of self-controls in men never completely totally self-represses individuals: men develop self-restraints in themselves to a greater or lesser extent depending on the social context and level of social development and on other factors which are empirically delineable. Horkheimer and Adorno were correct to locate humanness in the level and types of self-restraints historically admixed with the 'natural' 'animal' responses in social human beings, but wrong to trace in it either the reality of a total self-domination or even its danger given that the existence of self-restraints is necessarily always a more-or-less phenomenon, defining what it is to be human at any stage. Enlightenment from compulsive, coercive, unknown forces must be conceived of as a process *towards* greater demythologization in theory and *towards* greater freedom from hypostatized social forces in practice. To see the problem in absolute terms is itself a form of coercion since it is for ever unattainable. Adorno and Horkheimer's question "what is left of human desires after they have been totally scientised?" is abstract, the answer to which can only be criticism of the question. It is a philosophical question which rhetorically cries out in the context of a *given* oppressive human situation by going to one side of the extreme presupposition that human social life could function at either of the two extreme poles of totally scientized or totally unscientized desires or of total restraint or lack of it. Self-reflection on emotions is possible without the individual emasculating his emotions, in the same fashion that a science of human emotions is possible without totally neutralizing them. It is upon evidence for these propositions that moral imperatives must be formulated, propagated and if necessary acted upon.

29 The critical theoreticians also purged timeless philosophical-anthropological absolutes because these concepts would seem to hold men in their thrall even before they had acted and would also surreptitiously impose a pseudo-metaphysical harmony on a conflictual and unequal society. This position continued Marx's view that it is to the societal mediation of 'absolute' generalizable categories that we must look, i.e. to what Marx repeatedly described *ad nauseam* as "specific societies at specific stages of development", etc. One thing that Marx's methodology was designed strenuously to prove was that any economic categories that *appeared* applicable to all modes of production were only so at a certain level of summing up and were thus not eternal. And even then that was only possible because from a later stage of development they were seen to be applicable across time because the previously nascent structures, of which they were

originally the potential more abstract expression, were now preserved more concretized in the present structure. Marx purged eternal categories because they might deify a particular social order and, being absolute, render critique and the advocacy of change difficult or even impossible. The methodological fruitfulness of this principle for the sociology of knowledge needs to be assessed empirically but it must be remembered that it was originally informed by the interest of mounting a political critique of specific societies, which is a very different interest from that of scientificity. Informed by that evaluation at the present stage of development, however, the question of constant anthropological features of human societies or behaviour cannot be suppressed because it would potentially proscribe critique. Their existence, range of applicability and relationship to the type and level of social development which made their discovery possible are empirical questions.

30 One abstract, 'universal' conception of theological origin which Marx specifically rejected for similar reasons was that of 'Man', in favour of the analysis of specific groups and societies comprised of men. There is a qualification to be made here, too. It was Gramsci who saw an overall world-historical process towards the unity of mankind previously expressed in underdeveloped conditions as God, Spirit or Utopia, which would become a reality at the appropriate stage under socialism when "collective Man" would walk the earth in reality. Again, even though the absolute unity of mankind is an untenable projection, one might argue consistently within an historical perspective such as Gramsci's or Marx's for the retention of a sociological version of the postulate. At a certain level of development of productive forces and relations as these become more internationalized, Man or Mankind is placed in *reality* on the historical agenda, Issues begin to arise in the world which transcend specific groups of men distinguished on the class or nation-state level, which could properly therefore be called the concerns of Man. But to say that history was the road towards the progressive unity of Man through the historically developed successive societies of specific men would be to put the matter theologically or mythologically. Whereas to say that whether and to what extent this process consummates itself is an open question subject to possible reversals of development which are empirically delineable, is to put the matter sociologically.

31 The famous "cunning of Reason" in Hegel's *The Philosophy of History* "sets the passions" of individuals and the collective aspirations of nations "to work for itself" in the process of historical self-realization of what it essentially is, as comprehended and exemplified by Reason at later stages.[10] Strong teleological overtones are present in this conception as they are also in what we might analogously term Marx's implicit notion of a *cunning of praxis*, through which he dis-

cerned that history had a consciously appropriatable meaning in the blindly developing but ultimately self-rationalizing development of its successive social structures. In this process the development of forces of production for specific purposes by the practice of historically transitory social classes for their particular interests at particular times, furthered their own demise through the concealed significance of those accumulating productive forces – the conditions necessary for the full, universal development of mankind corresponding to the supplanting victory of the progressive proletariat. Historically transitory class societies systematically produced illusions about themselves until a condition which did not require illusions was made possible through that very social development. Also as in Hegel, in Marx no social order was ever superseded before it had exhausted its potential. Marx could not have seen, however, due to the horizon of the period in which he wrote and his particular theoretico-political context, that the same cunning of praxis was laying down concealed foundations which would enable at a later stage the appropriation of the further historical significance of his own Marxian project which he could not have known and that would permit its theoretical transcendence to incorporate the next stage of social development.

32 The succession of societies, social configurations and epochs which historical development continually bequeaths generally makes possible a potentially more extensive and intensive self-understanding of their succession from higher stages, although it need not necessarily do so. But a unified state of man in a harmonious end-state of total self-recognition, equality and planful rationality cannot be inferred from the study of historical processes and their tendencies (even though it might serve as an appealing and galvanizing myth in certain circumstances). Nor can we assume *a priori* the directionality of any particular or overall process of society as the Marxists tend to do. The 'choice' of conceptual frameworks for analysing historical social processes is not whimsical or heuristic but should be dictated by the changing nature of the structure of the 'object' being theorized, which makes possible its own conceptualization which then appropriately articulates the process. The theoreticians who hold out for a caesural or discontinuous interpretation of historical development should not be challenged by the dogmatic counter-assertion of a juxtaposed continuity approach. They should instead be faced with empirical evidence of progress or regress or relative stagnation in particular processes in relation to a previously demonstrably attained stage and the implications of this for a general theory. Without these provisos there can be no reliable, undogmatic conception of progress, nor a realistic appraisal of tendencies.

33 The nature of Western social development can be seen as entailing in the modern period that men must on many levels of the

social formation both individually and in groups always be less than totally informed as to the nature of the society which their actions reproduce. This is both because of its level of social differentiation, institutionalization and bureaucratization and the necessary discrepancy in these circumstances between the individual's purposiveness and the relatively reified society which defines his individuality. This will appear to the Marxist as a position which surreptitiously reinstates the bourgeois individual by declaring him to be eternal, but we must remember that the perspective which the Marxist would place up against that proposition implicitly presupposes an untenably total projected situation in which self-experienced individuality has become abolished in the institution of "collective man". But once we have eliminated this absolute from our concerns then, as in the case of the elimination of any historical absolutes we are dealing inevitably with *degrees* and *extents*, in this case, stated abstractly, of individual versus collective orientation and relative social reification versus relative individual self-determination. Since this general position more nearly articulates what we can observe of human societies, it is between these co-ordinates that political theory and practice must lie. It is a position thus hostile to both rampant egoism and Procrustean collectivism.

34 Furthermore, evidence suggests that there is something in the Hegelian insight that men only come to realize the fuller significance of their actions in their context after they have moved beyond the particular historical stage. To some extent they are condemned, like Marx, to fail to comprehend the total world-historical significance of their current praxis and to act in relative ignorance, *but this is not to be seen as a tragic circumstance.* The extent to which this is true is never constant, varies on different levels of society and is always subject to greater enlightenment and conscious praxis. *It provides a perennial justification for social theory to serve to minimize its extent.* And this standpoint feeds on the known historical tendency that whatever are the reversals, setbacks and progressions of the historical process as a totality and in its particular processes, the cunning of praxis must continue to 'allow' from here on the production and reproduction of a social level of integration for sociological enquiry. Later stages potentially enable us to know more about earlier stages, including those (known to us through archaeology and physical anthropology) before men completely constituted and experienced society as such. And there is always a later social stage: "World history did not always exist; history as world history is a result" (Marx).[11] New phases will tend, to various extents, to incorporate or to continue elements of the previous ones, although an omni-incorporative process cannot be assumed. But what is actually occurring, the structure of the real processes, will always potentially be accessible

to analysis on the basis of a relatively detached scientific evaluation although its degree of autonomy from other interests in any society may not be constant. From these kinds of investigations only can generalizations about mankind in general be legitimately posited. Such sociology must explain that which endures, that which becomes 'absolute' or relatively autonomous and lives on in and through successive particular social changes; implying conversely an explanation also of what perishes and why. A sociology of this kind must be detached to a degree which also permits a level of self-distanciation in order to assess the development of sociology itself and possibly to inform its more conscious direction. We study what social men historically either decided to perpetuate in society, had no choice in perpetuating or did not know they were perpetuating. This is to theorize (in addition to any given social configuration) what is in human history effectively eternal – the continuous in the discontinuous, the immortal in the mortal, the general in the particular, the autonomous in the heteronomous, the immutable in the mutable. Geared to this long-term perspective theory takes on a grandeur which transcends all particular social orders and particular group interests, even though it must perforce partake of their reality for its existence. It is sociology in the 'grand historical sense' through which the 'philosophical' questions are reformulated in a way more appropriate to the observed long-term character of social men.

35 Two objectors must be parried: (a) Karl Löwith argued that to be theoretically consistent the "trust" in continuity would have to come back to the classical theory of an endless circular movement because only on this basis is continuity demonstrable, since one cannot envisage a "linear progression without presupposing a discontinuing *terminus a quo* and *ad quem*, i.e. a beginning and an end".[12] But he has assumed abstract starting and finishing points of history, neither of which, as Marx rightly averred in 1844, are able to inform meaningful questions.[13] Löwith's argument requires also to be faced with empirical evidence for progression, regression or stagnation in relation to a level of development achieved up to a given stage in a given process. Without this, Löwith's view is of as much value as the blanket espousal of any particular philosophical assumption of the nature of the historical process (e.g. that it is linear, cyclical, caesural, teleological, finalist, etc.) irrespective of the inherent structure of observed processes. Whether continuity has occurred or is "linear" is an empirical question and must be related to given processes and the "trust" in continuity is, without evidence and specificity, no more than a vague faith. And (b) Theodor Adorno said that it was not enough to look for the permanent in the transient, or the archaic in the present, true dialectics being, rather, "the attempt to seek the new in the old instead of simply the old in the new" and that "it is

a mistaken conclusion that what endures is truer than what passes".[14] But he has polemically stated the problem one-sidedly and too abstractly. Adorno's propagandizing judgment is inspired by the negative dialectician's fear of deifying 'positivity' (the "old"), which might link him with what Is – the unequal *status quo*. But the argument can be inverted just as plausibly, i.e. it is a mistaken conclusion that what passes is "truer" than what endures. Bound up in the undiscriminating everyday language of "old" and "new" is the assumed legitimacy of employing the problematic notions of abstract potentiality and 'negative determination'. But aside from that, the elaboration of the whole issue presupposes knowledge and experience of the "old" against which the extent of the emerging "new" must be compared in order to be said to exist at all. Levels and examples must, however, be specified to get away from the undifferentiated way in which the problem has been posed and then we can more readily ascertain those "new" elements in society which actually endure and those that do not and *why*. Putting the matter in Adorno's language, human practice in general ultimately decides these questions since situations are continually created in which "old" and "new" are reversed, but without specification these notions remain unmanageably vague. As we have already argued, *positive dialectics* need not be necessarily conservative and unprogressive since some definite aspects of what Is must be 'rational' achievements and affirmed as such. Furthermore, it is possible to strengthen this position by possibly being able to show the extents to which men in society (on specified levels) not only unconsciously and blindly, but consciously, *choose* to perpetuate aspects of their society. We cannot assume that in so doing they are falsely conscious. On Adorno's stress, however, we would have to regard even these enduring elements as 'less true' simply because they endure. It is a dogmatic and one-sided stress to make the blanket assumption that the very problematic notion of the 'Otherness' or abstract potentiality of various social processes is 'more true' or more important or determinative in a given developed social configuration. This determination will in any case have been misconstrued if the observed historical dynamic has been wrongly delineated.

36 Evidence suggests that men cannot unmake their social relations at will and this theoretical result must be our starting point when considering the promotion of social changes and tendencies in various ways. Continuities of collective memory, customs, language, habits, norms, culture, personality types, and so on, across vast periods of time through many different and often monumental social changes, to say the least are in need of adequate explanation. They are by no means trivial, but are the very stuff of human social life. There are only aspects of society which are experienced as needing to be changed and in principle and in practice some aspects cannot be.

Theory and practice conceived in the post-Lukacsian totality mode often visualize and work towards an undifferentiated change of society from a supposed total determination to a visualized complete self-determination, so does not pose these problems. These theorists are blinded by the assumptions that society is completely imperfect, worthless and mystified against its 'rational' potentialities and that activity, institutions and consciousness in every nook and corner of it are permeated by, and explicable entirely in terms of, ruling-class hegemony. The historical presuppositions and implications of those characteristic post-Lukácsian Marxist assumptions about social reality have been critically laid bare in this study, but this preliminary task needs to be supplemented by empirical studies of the social processes they tried to grasp. If the conscious promoting of historical tendencies or the practical changing of social organization becomes an aim or a by-product of sociological research (although neither use is entailed nor an imperative in any absolute sense), it is essential to possess an adequate understanding of what forces actually determine men in societies. To what extent can society be changed? Who perceives the need for it? Why do things persist? What is already 'rational'? What must we fight to preserve? Instead of being dazzled by the fact that some groups of people have historically occasionally said 'no' to the social order, we should look more deeply into the significance of why so many people so genuinely, wholeheartedly and consistently have said 'yes'. Marxists, however, within their framework would tend to recoil from these matters for fear of conservatism, 'reformism', capitulation to established rationality, or losing sight of their monopoly of the theoretical grasp of the "totality". And in any case they would consider the matter subsumed under false consciousness. However, both in the interest of furthering human self-knowledge in general and/or promoting the practical removal of surplus reification on various levels (which may potentially constitute the same enterprise) our first step as sociologists at the present stage must be to undertake genetic, empirical investigations of long-term social processes which may provide answers to the kinds of questions posed above.

37 The Leninists have only imposed change on the world; the point, however, is to understand it.

Notes

Part one – Marx's theory of praxis

1 A starting point

1 Loyd Easton, 'Rationalism and Empiricism in Marx's Thought', *Social Research*, vol. 37, no. 3, 1970.
2 Respectively in Nicholas Lobkowicz, *Theory and Practice: History of a Concept from Aristotle to Marx*, Indiana, Notre Dame University Press, 1967, p. 422; C. Wright Mills, *The Marxists*, Harmondsworth, Penguin, 1967, p. 98; and Robert Vincent Daniels, 'Fate and Will in the Marxian Philosophy of History', *Journal of the History of Ideas*, vol. 21, 1960, p. 544.
3 Jean Hyppolite, *Studies on Marx and Hegel*, London, Heinemann, 1969, pp. 126–30.
4 Reinhard Bendix, *Embattled Reason: Essays on Social Knowledge*, New York, Oxford University Press, 1970, p. 40.
5 Eugene Kamenka, *Marxism and Ethics*, London, Macmillan, 1969, pp. 42–5.
6 *The Illusion of the Epoch: Marxism–Leninism as a Philosophical Creed*, London, Routledge & Kegan Paul, reprinted 1973, pp. 251–2.
7 Nathan Rotenstreich, 'On Human Historicity', *Proceedings of the Twelfth International Congress of Philosophy*, vol. 8, September 1958, pp. 215–22.
8 Shlomo Avineri, *The Social and Political Thought of Karl Marx*, Cambridge University Press, 1969, pp. 250–1.
9 Gianfranco Poggi, *Images of Society: Essays on the Sociological Theories of Tocqueville, Marx and Durkheim*, London, Oxford University Press, 1972, pp. 158–60; Zygmunt Bauman, Review of Poggi, *The Times Higher Education Supplement*, 13 April 1973, p. 16.
10 Chapter 8 of this study provides a brief discussion of aspects of these debates and of the work of Karl Korsch and carries footnotes covering studies of the Marxist controversies of the 1920s.
11 See John O'Neill, *Sociology as a Skin Trade*, London, Heinemann,

1972, Chapter 16 ('On Theory and Criticism in Marx') for an incisive comparison of Habermas and Althusser. Also George Lichtheim, *From Marx to Hegel and Other Essays*, London, Orbach & Chambers, 1971, *passim.*

2 *Praxis and practice in Hegel and Marx*

1 G. W. F. Hegel, *The Science of Logic*, translated by A. V. Miller, London, Allen & Unwin, 1969, p. 833.
2 G. W. F. Hegel, *The Logic* (Part One of the Encyclopaedia of the Philosophical Sciences, 1830) translated by William Wallace, second edition, London, Oxford University Press, 1892, reprinted 1972, paragraph 81, p. 152.
3 See particularly Chapter XXXII ('The Historical Tendency of Capital') in Karl Marx, *Capital*, vol. I, London, Lawrence & Wishart, 1970.
4 'Theses on Feuerbach', in T. Bottomore and M. Rubel (eds), *Karl Marx: Selected Writings in Sociology and Social Philosophy*, Harmondsworth, Penguin, 1967, p. 82.
5 See for example Michael Bakunin's heroic Hegelian revolutionism in his 'The Reaction in Germany' (1842), translated in James M. Edie, James P. Scanlan and Mary-Barbara Zeldin (eds), *Russian Philosophy*, vol. I, Chicago, Quadrangle, 1965, pp. 385–406.
6 *Capital*, vol. I, Afterword to the Second German Edition, 1873, *op. cit.*, p. 20.
7 See Part four, Chapter 15, for a discussion of further ramifications of this idea and its meaning in Soviet Marxism.
8 See Dick Howard, *The Development of the Marxian Dialectic*, Southern Illinois University Press, 1972, for a detailed Lukacsian reconstruction of the dialectical argumentation in Marx's overcoming of Hegel in the early writings which I have only sketched in the text.
9 Karl Marx and Frederick Engels, *The Holy Family*, Moscow, Progress Publishers, 1956, p. 186, quoted by Alfred Schmidt, *The Concept of Nature in Marx*, translated by Ben Fowkes, London, New Left Books, 1971, p. 31.
10 See Helmut Fleischer, *Marxism and History*, translated by Eric Mosbacher, London, Allen Lane, 1973, Chapter 4, for a useful account of the meanings of historical necessity in Marx and Marxism.
11 Karl Marx, letter to Weydemeyer, 5 March 1852, in *Karl Marx and Frederick Engels: Selected Correspondence*, Moscow, Progress Publishers, third revised edition, 1975, p. 64 (extensive italics deleted).
12 Karl Marx and Frederick Engels, *The German Ideology* (1845), London, Lawrence & Wishart, 1968, p. 48.
13 For example, Hiram Caton: "the socialist 'conclusions' of *Capital* are ideological because they flow from initial moral-political assumptions that cannot be logically integrated with a value-free science of economic value" ('Marx's Sublation of Philosophy into Praxis', *Review of Metaphysics*, vol. XXVI, December 1972, no. 2, p. 258).
14 In his *Prolegomena zur Historiosophie*, 1838. There is no major study

of Cieszkowski in English, but there is substantial commentary on his thought in at least the following studies: Lobkowicz, op. cit., Chapter 13; Georg Lukács, 'Moses Hess and the Problems of Idealist Dialectics' (1926) in Rodney Livingstone (ed.), *Georg Lukács, Political Writings, 1919–1929: The Question of Parliamentarianism and Other Essays*, London, New Left Books, 1972; Avineri, op. cit., pp. 124–30 (which contains a critique of Lukacs); Benoit P. Hepner, 'History and the Future: The Vision of August Cieszkowski', *Review of Politics*, vol. 15, no. 3, July 1953, pp. 328–49 which concentrates on the links with Messianism and Slavism in Cieszkowski's essentially Christian vision of action continuing man's religious peregrination towards the harmonious Kingdom of God on earth; Lawrence S. Stepelevich, 'August von Cieszkowski: From Theory to Praxis', *History and Theory*, vol. XIII, no. 1, 1974, pp. 39–52, presents Cieszkowski's relations with the Young Hegelians and expounds the essence of the *Prolegomena*; and N. O. Lossky, *Three Polish Messianists*, Prague, International Philosophical Library, 1937, covers Sigismund Krasinski and W. Lutoslawski, in addition to Cieszkowski, whose thought is treated as a whole, centring on his later master work, *Notre Père*. See Lobkowicz and Stepelevich for speculation on whether Marx had read Cieszkowski or knew of his thought via Moses Hess or Karl Werder. Marx did meet Cieszkowski in Paris in 1844 (Lobkowicz, op. cit., p. 205). The motto to this Part is from the *Prolegomena*, cited by Stepelevich, op. cit., p. 50.

15 Quoted by Lobkowicz, op. cit., p. 198.

16 Dick Howard has pointed out that the Feuerbachian *Umkehrungsmethode*, whereby Hegel's philosophy is subjected to a reformatory reversal of subject and predicate, to which Marx was undoubtedly deeply indebted in his critique of Hegel, is for some reason wrongly rendered as 'transformative method' in English, when 'invertive method' is closer to the German meaning ('On Marx's Critical Theory' *Telos*, no. 6, Autumn 1970, p. 224). This usage would indeed correspond more closely with Marx's frequent use of the image of Hegel's dialectic being 'on its head' or 'upside down'.

17 See Karl Löwith, 'Mediation and Immediacy in Hegel, Marx and Feuerbach' in Warren E. Steinkraus (ed.), *New Studies in Hegel's Philosophy*, New York, Holt, Rinehart & Winston, 1971.

18 *Hegel: An Illustrated Biography*, translated by Joachim Neugroschel, New York, Pegasus, 1968, p. 128. The validity of Marx's critique of Hegel and the implications of this for Marxian theory and its sociological legacy is an important area of enquiry, to which this study is partly intended to contribute. Apart from odd asides by Hegelians against the Marxian dialectic, one of the very few studies which attempts a specific and major challenge to Marx's position is the untranslated *Die Marxsche Theorie* by Klaus Hartmann (Berlin, De Gruyter, 1970). For discussions of Hartmann see Howard, *The Development of the Marxian Dialectic*, footnotes; Louis Dupré, 'Recent Literature on Marx and Marxism', *Journal of the History of Ideas*, October–December 1974, vol. XXXV, no. 4, pp. 703–14; and Allen W. Wood, 'Marx's Critical Anthropology: Three Recent Interpretations', *Review of Meta-*

physics, September 1972, vol. XXVI, no. 1, pp. 118–39. See also Hartmann's comments on Feuerbach and Marx in his 'Hegel: A Non-Metaphysical View', in Alasdair MacIntyre (ed.), *Hegel: A Collection of Critical Essays*, New York, Doubleday, 1972.

19 Bauer thus tried to dissuade Marx from political activity: "It would be folly if you would devote yourself to a practical career. Theory is nowadays the strongest praxis, and we still cannot forsee how much it can turn out to be practical in the long run." (Letter to Marx, 31 March 1841, quoted by Avineri, op. cit., p. 132.)

20 Quoted by David McLellan, *Karl Marx: His Life and Thought*, London, Macmillan, 1973, p. 143.

21 See Alfred Schmidt, *The Concept of Nature in Marx*, translated by Ben Fowkes, London, New Left Books, 1971, Chapter 1.

22 Alexis Khomyakov, 'On Recent Developments in Philosophy' (Letter to Y. F. Samarin) (1860) translated by Vladimir D. Pastuhov and Mary-Barbara Zeldin in James M. Edie, James P. Scanlan and Mary-Barbara Zeldin (eds), *Russian Philosophy*, vol. I, Chicago, Quadrangle, 1965, p. 234.

23 Karl Mannheim, *Essays on the Sociology of Knowledge* (1952) London, Routledge & Kegan Paul, fifth impression, 1972, pp. 154–79.

24 See Hegel, *The Logic*, paragraph 205, p. 346; *The Phenomenology of Mind* (1805), translated by J. B. Baillie, London, Allen & Unwin, 1966, p. 295; and G. W. F. Hegel, *The Philosophy of Nature* (Part Two of the Encyclopaedia of the Philosophical Sciences, 1830) translated by A. V. Miller, Oxford, Clarendon Press, 1970, paragraph 245, p. 4.

25 *The German Ideology*, p. 521.

26 Leszek Kolakowski, 'Marxism and the Classical Definition of Truth' in *Marxism and Beyond*, London, Paladin, 1971, p. 75.

27 Karl Marx, 'Theses on Feuerbach' in Bottomore and Rubel, op. cit., p. 82. (All unannotated quotations from the 'Theses' in the text are from this translation.)

28 *The German Ideology*, p. 28. Karl Löwith has however observed that "Marx . . . never asked how man could know a Nature which he had not himself produced; this question fell outside the exclusively anthropological-social area of his interest" ('Mediation and Immediacy', op. cit, p. 131). But it seems to me that this statement, inspired by both Vico and the *Geisteswissenschaft* tradition, implicitly assumes a separation of natural and social science and of 'man' and Nature which Marx never intended and which cannot be defended. It presupposes that men can understand historical-social reality because it is their creation but must perforce explain the processes of inanimate Nature in a different way. Löwith's position is formalistic and therefore unduly dualistic about conceiving the two types of enquiry and could lead us to minimize the human character of natural science knowledge as well as the partly natural character of human society. Nature and human society, as Marx correctly maintained, form a developing unity. Since men inevitably remain an evolving (biological) part of Nature, human knowledge of all aspects of that Nature is ultimately, seen developmentally and over long periods of time, the self-knowledge of Nature. Human

societies continue the self-development of Nature to a higher level because they enable men to know aspects of Nature which they did not create through the level of social development permitting the technical wherewithal to do so as men master Nature for their own purposes.

29 Ernst Bloch, *On Karl Marx*, translated by John Maxwell, New York, Herder & Herder, 1971 (from *Das Prinzip Hoffnung*, 1959).

30 Nathan Rotenstreich, *Basic Problems of Marx's Philosophy*, New York, Bobbs-Merrill, 1965.

31 Bottomore and Rubel, op. cit., p. 82 (*Diesseitgkeit* rendered as 'this-sidedness'). The Theses are best understood read alongside certain sections of Hegel's *Science of Logic*, notably the chapters on 'The Doctrine of the Notion', especially p. 577 ff. and p. 755 ff.

32 Hiram Caton rightly says that "In denying that the objective truth of thought can be decided within the scope of thought, Marx affiliates himself with all realists, for whom the object of thought provides the criterion of truth" ('Marx's Sublation of Philosophy into Praxis', op. cit., p. 248); cf. also Jean-Paul Sartre: ". . . in Marx's remarks on the *practical* aspect of truth and on the general relations of theory and *praxis*, it would be easy to discover the rudiments of a *realistic* epistemology which has never been developed". (*The Search for a Method*, translated by Hazel Barnes, New York, Vintage Books, 1968, p. 33, footnote 9.)

33 See Hegel, *The Science of Logic*, pp. 577–82.

34 Bloch, op. cit., p. 81. Thesis II is, however, far too cryptic to justify Bloch's conclusion that it is "quite original and new" because of departing from older definitions of truth as correspondence between concept and reality and that therefore for Marx " 'all previous' philosophy appears 'scholastic' " (p. 81). In Thesis I Marx talks of "all previous materialism" only. What is "scholastic" for Marx in Thesis II is only generalized "dispute" about what he calls the "reality or non-reality of thinking", not apparently all previous philosophy. Bloch leaves out of account that Hegel had already thrown the classical notion of truth into question: "In common life truth means the agreement of an object with our conception of it. We thus pre-suppose an object to which our conception must conform. In the philosophical sense of the word, on the other hand, truth may be described in general abstract terms as the agreement of a thought-content with itself . . . All finite things involve an untruth: they have a notion and an existence, but their existence does not meet the requirements of the notion." (*The Logic*, paragraph 24, pp. 51–2.) See also the references to Hegel's *Science of Logic* mentioned in Note 31, as well as his remarks on truth in the Preface to the *Phenomenology of Mind*. Bloch also sidesteps, as does Marx, the question of how the potentiality of men to create in practice conscious correspondences between "reality" and concepts or "thought" relates to the various aspects of socially imprinted natural objectivity and social objectivity referred to in the text and in Note 28. I have discussed some of these issues in relation to Herbert Marcuse as well as traced further ramifications of the Hegelian and Marxian

theories of truth in my paper 'On the Structure of Critical Thinking' *Leeds Occasional Papers in Sociology*, no. 2, Summer 1975.

35 'Theses on Feuerbach', p. 82.

36 Ibid., p. 83. Translation amended from "totality" to "ensemble".

37 Ibid.

38 Karl Marx, *The Poverty of Philosophy* (1847), New York, International Publications, 1969, p. 173.

39 Marx explained the abolition in practice of the theoretical construction of capitalism in *Capital* to Engels in the following terms: "Finally since these three (wages, rent, profit (interest)) constitute the respective sources of income of the three classes of landowners, capitalists and wage labourers, we have, in conclusion, the *class struggle* into which the movement and the analysis of the whole business resolves itself" (Marx, letter to Engels, 30 April 1868, in *Selected Correspondence*, third revised edition, Moscow, Progress, 1975, p. 195); cf. Gramsci: "The identification of theory and practice is a critical act, through which practice is demonstrated rational and necessary, and theory realistic and rational" (Antonio Gramsci, *Selections from the Prison Notebooks*, edited and translated by Quintin Hoare and Geoffrey Nowell-Smith, London, Lawrence & Wishart, 1971, p. 365).

40 Op. cit., p. 780. See also *The Science of Logic*, pp. 594–5, on the need critically to prove the truth of categories themselves to avoid arbitrariness.

41 Hegel, *The Phenomenology of Mind*, p. 515.

42 See Lucio Colletti, *Marxism and Hegel*, London, New Left Books, 1973, p. 210.

43 The quotations from Cieszkowski's *Prolegomena* in the text are cited by Stepelevich, op. cit., p. 50.

44 Several writers have also attempted to draw parallels between Marx's theory of praxis and pragmatist theories of truth of Peirce and James. Suggested by Stanley Moore in his formalistic 'Marx and the Origin of Dialectical Materialism', *Inquiry*, vol. 14, no. 4, Winter 1971, pp. 420–9 and argued at greater length by Norman D. Livergood in *Activity in Marx's Philosophy*, The Hague, Martinus Nijhoff, 1967. For a hostile critique of this equation see Bloch, op. cit., p. 90 ff. Bloch declares: "for Marx an idea is not true because it is useful, but useful because it is true" (p. 92). See also Rotenstreich, op. cit., pp. 51–3 for further critique: "Marx conceives of practice as realization while the pragmatist theory . . . conceives of practice as the decision as to what to do and what means to employ in the doing" (p. 53). See also Richard J. Bernstein, *Praxis and Action*, London, Duckworth, 1972, for an attempt to bring together the practical philosophy of pragmatism, analytic discussions of the concept of action and the concept of praxis in Marxist and existentialist thought.

45 Letter to Ferdinand Nieuwenhuis, 22 February 1881, in *Selected Correspondence*, pp. 317–18 (extensive italics deleted).

46 *Basic Problems of Marx's Philosophy*, p. 49.

Part two – Georg Lukács: theoretician of praxis

3 Lukács in context

1 Translated by Rodney Livingstone, London, Merlin Press, 1971. Text further cited as HCC. The discussion of Lukács's work in this Part is necessarily selective and not exhaustive because it is not intended as a study of Lukács's total *œuvre*. Since my focus is the sociological significance of the concept of praxis in the post-Lukácsian Marxists, I have made selections from their works (which often cover many fields) in accordance with this emphasis. This applies also to Lukács, from whose writings I have chosen to focus on HCC, and his writings of the 1920s on Bukharin and on the problems of Left Hegelian critique and praxis, as forming the stuff of basic sociological debate for subsequent writers in this Marxist tradition. This procedure has necessitated my leaving out of account Lukács's work on literary criticism and aesthetics as not directly relevant to my concerns. On these two aspects of Lukács's work see respectively G. H. R. Parkinson (ed.), *Georg Lukács, The Man, His Work and His Ideas*, London, Weidenfeld & Nicolson, 1970 and Stefan Morawski, 'Mimesis – Lukács' Universal Principle', *Science and Society*, vol. XXXII, Winter 1968, pp. 26–38.

2 See Istvan Mészáros, *Lukacs' Concept of Dialectic*, London, Merlin Press, 1972, pp. 112–14, on the influence of *History and Class Consciousness* on many thinkers in many different fields. Mészáros, however, includes Gramsci among these, but it is doubtful that this is directly true. Gramsci seems only to have known of Lukács's work through criticisms of it by Deborin and others. See *Selections from the Prison Notebooks of Antonio Gramsci*, edited and translated by Quintin Hoare and Geoffrey Nowell Smith, London, Lawrence & Wishart, 1971, editors' footnote p. 448. As is shown in Part three below, Gramsci and Lukács indeed reached remarkably similar conclusions against Bukharin's vulgar Marxism – but they did so independently of each other. See also Maurice Merleau-Ponty, *Adventures of the Dialectic*, translated by Joseph Bien, London, Heinemann, 1974, Chapter 2.

3 One might add here that whilst the Frankfurt School filtered out of Lukács's theoretical perspective its overtly party-political elements for reasons which will be discussed in Part four below, they can be said to have supplemented him by reinstating both the category of Nature and its autonomous role in human affairs, which Lukács later agreed he had blurred in 1923. See *Lukács*, 1967 Preface to the new edition of HCC, p. xvii, and Alfred Schmidt, *The Concept of Nature in Marx*, translated by Ben Fowkes, London, New Left Books, 1971, pp. 69–70.

4 Leszek Kolakowski, 'Lukács' Other Marx', *Cambridge Review*, 28, January 1972, p. 85. An exceptional counter-example to Kolakowski's judgment is Victor Zitta's very unfriendly and uncharitable assessment of Lukács's work as a whole, *Georg Lukács' Marxism: Alienation, Dialectics, Revolution: A Study in Utopia and Ideology*, The Hague, Martinus Nijhoff, 1964.

5 Karl Mannheim rightly pointed out long ago that immanent analysis of

the genesis of intellectual ideas – the history of ideas – needs to be supplemented by a "historical structural analysis", or the "existentially conditioned genesis of the various standpoints which encompass the patterns of thought available to any given epoch" (*Essays on the Sociology of Knowledge*, London, Routledge & Kegan Paul, 1952, fifth impression 1972, pp. 180–1) and I am aware of the limitations of the history of ideas. But for the limited purpose in Section (a) of this chapter of delineating the main concerns of the intellectual milieu in which Lukács initially operated, the history of ideas approach can serve as a first approximation towards a more comprehensive study. See also Mannheim's interesting comments on the 'lure of immanence' in German thought in *Essays on the Sociology of Culture*, London, Routledge & Kegan Paul, 1956, p. 25.

6 These themes also permeate Max Horkheimer's concepts of subjective and objective reason and instrumental versus critical reason. See *Eclipse of Reason* (1947), New York, Seabury Press, 1974, p. 6, for his comments on Weber and Chapter 17 below.

7 For Lukács's own biographical reflections on his intellectual mentors see the 1962 Preface to the new edition of his *Theory of the Novel*, London, Merlin Press, 1971. The outline of intellectual currents in the text draws mainly on the following sources: Lucio Colletti, *Marxism and Hegel*, translated by Lawrence Garner, London, New Left Books, 1973, Chapter X, 'From Bergson to Lukács'; George Lichtheim, *Lukács*, London, Fontana/Collins, 1970; Istvan Mészáros, *Lukács' Concept of Dialectic*; Gareth Stedman Jones, 'The Marxism of the Early Lukács: an Evaluation', *New Left Review*, no. 70, November–December 1971; H. Stuart Hughes, *Consciousness and Society: The Reorientation of European Social Thought 1890–1930*, London, MacGibbon & Kee, 1959, reprinted 1967.

8 Lichtheim, op. cit., p. 14.

9 For the record, Rudolf A. Makkreel points out that Dilthey's cultural and natural science dualism was not as sharp a distinction as Windelband's similarly conceived division between idiographic and nomothetic methods. Dilthey recognized in a Hegelian fashion a good deal of complementary interplay of explanation and description between the two kinds of science: "Dilthey makes it clear that *Verstehen* can be objective *only* if based on the knowledge of regularities that the natural sciences provide. And it is precisely this acknowledged relation with the natural sciences to which the phenomenologists have objected" (Review article on Dilthey, *Journal of the History of Philosophy*, April 1972, vol. X, no. 2, p. 233).

10 Lichtheim, op. cit., p. 26.

11 See Colletti, op. cit., p. 167.

12 For a useful short account of the culture and civilization theme in German social thought see *Aspects of Sociology* by the Frankfurt Institute for Social Research (with Preface by T. Adorno and M. Horkheimer), London, Heinemann, 1973, Chapter VI. Also Georg Iggers, *The German Conception of History*, Middletown, Connecticut, 1968, *passim*.

13 Bruce Mazlish, *The Riddle of History: The Great Speculators from Vico to Freud*, New York, Minerva Press, 1966, is good on Spengler's *Decline of the West*, stressing his belief in astrology, his relativism and the influence of his concept of culture on Ruth Benedict.
14 Henri Bergson, quoted by Hughes, op. cit., p. 118.
15 Quoted ibid., p. 117.
16 Quoted by Hayden White, *Metahistory*, Johns Hopkins University Press, London and Baltimore, 1973, p. 139.
17 Georg Lukács, *The Theory of the Novel* (1915), 1962 Preface, in 1971 translation, p. 21. Cf. also Lukács on the theoretical difficulty of surmounting positivism referred to in the text: "An attempt to overcome the flat rationalism of the positivists nearly always means a step in the direction of irrationalism; this applies especially to Simmel, but also to Dilthey himself' (ibid., p. 15).
18 Lichtheim, op. cit., p. 36.
19 Kolakowski, 'Lukács' Other Marx', *Cambridge Review*, 28, January 1972, and Lichtheim, op. cit., p. 69.
20 Lichtheim, op. cit., p. 70.
21 Kolakowski, op. cit., p. 88.
22 See Chapter 8.
23 Kolakowski, op. cit., p. 88.
24 Ibid., pp. 89–90. In the 1930s Franz Borkenau also perceived the elitism of what he called Lukács's "pure theory of communism". For Borkenau, Lukács "was one of the first men to study, in the West, Lenin's theory of the 'vanguard', of the organization of professional revolutionaries, and to draw . . . the logical conclusion that the proletariat had no 'proletarian class consciousness' but must get it through the leadership of intellectuals, who by theoretical understanding have learnt what the class-consciousness of the proletariat *ought* to be. There is no doubt that Lukács only expressed what was implicit in Lenin" (*The Communist International*, London, Faber & Faber, 1938, p. 172; now available in paperback reprint).
25 HCC, pp. 328–9. The ethical stance of Lukács is referred to again in relation to that of Gramsci in the Excursus to Part three and also in the latter part of Chapter 16 in Part four.
26 A qualification to Kolakowski's type of argument and to Borkenau's judgment in Note 24 above, comes from Istvan Mészáros, who says that Lukács's philosophy was always abstract-theoretical and "ought-ridden" in the absence of *real* socio-political mediations between the Soviet development and the universal perspectives of socialism: "We can single out here only one aspect of this development: the practical disintegration of all forms of effective political mediation, from the Workers' Councils to the Trade Unions. Even the Party, in the course of its adaptation to the requirements of Stalinistic policies, had largely lost its mediatory function and potential. If Lukács's idea of the Party as formulated in *History and Class Consciousness* contained a great deal of idealization, in the changed circumstances this idealization has become overwhelming. All the more because in *History and Class Consciousness* the institution of the Workers' Councils still appeared as a

necessary form of mediation and its effective instrumentality. Now, however, its place had to be left empty, as indeed all the other forms of political mediation too had to leave a vacuum behind them" (*Lukács' Concept of Dialectic*, p. 80).

27 H. H. Gerth and C. Wright Mills (eds), *From Max Weber: Essays in Sociology*, editors' introduction, p. 51. For Lukács's mature reflections on Max Weber, see his article 'Max Weber and German Sociology', *Economy and Society*, vol. I, no. 2, May 1972, pp. 386–98 (originally in *La Nouvelle Critique*, July–August 1955). Lukács says that Weber "commits sociology in the direction of Geisteswissenschaft, to the idealist interpretation of history" (p. 388) and he stresses Weber's irrationalism, subjectivism, formalism and attempt to prove the "ineluctability of capitalism" because he was one of the "ideologists of the bourgeoisie in the imperialist epoch" (p. 390).

28 Karl Löwith, 'Weber's Interpretation of the bourgeois-capitalistic world in terms of the guiding principle of "rationalization"', in Dennis Wrong (ed.), *Max Weber*, New Jersey, Prentice-Hall, 1970, pp. 114–15 (from 'Max Weber und Karl Marx', in Karl Löwith, *Gesammelte Abhandlungen*, Stuttgart, Verlag W. Kohlhammer, 1960).

29 Max Weber, *The Protestant Ethic and the Spirit of Capitalism* (1905), translated by Talcott Parsons, London, Unwin, 1968, pp. 180–3.

30 Weber, quoted by Löwith, op. cit., p. 110.

31 Wolfgang Mommsen, 'Max Weber's Political Sociology and his Philosophy of World History', in Dennis Wrong (ed.), op. cit., p. 186.

32 Weber, quoted by Mommsen, op. cit., p. 186.

33 Ibid., p. 188.

34 'Politics as a Vocation', in Gerth and Mills (eds), op. cit., p. 125, and Mommsen, op. cit., p. 188.

35 'Politics as a Vocation', p. 128.

36 Mommsen, op. cit., p. 184.

37 Friedrich Engels, 'Socialism: Utopian and Scientific', in Karl Marx and Frederick Engels, *Selected Works in one volume*, Lawrence & Wishart, London, 1968, p. 426.

38 Löwith, op. cit., p. 107.

39 Weber, *Methodology of the Social Sciences*, quoted by Löwith, op. cit., p. 104.

40 Löwith, ibid., p. 105.

41 Ibid., p. 103.

42 Ibid., p. 122.

43 Ibid., p. 108.

44 Quoted in ibid.

45 Löwith, op. cit., pp. 120–2. The position of the Frankfurt School critical theoreticians expounded in Part four below (especially in Chapter 14) on the question of the possible extent, dialectically speaking, of social 'dereification' clearly owes a great deal to Weber's views outlined in this chapter. Herbert Marcuse is wistful and ambiguous about the inevitability of Weber's "shell of bondage" arising from the processes of rationalization and specialization: "As political reason, technical reason is *historical*. If separation from the means of pro-

duction is a technical necessity, the bondage that it organizes is *not* . . . As technical reason, it can become the technique of liberation. For Max Weber this possibility was utopian. Today it looks as if he was right. But if contemporary industrial society defeats and triumphs over its own potentialities, then this triumph is no longer that of Max Weber's bourgeois reason. It is difficult to see reason at all in the ever more solid "shell of bondage" which is being constructed. Or is there perhaps already in Max Weber's concept of reason the irony that understands but disavows? Does he by any chance mean to say: And this you call 'reason'?" ('Industrialization and Capitalism in the Work of Max Weber', in Marcuse's *Negations: Essays in Critical Theory*, London, Allen Lane, 1968, pp. 225–6).

46 Löwith, op. cit., p. 122.

47 Karl Marx, notes to the German Ideology manuscript, in Addenda to *The German Ideology*, Lawrence & Wishart, London, 1965, p. 671.

48 Ibid., p. 672. Cf. the Fourth Thesis on Feuerbach: "the fact that the secular basis detaches itself from itself and establishes itself in the clouds as an independent realm can only be explained by the cleavage and self-contradictions within this secular basis" (ibid., p. 666).

49 *Capital*, vol. I, Lawrence & Wishart, London, 1970, p. 71.

50 Ibid., p. 72.

51 Marx may have been aided in developing his theory of fetishism by Hegel's description of African religion in the *Philosophy of History*. Talking about magicians trying to command the elements, Hegel reports: "The second element in their religion, consists in their giving an outward form to this supernatural power – projecting their hidden might into the world of phenomena by means of images. What they conceive of as the power in question, is therefore nothing really objective, having a substantial being and different from themselves, but the first thing that comes in their way . . . it may be an animal, a tree, a stone, or a wooden figure. This is their *Fetich* – a word to which the Portuguese first gave currency, and which is derived from *feitizo*, magic. Here, in the Fetich, a kind of objective independence as contrasted with the arbitrary fancy of the individual seems to manifest itself; but as the objectivity is nothing other than the fancy of the individual projecting itself into space, the human individuality remains master of the image it has adopted" (Hegel, *Philosophy of History*, p. 94). Hegel returns to this theme in the *Lectures on the Philosophy of Religion*, London, Kegan Paul, 1895, vol. I, pp. 308–9.

52 Afterword to the second German edition of *Capital*, 1873, p. 19.

53 'Structure and Contradiction in *Capital*', in Robin Blackburn (ed.), *Ideology in Social Science: Readings in Critical Social Theory*, London, Fontana/Collins, 1972, p. 337. See also Norman Geras, 'Essence and Appearance: Aspects of Fetishism in Marx's *Capital*', *New Left Review*, no. 65, January–February 1971: "where commodity production prevails, relations between persons really do take the form of relations between things" (p. 76). Alfred Söhn-Rethel says rightly that the general importance of Marx's theory of the fetishism of commodities was that it showed how processes of abstraction can occur in social reality itself

and are not restricted solely to the process of thought. ('Intellectual and Manual Labour: An Attempt at a Materialist Theory', *Radical Philosophy*, no. 6, Winter 1973, pp. 30–7).

54 'The Concept of Ideology', *History and Theory*, vol. 4, 1965, p. 177.

55 On the terminology of the moments of alienation see Istvan Mészáros, *Marx's Theory of Alienation*, London, Merlin Press, third edition, January 1972, p. 313. The concept of reification was used by Georg Simmel in his *Die Philosophie des Geldes*, Leipzig, Düncker & Humblot, 1900 – see Lukács, HCC, pp. 156–7.

56 Two interesting applications of the concept of reification deriving directly from Lukács are Peter L. Berger and Thomas Luckmann, *The Social Construction of Reality*, London, Allen Lane, 1967, pp. 106–9 and Peter L. Berger and Stanley Pullberg, 'Reification and the Sociological Critique of Consciousness', *History and Theory*, IV, 2, 1965. On the early Frankfurt School's notion of the necessity of reification see Chapter 14 below.

57 HCC, p. 84.

58 Ibid., p. 87.

59 Ibid., p. 88.

60 Ibid.

61 Ibid., p. 89.

62 Ibid., p. 92.

63 In the recent interview with Lukács (in Theo Pinkus (ed.), *Conversations with Lukács*, London, Merlin Press, 1974) he returned to the theme of the tragedy of existence in German thought which he called the "tragic ideology" (p. 93) and commented that: "it is false, and a form of ideology that supports the bad reality, to transform the social form of manipulation into the *condition humaine*. Indeed, at earlier stages of capitalism its ideologists also attempted over and over again to erect the objective economic conditions that led to class struggle into general conditions of human existence" (p. 90). See the Excursus on historical invariants in Part four below for a short discussion of this idea in early Critical Theory.

64 HCC, p. 101.

65 Ibid.

66 For an interesting critical humanist justification for retaining in sociological study a synthesis of explanation and *Verstehen* as two special and complementary moments of dialectic, see Mihailo Markovic, 'The Problem of Reification and the *Verstehen-Erklären* Controversy', *Acta Sociologica*, vol. 15, no. 1, March 1972, pp. 27–38.

67 HCC, p. 102.

4 Subject and object in bourgeois philosophy

1 HCC, pp. 110–11.

2 Ibid., p. 112.

3 Ibid., p. 219, footnote 40. This principle was also applicable to the thought and society of the Ancients, particularly that of Heraclitus (ibid.).

4 See HCC, p. 112, and footnote 40, p. 219.
5 G. W. F. Hegel, *The Science of Logic* (1812), translated by A. V. Miller, London, Allen & Unwin, 1969, p. 51.
6 HCC, p. 117.
7 Ibid., p. 118.
8 See Herbert Marcuse, 'Industrialization and Capitalism in the Work of Max Weber', op. cit., p. 204. Lukács's argument expounded in the text also probably draws on Hegel's derogatory remarks on the method and pretensions of mathematics in the Preface to G. W. F. Hegel, *The Phenomenology of Mind* (1805), translated by J. B. Baillie, London, Allen & Unwin, 1966, pp. 100–5.
9 HCC, p. 119.
10 Ibid.
11 Cf. Hegel: "The process of mathematical proof does not belong to the object; it is a function that takes place outside the matter in hand" (*The Phenomenology of Mind*, p. 101).
12 HCC, p. 119.
13 Cf. Leszek Kolakowski's surprisingly Kantian statement about Lukács: "This does not mean that he was right in accepting the mythology of the 'totality'. 'Totality' cannot be the object of any scientific enquiry" (Leszek Kolakowski, 'Lukács's Other Marx', *Cambridge Review* 28, January 1972, p. 90). Although he is probably correct about totality, Kolakowski presumably would not also exclude concepts such as 'social formation', 'social system', 'social configuration', etc., from scientific enquiry?
14 HCC, p. 142.
15 Ibid., p. 144.
16 Ibid., p. 146
17 Ibid., p. 147.
18 Ibid., p. 148.
19 Ibid.
20 Ibid., p. 102.
21 Ibid., pp. 121–2.
22 Ibid., p. 126.
23 Ibid.
24 Ibid., p. 128.
25 Ibid., my emphasis.
26 Zygmunt Bauman, *Culture as Praxis*, London, Routledge & Kegan Paul, 1973, p. 163.
27 See Chapter 17 below.
28 HCC, pp. 129–30.
29 G. W. F. Hegel, *Philosophy of Right*, translated by T. M. Knox, Oxford University Press, 1967, p. 35.
30 Cf. Hegel: "It is the fashion of youth to dash about in abstractions: but the man who has learnt to know life steers clear of the abstract 'either-or' and keeps to the concrete" (G. W. F. Hegel, *The Logic* (Part one of the Encyclopaedia of the Philosophical Sciences, 1830), translated by William Wallace, second edition, Oxford University Press, London, 1892, reprinted 1972, paragraph 80, p. 146). Cf. also: ". . . what is said

of the diversity in philosophies as if the manifold were fixed and stationary and composed of what is mutually exclusive, is at once refuted . . . the manifold or diverse is in a state of flux; it must really be conceived of as in the process of development, and as but a passing moment. Philosophy in its concrete Idea is the activity of development in revealing the differences which it contains within itself . . . The concrete alone as including and supporting the distinctions, is the actual; it is thus, and thus alone, that the differences are in their form entire" (G. W. F. Hegel, *Lectures on the History of Philosophy* (*1819–1830*), translated by E. S. Haldane, London, Kegan Paul, Trench, Trübner & Co., 1892, vol. I, pp. 34–5).

31 Karl Marx, *Economic and Philosophic Manuscripts of 1844*, translated by Martin Milligan, Moscow, Progress Publishers, 1967, p. 102.

32 Ibid., p. 95.

5 *From Lukács to Hegel and back*

1 'Base and Superstructure in Marxist Cultural Theory', *New Left Review*, 82, November/December 1973, p. 9.

2 G. W. F. Hegel, *The Logic* (Part one of the Encyclopaedia of the Philosophical Sciences, 1830), translated by William Wallace, London, Oxford University Press, 1892, reprinted 1972, paragraphs 213–15, pp. 352–8.

3 Ibid., paragraph 213, p. 353.

4 Ibid., p. 354.

5 Elaborated by Hegel at length in the Introduction to the *Lectures on the History of Philosophy* (*1819–1830*), translated by Elizabeth S. Haldane and Frances H. Simson, London, Kegan Paul, Trench, Trübner & Co., 1892, alongside the related concepts of the abstract and the concrete in their special Hegelian meaning. Marx's theoretical treatises are all permeated by these two dualisms. See Introduction to the *Grundrisse* (1857), translated by Martin Nicolaus, Harmondsworth, Penguin, 1973.

6 G. W. F. Hegel, *The Philosophy of Nature* (Part Two of the Encyclopaedia of the Philosophical Sciences, 1830), translated by A. V. Miller, Oxford, Clarendon Press, 1970, paragraph 245, p. 4.

7 *The Science of Logic* (1812), translated by A. V. Miller, London, Allen & Unwin, 1969, pp. 58–9.

8 Ibid., p. 64.

9 HCC, p. 147.

10 See Gustav E. Mueller, 'The Hegel Legend of "Thesis-Antithesis-Synthesis" ', *Journal of the History of Ideas*, vol. 19, 1958, pp. 411–14.

11 Hegel mentions "subject-object" at least in the lesser *Logic*, paragraph 214, p. 355, quoted in its context further on in this chapter.

12 *From Substance to Subject: Studies in Hegel*, The Hague, Martinus Nijhoff, 1974, pp. 1–2.

13 Ibid., p. 2.

14 *The Logic*, paragraph 214, p. 355.

15 Ibid.

16 Ibid., paragraph 173, p. 305.

17 Hegel, *The Science of Logic*, pp. 237–8.
18 Paul Connerton, 'The Collective Historical Subject: Reflections on Lukács' History and Class Consciousness', *British Journal of Sociology*, vol. XXV, no. 2, June 1974, p. 176.
19 Gareth Stedman Jones, 'The Marxism of the Early Lukács: An Evaluation', *New Left Review*, no. 70, November–December 1971, pp. 40 and 53.
20 Morris Watnick, 'Relativism and Class Consciousness: Georg Lukács', in Leopold Labedz (ed.), *Revisionism: Essays in the History of Marxist Ideas*, London, Allen & Unwin, 1962, p. 163.
21 Stanislaw Ossowski, *Class Structure in the Social Consciousness*, London, Routledge & Kegan Paul, 1967, p. 168.
22 See A. C. Ewing, *The Idealist Tradition from Berkeley to Blanshard*, Glencoe, Free Press, 1957, for a useful selection of readings, bibliography and an introductory essay on idealist philosophy.
23 *The Development of the Marxian Dialectic*, Carbondale and Edwardsville, Southern Illinois University Press, 1972, p. 188.
24 See Alfred Schmidt, *The Concept of Nature in Marx*, London, New Left Books, 1971, p. 29.
25 Connerton, op. cit., p. 177.
26 See 14.
27 HCC, p. 175.
28 Ibid., p. 188.
29 Jones, op. cit., p. 46.
30 *The Phenomenology of Mind* (1805), translated by J. B. Baillie, London, Allen & Unwin, 1966, p. 276.
31 HCC, p. 169.
32 Ibid., p. 177.
33 Jones, op. cit., pp. 52, 54. This article is particularly replete with static metaphysical dualisms, into the 'ideal' sides of which Lukács's complex mediations are crushed: 'ethereal/material', 'spiritual/terrestrial', 'ghostly/corporeal', etc., are all deployed in a manner which exemplifies a pre-Hegelian metaphysics. Moreover, Jones shows a basic misunderstanding of the Hegelian-Marxian concepts of the abstract and the concrete which Lukács employs in that meaning as a matter of course. He talks of Lukács's "abstract and ethereal role assigned to the proletariat" against his "contempt for . . . concrete facts" (pp. 46, 47) which completely erroneously gives the dualism the meaning of ideas versus what is tangible or material, revealing again a dualistic, positivist frame of mind. See note 5 above.
34 HCC, p. 169.
35 Ibid.
36 Ibid., p. 175.
37 Ibid.
38 Ibid., p. 177.
39 Ibid.
40 Ibid., p. 175. See Chapter 15 below.
41 HCC, p. 178.
42 Ibid., p. 177.

43 Jones, op. cit., p. 45.
44 HCC, p. 132.
45 Lukács is quite clear on the relationship between contemplation and praxis: "As long as man adopts a stance of intuition and contemplation he can only relate to his own thought and to the objects of the empirical world in an immediate way. He accepts both as ready-made – produced by historical reality. As he wishes only to know the world and not to change it he is forced to accept both the empirical, material rigidity of existence and the logical rigidity of concepts as unchangeable" (HCC, p. 202). It is the application of the method of contemplation in social science that Lukács fears will cut men off from their history, wed them to the reified appearance of processes as things, and blind tl em to the essence of commodity fetishism. Its validity, applicability or desirability in natural science is not at issue. Moreover, the affinity of this conception with some of the central propositions of the *Geisteswissenschaft* and *Lebensphilosophie* does not, as Stedman Jones effectively states, by definition render it implausible.
46 HCC, p. 133.
47 Chapter 8.
48 Jones, op. cit., p. 47.
49 HCC, p. xvii.
50 See Part four, especially Chapter 14 for a discussion of the issue raised in the text but in relation to Horkheimer and the early Frankfurt School.
51 HCC, pp. xvii–xviii.
52 HCC, pp. xxii–xxiv.
53 Hegel, *The Science of Logic*, p. 842.
54 *The Phenomenology of Mind*, p. 79.
55 Ibid., p. 807.
56 The passage in full from Hegel's *The Phenomenology* is as follows: "In thus concentrating itself on itself, Spirit is engulfed in the night of its own self-consciousness; its vanished existence is, however, conserved therein; and this superseded existence – the previous state, but born anew from the womb of knowledge – is the new stage of existence, a new world, and a new embodiment or mode of Spirit. Here it has to begin all over again at its immediacy, as freshly as before, and thence rise once more to the measure of its stature, as if, for it, all that preceded were lost, and as if it had learned nothing from the experience of the spirits that preceded" (ibid., p. 807).
57 Ibid., pp. 78–9.
58 HCC, p. xxxvi.

6 Towards conscious mediations

1 Cf. Hegel: "But the term subjectivity is not to be confined merely to the bad and finite kind of it which is contrasted with the thing (fact). In its truth subjectivity is immanent in the fact, and as a subjectivity thus infinite is the very truth of the fact" (G. W. F. Hegel, *The Logic* (Part One of the Encyclopaedia of the Philosophical Sciences, 1830), trans-

lated by William Wallace, second edition, London, Oxford University Press, 1892, reprinted 1972, paragraph 147, p. 270). For Lukacs, the "infinite" here would be the potential victory of the proletariat implicit in the tendencies of history but requiring to be mobilized by the act of transforming contradictions into conscious dialectical contradictions. To paraphrase Marx, the victory of the proletariat 'proves the truth', i.e. the 'reality' of its factual existence in practice.

2 HCC, p. 151.

3 Cf. Marx: "all science would be superfluous if the outward appearance and the essence of things directly coincided" (*Capital* (1867), in three volumes, London, Lawrence & Wishart, 1967–70, vol. III, p. 817). See also Marx's letter to Kugelmann, 11 July 1868, *Selected Correspondence of Marx and Engels*, Moscow, third edition, 1975, p. 195.

4 See Karl Löwith, *From Hegel to Nietzsche* (1941), translated by David E. Green, London, Constable, 1965, pp. 103–5, 110–15 and 147 ff.

5 Cf. Marx: "But here individuals are dealt with only in so far as they are the personifications of economic categories, embodiments of particular class-relations and class-interests. My standpoint, from which the evolution of the economic formation of society is viewed as a process of natural history, can less than any other make the individual responsible for relations whose creature he socially remains, however much he may subjectively raise himself above them" (*Capital*, vol. I, Preface to the first German edition, 1867, p. 10).

6 Max Stirner, *The Ego and His Own* (1844), quoted in William Brazill, *The Young Hegelians*, New Haven, Yale University Press, 1970, p. 223. See also Nicholas Lobkowicz, *Theory and Practice: History of a Concept from Aristotle to Marx*, Indiana, Notre Dame University Press, 1967, p. 390 ff., who argues that Marx devoted almost a half of *The German Ideology* to a critique of Stirner's relatively obscure book because its dissolution of all notions of history, communism, mankind, socialism, Christ, bourgeois society, etc., into "loose screws" and "phantoms" in the name of the sovereign Ego undermined Marx's grounding of critique of the present social order in terms of immanent laws of history, scientifically investigatable. For a defence of Stirner against Marx, see Eugène Fleischmann, 'The Role of the Individual in Pre-revolutionary Society: Stirner, Marx and Hegel', in Z. A. Pelczynski (ed.), *Hegel's Political Philosophy: Problems and Perspectives*, Cambridge University Press, 1971.

7 Max Horkheimer, *Eclipse of Reason* (1947), New York, Seabury Press, 1974, Chapter I. See also Part four below.

8 HCC, p. 193.

9 Ibid.

10 HCC, pp. 193–4. Cf. Marx's Eighth Thesis on Feuerbach: "All mysteries which mislead theory into mysticism find their rational solution in human practice and in the comprehension of this practice" (in Addenda to Karl Marx and Frederick Engels, *The German Ideology* (1845), London, Lawrence & Wishart, 1965, p. 667).

11 Ibid., p. 149.

12 Cf. Alfred Schutz: "We must, then, leave unsolved the notoriously

difficult problems which surround the constitution of the Thou within the subjectivity of private experience. We are not going to be asking, therefore, how the Thou is constituted in an Ego, whether the concept of "human being" presupposes a transcendental ego in which the transcendental alter ego is already constituted, or how universally valid intersubjective knowledge is possible. As important as these questions may be for epistemology and, therefore, for the social sciences, we may safely leave them aside in the present work" (*The Phenomenology of the Social World* (1932), translated by George Walsh and Frederick Lehnert, London, Heinemann, 1972, p. 98).

13 See Part four below, especially chapters 14 and 16.

14 See Part three below, especially Chapter 10.

15 On the role of mediation in the writings of the founders of German dialectics see Karl Löwith, 'Mediation and Immediacy in Hegel, Marx and Feuerbach', in Warren E. Steinkraus (ed.), USA, Holt, Rinehart & Winston, 1971, and in relation to aesthetics in Lukács, Marx and Max Raphael see Willis H. Truitt, 'Ideology, Expression and Mediation', *The Philosophical Forum*, Spring–Summer 1972, vol. III, nos. 3–4, pp. 468–97. On mediation in the work of Lukács see Istvan Mészáros, *Lukács' Concept of Dialectic*, London, Merlin Press, Chapter 6.

16 HCC, p. 154.

17 Ibid., p. 155. See Chapter 15, which deals in detail with the point about the logic of history and the logic of method which Lukács makes here.

18 See *The Logic*, paragraphs 38–58.

19 *Theories of Surplus Value* (1862–63), translated by J. Cohen, London, Lawrence & Wishart, 1969–72, vol. III, p. 500.

20 Karl Marx and Frederick Engels, *Selected Works in One Volume*, London, Lawrence & Wishart, 1968, pp. 405–11.

21 See Engels's letter to Kautsky, 20 September 1884, on this issue and on the nature of abstraction in Marx, in Karl Marx and Frederick Engels, *Selected Correspondence*, Moscow, third edition, 1975, p. 357.

22 HCC, p. 154.

23 Ibid., p. 155.

24 G. W. F. Hegel, *Lectures on the Philosophy of Religion* (1832), translated by E. B. Speirs and J. Burdon Sanderson, London, Kegan Paul, Trench, Trübner & Co., 1895, vol. I, p. 163.

25 Ibid., pp. 161–2. The Hegelian theory expounded in the text that world-historical truth is a concretizing process tending towards its abstract potentiality, in which process immediacy occupies but a transitory moment, partly determined by its universal Other, informs Marx's famous statement in *The Holy Family* (translated by R. Dixon, Moscow, 1956) that the point is not what the proletariat thinks are its aims but "*what the proletariat is*, and what, consequent on that *being*, it will be compelled to do" (p. 53). Lukács's 'actual' and 'imputed' class-consciousness is predicated on a similar philosophy of history, in Lukács's case it being the party which enshrines the imputed consciousness. This can be seen as having made explicit with an epistemological gloss what was already implicit in Marx. In Marx, his long-term view of historical processes also informed his view of the party. Marx distinguishes a particu-

lar Party from the historical party in general. As he explained in a rarely quoted letter to Ferdinand Freiligrath on 29 February 1852: "The League, like the Société des Saisons in Paris or like a hundred other societies, was only one episode in the history of the Party, which sprang naturally from the soil of modern society. [I have] . . . tried to explain the mistake you make in thinking that by 'Party' I mean a 'League' that has been dead for eight years, or an editorial board that was dissolved twelve years ago. By Party I mean the Party in the grand historical sense" (quoted by Werner Blumenberg, *Karl Marx* (1962), translated by Douglas Scott, London, New Left Books, 1972, p. 134).

26 *The German Ideology*, p. 48.

27 HCC, pp. 150–1.

28 Istvan Mészáros, *Lukács' Concept of Dialectic*, London, Merlin Press, 1972, pp. 70–1.

29 HCC, p. 181.

30 On the problem of sociological relativism in Lukács and Mannheim, see Morris Watnick, 'Relativism and Class Consciousness: Georg Lukács', in Leopold Labedz (ed.), *Revisionism: Essays in the History of Marxist Ideas*, London, Allen & Unwin, 1962, p. 156ff.

31 HCC, p. 163.

32 Watnick, op. cit., p. 158.

33 *The Phenomenology of Mind* (1805), translated by J. B. Baillie, London, Allen & Unwin, 1966, p. 273.

34 The notions of socio-genesis and the reclamation of the living past are discussed at length in Chapter 15 below.

35 HCC, p. 179.

7 *Sociology and mythology in Lukács*

1 HCC, p. 51.

2 Ibid.

3 Ibid., pp. 70 and 313.

4 See also the further discussion in the Excursus in Part three below of both Gramsci and Lukács's belief in a long-term fundamental historical process prevailing in the end.

5 G. W. F. Hegel, *The Phenomenology of Mind* (1805), translated by J. B. Baillie, London, Allen & Unwin, 1966, p. 289.

6 Morris Watnick, 'Relativism and Class Consciousness: Georg Lukács', in Leopold Labedz (ed.), *Revisionism: Essays in the History of Marxist Ideas*, London, Allen & Unwin, 1962, p. 161.

7 HCC, p. 205.

8 Ibid., p. 1.

9 Ibid.

10 See especially Part three, Chapter 8 and Chapter 17 of Part four.

11 An example of this tendency, in addition to the critique by Stedman Jones we have discussed in previous chapters, is the later assessment of Lukács's work in general by Bela Fogarasi: "The key principles of Marxian philosophical materialism play but a minor role in his works, whereas a definite stand on these issues is the first duty of the Marxist

philosopher. It follows, then, that the political bankruptcy which he displayed in 1956 was the outcome not of an accidental error, but the result of his entire previous socio-political and scientific activity" ('Reflections on the Philosophical Views of Georg Lukacs', *World Marxist Review*, June 1959, p. 42).

12 *History of the Last Systems of Philosophy in Germany* (1837), quoted by Nicholas Lobkowicz, *Theory and Practice: History of a Concept from Aristotle to Marx*, Notre Dame, 1967, p. 193.
13 Ibid., p. 198.
14 Cieszkowski, quoted by Lobkowicz, p. 202.
15 Lukács's judgment of the moralizing position of Moses Hess is in terms of the conception of the world-historical class truth of the proletariat mentioned in the text. For Lukács, Hess's position was "that of an intellectual who merely enters into an 'alliance' with the revolutionary proletariat but is never capable of thinking from the standpoint of the proletariat in its actual class situation" (Georg Lukács, 'Moses Hess and the Problems of Idealist Dialectics', (1926), in Rodney Livingstone (ed.), *Georg Lukács, Political Writings, 1919–1929: The Question of Parliamentarianism and Other Essays*, London, New Left Books, 1972, p. 201).
16 Ibid., p. 197.
17 Ibid., p. 186.
18 Ibid., *passim*.
19 HCC, p. 190.
20 Marx's persistent rejection of the concept of 'Man' in favour of the analysis of specific social men in given societies occurs especially in the following places: 'Excerpt-Notes of 1844', in Loyd D. Easton and Kurt H. Guddat (eds), *Writings of the Young Marx on Philosophy and Society*, New York, Doubleday, 1967, p. 272; Karl Marx and Frederick Engels, *The German Ideology* (1845), London, Lawrence & Wishart, 1965, p. 53ff.; Karl Marx, *Capital* (1867), London, Lawrence & Wishart, 1967–70, vol. I, p. 79; and in Karl Marx, 'Marginal Notes on Adolph Wagner's "Lehrbruch der politischen Ökonomie" ' (1880) in *Theoretical Practice*, issue 5, Spring 1972. See also Istvan Mészáros, *Marx's Theory of Alienation*, London, Merlin Press, 1970, pp. 110–11.
21 HCC, p. 208.
22 Ibid., p. 204.
23 Ibid., p. 155.
24 Livingstone (ed.), op. cit.
25 'Moses Hess', op. cit., p. 195.
26 *The Phenomenology of Mind*, p. 597.
27 Ibid. Also quoted by Lukács, in Livingstone (ed.), op. cit., p. 213.
28 Ibid.
29 Ibid., p. 214.
30 HCC., p. 61.
31 See the Excursus in Part three below and chapter 16 for further discussions of this question.
32 Theodor Adorno, *Negative Dialectics*, translated by E. B. Ashton, London, Routledge & Kegan Paul, p. 129. See Part four below,

Chapter 15, for a discussion of the nature of knowledge of the past and its relation to human praxis.

33 'A Review of Georg Lukács's 'History and Class Consciousness' '(1924), *Theoretical Practice*, no. 1, 1971.

34 HCC, p. 197; my emphasis.

35 Ibid., p. 199.

36 Stanley Rosen, *G. W. F. Hegel: An Introduction to the Science of Wisdom*, New Haven, Yale University Press, 1974, p. 256.

Part three – Antonio Gramsci: practical theoretician

8 Gramsci in context

1 English edition, *Historical Materialism: A System of Sociology*, with introduction by Alfred G. Meyer, Ann Arbor, University of Michigan Press, 1969.

2 Lukács's review of the 'Manual' appeared in *Archiv für die Geschichte des Socializmus und der Arbeiterbewegung*, XII, 1926, and is translated into English as 'Technology and Social Relations' in E. San Juan Jr (ed.), *Marxism and Human Liberation: Essays on History, Culture and Revolution*, by Georg Lukács, New York, Delta, 1973. (Also in R. Livingstone (ed.), *Georg Lukács: Political Writings 1919–1929: The Question of Parliamentarianism, and Other Essays*, New Left Books, London, 1972.)

3 *Selections from the Prison Notebooks of Antonio Gramsci*, edited and translated by Quintin Hoare and Geoffrey Nowell-Smith, Lawrence & Wishart, London, 1971, editor's introduction to Part III, Chapter 2, p. 379. (Text further cited as PN.)

4 See for example Iring Fetscher, 'From the Philosophy of the Proletariat to Proletarian Weltanschauung' in his *Marx and Marxism*, New York, Herder & Herder, 1971; cf. Zygmunt Bauman on the 'deterministic' trend in Marxian theory: ". . . I think it can be traced to functional prerequisities of a mass social movement: the necessity to bring the guiding philosophical doctrine closer to the natural cognitive set of the mass following" ('Modern Times: Modern Marxism', in P. Berger (ed.), *Marxism and Sociology: Views from Eastern Europe*, New York, Appleton Century-Crofts, 1969, p. 15); also Gramsci: " 'Politically' the materialist conception is close to the people, to 'common sense'. It is closely linked to many beliefs and prejudices, to almost all popular superstitions" (PN, p. 396).

5 PN, p. 419.

6 Ibid., p. 420.

7 Ibid., p. 421.

8 Lukács, Review of Bukharin, in San Juan Jr, op. cit., p. 50.

9 Nikolai Bukharin, *Historical Materialism: A System of Sociology*, Michigan, Ann Arbor Paperbacks, 1969, Chapter Six, particularly sections (e) 'Social Psychology and Social Ideology' and (h) 'The Formative Principles of Social Life'.

10 Ibid., p. 215.

11 Ibid., p. 216.
12 Ibid., p. 208. In a similar vein, in a recent interview (1967) Lukács saw Mannheim as being "extraordinarily harsh towards ideology while he has a charming indulgence, towards utopia" (Theo Pinkus (ed.), *Conversations with Lukács*, London, Merlin Press, 1974, p. 66).
13 Bukharin, op. cit., p. 208.
14 Alfred Meyer sees Bukharin's consensus-equilibrium interpretation of Marxism as more easily reconcilable with the philosophy and policies of the New Economic Policy (Introduction to the 1969 translation of Bukharin, op. cit., p. 6A).
15 Ibid., p. 264.
16 Ibid., p. 292.
17 PN, p. 424.
18 Ibid., p. 425.
19 Ibid., p. 425.
20 Lukács, too, saw Bukharin's position this way: "Bukharin is suspiciously close to what Marx aptly called bourgeois materialism", review of Bukharin, op. cit., p. 51).
21 Bukharin, op. cit., pp. 180–1 and 227. See L. Kolakowski, *Positivist Philosophy: From Hume to the Vienna Circle*, Harmondsworth, Pelican, 1972, particularly Chapter 8 on the logical empiricist view on philosophy: "Philosophy, if it is to exist as an independent discipline alongside the other branches of knowledge, cannot take the place of science in any question concerning the structure of the world . . . philosophy in this sense becomes a discipline dealing with methods of scientific procedure . . ." (p. 206). Kolakowski relates this view to the development at the beginning of this century of the theory of relativity and "the study of antinomies in the theory of classes" (p. 227). Cf. also L. Wittgenstein: "Philosophy sets limits to the much disputed sphere of natural science" (*Tractatus Logico-Philosophicus*, 1922, translated by D. F. Pears and B. F. McGuinness, London, Routledge & Kegan Paul, 1961: reprinted 1972, p. 49).
22 Karl Korsch's *Marxism and Philosophy* (1923), English translation, London, New Left Books, 1970, also put back on the Marxist agenda philosophy in the sense intended by Gramsci here. It is discussed later in this chapter.
23 PN, p. 345.
24 Ibid., p. 426.
25 In his review of Bukharin Lukács attributes this scientism to Bukharin's bias towards the natural sciences leading him to apply their methods to the study of society "uncritically, unhistorically and undialectically" (op. cit., p. 60). Gramsci makes exactly this point too (PN, p. 438).
26 Translated by Douglas Ainslie, London, Macmillan, 1913, pp. 364–82.
27 Ibid., pp. 374–5.
28 Ibid., p. 371.
29 PN, p. 427; my emphasis.
30 See Alfred Schmidt, *The Concept of Nature in Marx*, London, New Left Books, 1970, pp. 51–63 for a critique of Engels's 'laws of dialectics' on the grounds of their being an empty formalism, imposed or 'applied'

externally to their subject matter: "Whereas Marx, in very Hegelian fashion, allowed the dialectically presented science to emerge first from the criticism of its present state, and therefore at no point detached the materialist dialectic from the content of political economy, Engels's dialectic of nature necessarily remained external to its subject-matter" (p. 52).

31 PN, p. 427.
32 V. G. Kiernan, 'Gramsci and Marxism', *The Socialist Register*, London, Merlin Press, 1972, p. 2.
33 PN, p. 428.
34 Ibid., p. 429.
35 Croce, *The Philosophy of the Practical: Economic and Ethic*, London, Macmillan, 1913, p. 184.
36 PN, p. 429.
37 Ibid., p. 429.
38 Ibid., p. 429.
39 Lukács's review of Bukharin, 'The Theory of Historical Materialism: A Manual of Popular Sociology' (1926), translated as 'Technology and Social Relations' in E. San Juan Jr (ed.), *Marxism and Human Liberation: Essays on History, Culture and Revolution by Georg Lukacs*, New York, Delta, 1973, p. 52.
40 PN, p. 458.
41 Ibid., pp. 457–8.
42 Introduction to Bukharin, op. cit., p. 7A.
43 Who said that reflection materialism was "Platonism with a changed sign" (quoted in Iring Fetscher, *Marx and Marxism*, New York, Herder & Herder, 1971, p. 82.)
44 PN, p. 437.
45 Lukács, op. cit., p. 59.
46 PN, p. 436.
47 Lukács, op. cit., p. 58.
48 PN, p. 438.
49 Ibid., p. 438. Cf. Lenin: "To try to 'prove' in advance that there is 'absolutely' no way out of the situation would be sheer pedantry, or playing with concepts and catchwords. Practice alone can serve as real 'proof' in this and similar questions" (*Collected Works*, XXXI, quoted by Lukács, op. cit., p. 59).
50 'The Specificity of Marxist Sociology in Gramsci's Theory', in *The Sociological Quarterly*, 16, Winter 1975, pp. 65–86.
51 Editorial in *Avanti!*, quoted in Giuseppe Fiori, *Antonio Gramsci: Life of a Revolutionary*, New York, Dutton, 1971, p. 112 (Fiori's emphasis).
52 PN, p. 336.
53 Leonardo Salamini, 'The Specificity of Marxist Sociology in Gramsci's Theory', *Sociological Quarterly*, 16, Winter 1975, p. 72.
54 See H. Stuart Hughes, *Consciousness and Society: The Reorientation of European Social Thought 1890–1930*, London, Macgibbon & Kee, 1967, Chapter 3, for a discussion of the *fin de siècle* anti-positivist critics of Marxism in its economic determinist mode. Also Edmund E. Jacobitti, 'Labriola, Croce and Italian Marxism (1895–1910)' in *Journal of the*

History of Ideas, April–June 1975, pp. 297–318, for an interesting account of Antonio Labriola's "fiery critique of deterministic, positivistic, Marxism" (p. 305) and its initial influence on Croce who later turned against Labriola's practical Marxism feeling there was a higher justification, "more to life than simple satisfaction of practical needs" (p. 306). According to Jacobitti he then assumed the role of the most influential interpreter of Marxism in Italy. See also the useful survey of the social, political and cultural factors which favoured the development of social theory in Italy in Renato Treves, 'Sociological Study and Research in Italy', *Transactions of the Fourth World Congress of Sociology*, 1959, London, International Sociological Association, 1959, vol. I, pp. 73–94 and Chapter 3 of this study.

55 Piero Gobetti, in his powerful contemporary profile of Gramsci written in 1924 (translated by Hamish Henderson and Tom Nairn, *New Edinburgh Review*, double issue on Gramsci, vol. II, 1974, p. 45).

56 Quoted by Giuseppe Fiori, *Antonio Gramsci: Life of a Revolutionary*, New York, Dutton, 1971, p. 93.

57 Benedetto Croce, *The Philosophy of the Practical: Economic and Ethic*, translated by Douglas Ainslie, London, Macmillan, 1913, p. 302. Cf. also Croce's aphorism: "In the beginning was neither the Word nor the Act; but the Word of the Act and the Act of the Word" (ibid., p. 302).

58 Ibid., p. 33.

59 PN, p. 363.

60 Croce, op. cit., p. 34.

61 'Theory and Practice in Gramsci's Marxism', *Socialist Register*, London, Merlin Press, 1968, p. 162.

62 See John M. Cammett, *Antonio Gramsci and the Origins of Italian Communism*, California, Stanford University Press, 1967, Part II, for an excellent account of Gramsci's activities in the Turin factory councils movement.

63 'La Città Futura', 11 February 1917, quoted by Fiori, op. cit., p. 107.

64 PN, p. 366.

65 John Merrington, 'Theory and Practice in Gramsci's Marxism' in R. Miliband and J. Saville (eds), *The Socialist Register*, London, Merlin Press, 1968, p. 161.

66 PN, p. 407.

67 Ibid., p. 365.

68 Ibid., pp. 366–7.

69 Ibid., pp. 366–7, editors' footnote 59.

70 Ibid.

71 It is clear from Hoare and Nowell-Smith's Introduction to the Prison Notebooks that they have seen Gramsci's intellectual predecessors through the same static, metaphysical materialist spectacles. Antonio Labriola for them distinguished himself from the Hegelians mainly by his "insistence on the primacy of concrete relations over consciousness" (ibid., p. xxi). The simplistic dualism of 'ideas' and 'materialist base' is apparent again when they say that Labriola's ideas were often distorted to emphasize their "latent idealism at the expense of their materialist base" (p. xxi).

72 See Gramsci's comments on this, PN, pp. 366–7.
73 PN, p. 377.
74 Ibid., also cf. pp. 407 and 364–5.
75 Ibid., p. 407.
76 English translation by Sylvia Sprigge, London, Allen & Unwin, 1941.
77 Letter to Tatania Schucht, 9 May 1932 in *New Edinburgh Review*, op. cit. vol. II, p. 19.
78 PN, p. 431.
79 Ibid., p. 434.
80 Ibid., p. 420.
81 Op. cit.
82 Karl Korsch, *Marxism and Philosophy* (1924), English translation, London, New Left Books, 1970.
83 Ibid., p. 68.
84 Ibid., p. 83.
85 Ibid., p. 64.
86 Ibid., p. 73; my emphasis.
87 Ibid., p. 63.
88 The denigration of the young Lukács and Korsch as well as Revai and others by the Soviet orthodoxy is well known and the tradition is kept alive, as we have seen, in relation to Lukács by Stedman Jones, and in relation to Gramsci by Merrington and Hoare and Nowell Smith. See also Victor Zitta's unremittingly hostile assessment of Lukács's work in *Georg Lukács' Marxism: Alienation, Dialectics, Revolution: A Study in Utopia and Ideology*, The Hague, Martinus Nijhoff, 1964. A good brief study of the Lukács-Korsch controversy in the 1920s is Paul Brienes, 'Praxis and its Theorists: The Impact of Lukacs and Korsch in the 1920's' in *Telos*, no. 11, Spring 1972, pp. 67–105.
89 A common position among Marxists in general including elements of the New Left, and with many variants. See M. Merleau-Ponty, *Adventures of the Dialectic*, London, Heinemann, 1974, Chapter 2; Iring Fetscher, *Marx and Marxism*, New York, Herder & Herder, 1971; D. Howard and K. Klare (eds), *The Unknown Dimension: Post Leninist Marxism*, New York, Basic Books, 1972; and the tellingly titled Bart Grahl and Paul Piccone (eds), *Towards a New Marxism*, St Louis, Telos Press, 1973, particularly Piccone's Introduction, which sees the Western Marxist tradition as the *only* liberative alternative to Stalinism or "official bourgeois ideology" (p. 1). My point is that it is not a *new* Marxism that is required, but its transcendence altogether *qua* Marxism.
90 Lukács uses this term when he talks of the "spirit of historical materialism" in his critique of Bukharin in E. San Juan Jr (ed.), *Marxism and Human Liberation: Essays on History, Culture and Revolution*, New York, Delta, 1973, p. 52, and R. Livingstone (ed.), op. cit., p. 136.
91 Letter to Tatania Schucht, 2 May 1932 in *Edinburgh Review*, op. cit. vol. II, p. 18.

9 Hegemony and civil society

1 PN, p. 449. Karl Korsch in his remarks on Marx's *Critique of the Gotha*

Programme, 1922, also affirms the essentially *positive* result of dialectical critique: "Karl Marx was a *positive dialectician and revolutionary* and the magnificent character of his spirit is very evident in the 'Critique': he never allows his critical work to become a mere *negation* of the errors and superficialities analysed in his letter. He always goes on to expound or briefly indicate the *positive* and *true* concepts which should replace the error and illusion he criticises" (in *Marxism and Philosophy* (1923), English translation, London, New Left Books, 1970, p. 140).

2 The quotation from Bukharin is from a work contemporary to the Manual, the *ABC of Communism*, written with E. Preobrazhensky in 1922 (Harmondsworth, Penguin, 1969, p. 307) and the one from Gramsci is attributed to him from his period as assistant editor of *El Grido del Popolo* in 1917 (quoted in Giuseppe Fiori, *Antonio Gramsci: Life of a Revolutionary*, New York, Dutton, 1971, p. 105). Although of course said in very different socio-political circumstances, a fact which clearly makes one careful of making too much of such statements as comparable expressions of a general viewpoint, juxtaposing them is perhaps justified on the ground that they are symptomatic of two very different attitudes towards popular, 'ideological' beliefs found within Marxist theory. Also, the quotation from Bukharin exemplifies well his naïve scientism. See A. Pozzolini, *Antonio Gramsci: An Introduction to His Thought*, translated by Anne F. Showstack, London, Pluto Press, 1970, Chapter IX, for a brief account of Gramsci's views on religion.

3 *The Communist Manifesto* (1848), London, Penguin, 1967, p. 91.

4 See Thomas R. Bates, 'Gramsci and the Theory of Hegemony' in *Journal of the History of Ideas*, vol. XXXVI, April–June 1975, pp. 351–66, who points out (p. 352) that the term 'hegemony' can be traced to its introduction in Western political discourse by the first three writers mentioned in the text at the turn of the century in their dispute with the 'Economists' over the issue of spontaneity, when it meant political leadership. Lukács, in *History and Class Consciousness* (1923), translated by R. Livingstone, London, Merlin Press, 1971, pp. 52–4, employs the term hegemony in this Leninist sense: "For a class to be ripe for hegemony means that its interests and consciousness enable it to organise the whole of society in accordance with those interests. The crucial question in every class struggle is this: which class possesses this capacity and this consciousness at the decisive moment?" (p. 52). See also Lukács's essay 'Legality and Illegality', ibid., p. 256–f.

5 *Philosophy of Right*, addition to paragraph 268, p. 282.

6 *Capital*, London, Lawrence & Wishart, 1967–70, vol. I, p. 737.

7 Z. Bauman, *Between Class and Elite: The Eevolution of the British Labour Movement: A Sociological Study*, Manchester University Press, 1972, p. 3.

8 Preface to *A Contribution to the Critique of Political Economy*, 1859, in T. Bottomore and M. Rubel (eds), *Karl Marx: Selected Writings in Sociology and Social Philosophy*, Harmondsworth, Penguin, 1967, p. 68.

9 Bauman, op. cit., pp. 3–4.

10 Marx, Preface to *A Contribution* . . ., in Bottomore and Rubel, op. cit., p. 67.
11 PN, editors' introduction to Section II, Chapter 2, pp. 206–9. Important sections of Gramsci's writings with regard to the meanings of the terms discussed in my interpretative remarks in the text at this point are on PN, pp. 208, 170 (footnote 71), and 12–13, and in Gramsci's letter to Tatania Schucht, 7 September 1931, *New Edinburgh Review*, double issue on Gramsci, vol. I, 1974, pp. 46–7.
12 PN, p. 12.
13 Ibid., p. 12.
14 Letter to Tatania Schucht, 7 September 1931, op. cit., p. 47.
15 This is a formalistic error that the editors of the Prison Notebooks make in accusing Gramsci of such an inconsistency and a false synonymity of concepts. See PN, editors' introduction to Section II, Chapter 2, pp. 207–8.
16 PN, p. 13.
17 Ibid., p. 13.
18 Ibid., p. 366.
19 In the 1960s a number of English Marxists became influenced by Gramsci and some very useful studies were produced which applied some of his ideas to the development of British society. See for example Perry Anderson's articles 'Origins of the Present Crisis', *New Left Review*, no. 23, January–February 1964, pp. 26–53, reprinted in Perry Anderson and Robin Blackburn (eds), *Towards Socialism*, London, Fontana Library, 1965, pp. 11–52; 'Problems of Socialist Strategy', in Anderson and Blackburn (eds), *Towards Socialism*, pp. 221–90; 'Socialism and Pseudo-Empiricism', *New Left Review*, no. 35, January–February 1966, pp. 2–42; 'A Reply to E. P. Thompson, "The Peculiarities of the English" ', in Ralph Miliband and John Saville (eds), *The Socialist Register 1965*, London, Merlin Press, 1965, pp. 311–62; and 'The Limits and Possibilities of Trade Union Action', in Robin Blackburn and Alexander Cockburn (eds), *The Incompatibles: Trade Union Militancy and the Consensus*, Harmondsworth, Penguin, 1967, pp. 263–80. Also Quintin Hoare, 'What is Fascism?', *New Left Review*, no. 20, Summer 1963, pp. 99–111.
20 Fundamental categories which Gramsci inherited from the 'Machiavellian School' of political theorists, particularly Mosca and Pareto. (See Bates, op. cit.) See also PN, p. 80, footnote 49, for a further elaboration by Gramsci of the force-consent combination as characterizing the exercise of hegemony but sometimes supplemented by corruption and fraud when the exercise of force is too risky.
21 'The Concept of "Egemonia" in the Thought of Antonio Gramsci: Some Notes on Interpretation', *Journal of the History of Ideas*, vol. 21, 1960, p. 591.
22 PN, p. 184.
23 Ibid., p. 167; my emphasis.
24 Ibid., p. 12.
25 Bates, op. cit., p. 357, quoting Croce's *Etica e Politica*.
26 PN, p. 238.

27 Ibid., p. 180.
28 Ibid., p. 182.
29 G. W. F. Hegel, *The Philosophy of History*, New York, Dover, 1956, p. 74.
30 Ibid., p. 74. Another example of Gramsci's tolerance towards idealism is relevant to Hegel's quoted remark about deeds. Gramsci gives an activistic Marxist gloss to Croce's acceptance of the idealist principle that one knows that which one does, by warning that it must not be allowed to be reduced merely to the 'know' element. Provided the principle is translated into accelerating the historical process that is going on, so that theory and practice can be unified through the practical mobilizing of social potentials, then the idealist principle of the "adhesion of theory to practice" can be said to exist (PN, pp. 364–5).
31 Hegel, ibid., p. 74.
32 Ibid., p. 75.
33 Ibid., p. 75.
34 Lukács made the same point: "In the period of the 'pre-history of human society' and of the struggles between classes the only possible function of truth is to establish the various possible attitudes to an essentially uncomprehended world in accordance with man's needs in the struggle to master his environment. Truth could only achieve an 'objectivity' relative to the standpoint of the individual classes and the objective realities corresponding to it" (*History and Class Consciousness* (1923), translated by R. Livingstone, London, Merlin Press, 1971, p. 189).
35 PN, p. 445.
36 Ibid., p. 445.
37 Ibid., p. 201.
38 Hegel, op. cit., p. 75.
39 PN, pp. 365–6.
40 Ibid., p. 445.
41 Ibid., p. 446.
42 A. Schmidt, *The Concept of Nature in Marx*, translated by Ben Fowkes, London, New Left Books, 1971, p. 77.
43 Hegel, op. cit., p. 78.

10 Analysing the historical bloc (including Excursus)

1 PN, pp. 181, 366.
2 Ibid., p. 326.
3 Ibid., p. 9.
4 Ibid., p. 377.
5 Ibid.
6 Ibid., p. 366.
7 Ibid., p. 177.
8 Ibid., pp. 177–9.
9 Ibid., p. 177.
10 Ibid., p. 177, footnote 79.
11 Ibid., p. 181.

12 Ibid., p. 184.
13 Ibid., p. 181; my emphasis.
14 Ibid., pp. 181–2.
15 Ibid., p. 183.
16 Ibid., p. 183.
17 See Thomas R. Bates, 'Gramsci and the Theory of Hegemony', *Journal of the History of Ideas*, vol. XXXVI, April–June 1975, p. 354; also PN, p. 58, editors' note, footnote 8.
18 PN, p. 58.
19 Ibid., footnote 8.
20 Ibid., p. 59.
21 Ibid., p. 244.
22 Ibid., p. 244.
23 Ibid., p. 245.
24 Ibid., p. 245.
25 Ibid., p. 185.
26 *History and Class Consciousness* (1923), translated by R. Livingstone, London, Merlin Press, 1971, p. 197.
27 PN, p. 57, footnote 5.
28 See Fiori, op. cit., pp. 105 and 237–8.
29 PN, p. 185.
30 Ibid., p. 342.
31 Adolf Hitler, *Mein Kampf*, Munich, Eher, 1935. Quoted in Alan Bullock, *Hitler: A Study in Tyranny*, Harmondsworth, Pelican, 1967, p. 69.
32 PN, pp. 326–43.
33 Ibid., p. 340.
34 Ibid., p. 341.
35 Ibid., p. 365.
36 Ibid., pp. 128–30.
37 See, for example, PN, pp. 53, 55, 130, 189, 194, 198, 267, 345, 409, 410–13.
38 Herbert Marcuse, *Reason and Revolution: Hegel and the Rise of Social Theory*, second edition, London, Routledge & Kegan Paul, 1968, p. 322.
39 *History and Class Consciousness*, pp. 178–9.
40 Ibid., p. 199. See Chapter 3 above for a further discussion of the ethical dimension of Lukács's *History and Class Consciousness*.
41 PN, pp. 409–10.
42 Ibid., p. 133.
43 *History and Class Consciousness*, p. 198.
44 Ibid., p. 328.
45 Ibid., pp. 312–13.
46 Ibid., pp. 197–8.
47 Ibid., p. 313.
48 Ibid.
49 Ibid., p. 198.
50 PN, p. 406.
51 Ibid.
52 *Images of Society: Essays on the Sociological Theories of Tocqueville,*

Marx and Durkheim, California and Oxford, Stanford University Press, 1972, pp. 158–61. Robert Vincent Daniels (in 'Fate and Will in the Marxian Philosophy of History', *Journal of the History of Ideas*, vol. 21, 1960, pp. 538–52) makes a basic misunderstanding of the processual nature of the unity of theory and practice in the conscious harnessing of blindly necessary historical tendencies in Marx when he formalistically asserts that "The logical contradiction between a determinist philosophy of history and the vigorous pursuit of political action is obvious" (p. 545). He consequently erroneously concludes that which of these exclusive options is chosen as the basis of a political ideology solely depends upon the aim and intention of the individual revolutionary in various circumstances.

53 PN, p. 191.

54 Ibid., p. 405.

55 Ibid., p. 405. Zygmunt Bauman has argued, on the other hand, that the existence of such affirmations of Utopia performs a positive function as a necessary condition for critique in general as well as for historical change to transform society: "Utopias relativise the present. One cannot be critical about something that is believed to be an absolute. By exposing the partiality of current reality, by scanning the field of the possible in which the real occupies merely a tiny plot, utopias pave the way for a critical attitude and a critical activity which alone can transform the present predicament of man. The presence of a utopia, the ability to think of alternative solutions to the festering problems of the present, may be seen therefore as a necessary condition of historical change" (*Socialism: The Active Utopia*, London, Allen & Unwin, 1975, p. 13).

11 Towards the ethical State

1 PN, pp. 5–11.

2 Ibid., p. 9.

3 'The Concept of "Egemonia" in the Thought of Antonio Gramsci: Some Notes on Interpretation', *Journal of the History of Ideas*, vol. 21, 1960, p. 590.

4 PN, p. 14.

5 Ibid.

6 Ibid., p. 15.

7 Ibid.

8 Ibid., p. 16

9 Ibid.

10 Ibid.

11 Ibid., pp. 181–2.

12 Ibid., p. 268.

13 Ibid., p. 129.

14 Benedetto Croce, *Aesthetic as Science of Expression and General Linguistic*, translated by Douglas Ainslie, London, Macmillan, 1909, p. 92.

15 PN, p. 259.

16 Ibid., p. 227

17 Ibid., p. 268.
18 Ibid.
19 Ibid.
20 Ibid., p. 263.
21 See John Merrington, 'Theory and Practice in Gramsci's Marxism', in R. Miliband and J. Saville (eds), *The Socialist Register*, London, Merlin Press, 1968, p. 151.
22 *Il Grido del Popolo*, 2 March 1918, quoted by A. Pozzolini, *Antonio Gramsci: An Introduction to His Thought*, translated by Anne F. Showstack, London, Pluto Press, 1970, p. 76. During this period Gramsci wrote that his model of the ideal State was the factory council, in which "the concept of the citizen declines, and that of comrade takes its place" and "everyone is indispensable" (from 'Unions and Councils', *L'Ordine Nuovo*, 11 October 1919, in *New Edinburgh Review*, Vol. II, 1974, p. 59.)
23 PN, p. 226.
24 Ibid., pp. 132–3, 349 and 429.
25 Ibid., p. 429.
26 Ibid., p. 349.
27 V. I. Lenin, *What Is To Be Done?* Peking, Foreign Languages Press, 1973 edition, p. 86.
28 Ibid.
29 A position exemplified by George Lichtheim, who said, surely wrongly, of Gramsci that in prison he went on "to develop a doctrine more totalitarian than that of his gaolers" (in *Marxism: An Historical and Critical Study*, London, Routledge & Kegan Paul, 1961, p. 368).
30 Pozzolini, op. cit., pp. 76–88.
31 Ibid., p. 80.
32 Giuseppe Fiori, *Antonio Gramsci: Life of a Revolutionary*, New York, Dutton, 1971, p. 103.
33 Ibid., p. 237 *et seq.*
34 PN, p. 273.
35 'Antonio Gramsci: The Subjective Revolution', in Dick Howard and Karl E. Klare (eds), *The Unknown Dimension: European Marxism since Lenin*, New York, Basic Books, 1972, p. 165.
36 PN, p. 268.
37 See PN, pp. 261–4.
38 *Antonio Gramsci: The Man, His Ideas*, Sidney, Australian Left Review Publications, 1968, p. 41.
39 PN, pp. 262–3.
40 Ibid., p. 267.
41 Ibid., p. 9.
42 Ibid., p. 10.
43 Ibid., p. 355.

12 The unity of commonsense and philosophy

1 PN, p. 323.
2 Ibid.

3 Ibid., p. 326, footnote 5.
4 Ibid., p. 324.
5 Ibid., p. 347.
6 Ibid., p. 344.
7 Ibid., p. 345.
8 Ibid.
9 Ibid., pp. 325–6.
10 Ibid., p. 326.
11 Ibid., p. 328.
12 Ibid., p. 329.
13 Ibid., p. 325.
14 Ibid., p. 328.
15 Ibid., pp. 197, 323, 396.
16 Ibid., p. 197.
17 Ibid., pp. 325 and 450.
18 Ibid., p. 349.
19 Ibid.
20 Ibid., pp. 451–2.
21 Ibid., p. 453.
22 Ibid., p. 325.
23 Ibid., p. 326, footnote 5. Compare: "Common sense contains innumerable pre- and quasi-scientific interpretations about everyday life which it takes for granted" (P. Berger and T. Luckmann, *The Social Construction of Reality*, London, Allen Lane, 1967, p. 34).
24 PN, p. 326.
25 Ibid., p. 327.
26 Ibid.
27 Ibid., p. 33.
28 Ibid., p. 327.
29 Ibid., p. 332.
30 Ibid., pp. 332–3.
31 Ibid., pp. 330–1.
32 Ibid., p. 331.
33 Ibid., p. 330.
34 Ibid., p. 330.
35 Ibid., pp. 333–4; my emphasis. See also pp. 420–1.
36 4 September 1920, article entitled 'The Communist Party', in *New Edinburgh Review*, Vol. II, p. 104.
37 PN, p. 334.
38 Ibid., p. 342.

13 Inequality and the unity of mankind

1 PN, p. 340.
2 Ibid., p. 372.
3 *Class Inequality and Political Order: Social Stratification in Capitalist and Communist Societies*, London, Paladin, 1972, p. 81.
4 Ibid., Chapter 3.
5 Against Bukharin Gramsci comments: "It has been forgotten that in

the case of a very common expression [historical materialism] one should put the accent on the first term – "historical" – and not on the second, which is of metaphysical origin" (PN, p. 465).

6 'Base and Superstructure in Marxist Cultural Theory', *New Left Review*, no. 82, November–December 1973, p. 8.
7 PN, p. 465.
8 Ibid., p. 333.
9 Ibid., p. 357.
10 Ibid., p. 356.
11 Ibid., pp. 355–6.
12 Ibid., pp. 356 and 370.
13 Ibid., p. 360.
14 Ibid.
15 Ibid., p. 367.
16 Ibid., p. 356.
17 Ralf Dahrendorf, 'On the Origin of Inequality among Men', in André Béteille (ed.), *Social Inequality: Selected Readings*, Harmondsworth, Penguin, 1969, p. 40.
18 PN, p. 340. See also p. 371 where Gramsci suggests the writing of an "Anti-Croce" to function like Engels's *Anti-Dühring* but in this case in order to criticize "historicist theories of a speculative character".
19 Ibid., p. 340.
20 Ibid., pp. 418–19.
21 Ibid., p. 397.
22 Ibid., p. 369.
23 Ibid., p. 348.
24 Ibid., pp. 369 and 333.
25 Ibid., p. 349.
26 Ibid., p. 370.
27 Ibid.
28 See H. Stuart Hughes, *Consciousness and Society: The Reorientation of European Social Thought 1890–1930*, London, MacGibbon & Kee, 1959, reprinted 1967, p. 103; also PN, p. 465.
29 PN, pp. 396 and 465.
30 Ibid., p. 398.

Part four – Early critical theory: the sociology of praxis

14 Horkheimer in context

1 In *Critical Theory: Selected Essays* by Max Horkheimer, translated by Matthew J. O'Connell and others, New York, Herder & Herder, 1972. ('Traditional and Critical Theory' essay further cited as T & CT.) Two studies which give short accounts from a history of ideas perspective of early critical theory are Martin Jay, *The Dialectical Imagination: A History of the Frankfurt School and the Institute of Social Research 1923–1950*, London, Heinemann, 1973, Chapter 2, and William Leiss, 'The Critical Theory of Society: Present Situation and Future Tasks',

in Paul Brienes (ed.), *Critical Interruptions: New Left Perspectives on Herbert Marcuse*, New York, Herder & Herder, 1970. In addition Jay gives extensive coverage of the wide range of other cultural themes studied by the Frankfurt School, including mass culture, family, personality, Nazism, and psychoanalysis, and provides extensive bibliographies of the main writers of the School such as Adorno, Horkheimer, Kirchheimer, Marcuse, Fromm, and Benjamin. On the recent developments in critical theory, particularly the work of Habermas, see Albrecht Wellmer, *Critical Theory of Society*, translated by John Cumming, New York, Herder & Herder, 1971; Trent Schroyer, *The Critique of Domination: The Origins and Development of Critical Theory*, New York, George Braziller, 1973; and William Leiss, *The Domination of Nature*, New York, George Braziller, 1972, Part Two.

2 T & CT, pp. 192–3.
3 Ibid., p. 205.
4 Ibid., p. 194.
5 Ibid., p. 200.
6 Ibid.
7 Ibid., p. 202.
8 Ibid.
9 Ibid., p. 210.
10 Ibid., p. 204.
11 Ibid.
12 Ibid., p. 206.
13 Ibid., p. 207. In my paper 'On the Structure of Critical Thinking', *Leeds Occasional Papers in Sociology*, no. 2, Summer 1975, I trace the "critical attitude" and its dialectical opposite of positivism back to their Hegelian origins in the conceptions of Reason and the Understanding, as perpetuated by Marx in his methodological critique of the political economists. See also Martin Jay, *The Dialectical Imagination: A History of the Frankfurt School and the Institute of Social Research 1923–1950*, London, Heinemann, 1973, p. 60 ff.
14 T & CT, p. 207.
15 Ibid., p. 208.
16 Ibid.
17 Ibid.
18 Ibid., p. 209.
19 Horkheimer was also critical of this school as well as the logical empiricists. See his essay 'The Latest Attack on Metaphysics' in *Critical Theory: Selected Essays*, translated by Matthew J. O'Connell, *et al.*, New York, Herder & Herder, 1972 and Albrecht Wellmer, *Critical Theory of Society*, translated by John Cumming, New York, Herder & Herder, 1971, pp. 16–26.
20 'The Concept of Essence', in Herbert Marcuse, *Negations*, London, Allen Lane, 1969, p. 85.
21 Ibid., p. 66.
22 Ibid., p. 67.
23 Ibid., p. 72.
24 T & CT, p. 210.

25 Ibid., p. 211.
26 Ibid., p. 214.
27 Ibid.; my emphasis.
28 Ibid., p. 215.
29 Ibid., p. 216.
30 Karl Marx, *Capital* (1867) London, Lawrence & Wishart, 1970, Vol. III, p. 820.
31 T & CT, p. 210.
32 There have been some writers, such as Ernst Bloch, Walter Benjamin and Norman O. Brown, who have on the other hand believed that the distinction between subject and object in the broadest sense can be totally obliterated. In the *Dialectic of Enlightenment* Horkheimer and Adorno argued that it was the reflective opposition between them that preserved the Utopia, i.e. the continual possibility of their reconciliation. See *Martin Jay*, op. cit., p. 267, and the subsequent remarks on Marcuse and Brown in this chapter. Karl Mannheim made the same point as Horkheimer and Adorno in two different contexts in *Ideology and Utopia* (1929), London, Routledge & Kegan Paul, 1968, pp. 170 and 236.
33 T & CT, p. 230.
34 London, New Left Books, 1971.
35 *Prisms*, translated by Samuel and Shierry Weber, London, Neville Spearman, 1967, p. 106. Adorno is following Hegel here who also saw the life process of human beings as endemically contradictory: 'First' the living being determines itself, in so doing posits itself as denied, and thereby relates itself to an *other* to it, to the indifferent objectivity; but secondly, it is equally not lost in this loss of itself but maintains itself therein . . . thus it is the urge to posit this *other* world *as its own*, as similar to itself, to sublate it and to objectify *itself*. By doing this, its self-determination has the form of objective externality, and as it is at the same time identical with itself it is absolute contradiction, (*Science of Logic*, translated by A. V. Miller, London, Allen & Unwin, 1969, p. 770).
36 'Love Mystified: A Critique of Norman O. Brown, in Marcuse, *Negations*, p. 238.
37 Ibid., p. 241.
38 Ibid., p. 243.
39 Ibid., p. 241.
40 T & CT, p. 216.
41 Ibid., p. 229.
42 Ibid., pp. 240–1.
43 Ibid., p. 220.
44 Ibid., p. 232.
45 T & CT, p. 222. Both Marcuse and Adorno also made the same point against the sociology of knowledge. See Martin Jay, op. cit., pp. 64 and 313.
46 T & CT, p. 209.
47 Ibid., p. 223.
48 Ibid., p. 221.
49 Karl Mannheim, *Ideology and Utopia: An Introduction to the Sociology*

of Knowledge (1929), London, Routledge & Kegan Paul, 1969, p. 137. Mannheim's posthumously published essays from the 1930's on the question of the intelligentsia carry replies to the critics of *Ideology and Utopia* and are most instructive. See *Essays on the Sociology of Culture*, London, Routledge & Kegan Paul, 1971, Part Two.

50 T & CT, p. 22.

51 In my paper 'On the Structure of Critical Thinking', *Leeds Occasional Papers in Sociology*, no. 2, Summer 1975, Section V, I discuss this issue in relation to the "positivist moment" in all sociological analysis.

52 The allusion is to Engels's popular gloss on the relationship between action and the sense-perception of objects in the Special Introduction to the English Edition of 'Socialism: Utopian and Scientific', 1892. In Karl Marx and Frederick Engels, *Selected Works in one volume* Lawrence & Wishart, London, 1968, p. 385.

53 See Karl Mannheim, *Ideology and Utopia*, pp. 112–13, Horkheimer, T & CT, pp. 220–1 and Georg Lukács, *History and Class Consciousness* (1923), translated by R. Livingstone, London, Merlin Press, 1971, pp. 197–9 for accounts of this aspect of Marxist thought.

54 T & CT, p. 210.

55 Ibid., p. 209.

56 From a letter to Niethammer, 28 October 1808, quoted by Shlomo Avineri, *Hegel's Theory of the Modern State*, Cambridge University Press, 1972, p. 68. For an account of Hegel's conception of the unity of thinking and willing and of the primacy of the infinite over the finite implied in this statement, see George Armstrong Kelly, *Idealism, Politics and History: Sources of Hegelian Thought*, Cambridge University Press, 1969, p. 309 ff.

57 T & CT, p. 229.

58 Ibid. See F. Engels, 'Socialism: Utopian and Scientific' (1892), in *Karl Marx and Frederick Engels, Selected Works in One Volume*, London, Lawrence & Wishart, 1968, pp. 428–9.

59 T & CT, p. 231.

60 Ibid., p. 241.

61 Ibid.

62 On this issue see George Lichtheim, *Marxism: An Historical and Critical Study*, London, Routledge & Kegan Paul, 1961, pp. 238–40.

63 It is taken from Mannheim's *Ideology and Utopia*, p. 43.

64 T & CT, p. 239.

15 Praxis and method

1 T & CT, p. 228. Hence Göran Therborn, in his zeal to write off critical theory as anti-scientific, wrongly asserts that since critical theory sees itself as humanity's self-knowledge it "cannot and must not have a structure which is (formally) logical and systematic" ('A Critique of the Frankfurt School', *New Left Review*, no. 63, September–October 1970, p. 78).

2 In Herbert Marcuse, *Negations: Essays in Critical Theory*, London, Allen Lane, 1968. See also my paper 'On The Structure of Critical

Thinking', *Leeds Occasional Papers in Sociology* no. 2, Summer 1975.

3 E. Mandel, in *The Formation of the Economic Thought of Karl Marx, 1843 to Capital*, translated by B. Pearce, New York, Monthly Review Press, 1971, pp. 91–9, explains the point about labour power in order to show how some critics of Marx's economic theories have wrongly assumed that he was searching for an immutable and invariable measure of value which he found in labour.

4 'The Concept of Essence', in *Negations*, p. 85.

5 T & CT, p. 218.

6 Ibid., p. 224.

7 Ibid., p. 225.

8 Ibid.

9 Ibid.

10 Ibid., p. 227.

11 Ibid.

12 See John Lachs, *Marxist Philosophy: A Bibliographical Guide*, Chapel Hill, North Carolina Press, 1967, pp. 90–2; Alfred G. Meyer, *Marxism: The Unity of Theory and Practice*, Cambridge, Mass., Harvard University Press, 1954, especially pp. 104–7; and Gustav A. Wetter, *Dialectical Materialism: A Historical and Systematic Survey of Philosophy in the Soviet Union*, London, Routledge & Kegan Paul, 1958, pp. 256–67.

13 T & CT, p. 242.

14 Ibid., p. 229.

15 Ibid.

16 Albrecht Wellmer in *Critical Theory of Society*, translated by John Cumming, New York, Herder & Herder, 1971, p. 10, makes a similar point to this about the early Horkheimer but misses the significance of his concession to 'traditional' principles of verification for certain aspects of the totality whose location and function are difficult to determine.

17 T & CT, pp. 218–19.

18 Ibid., p. 220.

19 Ibid., p. 218.

20 Ibid., p. 220.

21 *The Dialectical Imagination: A History of the Frankfurt School and the Institute of Social Research 1923–1950*, London, Heinemann, 1973, p. 63.

22 T & CT, p. 242.

23 *Culture as Praxis*, London and Boston, Routledge & Kegan Paul, 1973, p. 146.

24 This dualism is stated explicitly as characterizing two sides of human existence in Zygmunt Bauman's 'Culture, Values and Science of Society', Inaugural Lecture, University of Leeds, 1972.

25 Bauman, op. cit., p. 176.

26 Zygmunt Bauman, '*Between Class and Elite* . . .', op. cit., Preface to the English Edition, p. ix.

27 R. G. Collingwood, *The Idea of History* (1946), Oxford University Press, 1973, p. 226.

28 Karl Marx, 'Introduction' (originally unpublished draft, 1857, part of the *Grundrisse* manuscripts) to the 1859 *A Contribution to the Critique*

of Political Economy, translated by S. W. Ryazanskaya in Appendices to the English edition of the 'Contribution', Maurice Dobb (ed.), London, Lawrence & Wishart, 1971, pp. 209–14. Now included in Martin Nicolaus's English translation of the entire *Grundrisse* (*Foundations of the Critique of Political Economy* (rough draft)), Harmondsworth, Penguin, 1973.

29 Ibid., p. 212.

30 Jean-Paul Sartre, *Search for a Method*, New York, Vintage Books, 1968, p. 91, footnote 2.

31 Ibid., p. 123.

32 Ibid., p. 133. He has in mind particularly one of Lukacs's more dogmatic works, *Existentialisme ou Marxisme*, trans. E. Keleman, Paris, Nagel, 1948, which situates existentialism as an attempt by bourgeois consciousness in the imperialistic period to construct a 'third way' between materialism and idealism through a system of fetishized interiority which ill-disguises its idealism (Sartre, op. cit., pp. 21 and 35–9.) See also Paul Piccone, 'Phenomenological Marxism' in Bart Grahl and Paul Piccone (eds), *Towards a New Marxism*, St Louis, Telos Press, 1973.

33 Sartre, op. cit., p. 90.

34 For the elaboration of the joint necessity of the 'internalization of the external' and the 'externalization of the internal' and the dialectics of the "project" as the praxis mediating these two moments of objectivity, which backs up Sartre's argument here, see ibid., pp. 97–9.

35 Ibid., pp. 98–9, footnote 4.

16 Sociological facts and mass praxis (including Excursus)

1 F. Engels, 'Ludwig Feuerbach and the End of Classical German Philosophy', in Karl Marx and Frederick Engels, *Selected Works in One Volume*, London, Lawrence & Wishart, 1968, p. 620.

2 Horkheimer, quoted by Martin Jay, *The Dialectical Imagination: A History of the Frankfurt School and the Institute of Social Research 1923–1950*, London, Heinemann, 1973, p. 48.

3 See Martin Jay, op. cit., pp. 61–3, and Max Horkheimer, 'The Latest Attack on Metaphysics', in *Critical Theory: Selected Essays*, translated by Matthew J. O'Connell *et al.*, New York, Herder & Herder, 1972.

4 Adorno quoted by Jay, op. cit., p. 70.

5 'Philosophy and Critical Theory', in Herbert Marcuse, *Negations: Essays in Critical Theory*, London, Allen Lane, 1968, p. 156.

6 Horkheimer quoted by Jay, op. cit., p. 83.

7 G. W. F. Hegel, *Science of Logic* (1812), translated by A. V. Miller, London, Allen & Unwin, 1969, p. 50.

8 T. W. Adorno, 'Contemporary German Sociology', *Transactions of the Fourth World Congress of Sociology 1959*, International Sociological Association, London, Vol. I, 1959, p. 38.

9 Foreword to the English edition of T. W. Adorno, *Prisms*, translated by Samuel and Shierry Weber, London, Neville Spearman, 1967, p. 7.

10 'Contemporary German Sociology', p. 35.

11 See Trent Schroyer, 'Towards a Critical Theory for Advanced Industrial

Society', in Hans Peter Dreitzel (ed.), *Recent Sociology No. 2: Patterns of Communicative Behaviour*, New York, Macmillan, 1970, pp. 213–14 for a short clear account of scientism.

12 For a fuller elucidation of this view of sciences see Norbert Elias, 'The Sciences: Towards a Theory', in R. Whitley (ed.), *Social Processes of Scientific Development*, Routledge & Kegan Paul, London, 1974, and his 'Theory of Science and History of Science: Comments on a Recent Discussion', in *Economy and Society*, vol. I, no. 2, May 1972.

13 Karl Marx, *Critique of Hegel's 'Philosophy of Right'* (1843), edited with an introduction by Joseph O'Malley, Cambridge University Press, 1970, p. 92.

14 See Norbert Elias, 'Problems of Involvement and Detachment', *British Journal of Sociology*, vol. 7, 1956, pp. 226–52.

15 *Knowledge and Human Interests*, London, Heinemann, 1973, p. 315.

16 'Mental Illness *Is* Illness', *Salmagundi*, Fall 1972.

17 Georg Lukács, *History and Class Consciousness*, translated by Rodney Livingstone, London, Merlin Press, 1971, pp. 328–9.

18 Herbert Marcuse, *Reason and Revolution: Hegel and the Rise of Social Theory*, London, Routledge & Kegan Paul, 1941, Second edition, 1968, p. 322.

19 T. W. Adorno, *Negative Dialectics*, translated by E. B. Ashton, London, Routledge & Kegan Paul, 1973, p. 3.

20 In *Critical Theory: Selected Essays*, translated by Matthew J. O'Connell *et al.*, New York, Herder & Herder, 1972.

21 Ibid., p. 21.

22 Quoted by Jay, op. cit., p. 56.

23 Ibid., Chapter 2.

24 See ibid., pp. 71–4. Also P. Piccone and A. Delfini, 'Marcuse's Heideggerian Marxism', *Telos*, no. 6, Autumn 1970, and Russell Jacoby, 'Towards a Critique of Automatic Marxism: The Politics of Philosophy from Lukács to the Frankfurt School', *Telos*, no. 10, Winter 1971, section IV.

25 Quoted by Jay, op. cit., p. 47.

26 Theodor Adorno, *Negative Dialectics*, translated by E. B. Ashton, London, Routledge & Kegan Paul, 1973, pp. 129–30. Adorno is also concerned about the political implications which flow from the Heideggerian view that the existence of the contemporary world is ultimately absorbed into the category of Being since this could justify submission to actual historical situations (pp. 128–31). See also Adorno's *The Jargon of Authenticity*, translated by Knut Tarnowski and Frederic Will, London, Routledge & Kegan Paul, 1973, for a critique of post-First World War German existentialism in general, including that of Heidegger.

27 Cf. Marx in one of the very few passages where he mentions the category of ontology, only to sociologize and historicize it in the same manner as Horkheimer: "If man's feelings, passions, etc., are not merely anthropological phenomena in the narrower sense, but truly *ontological* affirmations of essential being (of nature) . . . Only through developed industry – i.e. through the medium of private property –

does the ontological essence of human passion come to be both in its totality and in its humanity" (*Economic and Philosophic Manuscripts of 1844*) translated by Martin Milligan, Moscow, 1967, p. 126.

28 Max Horkheimer, *Eclipse of Reason*, New York, Seabury Press, 1947; new edition, 1974, pp. 181–2.

29 Written in 1928, quoted by Jay, op. cit., pp. 72–3.

30 A. Schmidt, *The Concept of Nature in Marx*, translated by Ben Fowkes, London, New Left Books, 1971, p. 29. See also L. Kolakowski, 'Karl Marx and the Classical Definition of Truth', in *Marxism and Beyond*, London, Paladin, 1971, for a similarly 'revisionist' interpretation of Marx's practical materialism, especially its epistemological implications. Adam Schaff replied to this from the orthodox camp in his barbarous 'Studies of the Young Marx: a Rejoinder', in Leopold Labedz (ed.), *Revisionism: Essays on the History of Marxist Ideas*, London, Allen & Unwin, 1962.

31 Quoted by Jay, op. cit., pp. 55–6.

32 'Materialism and Metaphysics', in *Critical Theory: Selected Essays*, p. 25.

17 Philosophical sociology and sociological philosophy

1 Herbert Marcuse, *Soviet Marxism: A Critical Analysis* (1958), Harmondsworth, Penguin, 1971, p. 106. See also Karl Korsch, *Marxism and Philosophy* (1923), English translation, London, New Left Books, 1970, pp. 66–7.

2 See Max Horkheimer, 'The Social Function of Philosophy', in *Critical Theory: Selected Essays*, translated by Matthew J. O'Connell, *et al.*, New York, Herder & Herder, 1972, pp. 253–4 and my discussion of Bukharin in Chapter 8.

3 Ibid., p. 256.

4 Ibid., p. 257.

5 Max Horkheimer, *Eclipse of Reason* (1947), New York, Seabury Press, 1974, Chapter 1.

6 'On Science and Phenomenology', in Anthony Giddens (ed.), *Positivism and Sociology*, London, Heinemann, 1974, p. 225 ff., and Jürgen Habermas, *Knowledge and Human Interests*, London, Heinemann, 1973, p. 301.

7 Marcuse, op. cit.

8 *Eclipse of Reason*, pp. 6–7.

9 Ibid., p. 11.

10 Ibid., p. 12.

11 'The Social Function of Philosophy', in *Critical Theory: Selected Essays*, p. 268.

12 Ibid.

13 *Eclipse of Reason*, p. 6, footnote 1. See also my remarks on Max Weber in the Lukacs chapters in Part two.

14 Ibid., p. 6.

15 Herbert Marcuse, 'Philosophy and Critical Theory' in *Negations: Essays in Critical Theory*, London, Allen Lane, 1968, pp. 148–9.

16 Göran Therborn, 'A Critique of the Frankfurt School', *New Left Review*, no. 63, September–October 1970.
17 Letter to Lowenthal, 1946, quoted by Martin Jay, *The Dialectical Imagination: A History of the Frankfurt School and the Institute of Social Research 1923–1950*, London, Heinemann, 1973, p. 274.
18 Göran Therborn, 'A Critique of the Frankfurt School', *New Left Review*, no. 63, September–October 1970, p. 74.
19 Karl Marx, *Capital*, vol. I, Afterword to the Second German Edition, p. 15. George Lichtheim, too, saw Althusser's work as an "attempt to transform Marxism into a rigorously 'scientific' doctrine cut off from its author's own philosophical postulates". He added that "The concept of 'exploitation' hinges upon an understanding of the labour theory of value which links an anthropological critique of society to a scientific analysis of capitalism. If this link is severed, Marxism becomes a 'value-free' theory . . . If there can be a scientific theory of language, why not a scientific theory of society? Indeed, why not? Althusser is the Talcott Parsons of Marxism" (*From Marx to Hegel and Other Essays*, London, Orbach & Chambers, 1971, pp. 198–9).
20 *Eclipse of Reason*, p. 18.
21 'The Social Function of Philosophy', in *Critical Theory: Selected Essays*, p. 262.
22 Ibid., p. 264.
23 Ibid., pp. 264–5.
24 Ibid., p. 268.
25 Herbert Marcuse, 'Philosophy and Critical Theory', *Negations: Essays in Critical Theory*, p. 135.
26 *Eclipse of Reason*, p. 168. Both Marcuse and Horkheimer are drawing here on Hegel's critique of the Kantian critical philosophy as being subjective idealism and open to the charge of reducing categories to the arbitrary creations of individual knowers rather than seeing them as simultaneously embodied in the object itself. Hegel said of his position that: "it is assumed . . . that the determinations contained in definitions do not belong only to the knower, but are determinations of the object, constituting its innermost essence and its very own nature" (*Science of Logic* (1812), translated by A. V. Miller, London, Allen & Unwin, 1969, p. 50).
27 'Philosophy and Critical Theory', pp. 141–2. In the *Grundrisse* Marx comments on the conditions under which true individuality could be realized in the sense intended by Marcuse and Horkheimer as expounded in this chapter. He writes: "Universally developed individuals, whose social relations, as their communal (*gemeinschaftlich*) relations, are hence also subordinated to their own communal control, are no product of nature, but of history. The degree and the universality of the development of wealth where *this* individuality becomes possible supposes production on the basis of exchange values as a prior condition, whose universality produces not only the alienation of the individual from himself and from others, but also the universality and the comprehensiveness of his relations and capacities. In earlier stages of development the single individual seems to be developed more fully,

because he has not yet worked out his relationships in their fullness, or erected them as independent social powers and relations opposite himself" (*Grundrisse* (*Foundations of the Critique of Political Economy*, rough draft 1857) translated by Martin Nicolaus, Harmondsworth, Penguin, 1973, p. 162).

18 Conclusion: The cunning of praxis

1 Karl Marx and Frederick Engels, *The Holy Family* (1845), translated by R. Dixon, Moscow, 1956, p. 164, as quoted by Alfred Schmidt, *The Concept of Nature in Marx*, translated by Ben Fowkes, London, New Left Books, 1971, p. 31.
2 Karl Marx, *Capital* (1867), London, Lawrence & Wishart, 1967–70, vol. III, p. 819.
3 Max Weber, 'Politics as a Vocation', in H. H. Gerth and C. Wright Mills (eds), *From Max Weber: Essays in Sociology*, London, Routledge & Kegan Paul, 1970, p. 120 ff.
4 Max Horkheimer and Theodor Adorno, *Dialectic of Enlightenment* (1944), translated by John Cumming, New York, Herder & Herder, 1972.
5 Ibid., p. 6.
6 See Albrecht Wellmer, *Critical Theory of Society*, translated by J. Cumming, New York, Herder & Herder, 1971, p. 128 ff.
7 *Conversations with Lukács*, edited by Theo Pinkus, London, Merlin Press, 1974, p. 93.
8 Max Horkheimer and Theodor Adorno, *Dialectic of Enlightenment* (1944), translated by J. Cumming, New York, Herder & Herder, 1972, p. 54.
9 Ibid.
10 G. W. F. Hegel, *The Philosophy of History* (1830–1), translated by J. Sibree, New York, Dover, 1956, p. 33.
11 Karl Marx, Introduction to the *Grundrisse*, in Appendix to the 1859 *Contribution to the Critique of Political Economy*, translated by S. W. Ryazanskaya, Maurice Dobb (ed.), London, Lawrence & Wishart, 1971, p. 215.
12 *Meaning in History* (1949) Chicago University Press, 1970, p. 207.
13 Karl Marx, *Economic and Philosophic Manuscripts of 1844*, translated by Martin Milligan, Moscow, 1967, pp. 65 and 77–8.
14 Quoted by Martin Jay, *The Dialectical Imagination: A History of the Frankfurt School and the Institute of Social Research 1923–1950*, London, Heinemann, 1973, p. 69.

Bibliography

Acton, H. B., *The Illusion of the Epoch: Marxism–Leninism as a Philosophical Creed* (1955), London, Routledge & Kegan Paul, reprinted 1973.

Adorno, Theodor W., 'Contemporary German Sociology', *Transations of the Fourth World Congress of Sociology*, International Sociological Association, London, vol. I, 1959.

Adorno, Theodor W., *Prisms*, translated by Samuel and Shierry Weber, London, Neville Spearman, 1967.

Adorno, Theodor W., *The Jargon of Authenticity*, translated by Knut Tarnowski and Frederic Will, London, Routledge & Kegan Paul, 1973.

Adorno, Theodor W., *Negative Dialectics*, translated by E. B. Ashton, London, Routledge & Kegan Paul, 1973.

Anderson, Perry, 'Origins of the Present Crisis', *New Left Review*, no. 23, Jan.–Feb. 1964, pp. 26–53; reprinted in P. Anderson and R. Blackburn (eds), *Towards Socialism*, London, Fontana Library, 1965, pp. 11–52.

Anderson, Perry, 'Problems of Socialist Strategy', in P. Anderson and R. Blackburn (eds), *Towards Socialism*, London, Fontana Library, 1965.

Anderson, Perry, 'A Reply to E. P. Thompson, "The Peculiarities of the English" ', in R. Miliband and J. Saville (eds), *The Socialist Register*, London, Merlin Press, 1965, pp. 311–62.

Anderson, Perry, 'Socialism and Pseudo Empiricism', *New Left Review*, no. 35, Jan.–Feb. 1966, pp. 2–42.

Anderson, Perry, 'The Limits and Possibilities of Trade Union Action', in R. Blackburn and Alexander Cockburn (eds), *The Incompatibles: Trade Union Militancy and the Consensus*, Harmondsworth, Penguin, 1967, pp. 263–80.

Avineri, Shlomo, *The Social and Political Thought of Karl Marx*, Cambridge University Press, 1969.

Avineri, Shlomo, *Hegel's Theory of the Modern State*, Cambridge University Press, 1972.

Bakunin, Michael, 'The Reaction in Germany: A Fragment from a Frenchman' (1842), translated by Mary-Barbara Zeldin in James M. Edie,

James P. Scanlan and Mary-Barbara Zeldin (eds), *Russian Philosophy*, vol. I, Chicago, Quadrangle, 1965, pp. 385–406.

Bates, Thomas R., 'Gramsci and the Theory of Hegemony', *Journal of the History of Ideas*, vol. XXXVI, April–June 1975, pp. 351–66.

Bauman, Zygmunt, 'Modern Times: Modern Marxism', in Peter Berger (ed.), *Marxism and Sociology: Views from Eastern Europe*, New York, Appleton-Century-Crofts, 1969.

Bauman, Zygmunt, *Between Class and Elite: The Evolution of the British Labour Movement: A Sociological Study*, Manchester University Press, 1972.

Bauman, Zygmunt, 'Culture, Values and Science of Society', Inaugural Lecture, University of Leeds, 1972.

Bauman, Zygmunt, *Culture as Praxis*, London and Boston, Routledge & Kegan Paul, 1973.

Bauman, Zygmunt, Review of *Images of Society* by G. Poggi, *Times Higher Education Supplement*, 13 April 1973.

Bauman, Zygmunt, *Socialism: The Active Utopia*, London, Allen & Unwin, 1975.

Bendix, Reinhard, *Embattled Reason: Essays on Social Knowledge*, New York, Oxford University Press, 1970.

Berger, Peter L. and Luckmann, Thomas, *The Social Construction of Reality*, London, Allen Lane, 1967.

Berger, Peter L. and Pullberg, Stanley, 'Reification and the Sociological Critique of Consciousness', *History and Theory*, vol. IV, no. 2, 1965.

Bernstein, Richard J., *Praxis and Action*, London, Gerald Duckworth, 1972.

Bloch, Ernst, *On Karl Marx* (1968), translated by John Maxwell, New York, Herder & Herder, 1971.

Blumenberg, Werner, *Karl Marz* (1962), translated by Douglas Scott, London, New Left Books, 1972.

Borkenau, Franz, *The Communist International*, London, Faber & Faber, 1938.

Bottomore, T. and Rubel, M. (eds), *Karl Marx: Selected Writings in Sociology and Social Philosophy*, Harmondsworth, Penguin, 1967.

Brazill, William, *The Young Hegelians*, New Haven, Yale University Press, 1970.

Brienes, Paul, 'Praxis and its Theorists: The Impact of Lukács and Korsch in the 1920's', *Telos*, no. 11, Spring 1972, pp. 67–105.

Bukharin, Nikolai, *Historical Materialism: A System of Sociology*, with an Introduction by Alfred G. Meyer, Michigan, Ann Arbor Paperbacks, 1969, (originally *The Theory of Historical Materialism: A Manual of Popular Sociology*, 1921).

Bukharin, Nikolai and Preobrazhensky, E., *ABC of Communism* (1922), Harmondsworth, Penguin Books, 1969.

Bullock, Alan, *Hitler: A Study in Tyranny*, Harmondsworth, Pelican, reprinted 1967.

Cammett, John M., *Antonio Gramsci and the Origins of Italian Communism*, California, Stanford University Press, 1967.

Caton, Hiram, 'Marx's Sublation of Philosophy into Praxis', *Review of Metaphysics*, vol. XXVI, no. 2, Dec. 1972, pp. 233–59.

Colletti, Lucio, *Marxism and Hegel*, translated by Lawrence Garner, London, New Left Books, 1973.

Collingwood, R. G., *The Idea of History* (1946), Oxford University Press, 1973.

Connerton, Paul, 'The Collective Historical Subject: Reflections on Lukacs' History and Class Consciousness', *British Journal of Sociology*, vol. XXV, no. 2, June 1974.

Croce, Benedetto, *Aesthetic as Science of Expression and General Linguistic*, translated by Douglas Ainslie, London, Macmillan, 1909.

Croce, Benedetto, *The Philosophy of the Practical: Economic and Ethic* (1913), translated by Douglas Ainslie, London, Macmillan, 1913.

Croce, Benedetto, *History as the Story of Liberty* (1941), English translation by Sylvia Sprigge, London, Allen & Unwin, 1941.

Dahrendorf, Ralf, 'On the Origin of Inequality Among Men', in André Beteille (ed.), *Social Inequality: Selected Readings*, Harmondsworth, Penguin, 1969.

Daniels, Robert Vincent, 'Fate and Will in the Marxian Philosophy of History', *Journal of the History of Ideas*, vol. 21, 1960, pp. 538–52.

Davidson, Alastair, *Antonio Gramsci: The Man, His Ideas*, Sidney, Australian Left Review Publications, 1968.

Dupré, Louis, 'Recent Literature on Marx and Marxism', *Journal of the History of Ideas*, vol. XXXV, no. 4, Oct.–Dec. 1974, pp. 703–14.

Easton, Loyd, 'Rationalism and Empiricism in Marx's Thought', *Social Research*, vol. 37, no. 3, 1970.

Easton, Loyd and Guddat, Kurt H. (eds), *Writings of the Young Marx on Philosophy and Society*, New York, Doubleday, 1967.

Elias, Norbert, 'Problems of Involvement and Detachment', *British Journal of Sociology*, vol. 7, 1956, pp. 226–52.

Elias, Norbert, 'Theory of Science and History of Science: Comments on a Recent Discussion', *Economy and Society*, vol. I, no. 2, May 1972.

Elias, Norbert, 'The Sciences: Towards a Theory', in R. Whitley (ed.), *Social Processes of Scientific Development*, London and Boston, 1974.

Engels, Frederick, 'Ludwig Feuerbach and the End of Classical German Philosophy' (1888), in Karl Marx and Frederick Engels, *Selected Works in one Volume*, London, Lawrence & Wishart, 1968.

Engels, Frederick, 'Socialism: Utopian and Scientific' (1892), in Karl Marx and Frederick Engels, *Selected Works in one Volume*, London, Lawrence & Wishart, 1968.

Ewing, A. C., *The Idealist Tradition from Berkeley to Blanshard*, Glencoe, Free Press, 1957.

Fetscher, Iring, *Marx and Marxism*, New York, Herder & Herder, 1971.

Fiori, Giuseppe, *Antonio Gramsci: Life of a Revolutionary*, New York, Dutton, 1971.

Fleischer, Helmut, *Marxism and History* (1969), translated by Eric Mosbacher, London, Allen Lane, 1973.

Fleischmann, Eugène, 'The Role of the Individual in Pre-Revolutionary Society: Stirner, Marx and Hegel', in Z. A. Pelczynski (ed.), *Hegel's Political Philosophy: Problems and Perspectives*, Cambridge University Press, 1971.

Fogarasi, Bela, 'Reflections on the Philosophical Views of Georg Lukács', *World Marxist Review*, June 1959.

Frankfurt Institute for Social Research, *Aspects of Sociology* (Preface by T. Adorno and M. Horkheimer), London, Heinemann, 1973.

Geras, Norman, 'Essence and Appearance: Aspects of Fetishism in Marx's *Capital*', *New Left Review*, no. 65, Jan.–Feb. 1971.

Gerth, H. H. and Mills, C. Wright (eds), *From Max Weber: Essays in Sociology*, London, Routledge & Kegan Paul, 1970.

Giachetti, Romano, 'Antonio Gramsci: The Subjective Revolution', in Dick Howard and Karl E. Klare (eds), *The Unknown Dimension: European Marxism since Lenin*, New York, Basic Books, 1972.

Gobetti, Piero, 'Gramsci: A 1924 Profile', translated by H. Henderson and Tom Nairn, in *New Edinburgh Review*, double issue on Gramsci, no. II, 1974.

Godelier, Maurice, 'Structure and Contradiction in *Capital*', in Robin Blackburn (ed.), *Ideology in Social Science: Readings in Critical Social Theory*, London, Fontana/Collins, 1972.

Grahl, Bart and Piccone, Paul (eds), *Towards a New Marxism*, St Louis, Telos Press, 1973.

Gramsci, Antonio, *Selections from the Prison Notebooks of Antonio Gramsci*, edited and translated by Quintin Hoare and Geoffrey Nowell-Smith, London, Lawrence & Wishart, 1971.

Gramsci, Antonio, 'Lettere dal Carcere', translated by Hamish Henderson, in *New Edinburgh Review*, double issue on Gramsci, nos I and II, 1974.

Habermas, Jürgen, *Knowledge and Human Interests*, London, Heinemann, 1973.

Hartmann, Klaus, 'Hegel: A Non-Metaphysical View', in Alasdair MacIntyre (ed.), *Hegel: A Collection of Critical Essays*, New York, Doubleday, 1972.

Hegel, G. W. F., *The Phenomenology of Mind* (1805), translated by J. B. Baillie, London, Allen & Unwin, 1966.

Hegel, G. W. F., *Science of Logic* (1812), translated by A. V. Miller, London, Allen & Unwin, 1969.

Hegel, G. W. F., *Lectures on the History of Philosophy* (*1819–1830*), translated by Elizabeth S. Haldane and Francis H. Simson, London, Kegan Paul, Trench, Trübner & Co., 1892.

Hegel, G. W. F., *The Philosophy of Right* (1821), translated by T. M. Knox, Oxford University Press, 1967.

Hegel, G. W. F., *The Logic* (Part One of The Encyclopaedia of the Philosophical Sciences, 1830), translated by William Wallace, second edition, London, Oxford University Press, 1892, reprinted 1972.

Hegel, G. W. F., *The Philosophy of Nature* (Part Two of the Encyclopaedia of the Philosophical Sciences, 1830), translated by A. V. Miller, Oxford, Clarendon Press, 1970.

Hegel, G. W. F., *The Philosophy of History* (1830–1), translated by J. Sibree, New York, Dover, 1956.

Hegel, G. W. F., *Lectures on the Philosophy of Religion* (1832), translated by E. B. Speirs and J. Burdon Sanderson, London, Kegan Paul, Trench Trübner & Co., 1895 (three vols).

Hepner, Benoit P., 'History and the Future: The Vision of August Cieszkowski', *Review of Politics*, vol. 15, no. 3, July 1953, pp. 328–49.

Hoare, Quintin, 'What is Fascism?', *New Left Review*, no. 20, Summer 1963, pp. 99–111.

Horkheimer, Max, *Critical Theory: Selected Essays*, translated by Matthew J. O'Connell, *et al.*, New York, Herder & Herder, 1972.

Horkheimer, Max, *Eclipse of Reason* (1947), New York, Seabury Press, 1974.

Horkheimer, Max and Adorno, Theodor, *Dialectic of Enlightenment* (1944), translated by John Cumming, New York, Herder & Herder, 1972.

Howard, Dick, 'On Marx's Critical Theory', *Telos*, no. 6, Autumn 1970, pp. 224–33.

Howard, Dick, *The Development of the Marxian Dialectic*, Carbondale and Edwardsville, Southern Illinois University Press, 1972.

Howard, Dick and Klare, E. Karl (eds), *The Unknown Dimension: European Marxism Since Lenin*, New York, Basic Books, 1972.

Hughes, H. Stuart, *Consciousness and Society: The Reorientation of European Social Thought 1890–1930*, London, Macgibbon & Kee, 1959, reprinted 1967.

Hyppolite, Jean, *Studies on Marx and Hegel*, London, Heinemann, 1969.

Iggers, Georg, *The German Conception of History*, Connecticut, Middletown, 1968.

Jacobitti, Edmund E., 'Labriola, Croce and Italian Marxism (1895–1910)', *Journal of the History of Ideas*, vol. XXXVI, April–June 1975.

Jacoby, Russell, 'Towards a Critique of Automatic Marxism: The Politics of Philosophy from Lukács to the Frankfurt School', *Telos*, no. 10, Winter 1971.

Jay, Martin, *The Dialectical Imagination: A History of the Frankfurt School and the Institute of Social Research 1923–1950*, London, Heinemann, 1973.

Jones, Gareth Stedman, 'The Marxism of the Early Lukács: An Evaluation', *New Left Review*, no. 70, Nov.–Dec. 1971.

Kamenka, Eugene, *Marxism and Ethics*, London, Macmillan, 1969.

Kelly, G. A., *Idealism, Politics and History: Sources of Hegelian Thought*, Cambridge University Press, 1969.

Khomyakov, Alexis, 'On Recent Developments in Philosophy (Letter to Y.F. Samarin)' (1860), translated by Vladimir D. Pastuhov and Mary-Barbara Zeldin, in James M. Edie, James P. Scanlan and Mary-Barbara Zeldin (eds), *Russian Philosophy*, vol. 1, Chicago, Quadrangle 1965, pp. 221–45.

Kiernan, V. G., 'Gramsci and Marxism', in *The Socialist Register*, R. Miliband and J. Saville (eds), London, Merlin, 1972.

Kilminster, Richard, 'On the Structure of Critical Thinking', *Leeds Occasional Papers in Sociology*, no. 2, Summer 1975.

Kolakowski, Leszek, *Marxism and Beyond*, London, Paladin, 1971.

Kolakowski, Leszek, 'Lukács's Other Marx', *Cambridge Review*, 28, Jan. 1972.

Kolakowski, Leszek, *Positivist Philosophy: From Hume to the Vienna Circle*, Harmondsworth, Penguin, 1972.

Korsch, Karl, *Marxism and Philosophy* (1923), English translation, London, New Left Books, 1970.

Lachs, J., *Marxist Philosophy: A Bibliographical Guide*, Chapel Hill, North Carolina Press, 1967.

Leiss, William, 'The Critical Theory of Society: Present Situation and Future Tasks', in Paul Brienes (ed.), *Critical Interruptions: New Left Perspectives on Herbert Marcuse*, New York, Herder & Herder, 1970.

Leiss, William, *The Domination of Nature*, New York, George Braziller, 1972.

Lenin, V. I., *What Is To Be Done?* Peking, Foreign Languages Press, 1973.

Lichtheim, George, *Marxism: An Historical and Critical Study*, London, Routledge & Kegan Paul, 1961.

Lichtheim, George, 'The Concept of Ideology', *History and Theory*, vol. 4, 1965.

Lichtheim, George, *Lukács*, London, Fontana/Collins, 1970.

Lichtheim, George, *From Marx to Hegel and Other Essays*, London, Orbach & Chambers, 1971.

Livergood, Norman D., *Activity in Marx's Philosophy*, The Hague, Martinus Nijhoff, 1967.

Lobkowicz, Nicholas, *Theory and Practice: History of a Concept from Aristotle to Marx*, Indiana, Notre Dame University Press, 1967.

Lossky, N. O., *Three Polish Messianists*, Prague, International Philosophical Library, 1937.

Löwith, Karl, *From Hegel to Nietszche* (1941), translated by David E. Green, London, Constable, 1965.

Löwith, Karl, *Meaning in History* (1949), Chicago University Press, 1970.

Löwith, Karl, 'Weber's Interpretation of the Bourgeois-Capitalistic World in Terms of the Guiding Principle of "Rationalization" ', in Dennis Wrong (ed.), *Max Weber*, New Jersey, Prentice-Hall, 1970.

Löwith, Karl, 'Mediation and Immediacy in Hegel, Marx and Feuerbach', in Warren E. Steinkraus, ed.*New Studies in Hegel's Philosophy*, New York, Holt, Rinehart & Winston, 1971.

Lukács, Georg, *The Theory of the Novel* (1915), translated by Ann Bostock, London, Merlin Press, 1971.

Lukács, Georg, *History and Class Consciousness* (1923), translated by Rodney Livingstone, London, Merlin Press, 1971.

Lukács, Georg, 'Moses Hess and the Problems of Idealist Dialectics' (1926), in Rodney Livingstone (ed.), *Georg Lukács, Political Writings, 1919–1929: The Question of Parliamentarianism and Other Essays*, London, New Left Books, 1972.

Lukács, Georg, Review of N. Bukharin's 'The Theory of Historical Materialism: A Manual of Popular Sociology' (1926), translated as 'Technology and Social Relations' in E. San Juan Jr (ed.), *Marxism and Human Liberation: Essays on History, Culture and Revolution by Georg Lukacs*, New York, Delta, 1973.

Lukács, Georg, *Existentialisme ou Marxisme* (1948), trans. E. Keleman, Paris, Nagel, 1948.

Lukács, Georg, 'Max Weber and German Sociology', *Economy and Society*, vol. I, no. 2, May 1972, pp. 386–98.

Makkreel, Rudolf A., 'Review Article on Dilthey', *Journal of the History of Philosophy*, vol. X, no. 2, April 1972, pp. 232–7.

Mandel, E., *The Formation of the Economic Thought of Karl Marx, 1843 to Capital*, translated by B. Pearce, New York, Monthly Review Press, 1971.

Mannheim, Karl, *Essays on the Sociology of Knowledge* (1952), London, Routledge & Kegan Paul, fifth impression, 1972.

Mannheim, Karl, *Ideology and Utopia: An Introduction to the Sociology of Knowledge* (1929), London, Routledge & Kegan Paul, 1968.

Mannheim, Karl, *Essays on the Sociology of Culture*, London, Routledge & Kegan Paul, 1956.

Marcuse, Herbert, *Reason and Revolution: Hegel and the Rise of Social Theory*, London, Routledge & Kegan Paul (1941) second edition, 1968.

Marcuse, Herbert, *Soviet Marxism: A Critical Analysis* (1958), Harmondsworth, Penguin, 1971.

Marcuse, Herbert, *Negations: Essays in Critical Theory*, London, Allen Lane, 1968.

Marcuse, Herbert, 'On Science and Phenomenology', in Anthony Giddens (ed.), *Positivism and Sociology*, London, Heinemann, 1974.

Markovic, Mihailo, 'The Problem of Reification and the Verstehen-Erklären Controversy', *Acta Sociologica*, vol. 15, no. 1, March 1972.

Marx, Karl, *Critique of Hegel's* The Philosophy of Right (1843), edited and with an Introduction by J. O'Malley, Cambridge University Press, 1970.

Marx, Karl, *Economic and Philosophic Manuscripts of 1844*, translated by Martin Milligan, Moscow, Progress Publishers, 1967.

Marx, Karl and Engels, Frederick, *The German Ideology* (1845), London, Lawrence & Wishart, 1965.

Marx, Karl and Engels, Frederick, *The Holy Family* (1845), translated by R. Dixon, Moscow, Progress Publishers, 1956.

Marx, Karl, *The Poverty of Philosophy* (1847), New York, International Publishers, 1969.

Marx, Karl, *The Communist Manifesto* (1848), Harmondsworth, Penguin, 1967.

Marx, Karl, *Grundrisse* (*Foundations of the Critique of Political Economy*, (rough draft 1857), translated by Martin Nicolaus, Harmondsworth, Penguin, 1973.

Marx, Karl, 'Introduction' (originally unpublished draft, 1857, part of the *Grundrisse* manuscripts) to the 1859 *A Contribution to the Critique of Political Economy*, translated by S. W. Ryazanskaya in Appendices to the English edition of the Contribution, Maurice Dobb (ed.), London, Lawrence & Wishart, 1971.

Marx, Karl, *Theories of Surplus Value* (1862–3), in three volumes, translated by J. Cohen, London, Lawrence & Wishart, 1969–72.

Marx, Karl, *Capital* (1867), in three volumes, London, Lawrence & Wishart, 1967–70.

Marx, Karl, 'Marginal Notes on Adolph Wagner's *Lehrbruch der politischen Ökonomie*' (1880), *Theoretical Practice*, issue 5, Spring 1972.

Marx, Karl and Engels, Frederick, *Selected Works in One Volume*, London, Lawrence & Wishart, 1968.

Marx, Karl and Engels, Frederick, *Selected Correspondence*, Moscow, Progress Publishing, third edition, 1975.
Mazlish, Bruce, *The Riddle of History: The Great Speculators from Vico to Freud*, New York, Minerva Press, 1966.
McLellan, David, *Karl Marx: His Life and Thought*, London, Macmillan, 1973.
Merleau-Ponty, Maurice, *Adventures of the Dialectic*, translated by Joseph Bien, London, Heinemann, 1974.
Merrington, John, 'Theory and Practice in Gramsci's Marxism', in R. Miliband and J. Saville (eds), *The Socialist Register*, London, Merlin Press, 1968.
Mészáros, Istvan, *Lukács' Concept of Dialectic*, London, Merlin Press, 1972.
Mészáros, Istvan, *Marx's Theory of Alienation*, London, Merlin Press, third edition, Jan. 1972.
Meyer, Alfred G., *Marxism: The Unity of Theory and Practice*, Cambridge, Mass., Harvard University Press, 1954.
Mills, C. Wright, *The Marxists*, Harmondsworth, Penguin, 1967.
Mommsen, Wolfgang, 'Max Weber's Political Sociology and his Philosophy of World History', in Dennis Wrong (ed.), *Max Weber*, New Jersey, Prentice-Hall, 1970.
Moore, Stanley, 'Marx and the Origin of Dialectical Materialism', *Inquiry* 14, no. 4, vol. 14, Winter 1971, pp. 420–9.
Morawski, Stefan, 'Mimesis – Lukács' Universal Principle', *Science and Society*, vol. XXXII, Winter 1968, pp. 26–38.
Mueller, Gustav E., 'The Hegel Legend of "Thesis-Antithesis-Synthesis" ', *Journal of the History of Ideas*, vol. 19, 1958, pp. 411–14.
O'Neill, John, *Sociology as a Skin Trade*, London, Heinemann, 1972.
Ossowski, Stanislaw, *Class Structure in the Social Consciousness*, London, Routledge & Kegan Paul, 1967.
Parkin, Frank, *Class Inequality and Political Order: Social Stratification in Capitalist and Communist Societies*, London, Paladin, 1972, reprinted 1973.
Parkinson, G. H. R. (ed.), *Georg Lukács, The Man, His Work and His Ideas*, London, Weidenfeld & Nicolson, 1970.
Piccone, Paul, 'Phenomenological Marxism' in Bart Grahl and Paul Piccone (eds), *Towards a New Marxism*, St Louis, Telos Press, 1973.
Piccone, Paul and Delfini, A., 'Marcuse's Heideggerian Marxism', *Telos*, no. 6, Autumn 1970.
Pinkus, Theo (ed.), *Conversations with Lukács*, London, Merlin Press, 1974.
Poggi, Gianfranco, *Images of Society: Essays on the Sociological Theories of Tocqueville, Marx and Durkheim*, Stanford University Press and Oxford, 1972.
Pozzolini, A., *Antonio Gramsci: An Introduction to His Thought*, translated by Anne F. Showstack, London, Pluto Press, 1970.
Revai, Jozsef, 'A Review of Georg Lukács' *History and Class Consciousness*' (1924), *Theoretical Practice*, no. 1, Jan. 1971.
Rosen, Stanley, *G. W. F. Hegel: An Introduction to the Science of Wisdom*, Yale University Press, 1974.

Rotenstreich, Nathan, 'On Human Historicity', *Proceedings of the Twelfth International Congress of Philosophy*, vol. 8, Sept. 1958, pp. 215–22.
Rotenstreich, Nathan, *Basic Problems of Marx's Philosophy*, New York, Bobbs-Merrill, 1965.
Rotenstreich, Nathan, *From Substance to Subject: Studies in Hegel*, The Hague, Martinus Nijhoff, 1974.
Salamini, Leonardo, 'The Specificity of Marxist Sociology in Gramsci's Theory', *Sociological Quarterly*, 16, Winter 1975, pp. 65–86.
Sartre, Jean-Paul, *Search for a Method*, New York, Vintage Books, 1968.
Schaff, Adam, 'Studies of the Young Marx: A Rejoinder', in Leopold Labedz (ed.), *Revisionism: Essays on the History of Marxist Ideas*, London, Allen & Unwin, 1962.
Schmidt, Alfred, *The Concept of Nature in Marx*, translated by Ben Fowkes, London, New Left Books, 1971.
Schroyer, Trent, 'Towards a Critical Theory for Advanced Industrial Society', in Hans Peter Dreitzel (ed.), *Recent Sociology, No. 2: Patterns of Communicative Behaviour*, New York, Macmillan, 1970.
Schroyer, Trent, *The Critique of Domination: The Origins and Development of Critical Theory*, New York, George Braziller, 1973.
Schutz, Alfred, *The Phenomenology of the Social World* (1932), translated by George Walsh and Frederick Lehnert, London, Heinemann, 1972.
Sedgwick, Peter, 'Mental Illness *Is* Illness', *Salmagundi*, Fall 1972.
Simmel, Georg, *Die Philosophie des Geldes*, Leipzig, Düncker & Humblot, 1900.
Söhn-Rethel, Alfred, 'Intellectual and Manual Labour: An Attempt at a Materialist Theory', *Radical Philosophy*, no. 6, Winter 1973.
Stepelevich, Lawrence S., 'August Von Cieszkowski: From Theory to Praxis', *History & Theory*, vol XIII, no. 1, 1974, pp. 39–52.
Therborn, Göran, 'A Critique of the Frankfurt School', *New Left Review*, no. 63, Sept.–Oct. 1970.
Treves, Renato, 'Sociological Study and Research in Italy', *Transactions of the Fourth World Congress of Sociology, 1959*, vol. 1, International Sociological Association, London, 1959, pp. 73–94.
Truitt, Willis H., 'Ideology, Expression and Mediation', *The Philosophical Forum*, vol. III, nos. 3–4, Spring-Summer 1972, pp. 468–97.
Watnick, Morris, 'Relativism and Class Consciousness: Georg Lukács', in Leopold Labedz (ed.), *Revisionism: Essays in the History of Marxist Ideas*, London, Allen & Unwin, 1962.
Weber, Max, *The Protestant Ethic and the Spirit of Capitalism* (1905), translated by Talcott Parsons, London, Allen & Unwin, 1968.
Weber, Max, 'Politics as a Vocation', in H. Gerth and C. Wright Mills, *From Max Weber: Essays in Sociology*, London, Routledge & Kegan Paul, 1970.
Wellmer, Albrecht, *Critical Theory of Society*, translated by John Cumming, New York, Herder & Herder, 1971.
Wetter, G. A., *Dialectical Materialism: A Historical and Systematic Survey of Philosophy in the Soviet Union*, London, Routledge & Kegan Paul, 1958.
White, Hayden, *Metahistory*, London and Baltimore, Johns Hopkins University Press, 1973.

Wiedmann, Franz, *Hegel: An Illustrated Biography*, translated by Joachim Neugroschel, New York, Pegasus, 1968.
Williams, Gwyn A., 'The Concept of 'Egemonia' in the Thought of Antonio Gramsci: Some Notes on Interpretation', *Journal of the History of Ideas*, vol. 21, 1960.
Williams, Raymond, 'Base and Superstructure in Marxist Cultural Theory', *New Left Review*, 82, Nov.–Dec. 1973.
Wittgenstein, Ludwig, *Tractatus Logico-Philosophicus* (1922), translated by D. F. Pears and B. F. McGuinness, London, Routledge & Kegan Paul, 1961, reprinted 1972.
Wood, Allen W., 'Marx's Critical Anthropology: Three Recent Interpretations', *Review of Metaphysics*, vol. XXVI, no. 1, Sept. 1972, pp. 118–39.
Zitta, Victor, *Georg Lukács' Marxism: Alienation, Dialectics, Revolution: A Study in Utopia and Ideology*, The Hague, Martinus Nijhoff, 1964.

Index

Routledge Social Science Series

Routledge & Kegan Paul London, Henley and Boston

39 Store Street, London WC1E 7DD
Broadway House, Newtown Road,
Henley-on-Thames, Oxon RG9 1EN
9 Park Street, Boston, Mass. 02108

Contents

Authors wishing to submit manuscripts for any series in this catalogue should send them to the Social Science Editor, Routledge & Kegan Paul Ltd, 39 Store Street, London WC1E 7DD

●*Books so marked are available in paperback*
All books are in Metric Demy 8vo format (216 × 138mm approx.)

International Library of Sociology

General Editor John Rex

GENERAL SOCIOLOGY

Barnsley, J. H. The Social Reality of Ethics. *464 pp.*
Brown, Robert. Explanation in Social Science. *208 pp.*
● Rules and Laws in Sociology. *192 pp.*
Bruford, W. H. Chekhov and His Russia. *A Sociological Study. 244 pp.*
Burton, F. and **Carlen, P.** Official Discourse. *On Discourse Analysis, Government Publications, Ideology. About 140 pp.*
Cain, Maureen E. Society and the Policeman's Role. *326 pp.*
● **Fletcher, Colin.** Beneath the Surface. *An Account of Three Styles of Sociological Research. 221 pp.*
Gibson, Quentin. The Logic of Social Enquiry. *240 pp.*
Glucksmann, M. Structuralist Analysis in Contemporary Social Thought. *212 pp.*
Gurvitch, Georges. Sociology of Law. *Foreword by Roscoe Pound. 264 pp.*
Hinkle, R. Founding Theory of American Sociology 1883-1915. *About 350 pp.*
Homans, George C. Sentiments and Activities. *336 pp.*
Johnson, Harry M. Sociology: *a Systematic Introduction. Foreword by Robert K. Merton. 710 pp.*
● **Keat, Russell** and **Urry, John.** Social Theory as Science. *278 pp.*
Mannheim, Karl. Essays on Sociology and Social Psychology. *Edited by Paul Keckskemeti. With Editorial Note by Adolph Lowe. 344 pp.*
Martindale, Don. The Nature and Types of Sociological Theory. *292 pp.*
● **Maus, Heinz.** A Short History of Sociology. *234 pp.*
Myrdal, Gunnar. Value in Social Theory: *A Collection of Essays on Methodology. Edited by Paul Streeten. 332 pp.*
Ogburn, William F. and **Nimkoff, Meyer F.** A Handbook of Sociology. *Preface by Karl Mannheim. 656 pp. 46 figures. 35 tables.*
Parsons, Talcott, and **Smelser, Neil J.** Economy and Society: *A Study in the Integration of Economic and Social Theory. 362 pp.*
Podgórecki, Adam. Practical Social Sciences. *About 200 pp.*
Raffel, S. Matters of Fact. *A Sociological Inquiry. 152 pp.*
● **Rex, John.** (Ed.) Approaches to Sociology. *Contributions by Peter Abell,* Sociology and the Demystification of the Modern World. *282 pp.*
● **Rex, John** (Ed.) Approaches to Sociology. *Contributions by Peter Abell, Frank Bechhofer, Basil Bernstein, Ronald Fletcher, David Frisby, Miriam Glucksmann, Peter Lassman, Herminio Martins, John Rex, Roland Robertson, John Westergaard and Jock Young. 302 pp.*
Rigby, A. Alternative Realities. *352 pp.*
Roche, M. Phenomenology, Language and the Social Sciences. *374 pp.*
Sahay, A. Sociological Analysis. *220 pp.*

Strasser, Hermann. The Normative Structure of Sociology. *Conservative and Emancipatory Themes in Social Thought. About 340 pp.*
Strong, P. Ceremonial Order of the Clinic. *About 250 pp.*
Urry, John. Reference Groups and the Theory of Revolution. *244 pp.*
Weinberg, E. Development of Sociology in the Soviet Union. *173 pp.*

FOREIGN CLASSICS OF SOCIOLOGY

● **Gerth, H. H.** and **Mills, C. Wright.** From Max Weber: *Essays in Sociology. 502 pp.*
● **Tönnies, Ferdinand.** Community and Association. *(Gemeinschaft and Gesellschaft.) Translated and Supplemented by Charles P. Loomis. Foreword by Pitirim A. Sorokin. 334 pp.*

SOCIAL STRUCTURE

Andreski, Stanislav. Military Organization and Society. *Foreword by Professor A. R. Radcliffe-Brown. 226 pp. 1 folder.*
Carlton, Eric. Ideology and Social Order. *Foreword by Professor Philip Abrahams. About 320 pp.*
Coontz, Sydney H. Population Theories and the Economic Interpretation. *202 pp.*
Coser, Lewis. The Functions of Social Conflict. *204 pp.*
Dickie-Clark, H. F. Marginal Situation: *A Sociological Study of a Coloured Group. 240 pp. 11 tables.*
Giner, S. and **Archer, M. S.** (Eds.). Contemporary Europe. *Social Structures and Cultural Patterns. 336 pp.*
● **Glaser, Barney** and **Strauss, Anselm L.** Status Passage. *A Formal Theory. 212 pp.*
Glass, D. V. (Ed.) Social Mobility in Britain. *Contributions by J. Berent, T. Bottomore, R. C. Chambers, J. Floud, D. V. Glass, J. R. Hall, H. T. Himmelweit, R. K. Kelsall, F. M. Martin, C. A. Moser, R. Mukherjee, and W. Ziegel. 420 pp.*
Kelsall, R. K. Higher Civil Servants in Britain: *From 1870 to the Present Day. 268 pp. 31 tables.*
● **Lawton, Denis.** Social Class, Language and Education. *192 pp.*
McLeish, John. The Theory of Social Change: *Four Views Considered. 128 pp.*
● **Marsh, David C.** The Changing Social Structure of England and Wales, 1871-1961. *Revised edition. 288 pp.*
Menzies, Ken. Talcott Parsons and the Social Image of Man. *About 208 pp.*
● **Mouzelis, Nicos.** Organization and Bureaucracy. *An Analysis of Modern Theories. 240 pp.*
Ossowski, Stanislaw. Class Structure in the Social Consciousness. *210 pp.*
● **Podgórecki, Adam.** Law and Society. *302 pp.*
Renner, Karl. Institutions of Private Law and Their Social Functions. *Edited, with an Introduction and Notes, by O. Kahn-Freud. Translated by Agnes Schwarzschild. 316 pp.*

Rex, J. and **Tomlinson, S.** Colonial Immigrants in a British City. *A Class Analysis. 368 pp.*
Smooha, S. Israel: Pluralism and Conflict. *472 pp.*
Wesolowski, W. Class, Strata and Power. *Trans. and with Introduction by G. Kolankiewicz. 160 pp.*
Zureik, E. Palestinians in Israel. *A Study in Internal Colonialism. 264 pp.*

SOCIOLOGY AND POLITICS

Acton, T. A. Gypsy Politics and Social Change. *316 pp.*
Burton, F. Politics of Legitimacy. *Struggles in a Belfast Community. 250 pp.*
Etzioni-Halevy, E. Political Manipulation and Administrative Power. *A Comparative Study. About 200 pp.*
● **Hechter, Michael.** Internal Colonialism. *The Celtic Fringe in British National Development, 1536–1966. 380 pp.*
Kornhauser, William. The Politics of Mass Society. *272 pp. 20 tables.*
Korpi, W. The Working Class in Welfare Capitalism. *Work, Unions and Politics in Sweden. 472 pp.*
Kroes, R. Soldiers and Students. *A Study of Right- and Left-wing Students. 174 pp.*
Martin, Roderick. Sociology of Power. *About 272 pp.*
Myrdal, Gunnar. The Political Element in the Development of Economic Theory. *Translated from the German by Paul Streeten. 282 pp.*
Wong, S.-L. Sociology and Socialism in Contemporary China. *160 pp.*
Wootton, Graham. Workers, Unions and the State. *188 pp.*

CRIMINOLOGY

Ancel, Marc. Social Defence: *A Modern Approach to Criminal Problems. Foreword by Leon Radzinowicz. 240 pp.*
Athens, L. Violent Criminal Acts and Actors. *About 150 pp.*
Cain, Maureen E. Society and the Policeman's Role. *326 pp.*
Cloward, Richard A. and **Ohlin, Lloyd E.** Delinquency and Opportunity: *A Theory of Delinquent Gangs. 248 pp.*
Downes, David M. The Delinquent Solution. *A Study in Subcultural Theory. 296 pp.*
Friedlander, Kate. The Psycho-Analytical Approach to Juvenile Delinquency: *Theory, Case Studies, Treatment. 320 pp.*
Gleuck, Sheldon and **Eleanor.** Family Environment and Delinquency. *With the statistical assistance of Rose W. Kneznek. 340 pp.*
Lopez-Rey, Manuel. Crime. *An Analytical Appraisal. 288 pp.*
Mannheim, Hermann. Comparative Criminology: *a Text Book. Two volumes. 442 pp. and 380 pp.*
Morris, Terence. The Criminal Area: *A Study in Social Ecology. Foreword by Hermann Mannheim. 232 pp. 25 tables. 4 maps.*
Podgorecki, A. and **Łos, M.** *Multidimensional Sociology. About 380 pp.*
Rock, Paul. Making People Pay. *338 pp.*

● **Taylor, Ian, Walton, Paul,** and **Young, Jock.** The New Criminology. *For a Social Theory of Deviance. 325 pp.*

● **Taylor, Ian, Walton, Paul** and **Young, Jock.** (Eds) Critical Criminology. *268 pp.*

SOCIAL PSYCHOLOGY

Bagley, Christopher. The Social Psychology of the Epileptic Child. *320 pp.*

Brittan, Arthur. Meanings and Situations. *224 pp.*

Carroll, J. Break-Out from the Crystal Palace. *200 pp.*

● **Fleming, C. M.** Adolescence: Its Social Psychology. *With an Introduction to recent findings from the fields of Anthropology, Physiology, Medicine, Psychometrics and Sociometry. 288 pp.*

● The Social Psychology of Education: *An Introduction and Guide to Its Study. 136 pp.*

Linton, Ralph. The Cultural Background of Personality. *132 pp.*

● **Mayo, Elton.** The Social Problems of an Industrial Civilization. *With an Appendix on the Political Problem. 180 pp.*

Ottaway, A. K. C. Learning Through Group Experience. *176 pp.*

Plummer, Ken. Sexual Stigma. *An Interactionist Account. 254 pp.*

● **Rose, Arnold M.** (Ed.) Human Behaviour and Social Processes: *an Interactionist Approach. Contributions by Arnold M. Rose, Ralph H. Turner, Anselm Strauss, Everett C. Hughes, E. Franklin Frazier, Howard S. Becker et al. 696 pp.*

Smelser, Neil J. Theory of Collective Behaviour. *448 pp.*

Stephenson, Geoffrey M. The Development of Conscience. *128 pp.*

Young, Kimball. Handbook of Social Psychology. *658 pp. 16 figures. 10 tables.*

SOCIOLOGY OF THE FAMILY

Bell, Colin R. Middle Class Families: *Social and Geographical Mobility. 224 pp.*

Burton, Lindy. Vulnerable Children. *272 pp.*

Gavron, Hannah. The Captive Wife: *Conflicts of Household Mothers. 190 pp.*

George, Victor and **Wilding, Paul.** Motherless Families. *248 pp.*

Klein, Josephine. Samples from English Cultures.

1. Three Preliminary Studies and Aspects of Adult Life in England. *447 pp.*
2. Child-Rearing Practices and Index. *247 pp.*

Klein, Viola. The Feminine Character. *History of an Ideology. 244 pp.*

McWhinnie, Alexina M. Adopted Children. *How They Grow Up. 304 pp.*

● **Morgan, D. H. J.** Social Theory and the Family. *About 320 pp.*

● **Myrdal, Alva** and **Klein, Viola.** Women's Two Roles: *Home and Work. 238 pp. 27 tables.*

Parsons, Talcott and **Bales, Robert F.** Family: Socialization and Interaction Process. *In collaboration with James Olds, Morris Zelditch and Philip E. Slater. 456 pp. 50 figures and tables.*

SOCIAL SERVICES

Bastide, Roger. The Sociology of Mental Disorder. *Translated from the French by Jean McNeil. 260 pp.*

Carlebach, Julius. Caring For Children in Trouble. *266 pp.*

George, Victor. Foster Care. *Theory and Practice. 234 pp.*

Social Security: *Beveridge and After. 258 pp.*

George, V. and **Wilding, P.** Motherless Families. *248 pp.*

● **Goetschius, George W.** Working with Community Groups. *256 pp.*

Goetschius, George W. and **Tash, Joan.** Working with Unattached Youth. *416 pp.*

Heywood, Jean S. Children in Care. *The Development of the Service for the Deprived Child. Third revised edition. 284 pp.*

King, Roy D., Ranes, Norma V. and **Tizard, Jack.** Patterns of Residential Care. *356 pp.*

Leigh, John. Young People and Leisure. *256 pp.*

● **Mays, John.** (Ed.) Penelope Hall's Social Services of England and Wales. *About 324 pp.*

Morris, Mary. Voluntary Work and the Welfare State. *300 pp.*

Nokes, P. L. The Professional Task in Welfare Practice. *152 pp.*

Timms, Noel. Psychiatric Social Work in Great Britain (1939-1962). *280 pp.*

● Social Casework: *Principles and Practice. 256 pp.*

SOCIOLOGY OF EDUCATION

Banks, Olive. Parity and Prestige in English Secondary Education: a Study in Educational Sociology. *272 pp.*

● **Blyth, W. A. L.** English Primary Education. *A Sociological Description.* 2. Background. *168 pp.*

Collier, K. G. The Social Purposes of Education: *Personal and Social Values in Education. 268 pp.*

Evans, K. M. Sociometry and Education. *158 pp.*

● **Ford, Julienne.** Social Class and the Comprehensive School. *192 pp.*

Foster, P. J. Education and Social Change in Ghana. *336 pp. 3 maps.*

Fraser, W. R. Education and Society in Modern France. *150 pp.*

Grace, Gerald R. Role Conflict and the Teacher. *150 pp.*

Hans, Nicholas. New Trends in Education in the Eighteenth Century. *278 pp. 19 tables.*

● Comparative Education: *A Study of Educational Factors and Traditions. 360 pp.*

● **Hargreaves, David.** Interpersonal Relations and Education. *432 pp.*

● Social Relations in a Secondary School. *240 pp.*

School Organization and Pupil Involvement. *A Study of Secondary Schools.*

● **Mannheim, Karl** and **Stewart, W.A.C.** An Introduction to the Sociology of Education. *206 pp.*

● **Musgrove, F.** Youth and the Social Order. *176 pp.*

● **Ottaway, A. K. C.** Education and Society: An Introduction to the Sociology of Education. *With an Introduction by W. O. Lester Smith. 212 pp.*

Peers, Robert. Adult Education: *A Comparative Study. Revised edition. 398 pp.*

Stratta, Erica. The Education of Borstal Boys. *A Study of their Educational Experiences prior to, and during, Borstal Training. 256 pp.*

● **Taylor, P. H., Reid, W. A.** and **Holley, B. J.** The English Sixth Form. *A Case Study in Curriculum Research. 198 pp.*

SOCIOLOGY OF CULTURE

Eppel, E. M. and **M.** Adolescents and Morality: *A Study of some Moral Values and Dilemmas of Working Adolescents in the Context of a changing Climate of Opinion. Foreword by W. J. H. Sprott. 268 pp. 39 tables.*

● **Fromm, Erich.** The Fear of Freedom. *286 pp.*

● The Sane Society. *400 pp.*

Johnson, L. The Cultural Critics. *From Matthew Arnold to Raymond Williams. 233 pp.*

Mannheim, Karl. Essays on the Sociology of Culture. *Edited by Ernst Mannheim in co-operation with Paul Kecskemeti. Editorial Note by Adolph Lowe. 280 pp.*

Zijderfeld, A. C. On Clichés. *The Supersedure of Meaning by Function in Modernity. About 132 pp.*

SOCIOLOGY OF RELIGION

Argyle, Michael and **Beit-Hallahmi, Benjamin.** The Social Psychology of Religion. *About 256 pp.*

Glasner, Peter E. The Sociology of Secularisation. *A Critique of a Concept. About 180 pp.*

Hall, J. R. The Ways Out. *Utopian Communal Groups in an Age of Babylon. 280 pp.*

Ranson, S., Hinings, B. and **Bryman, A.** Clergy, Ministers and Priests. *216 pp.*

Stark, Werner. The Sociology of Religion. *A Study of Christendom.*

Volume II. *Sectarian Religion. 368 pp.*

Volume III. *The Universal Church. 464 pp.*

Volume IV. *Types of Religious Man. 352 pp.*

Volume V. *Types of Religious Culture. 464 pp.*

Turner, B. S. Weber and Islam. *216 pp.*

Watt, W. Montgomery. Islam and the Integration of Society. *320 pp.*

SOCIOLOGY OF ART AND LITERATURE

Jarvie, Ian C. Towards a Sociology of the Cinema. *A Comparative Essay on the Structure and Functioning of a Major Entertainment Industry. 405 pp.*

Rust, Frances S. Dance in Society. *An Analysis of the Relationships between the Social Dance and Society in England from the Middle Ages to the Present Day. 256 pp. 8 pp. of plates.*

Schücking, L. L. The Sociology of Literary Taste. *112 pp.*

Wolff, Janet. Hermeneutic Philosophy and the Sociology of Art. *150 pp.*

SOCIOLOGY OF KNOWLEDGE

Diesing, P. Patterns of Discovery in the Social Sciences. *262 pp.*

● **Douglas, J. D.** (Ed.) Understanding Everyday Life. *370 pp.*

Glasner, B. Essential Interactionism. *About 220 pp.*

● **Hamilton, P.** Knowledge and Social Structure. *174 pp.*

Jarvie, I. C. Concepts and Society. *232 pp.*

Mannheim, Karl. Essays on the Sociology of Knowledge. *Edited by Paul Kecskemeti. Editorial Note by Adolph Lowe. 353 pp.*

Remmling, Gunter W. The Sociology of Karl Mannheim. *With a Bibliographical Guide to the Sociology of Knowledge, Ideological Analysis, and Social Planning. 255 pp.*

Remmling, Gunter W. (Ed.) Towards the Sociology of Knowledge. *Origin and Development of a Sociological Thought Style. 463 pp.*

URBAN SOCIOLOGY

Aldridge, M. The British New Towns. *A Programme Without a Policy. About 250 pp.*

Ashworth, William. The Genesis of Modern British Town Planning: *A Study in Economic and Social History of the Nineteenth and Twentieth Centuries. 288 pp.*

Brittan, A. The Privatised World. *196 pp.*

Cullingworth, J. B. Housing Needs and Planning Policy: *A Restatement of the Problems of Housing Need and 'Overspill' in England and Wales. 232 pp. 44 tables. 8 maps.*

Dickinson, Robert E. City and Region: *A Geographical Interpretation. 608 pp. 125 figures.*

The West European City: *A Geographical Interpretation. 600 pp. 129 maps. 29 plates.*

Humphreys, Alexander J. New Dubliners: *Urbanization and the Irish Family. Foreword by George C. Homans. 304 pp.*

Jackson, Brian. Working Class Community: *Some General Notions raised by a Series of Studies in Northern England. 192 pp.*

● **Mann, P. H.** An Approach to Urban Sociology. *240 pp.*

Mellor, J. R. Urban Sociology in an Urbanized Society. *326 pp.*

Morris, R. N. and **Mogey, J.** The Sociology of Housing. *Studies at Berinsfield. 232 pp. 4 pp. plates.*

Rosser, C. and **Harris, C.** The Family and Social Change. *A Study of Family and Kinship in a South Wales Town. 352 pp. 8 maps.*

● **Stacey, Margaret, Batsone, Eric, Bell, Colin** and **Thurcott, Anne.** Power, Persistence and Change. *A Second Study of Banbury. 196 pp.*

RURAL SOCIOLOGY

Mayer, Adrian C. Peasants in the Pacific. *A Study of Fiji Indian Rural Society. 248 pp. 20 plates.*

Williams, W. M. The Sociology of an English Village: *Gosforth. 272 pp. 12 figures. 13 tables.*

SOCIOLOGY OF INDUSTRY AND DISTRIBUTION

Dunkerley, David. The Foreman. *Aspects of Task and Structure. 192 pp.*

Eldridge, J. E. T. Industrial Disputes. *Essays in the Sociology of Industrial Relations. 288 pp.*

Hollowell, Peter G. The Lorry Driver. *272 pp.*

● **Oxaal, I., Barnett, T.** and **Booth, D.** (Eds) Beyond the Sociology of Development. *Economy and Society in Latin America and Africa. 295 pp.*

Smelser, Neil J. Social Change in the Industrial Revolution: *An Application of Theory to the Lancashire Cotton Industry, 1770–1840. 468 pp. 12 figures. 14 tables.*

Watson, T. J. The Personnel Managers. *A Study in the Sociology of Work and Employment. 262 pp.*

ANTHROPOLOGY

Brandel-Syrier, Mia. Reeftown Elite. *A Study of Social Mobility in a Modern African Community on the Reef. 376 pp.*

Dickie-Clark, H. F. The Marginal Situation. *A Sociological Study of a Coloured Group. 236 pp.*

Dube, S. C. Indian Village. *Foreword by Morris Edward Opler. 276 pp. 4 plates.*

India's Changing Villages: *Human Factors in Community Development. 260 pp. 8 plates. 1 map.*

Firth, Raymond. Malay Fishermen. *Their Peasant Economy. 420 pp. 17 pp. plates.*

Gulliver, P. H. Social Control in an African Society: a Study of the Arusha, Agricultural Masai of Northern Tanganyika. *320 pp. 8 plates. 10 figures.*

Family Herds. *288 pp.*

Jarvie, Ian C. The Revolution in Anthropology. *268 pp.*

Little, Kenneth L. Mende of Sierra Leone. *308 pp. and folder.*

Negroes in Britain. *With a New Introduction and Contemporary Study by Leonard Bloom. 320 pp.*

Madan, G. R. Western Sociologists on Indian Society. *Marx, Spencer, Weber, Durkheim, Pareto. 384 pp.*

Mayer, A. C. Peasants in the Pacific. *A Study of Fiji Indian Rural Society. 248 pp.*

Meer, Fatima. Race and Suicide in South Africa. *325 pp.*

Smith, Raymond T. The Negro Family in British Guiana: *Family Structure and Social Status in the Villages. With a Foreword by Meyer Fortes. 314 pp. 8 plates. 1 figure. 4 maps.*

SOCIOLOGY AND PHILOSOPHY

Barnsley, John H. The Social Reality of Ethics. *A Comparative Analysis of Moral Codes. 448 pp.*

Diesing, Paul. Patterns of Discovery in the Social Sciences. *362 pp.*

● **Douglas, Jack D.** (Ed.) Understanding Everyday Life. *Toward the Reconstruction of Sociological Knowledge. Contributions by Alan F. Blum, Aaron W. Cicourel, Norman K. Denzin, Jack D. Douglas, John Heeren, Peter McHugh, Peter K. Manning, Melvin Power, Matthew Speier, Roy Turner, D. Lawrence Wieder, Thomas P. Wilson and Don H. Zimmerman. 370 pp.*

Gorman, Robert A. The Dual Vision. *Alfred Schutz and the Myth of Phenomenological Social Science. About 300 pp.*

Jarvie, Ian C. Concepts and Society. *216 pp.*

Kilminster, R. Praxis and Method. *A Sociological Dialogue with Lukács, Gramsci and the early Frankfurt School. About 304 pp.*

● **Pelz, Werner.** The Scope of Understanding in Sociology. *Towards a More Radical Reorientation in the Social Humanistic Sciences. 283 pp.*

Roche, Maurice. Phenomenology, Language and the Social Sciences. *371 pp.*

Sahay, Arun. Sociological Analysis. *212 pp.*

Slater, P. Origin and Significance of the Frankfurt School. *A Marxist Perspective. About 192 pp.*

Spurling, L. Phenomenology and the Social World. *The Philosophy of Merleau-Ponty and its Relation to the Social Sciences. 222 pp.*

Wilson, H. T. The American Ideology. *Science, Technology and Organization as Modes of Rationality. 368 pp.*

International Library of Anthropology

General Editor Adam Kuper

Ahmed, A. S. Millenium and Charisma Among Pathans. *A Critical Essay in Social Anthropology. 192 pp.*

Pukhtun Economy and Society. *About 360 pp.*

Brown, Paula. The Chimbu. *A Study of Change in the New Guinea Highlands. 151 pp.*

Foner, N. Jamaica Farewell. *200 pp.*

Gudeman, Stephen. Relationships, Residence and the Individual. *A Rural Panamanian Community. 288 pp. 11 plates, 5 figures, 2 maps, 10 tables.*

The Demise of a Rural Economy. *From Subsistence to Capitalism in a Latin American Village. 160 pp.*

Hamnett, Ian. Chieftainship and Legitimacy. *An Anthropological Study of Executive Law in Lesotho. 163 pp.*

Hanson, F. Allan. Meaning in Culture. *127 pp.*

Humphreys, S. C. Anthropology and the Greeks. *288 pp.*

Karp, I. Fields of Change Among the Iteso of Kenya. *140 pp.*

Lloyd, P. C. Power and Independence. *Urban Africans' Perception of Social Inequality. 264 pp.*

Parry, J. P. Caste and Kinship in Kangra. *352 pp. Illustrated.*

Pettigrew, Joyce. Robber Noblemen. *A Study of the Political System of the Sikh Jats. 284 pp.*

Street, Brian V. The Savage in Literature. *Representations of 'Primitive' Society in English Fiction, 1858–1920. 207 pp.*

Van Den Berghe, Pierre L. Power and Privilege at an African University. *278 pp.*

International Library of Social Policy

General Editor Kathleen Jones

Bayley, M. Mental Handicap and Community Care. *426 pp.*

Bottoms, A. E. and **McClean, J. D.** Defendants in the Criminal Process. *284 pp.*

Butler, J. R. Family Doctors and Public Policy. *208 pp.*

Davies, Martin. Prisoners of Society. *Attitudes and Aftercare. 204 pp.*

Gittus, Elizabeth. Flats, Families and the Under-Fives. *285 pp.*

Holman, Robert. Trading in Children. *A Study of Private Fostering. 355 pp.*

Jeffs, A. Young People and the Youth Service. *About 180 pp.*

Jones, Howard, and **Cornes, Paul.** Open Prisons. *288 pp.*

Jones, Kathleen. History of the Mental Health Service. *428 pp.*

Jones, Kathleen, with **Brown, John, Cunningham, W. J., Roberts, Julian** and **Williams, Peter.** Opening the Door. *A Study of New Policies for the Mentally Handicapped. 278 pp.*

Karn, Valerie. Retiring to the Seaside. *About 280 pp. 2 maps. Numerous tables.*

King, R. D. and **Elliot, K. W.** Albany: Birth of a Prison—End of an Era. *394 pp.*

Thomas, J. E. The English Prison Officer since 1850: *A Study in Conflict. 258 pp.*

Walton, R. G. Women in Social Work. *303 pp.*

● **Woodward, J.** To Do the Sick No Harm. *A Study of the British Voluntary Hospital System to 1875. 234 pp.*

International Library of Welfare and Philosophy

General Editors Noel Timms and David Watson

● **McDermott, F. E.** (Ed.) Self-Determination in Social Work. *A Collection of Essays on Self-determination and Related Concepts by Philosophers and Social Work Theorists. Contributors: F. B. Biestek, S. Bernstein, A. Keith-Lucas, D. Sayer, H. H. Perelman, C. Whittington, R. F. Stalley, F. E. McDermott, I. Berlin, H. J. McCloskey, H. L. A. Hart, J. Wilson, A. I. Melden, S. I. Benn. 254 pp.*

● **Plant, Raymond.** Community and Ideology. *104 pp.*

Ragg, Nicholas M. People Not Cases. *A Philosophical Approach to Social Work. About 250 pp.*

● **Timms, Noel** and **Watson, David.** (Eds) Talking About Welfare. *Readings in Philosophy and Social Policy. Contributors: T. H. Marshall, R. B. Brandt, G. H. von Wright, K. Nielsen, M. Cranston, R. M. Titmuss, R. S. Downie, E. Telfer, D. Donnison, J. Benson, P. Leonard, A. Keith-Lucas, D. Walsh, I. T. Ramsey. 320 pp.*

● (Eds). Philosophy in Social Work. *250 pp.*

● **Weale, A.** Equality and Social Policy. *164 pp.*

Primary Socialization, Language and Education

General Editor Basil Bernstein

Adlam, Diana S., *with the assistance of Geoffrey Turner and Lesley Lineker.* Code in Context. *About 272 pp.*

Bernstein, Basil. Class, Codes and Control. *3 volumes.*

● 1. *Theoretical Studies Towards a Sociology of Language. 254 pp.*

2. *Applied Studies Towards a Sociology of Language. 377 pp.*

● 3. *Towards a Theory of Educational Transmission. 167 pp.*

Brandis, W. and **Bernstein, B.** Selection and Control. *176 pp.*

Brandis, Walter and **Henderson, Dorothy.** Social Class, Language and Communication. *288 pp.*

Cook-Gumperz, Jenny. Social Control and Socialization. *A Study of Class Differences in the Language of Maternal Control. 290 pp.*

● **Gahagan, D. M** and **G. A.** Talk Reform. *Exploration in Language for Infant School Children. 160 pp.*

Hawkins, P. R. Social Class, the Nominal Group and Verbal Strategies. *About 220 pp.*

Robinson, W. P. and **Rackstraw, Susan D. A.** A Question of Answers. *2 volumes. 192 pp. and 180 pp.*

Turner, Geoffrey J. and **Mohan, Bernard A.** A Linguistic Description and Computer Programme for Children's Speech. *208 pp.*

Reports of the Institute of Community Studies

Baker, J. The Neighbourhood Advice Centre. A Community Project in Camden. *320 pp.*

● **Cartwright, Ann.** Patients and their Doctors. *A Study of General Practice. 304 pp.*

Dench, Geoff. Maltese in London.*A Case-study in the Erosion of Ethnic Consciousness. 302 pp.*

Jackson, Brian and **Marsden, Dennis.** Education and the Working Class: *Some General Themes raised by a Study of 88 Working-class Children in a Northern Industrial City. 268 pp. 2 folders.*

Marris, Peter. The Experience of Higher Education. *232 pp. 27 tables.*

● Loss and Change. *192 pp.*

Marris, Peter and **Rein, Martin.** Dilemmas of Social Reform. *Poverty and Community Action in the United States. 256 pp.*

Marris, Peter and **Somerset, Anthony.** African Businessmen. *A Study of Entrepreneurship and Development in Keyna. 256 pp.*

Mills, Richard. Young Outsiders: *a Study in Alternative Communities. 216 pp.*

Runciman, W. G. Relative Deprivation and Social Justice. *A Study of Attitudes to Social Inequality in Twentieth-Century England. 352 pp.*

Willmott, Peter. Adolescent Boys in East London. *230 pp.*

Willmott, Peter and **Young, Michael.** Family and Class in a London Suburb. *202 pp. 47 tables.*

Young, Michael and **McGeeney, Patrick.** Learning Begins at Home. *A Study of a Junior School and its Parents. 128 pp.*

Young, Michael and **Willmott, Peter.** Family and Kinship in East London. *Foreword by Richard M. Titmuss. 252 pp. 39 tables.*

The Symmetrical Family. *410 pp.*

Reports of the Institute for Social Studies in Medical Care

Cartwright, Ann, Hockey, Lisbeth and **Anderson, John J.** Life Before Death. *310 pp.*

Dunnell, Karen and **Cartwright, Ann.** Medicine Takers, Prescribers and Hoarders. *190 pp.*

Farrell, C. My Mother Said. . . . *A Study of the Way Young People Learned About Sex and Birth Control. 200 pp.*

Medicine, Illness and Society

General Editor W. M. Williams

Hall, David J. Social Relations & Innovation. *Changing the State of Play in Hospitals. 232 pp.*

Hall, David J., and **Stacey, M.** (Eds) Beyond Separation. *234 pp.*

Robinson, David. The Process of Becoming Ill. *142 pp.*

Stacey, Margaret *et al.* Hospitals, Children and Their Families. *The Report of a Pilot Study. 202 pp.*

Stimson G. V. and **Webb, B.** Going to See the Doctor. *The Consultation Process in General Practice. 155 pp.*

Monographs in Social Theory

General Editor Arthur Brittan

● **Barnes, B.** Scientific Knowledge and Sociological Theory. *192 pp.*

Bauman, Zygmunt. Culture as Praxis. *204 pp.*

● **Dixon, Keith.** Sociological Theory. *Pretence and Possibility. 142 pp.*

Meltzer, B. N., Petras, J. W. and **Reynolds, L. T.** Symbolic Interactionism. *Genesis, Varieties and Criticisms. 144 pp.*

● **Smith, Anthony D.** The Concept of Social Change. *A Critique of the Functionalist Theory of Social Change. 208 pp.*

Routledge Social Science Journals

The British Journal of Sociology. *Editor – Angus Stewart; Associate Editor – Leslie Sklair. Vol. 1, No. 1 – March 1950 and Quarterly. Roy. 8vo. All back issues available. An international journal publishing original papers in the field of sociology and related areas.*

Community Work. *Edited by David Jones and Marjorie Mayo. 1973. Published annually.*

Economy and Society. *Vol. 1, No. 1. February 1972 and Quarterly. Metric Roy. 8vo. A journal for all social scientists covering sociology, philosophy, anthropology, economics and history. All back numbers available.*

Ethnic and Racial Studies. *Editor – John Stone. Vol. 1 – 1978. Published quarterly.*

Religion. Journal of Religion and Religions. *Chairman of Editorial Board, Ninian Smart. Vol. 1, No. 1, Spring 1971. A journal with an inter-disciplinary approach to the study of the phenomena of religion. All back numbers available.*

Sociology of Health and Illness. *A Journal of Medical Sociology. Editor – Alan Davies; Associate Editor – Ray Jobling. Vol. 1, Spring 1979. Published 3 times per annum.*

Year Book of Social Policy in Britain, The. *Edited by Kathleen Jones. 1971. Published annually.*

Social and Psychological Aspects of Medical Practice

Editor Trevor Silverstone

Lader, Malcolm. Psychophysiology of Mental Illness. *280 pp.*

● **Silverstone, Trevor** and **Turner, Paul.** Drug Treatment in Psychiatry. *Revised edition. 256 pp.*

Whiteley, J. S. and **Gordon, J.** Group Approaches in Psychiatry. *256 pp.*

Printed in Great Britain by
Lowe & Brydone Printers Limited, Thetford, Norfolk